S0-BSU-230

International Handbook
on
Juvenile Justice

International Handbook on Juvenile Justice

Edited by
DONALD J. SHOEMAKER

GREENWOOD PRESS
Westport, Connecticut · London

0109317

141123

Library of Congress Cataloging-in-Publication Data

International handbook on juvenile justice / edited by Donald J.
  Shoemaker.
     p. cm.
  Includes bibliographical references and index.
  ISBN 0–313–28895–X (alk. paper)
   1. Juvenile justice, Administration of—Cross-cultural studies.
  2. Juvenile corrections—Government policy—Cross-cultural studies.
  I. Shoemaker, Donald J.
  HV9069.I665   1996
  364.3′6′0973—dc20   95–22980

British Library Cataloguing in Publication Data is available.

Copyright © 1996 by Donald J. Shoemaker

All rights reserved. No portion of this book may be
reproduced, by any process or technique, without the
express written consent of the publisher.

Library of Congress Catalog Card Number: 95–22980
ISBN: 0–313–28895–X

First published in 1996

Greenwood Press, 88 Post Road West, Westport, CT 06881
An imprint of Greenwood Publishing Group, Inc.

Printed in the United States of America

The paper used in this book complies with the
Permanent Paper Standard issued by the National
Information Standards Organization (Z39.48–1984).

10 9 8 7 6 5 4 3 2 1

CONTENTS

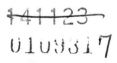
141123
010931 7

TABLES AND FIGURES

ACKNOWLEDGMENTS

No handbook of this nature could have been compiled without the generous assistance of many people. Of course, in a book such as this one, a most important component is the involvement of each of the contributors. In this case, all of the contributors were excellent colleagues to work with, and their persistent attention to my numerous requests made the project far easier to accomplish. However, many other contributors to the project do not appear in the text. I would like to acknowledge the assistance of these people, for their efforts contributed significantly to the publication of this book.

First, I would like to thank all of my colleagues who provided many names and addresses of possible contributors to this volume, especially those of foreign authors. While several colleagues provided this assistance, I would like to acknowledge the special assistance of Chris Birkbeck, who responded to my several requests with timely and very useful suggestions.

In addition, I would like to thank the very personable and professional secretarial staff in the Department of Sociology at Virginia Tech. I would like to acknowledge the work of Traci Starcher and, in particular, the outstanding work of Barbara Townley, who undertook the difficult and demanding task of organizing all of the chapters and putting them into standard order, including retyping many of the manuscripts into a standardized computer file.

Last, I would like to acknowledge the production assistance of Nita Romer and Jodie McCune and the encouragement of Mildred Vasan, Senior Editor with the Greenwood Publishing Group, without whose confidence and guidance this book would never have been produced.

INTRODUCTION

Donald J. Shoemaker

Social scientists and legal scholars have examined the structures and operations of juvenile justice systems in Western societies for several decades. These studies have included the factors that influence the establishment of laws affecting juveniles (Platt, 1977; Hagan and Leon, 1979; Sutton, 1985). In addition, many investigations have focused on the variables that influence decision making by officials working in different facets of the juvenile justice system (Cicourel, 1968; Emerson, 1969; Cohen and Kluegel, 1978; Bortner, 1984; Sampson, 1986; Mahoney, 1987).

The results of this research have contributed to a greater understanding of the forces that operate to establish and influence laws, policies, and procedures affecting the official processing of juvenile offenders in industrialized nations. We know, for example, that some laws and decisions are affected by considerations of social class and the demographic characteristics of defendants. In addition, the factors that may have an impact on decisions in urban jurisdictions may not be of import in rural areas. We know also that often the formal, legally established policies are not followed or enforced in practice. Rather, many less formal procedures develop and become more or less "ritualized." Sometimes these informal operations are reflective of individualized practices; at other times, they are products of organizational or cultural factors.

While this information is impressive in its scope and detail, there is a need for more knowledge concerning the laws and procedures that might affect the handling of juvenile offenders or suspects in other societies, particularly societies reflecting various sociocultural characteristics, geographic locations, and/or stages of development. The presentation of such information is the goal of this handbook (see Janeksela, 1992).

This handbook presents a description and discussion of the current system of juvenile justice in 19 countries. The countries selected for inclusion in this volume represent all the inhabitable continents of the world. In addition, the countries described in this book include societies that are highly industrialized, in middle stages of development, and what are termed Third World status. These chapters also represent various political and economic systems, such as capitalism, communism, socialism, and mixtures of governmental-economic categories.

Most chapters are divided into similar sections, beginning with an introductory and historical description, followed by discussions of the policies and procedures that characterize the formal structure of the juvenile justice system, as well as informal practices that deal with juvenile offenders, and then a summary and brief discussion of the implications and/or trends concerning juvenile justice or delinquency in the country.

The format of these chapters permits a comparative glance at diverse systems of justice for juvenile offenders across the governmental-economic divisions of the countries included in this volume. While detailed, systematic comparisons cannot always be accomplished from the discussions in this handbook, general points of similarity and difference are possible to ascertain from these chapters. For example, the influence of English laws and customs is evident in the systems of justice described in Australia, Canada, Hong Kong, India, Nigeria, South Africa, and the United States. A description of the juvenile justice system in England is also presented, which allows for more direct comparison with the countries influenced by England. Moreover, there is a discussion of juvenile justice in France, as well as a description of the juvenile justice system in Brazil, which is somewhat influenced by French legal codes.

Some systems reflect the influences of multiple countries, such as the United States and Spain in the Philippines and the United States and England in Australia. The influence of the United States can also be seen in the systems of justice in Canada and Japan. The discussion concerning Nigeria demonstrates the efforts of one society to manage the significant influences of many cultures, particularly the divergence between Western societies, represented primarily by the British, and Islam. The chapter on Egypt focuses on the impact of significant socioeconomic and political changes on delinquency, although these changes are not specifically tied to the influences of particular countries.

Besides facilitating comparative assessments of juvenile justice systems throughout the world, the chapters in this handbook also present a contemporary view of the impact of societal change on the treatment of juvenile offenders. Significant changes are reflected in the descriptions of juvenile justice in several countries, such as Canada, China, India, Germany, Mexico, and Russia. In addition, the discussion of juvenile justice in South Africa provides a basis of comparison and analysis for future analyses as this country experiences democratic reform. The simultaneous discussions of juvenile justice in Hong Kong, England, and China should also provide interesting comparative information as Hong Kong prepares for incorporation into the Chinese government in 1997.

Despite the influences of other societies, most of the systems of juvenile justice described in this volume also reflect cultural values and customs, organizational structures, financial situations, and other factors particular to each country. These more particularistic features of the country are often expressed in the informal patterns of juvenile justice that coexist with the formalized procedures and policies, such as with the arrests of juveniles in Mexico. In some instances, such as the Philippines, it seems as if these informal practices are more the norm than is the formalized system. Informal procedures are also found in more industrialized nations such as Australia and England, where there exists a process of police screening called "cautioning."

It is interesting to see, from this international perspective, how people from diverse backgrounds and settings have developed similar procedures for dealing with juvenile offenders in their countries. Certainly, the problem of delinquency is greater in some societies than in others, but no country has an absence of delinquency, and each of those included in this volume has developed formal procedures, often rather elaborate guidelines, for handling juvenile offenders. It is also interesting to learn that in virtually every country there is the goal of somehow rehabilitating young offenders and preventing further acts of crime and delinquency, apart from punitive correctional practices, especially the death penalty. A concern for educational rehabilitation of juvenile offenders would seem particularly pronounced in France, both historically and with proposed legislative reforms of juvenile delinquency codes. In addition, there seems to be nearly universal interest in protecting the rights of youths who become involved with the formal system of juvenile justice, and this issue is receiving significant interest in Japan.

However, many of the chapters, such as those concerning Brazil, Canada, England, and the United States, indicate growing public concern over violence committed by youth. In these countries, new legislation focuses on tougher sentencing laws and procedures for trying juveniles in adult courts.

Most of the chapters in this volume indicate the existence of efforts to include nonprofessional, communal influences in the handling of juvenile offenders, especially those charged with minor acts of illegality. This use of "lay" inputs is evident even in countries that are considered industrialized, such as France and Germany, but seems more pronounced in less industrialized countries, such as China.

In some societies, informal influences on juvenile justice are reflected in such institutions as the family and the school. The use of family conferences and informal panels in Australia, for example, represents significant lay involvement in the handling of juvenile offenders. In India, the importance of the family and kin in the handling of delinquent youth is pronounced and would appear to be preferred over more formal, governmental responses to delinquency. In Nigeria, the traditional culture emphasizes the importance of the extended family system in the control of youth. In Japan, school officials are a major source of informal controls of juveniles.

The chapters in this book also present differences in the procedures and pol-

icies for handling juvenile offenders. For example, while in many of these societies there is the possibility of treating youth either as juvenile offenders or
adult criminals, with specific rules and conditions applying to that decision, in
other countries, such as Greece, youthful offenders cannot receive the type of
severe penalties given to adult felons. In Russia, there is no formal juvenile
court system, and juvenile cases are processed in adult, "people's" courts, while
in Poland, there is a highly specialized juvenile justice system, which is highlighted by the Family Court.

Some chapters are written by legal experts and emphasize the formal and
legal aspects of juvenile justice. Other chapters are written by academic scholars
and emphasize the social and cultural aspects of juvenile justice in a particular
country. All of these contributions, however, contain both legal and sociocultural
points of interest concerning the juvenile justice system in a country. Hopefully,
therefore, the book will be of interest and use to both academic scholars and
legal practitioners.

Those interested in pursuing more information on juvenile offenders and/or
the system of juvenile justice in these countries may wish to use the list of
agencies and/or publications presented at the end of most chapters. Where available, these lists contain the names of specific representatives, but this list of
individuals, of course, is variable. In addition, legal and social changes can occur
quickly, which, of course, can dramatically affect current laws and policies.
Every effort was made to update material during the production process, however, in some countries new laws and policies may have developed during the
printing and, thus, do not appear in this book. This situation applies also to the
listing of names and addresses of key agencies and officials, presented in the
appendices of the chapters.

The countries included in this volume do not reflect a random sampling of
all possible combinations and categorizations of juvenile justice systems. Such
is not the purpose of this project. The countries included in this book, however,
do represent a broad collection of social, economic, and cultural conditions that
provide an opportunity for contemporary and comparative information on the
handling of juvenile offenders throughout the world. Perhaps this information
will be useful in establishing research questions for scholars, as well as intervention strategies for practitioners. At the least, it is hoped the contents of this
handbook will stimulate dialogue on these issues. If this occurs, the purpose of
the book will have been accomplished.

REFERENCES

Bortner, M. A. *Inside a Juvenile Court: The Tarnished Ideal of Individualized Justice.*
New York: New York University Press, 1984.
Cicourel, Aaron V. *The Social Organization of Juvenile Justice.* London: Heinemann
Educational Books, 1968.
Cohen, Lawrence E., and James R. Kluegel. "Determinants of Juvenile Court Disposi-

tions: Ascriptive and Achieved Factors in Two Metropolitan Courts.'' *American Sociological Review* 43 (1978): 162–176.

Emerson, Robert M. *Judging Delinquents: Context and Process in Juvenile Court.* New York: Aldine, 1969.

Hagan, John, and Jeffrey Leon. ''Rediscovering Delinquency: Social History, Political Ideology and the Sociology of Law.'' *American Sociological Review* 42 (1979): 587–598.

Janeksela, Galan M. ''The Significance of Comparative Analysis of Juvenile Delinquency and Juvenile Justice.'' *International Journal of Comparative and Applied Criminal Justice* 16 (1992): 137–150.

Mahoney, Anne Rankin. *Juvenile Justice in Context.* Boston: North University Press, 1987.

Platt, Anthony M. *The Child Savers,* 2d ed., enlarged. Chicago: University of Chicago Press, 1977.

Sampson, Robert J. ''Effects of Socioeconomic Context on Official Reaction to Juvenile Delinquency.'' *American Sociological Review* 51 (1986): 876–885.

Sutton, John R. ''The Juvenile Court and Social Welfare: Dynamics of Progressive Reform.'' *Law and Society Review* 19 (1985): 107–145.

International Handbook on Juvenile Justice

1

AUSTRALIA

John Seymour

BACKGROUND

The Commonwealth of Australia is a federation consisting of six states and two territories;[1] each state and territory has its own laws governing procedures for dealing with young offenders, and thus there are eight separate systems. All that can be undertaken here is a broad description of the more important features of the varying approaches adopted to young lawbreakers. Readers interested in fuller details should consult the relevant statutes.[2]

A proper understanding of current procedures demands some knowledge of their origins.[3] When, in 1788, European settlers arrived in the colony of New South Wales, they were regarded as bringing with them any applicable English laws. At that time and until the middle of the nineteenth century, the English criminal law made few concessions to youth. The most important of these was the concept of the age of criminal responsibility, which was then seven. Children over that age were tried in the same courts as adults and generally subject to the same penalties. The recognition of young offenders as a separate category deserving special treatment was very slow; in the early stages of settlement, neglected and vagrant children's needs attracted attention. The response to their plight—particularly the establishment of benevolent institutions—was, however, to have an important influence on the development of methods for dealing with young offenders. The measures adopted to assist destitute children represented the beginnings of a child welfare system and so provided the foundation on which juvenile justice procedures were later to be built.

The statutory framework for this system was erected in the second half of the nineteenth century, when the Australian colonies—the number of which had grown to six—enacted laws providing for industrial and reformatory schools.

Under these laws, which were based on English models, magistrates were empowered to commit neglected children to industrial schools and young offenders to reformatories. The resulting systems embodied many elements that were to remain features of the child welfare law for many years. Detention in the institutions was for an extended, indefinite period. This period could be reduced by such devices as release by way of apprenticeship, "at service," or "on licence," and thus provision was made for an element of flexibility. The fact that the powers conferred by the various acts were exercised by magistrates who had no special training in welfare matters and who presided in courts that were often referred to as "police courts" had a lasting effect on the later development of the system. Finally, the procedures introduced in the mid-nineteenth century depended on the making of a distinction between offenders and "neglected" children. Whether such a distinction can, and should, be made continues to trouble those concerned about the design of procedures for dealing with young offenders in Australia. Examination of the development of these procedures reveals constant uncertainty as to whether young lawbreakers are to be regarded as children whose needs should be addressed or as offenders whose conduct merits punishment.

After the establishment of an institutional system, the next major innovation was the creation of Children's Courts.[4] This step was taken in South Australia in the late nineteenth century and in the other five states (as the former colonies became after federation) early in the twentieth century. The influence of U.S. models was apparent both in South Australia and in other Australian jurisdictions. The parliamentary debates that preceded the enactment of the various statutes contained references to reforms undertaken in Massachusetts, Illinois, New York, and Colorado. As a result, the child-saving philosophy that underlay these reforms was absorbed into the emerging court system. What must be emphasized, however, is that the adoption of this philosophy did not lead to the copying of American procedures. The new Children's Courts had more in common with their English counterparts than with juvenile courts in the United States. The important corollary of this was that they employed criminal procedures; those appearing before the Children's Courts faced specific charges and were not dealt with by way of the delinquency petitions used in the United States. These courts were thus modified police courts rather than specialist tribunals. They therefore provided a somewhat unlikely setting in which to pursue the ideals of the child-savers.

Current practices must be examined against this background. This can best be begun by considering the role of the police in the juvenile justice system. Before this is done, it is necessary to identify the upper and lower age limits of the Children's Courts' criminal jurisdiction. In most states and territories the age of criminal responsibility is 10; in Tasmania it is 7, and in the Australian Capital Territory it is 8. In three states and one territory the Children's Courts' power to deal with young offenders ceases at the age of 17; in the remainder the age is 18.

POLICE PROCEDURES

Some of the eight state and territory police forces have special units for assisting children in trouble. These are variously named Juvenile Aid Bureaux (in Queensland and the Australian Capital Territory), Community Policing Squads (in Victoria), and the Youth Aid Section (in South Australia). In practice, these units have a limited role in processing young offenders, and the description that follows relates mainly to the work of nonspecialist officers.

Special rules[5] govern the arrest of young suspects, their interrogation, pretrial detention, photographing, and fingerprinting.[6] In all jurisdictions, controls are placed on the use of the power of arrest. In most, the law endeavors to encourage the police to proceed by way of summons, and in two states, efforts have been made to develop an informal procedure, known as a court attendance notice. This is a simple notice, handed to the suspect at a police station, specifying the date and time of the court hearing. Nevertheless, in spite of widespread acceptance of the view that juveniles should be arrested only when necessary, practices vary throughout Australia. In some parts of the country, a very high proportion of young suspects are dealt with by way of arrest. In others, proceedings are more likely to be initiated by way of summons. Even where court attendance notices may be employed, there is evidence that their use varies from one area to another. Juvenile arrest rates, it seems, are determined by "entrenched police behavior rather than policy directives" (Warner, 1992:9). It is clear that some police see the use of the power of arrest as a way of asserting their authority.

The rules governing the interviewing of young suspects require the presence of adult witnesses. Normally, an interview should not proceed unless a parent, guardian, or other independent adult is present. In some jurisdictions, provision is made for a police officer (not connected with the inquiry) to attend if no other witness is available. The fact that an interview is conducted in contravention of the rules does not necessarily mean that a juvenile's statement is inadmissible. The courts may exercise a wide discretion as to the admissibility of evidence obtained as a result of interviews conducted in violation of police standing orders and instructions. Further, even where the rules are in statutory form, the decision as to the admission of the evidence may be left to the court. In New South Wales, for example, the relevant provision contains a proviso that if there is sufficient reason for the absence of an adult witness, the evidence may be admitted.

Two aspects of the rules on interviewing deserve comment. In some states, the police adopt the view that they may decide when an "interview" begins. This allows them to take a preliminary statement in the absence of a witness and then arrange for the statement to be repeated in a formal interview that conforms to the rules. On some occasions the courts have condoned this practice and so diminished the protection given to juveniles when they are questioned by the police. The courts' approach has not, however, been uniform. In Tasmania, a judge has expressed the opinion that the rules should not be bypassed and that an adult witness should be present before the police ask "any investigatory questions" (Warner, 1992:6).

While the presence of an adult witness can ensure that the police do not exert undue pressure on a young suspect, the precise role that the witness (particularly one who lacks legal training) can play is unclear. In some jurisdictions it seems that the police expect the witness to be no more than a passive spectator and not to interfere in any way. If this view is accepted, the result is that the witness is regarded as "an appropriate piece of furniture" (Rees, 1982:69) rather than an active protector of the suspect's interests.

The subjects of pretrial detention and fingerprinting and photographing can be dealt with more briefly. Normally, juveniles who are not granted bail following arrest are detained in remand centers administered by welfare departments. Before transfer to these centers, they may occasionally be held in police cells. In some states, efforts are being made to encourage welfare officers to seek alternative placements for juveniles who would otherwise be held in remand centers. There are great variations in the rules governing fingerprinting and photographing of young suspects. In some jurisdictions, there are few restrictions, while in others, a court order must be obtained.

INFORMAL ALTERNATIVES TO THE COURT

Panels and Family Conferences

Although it is common for procedures designed to remove young offenders from the courts to be described as embodying a policy of "diversion," the term is a misleading one and will not be employed here. The use of the word suggests that when a child has allegedly committed an offense, the normal outcome will be a court appearance and that special efforts have to be made to "divert" the child. In practice, however, the various Australian systems have long reflected a recognition of the view that a substantial proportion of young offenders can appropriately be dealt with informally. The resulting informal procedures are considered here.

These procedures represent a particularly interesting and distinctive feature of the Australian system. At the time of writing, a great deal of energy was being devoted to their development and modification. This fact makes the task of describing them extremely difficult. Substantial changes are taking place. Until very recently, South Australia and Western Australia employed panels to deal with a wide range of juvenile offenders, and the remaining jurisdictions relied on a police caution as an alternative to a prosecution. In 1993, South Australia abandoned the use of panels in favor of procedures based on New Zealand's Family Group Conferences (described in Morris and Maxwell, 1993), and Western Australia is contemplating a similar change. Further, New South Wales and the Australian Capital Territory—which previously relied on police cautions as the sole informal measure—have, for some time, been experimenting with methods based on those used in the Family Group Conferences.

Although changes have been made (or are about to be made), a brief description of the panels will be provided, since they represented a valuable contribution to the development of alternative methods of dealing with young offenders. Further, no understanding of the current reforms is possible without an appreciation of the procedures on which they are built. In particular, the developments that have just taken place in South Australia illuminate both the panel system and the way that this system is being modified.

In that state, the case of an alleged offender (except one charged with homicide) was formerly considered by a Screening Panel. This panel—consisting of a social worker and a police officer—had four options. It could take no action, refer the child back to the police for a caution, refer the matter to a Children's Aid Panel, or recommend a prosecution. The Children's Aid Panel (which was also made up of a social worker and a police officer) was an informal tribunal that sat in the local offices of the Welfare Department. The child and parents appeared before it, and normally no other persons were present. The hearing was informal and typically lasted 20 to 30 minutes; after considering the allegations and obtaining an admission, the panel members discussed the offense, the family's reaction to it, and any problems that the child and parents were encountering. Sometimes, advice was offered, and the hearing commonly ended with a warning as to the high likelihood of a prosecution should the child again come to notice. In most cases this was where the matter ended, and the outcome was recorded as a warning and counseling. In a small number of cases, children were required to give undertakings (e.g., to accept supervision or to make restitution).

Eligibility for referral to Western Australia's Children's (Suspended Action) Panels is determined not by a Screening Panel but by legislative criteria. These panels deal with first offenders charged with offenses other than certain serious matters specified in the relevant act. As in South Australia, a panel consists of a social worker and a police officer, and its hearings are informal. In addition to the power to admonish the child or to require acceptance of supervision, a Western Australian panel may refer the matter to the Children's Court.

As has been noted, both South Australia and Western Australia are replacing the panel system. What is to be put in its place? The fullest answer to this question is offered by a South Australian Select Committee's report on Juvenile Justice (South Australia, 1992). While it must be emphasized that South Australia is simply one of Australia's eight jurisdictions (and by no means the largest), the committee's report merits close examination, since it offers a useful way of identifying a number of issues that are central to the current operation of Australia's juvenile justice systems.

To understand the changes recommended in this report (and since implemented), it is necessary to appreciate the objectives adopted by the committee. The most important of these include the following:

- to give the victim a more central role in the juvenile justice process;
- to ensure that the young offender is aware of the consequences of his or her behavior and takes responsibility for that behavior;
- to streamline the system and to provide a more immediate response to offending;
- to develop a broader range of sanctions;
- to involve the offender's family in the process and make them more directly responsible for their children's behavior; and
- to permit the police to play a greater part in procedures for dealing with juvenile lawbreakers.

A crucial element in the new approach is a commitment to what is described as "restorative justice." Earlier in this chapter, reference was made to the central problem of whether young lawbreakers are to be regarded as children whose needs should be addressed or as offenders whose conduct merits punishment. Although a crude oversimplification, another way of characterizing this dilemma is by drawing a contrast between the welfare and justice models. The significance of the reforms outlined in the South Australian report is that they reflect the adoption of a third—and genuinely new—model. This model is a product of a concern for the victim and a desire to compensate him or her for the loss or injury suffered. More is involved, however, than the making of restitution. The broader aim is to facilitate a healing process, to restore harmony in the community. This aim is pursued in an informal process of negotiation and mediation in which victim, offender, and family participate. The report recommended that the new policy be implemented by creating a new tribunal of the kind pioneered in New Zealand. The result was the establishment, under the Young Offenders Act, 1993 (SA), of a system of Family Conferences.

Before these are described, it should be noted that the Family Conference is no more than one element in the South Australian reforms. It would be wrong to regard these reforms as displaying a single-minded commitment to restorative justice. The objectives listed before also reveal the adoption of what can be described as "crime control" strategies. In particular, the references to immediacy of response, the protection of the community, and greater police involvement should not be overlooked. As will be seen, these aims are also reflected in the redesigned procedures embodied in the 1993 legislation.

The result of the decision to give more power to the police was the introduction of a formal police cautioning program. In the past, the Screening Panels and the Children's Aid Panels lay at the heart of the South Australian system, and consequently, the police played a minor role in the informal handling of young offenders. This has been changed by the creation of a range of cautioning options. Under the legislation, the police are authorized to administer a formal caution in respect of a "minor" offense.[7] A caution may require a young offender to enter into an undertaking to pay compensation to the victim, to perform up to 75 hours of community service, to apologize to the victim, or "to do anything else that may be appropriate in the circumstances of the case."[8] If an undertaking is broken, the police may refer the matter to a Family Conference.

Linked with these changes was the abolition of Children's Aid Panels. These were thought to result in overprocessing (in the sense that they constituted an unnecessarily elaborate response to much minor offending) and, consequently, produced an increased number of cases in the system (net widening). The panels were also considered unduly coercive and insufficiently concerned with due process. Finally, they were criticized for lacking effective sanctions and not allowing for victim participation.

The Family Conferences that replaced them were designed to overcome these deficiencies.[9] Membership of a conference varies, but it must include a youth justice coordinator (who chairs the conference), the juvenile, and a representative of the police. In addition, a range of other persons may be invited; these include the juvenile's parents or guardians, relatives, and other persons who have had a close association with the juvenile and the victim. The juvenile is entitled to have a legal adviser present at the conference. A conference may administer a formal caution or require an undertaking to pay compensation, to carry out up to 300 hours of community service, or to apologize to the victim. As with a police caution, the formula allowing for an undertaking to do "anything else that may be appropriate" is employed. If the juvenile fails to attend the conference or does not comply with an undertaking, the police may lay a charge in respect of the offense that led to the conference referral. The power of the police is further underlined by a provision that states that no arrangement reached at a conference is valid if the police representative does not concur in the decision.

Variants of the Family Conference have been introduced in New South Wales, Western Australia, and the Australian Capital Territory. In Wagga Wagga, a town in rural New South Wales, the family conferencing process that has been developed is seen as a variant of a police caution. The conferences are chaired by the local police officer responsible for the cautioning program. The scheme, which is the result of this officer's imaginative adaptation of existing practices, has yet to receive legislative recognition. The conference also takes other forms in New South Wales. In one area, there is a Community Justice Council, to which the police may refer Aboriginal offenders guilty of minor offenses. The council consists of five members of the local Aboriginal community. In another area, a similar initiative has led to the establishment of a Juvenile Justice Panel, again consisting of community members, although not necessarily Aborigines.

As has been explained, Western Australia has in the past relied on Children's (Suspended Action) Panels. As in South Australia, a recent report expressed dissatisfaction with the operation of the panels. It was thought that there was a need for less cumbersome, more flexible procedures. Hence, the introduction of a formal cautioning system was recommended (Western Australia, *Laws for People,* 1991:70–71). This is being supplemented by a form of conference, introduced by way of pilot projects. These established Juvenile Justice Teams accept cases previously handled by the police or by the local panels.

As in South Australia, descriptions of the conference procedures employed elsewhere emphasize the aim of involving members of the juvenile's family and immediate community, as well as the victim. There are numerous references to the need for the offender to make reparation to the victim and to accept responsibility for the offense. Equally, the goals of empowering families and reaching outcomes in which those affected genuinely participate are constantly stressed.

One further feature of the developing conference system must be identified. In some jurisdictions in which a variant of this system is in operation, it is possible for a court to refer a matter to a conference. In South Australia, the Youth Court may, after guilt has been established, direct that the case be dealt with by a police officer or Family Conference. In Western Australia, the Children's Court may remand a matter to a Juvenile Justice Team; if a satisfactory outcome is achieved, the court dismisses the case. In New South Wales, Community Aid Panels operate in many parts of the state. A magistrate may adjourn a case to a panel, which consists of a member of the police and representatives of the local community. Discussion at the panel is designed to obtain the juvenile's agreement to undertake some form of community work or appropriate educational or rehabilitative program. Special emphasis is placed on work as a form of restitution; one panel studied regularly required juveniles to perform between 25 and 35 hours of community work. When the juvenile's task is completed, the case is returned to court, and participation in the program is taken into account as a mitigating factor in sentencing (Bargen, 1992).

The existence of practices that have emerged in these jurisdictions makes it necessary to qualify the statement earlier in this chapter that the use of the term "diversion" should always be rejected. There it was pointed out that informal measures are best seen as free-standing alternatives to the court. This does not apply to procedures that allow the courts to refer cases for informal handling. Such matters can properly be described as having been "diverted."

Police Cautions

A less elaborate method of handling cases informally is by way of police caution. In Victoria, Queensland, Tasmania, and the Northern Territory, the caution is the sole alternative to a prosecution. In the remaining jurisdictions, it is employed for cases not serious enough to warrant referral to a panel, conference, or Juvenile Justice Team. A distinction must be made between informal cautions (which occur on the street and are normally not recorded) and formal cautions, administered at a police station. All states and territories employ both forms; formal cautions are considered here. Some states have more extensive cautioning programs than others. In Victoria and Queensland, for example, the legislation makes specific provision for formal cautions. This reflects the extensive use made of cautions in these two states.

As an example of the procedures employed, it is convenient to concentrate on Victoria, which has a well-established cautioning program. Cautioning is considered particularly suitable for first offenders, although it is not confined to this category. Most cautions are administered at the juvenile's local police station by a senior officer such as an inspector or sergeant. Usually a parent is required to be present. A typical caution takes about 15 minutes. There are variations in the approaches adopted. In the words of one Victorian police officer, cautions can vary "from gentle to table thumping, depending on the child" (Higgins, 1982:179). It is common for cautions to incorporate a stern warning designed to deter the child from further offending. The warning may be augmented by advice on such matters as the use of leisure time and the avoidance of undesirable companions. Most cautioning programs are not designed to provide continuing assistance to juveniles and their families. At most, a family in difficulty might be advised to contact the local welfare department. In short, while practices vary, in general, it is accurate to describe a caution as "a good talking-to" rather than a counseling session.

Queensland's cautioning program has recently been given additional emphasis, and special provisions are now embodied in the *Justice Juvenile Act* 1992 (Qld). In all cases the police are directed to consider the appropriateness of taking no action or of dealing with a matter by way of a caution. The legislation also echoes the policy pursued by the conference system, for it states that a caution may involve the juvenile's apologizing to the victim. An interesting feature of the legislation is that it provides for an Aboriginal child to be cautioned by an elder of the local Aboriginal community. It also underlines the importance of diversion by authorizing a Children's Court to dismiss a matter if it should have been dealt with by way of a caution.

THE CHILDREN'S COURTS

Constitution and Jurisdiction

Reference has already been made to the fact that the courts responsible for dealing with young offenders in Australia were originally called Children's Courts. They still bear this title in all states and territories except South Australia, where the name Youth Court has been adopted. To simplify the account that follows, the term "Children's Courts" will be used throughout.

These courts are presided over by magistrates or judges. They sit without a jury. In Australia, magistrates are the judicial officers who preside in the lowest tier of trial courts. They all hold legal qualifications. In some states, appointments to the Children's Courts are now made at the level of District Court (i.e., intermediate trial court) level. In Queensland, South Australia, and Western Australia, such judges have been appointed the senior judges of their respective courts. Both magistrates and judges hold general appointments as judicial officers; they are not specialists selected on the basis of their knowledge of children. Some, however, are appointed to the bench because they are thought to be well suited to work with children. They may sit primarily or exclusively in the Children's Courts.

The criminal jurisdiction of the Children's Courts is broad. In most states and territories, these courts may deal with all except the most serious offenses. Commonly, the legislation prevents the courts from hearing homicide charges or charges involving certain serious indictable offenses; sometimes the excluded offenses are specifically listed, and sometimes the statutes state that offenses carrying a certain penalty (e.g., life imprisonment) are not triable by a Children's Court. The Western Australian and Queensland Children's Courts are not subject to limitations of this kind; they may deal with all offenses. South Australia is distinctive, as provision is made for a prosecutor to apply to have a juvenile's case removed to an adult court. In some jurisdictions, it is open to Children's Courts to decline jurisdiction if a matter is thought too serious. In all states and territories, juveniles may elect trial by jury in circumstances where this right is available to adult defendants.

A feature of Australia's Children's Courts is that normally they are, by law, closed to the public. The courts in Victoria and the Northern Territory are an exception; they are conducted as open courts unless the presiding judge or magistrate orders the exclusion of members of the public. In all states and territories, except the Northern Territory, there are restrictions on the reporting of proceedings. A prohibition on the publication of a young offender's name or any identifying details is virtually universal.

The Measures Employed by Children's Courts

The range of measures employed by the Children's Courts after a finding of guilt is wide. In general, the legislation governing the courts lists all available penalties; the result is that judges and magistrates may exercise a broad discretion and make whatever orders seem appropriate. In this respect, the law contrasts with what applies to adult offenders; in the case of adults, maximum penalties are specified for most offenses.

The most lenient response is an unconditional discharge. The effect of this is to dismiss the matter without the infliction of any penalty. The process may be accompanied by a reprimand; depending on the personality of the judge or magistrate, a homily may also be delivered. It is debatable whether the majority of young offenders who receive such a homily are capable of understanding what is said to them. Much more comprehensible is the infliction of monetary penalties, which are employed in all states and territories. These may take the form of a fine or an order to pay compensation. The legislation commonly sets an upper limit, which must be observed when the defendant is a juvenile. In some jurisdictions, the courts are directed to have regard for the young offender's capacity to pay.

The most flexible and creative orders made by the Children's Courts depend on the use of the device of a conditional discharge. By employing this device—by which young offenders are released on condition that they fulfill certain obligations—the courts can fashion all sorts of measures designed to impose controls or to bring good influences to bear. At its simplest, the order can require a juvenile to enter into an undertaking (often referred to as a "recognizance") to be of good behavior or to return to court if called upon. A breach of the undertaking (e.g., committing another offense and so failing to display good behavior) can result in the imposition of a sentence for the original offense. The order can be more substantial. It might require the acceptance of supervision, the performance of community service, or attendance at a center in the evening and on weekends. When such conditions are imposed, the result tends to be seen as a discrete sentence (such as probation), and for this reason the various conditions will be discussed separately. It is important, however, not to overlook that each of the measures outlined is simply a particular form of a conditional discharge. In theory, each depends on the courts' power to suspend sentence and expose the offender to the possibility of being sentenced for the original offense if the conditions are not observed.

In all states and territories, the Children's Courts may make probation orders, although in some instances the legislation uses the term "supervision." The primary purpose of orders of this kind is to place young offenders under the supervision of probation or welfare officers. Normally these officers are professionals, employed by the local state department responsible for the provision of juvenile correctional services. In some states, however, reliance is occasionally placed on voluntary probation officers, and in South Australia there has been an interesting experiment under which intensive supervision is provided by members of the community. The various statutes set different maximum terms: one, two, or three years.

The probation order is an extremely flexible device. In addition to imposing an obligation to accept supervision, it may include a range of other conditions. A favorite formula is a requirement that the juvenile be of good behavior and obey all reasonable directions of the probation officer. The order may, however, be more far-reaching. There may be a direction that the juvenile refrain from specified activities or from associating with named persons. The juvenile may be required to live where directed (in practice, this will frequently mean residence in a hostel run by a voluntary organization) or to participate in a specified program (e.g., drug and alcohol counseling).

In most jurisdictions, juvenile offenders can be ordered to perform community service. This involves the performance of a specified number of hours of work; the maximum number is usually prescribed by the legislation. In New South Wales, for example, the upper limit is 100 hours, in Queensland it is 60 hours (if the juvenile is under 15) and 120 hours (if over that age), and in South

Australia it is 500 hours. The implementation of community service schemes varies. Usually, responsibility for the administration of work orders falls on members of the local correctional departments. Some schemes, however, are designed to allow young people to work with members of community organizations. Examples of activities that might be undertaken include maintenance for a bushfire brigade; gardening and maintenance work at preschools, community centers, old people's homes, and historic homesteads; and helping disadvantaged persons.

Perhaps the most innovative of the measures employed by the Children's Courts require periodic attendance at centers that operate in the evenings and on weekends. The legislation uses various terms to describe these facilities: attendance center, community youth center, activity center, and youth attendance project. In some cases, the law—instead of identifying a particular type of facility—simply provides for participation in a "program" to be ordered. Whatever term is used, the important feature of these measures is their flexibility. The form the programs take varies from place to place and from juvenile to juvenile. A typical program includes educational and recreational activities, counseling, and the provision of assistance in finding jobs. Some programs place particular emphasis on teaching practical and social skills.

The most restrictive type of measure is, of course, committal to an institution. In all states and territories, there are juvenile detention centers run by the state correctional departments. As in other areas, the laws governing the terms of committal vary; in most states and territories the maximum is two years, but in South Australia it is three years, and in Victoria a juvenile over the age of 15 may be committed to an institution for up to three years. In practice, the procedures employed are flexible, and release dates are determined by parole boards or equivalent bodies. As in all parts of the world, an examination of juvenile detention centers reveals continuing debate about their role and potential.

Institutions range from the sterile, repressive, and regimented (where little more than "warehousing" is achieved), to those in which genuine efforts are made to meet juveniles' social and developmental needs. All provide educational programs, trade and work-skill training, and facilities for the development of leisure interests. The success of these programs in achieving their objects is uncertain. One detailed examination of a Victorian youth training center revealed a high degree of skepticism among inmates; many of their comments suggested that they saw the center's regime as being devoted to discipline rather than training (Asher, 1986). This, however, is only one study; more research is needed to determine how representative these findings are.

In three jurisdictions (Tasmania, Western Australia, and the Northern Territory), the Children's Courts are empowered to imprison juveniles. In the remainder, the Children's Courts normally lack this power. There is, however, an additional, complicating factor, as the law in three states authorizes the transfer to prison of juveniles over 16 years old who have been sentenced to detention centers. Nor should it be thought that the provisions outlined represent the only means by which juveniles can be imprisoned. Such an outcome is possible for juveniles whose cases are removed to adult courts. These are the juveniles who have been convicted of very serious offenses, and we now turn to the practices employed in these cases.

SERIOUS OFFENSES

As has been explained, the Children's Courts lack the power to deal with certain matters, which must be heard in adult courts. When this occurs, the young offenders involved may be sentenced to adult penalties. A juvenile who has been convicted of murder or manslaughter, for example, may receive an indeterminate sentence, part of which will be served in a training center and part in a prison.

Although, in general, the problems that arise when a juvenile matter is removed to an adult court have not aroused the same concern as in the United States, recently, a series of serious crimes in Western Australia has focused attention on a previously neglected aspect of juvenile justice. Over an 18-month period in 1990 and 1991, a number of people died as a result of the police pursuit of juveniles driving stolen cars. In the incident that attracted the most publicity, on Christmas night, 1991, a pregnant woman and her baby son were killed when the car in which they were traveling was involved in a collision with a stolen car. The car, which was being pursued by the police, was driven by a 14-year-old Aboriginal youth. Naturally, the incident produced outrage in the media, and a public campaign was launched directed toward the introduction of a "get tough" policy. The state government reacted swiftly; within two weeks, it was announced that "hard-core" offenders would be targeted and "excised" from society.

The result was hurried and badly drafted legislation, designed to impose long custodial terms on repeat offenders.[10] The details of this legislation need not concern us here. The important point is that its enactment raised questions about the assumptions underlying society's reactions to serious offending by the young. At the heart of the government response was a belief that the incidence of certain types of criminal behavior could be reduced by a combination of selective incapacitation (locking up "the hard core") and the use of deterrent penalties. Indeed, government statements claimed that the introduction of the new laws was accompanied by a diminution in the rate of serious crime. Yet, as a thorough report on these laws has pointed out, any downward trend could be the result of the interaction of a number of factors; it is unwise to place reliance only on a sentencing statute (Harding, 1993:5). Further, the focus on this statute and the policy that it embodied had an unfortunate effect on the entire juvenile justice system in Western Australia. The report referred to the debate about youthful crime in that state as having been "debased" by the controversy; all the attention was given to increased punishment (Harding,

1993:11). As a result, other, more positive reforms that had been under consideration were deferred.

ABORIGINAL OFFENDERS

In common with many other countries, Australia is experiencing deep concern about the impact of the juvenile justice system on its indigenous peoples. Aboriginal youth are overrepresented in the system and—in comparison with non-Aboriginals—are more harshly dealt with at every stage of that system.

The most dramatic figures on overrepresentation relate to Aboriginal juveniles in custody. A survey conducted in Victoria in 1982 found that, while young Aboriginals made up less than 1 percent of the state's youth population, they constituted 8.3 percent of all young people in youth training centers (Victoria, Department of Community Welfare Services, 1982). In Western Australia, a study revealed that young Aborigines (who represented less than 3 percent of that state's population at the time of the study) accounted for 31.6 percent of all juveniles admitted to remand and assessment facilities over a 12-month period ending in 1974 (Western Australia, Department for Community Services, 1982). Similarly, in South Australia in 1985–1986, Aboriginals were the subject of 21.4 percent of all Children's Court detention orders. The rate of detention for Aborigines was 7.6 per 1,000, compared with 0.5 per 1,000 for non-Aborigines (Gale et al., 1990:32).

Disturbing findings emerge from studies that have analyzed the progress of Aboriginal juveniles through the juvenile justice system. Although these findings relate particularly to South Australia (where detailed research has recently been undertaken: Gale et al., 1990), there is no reason to suppose that the results obtained are not equally applicable to other parts of the country. Examination of police practices suggested that Aboriginal youths in South Australia were less likely to be cautioned than non-Aboriginals. Further—and this is most important—when the police made the decision to initiate formal proceedings, they were much more likely to use the power of arrest. The figures are striking. In 1985–1986, 29.5 percent of young Aborigines who were brought into the formal system came by way of arrest rather than by way of a police report to a Screening Panel. In contrast, 12.8 percent of non-Aborigines were arrested. For every 1,000 young Aborigines, 48.3 arrests occurred, compared with 3.5 arrests per 1,000 non-Aborigines.

Differences were also observed at the next stage of the process. As has been explained, at the time of the study it was the task of a Screening Panel to decide whether a juvenile was to be referred to a Children's Aid Panel or to the Children's Court. It was found that, in 1985–1986, 59.4 percent of Aboriginal offenders were referred to court rather than to an Aid Panel. The corresponding figure for non-Aborigines was 38.2 percent. The Children's Court appearance rate for young Aboriginals in that year was 97.5 per 1,000, compared with 10.4 per 1,000 for non-Aborigines. Finally, differences were also observable at the sentencing stage. In 1985–1986, the Children's Court sentenced 7.8 percent of young Aborigines to detention, compared with 4.5 percent of non-Aboriginal offenders (Gale et al., 1990:31–32).

What emerged from the study, therefore, was evidence of differential treatment at all major stages of the juvenile justice process. Further, the authors drew attention to the "compounding effect" of the various decisions made at each of these stages (Gale et al., 1990:88). This important insight is best explained by reference to the police use of the power of arrest. In the majority of cases, it was found that juveniles who had been arrested were almost certain to be referred to court by a Screening Panel. As has been shown, Aborigines were much more likely to be arrested than non-Aboriginals and therefore much more likely to be denied the opportunity to appear before a Children's Aid Panel. Further, as has also been shown, once an Aborigine was referred to the Children's Court, the likelihood of a custodial sentence was greater than was the case for a non-Aboriginal. Thus, a decision taken at one stage of the process was found to have significant repercussions at a later stage (Gale et al., 1990:119).

Explaining the juvenile justice system's response to Aborigines is difficult. That it is, to some extent, the product of racial discrimination is undeniable, although it is also clear that, both in South Australia and elsewhere, many persons "go to extreme lengths to try to give Aboriginal youth a fair opportunity for both justice and rehabilitation" (Gale et al., 1990:8). It seems that a number of factors combine. Aborigines are very visible, and police stereotypes can lead to unjustified intervention. When an Aboriginal youth has been stopped by the police, aggression and hostility (on both sides) may lead to an escalation of the situation. The confrontation can lead to the laying of charges such as the use of abusive language and resisting arrest. Charges of this kind are frequently the product of police intervention and may result in circumstances in which there are no grounds for suspecting that the youth has committed any other offense.

Once Aboriginal youths are known to the police, their chance of avoiding further contact with the system is greatly reduced; they are a relatively easy target. Not only do they stand a higher chance of being stopped by the police, but they can quickly acquire a record that will make arrest (and the consequent referral to court rather than to a Children's Aid Panel) more likely. Thus, "the process may be self-generating" (Gale et al., 1990:51). This, in its turn, helps to put the statistics into perspective: "[T]he repeated apprehension of a comparatively small number of Aborigines exaggerates their representation in the official records" (Gale et al., 1990:40).

SUMMARY

A distinctive juvenile justice system has existed in Australia for a little less than 100 years. During that time there have been many changes, but much continuity can also be discerned. The present Children's Courts are recognizable as the descendants of those established almost a century ago, and the measures available to them have not altered as much as might be expected. There are still training schools, although less use is made of them than in the past, their regimes are less rigorous, and the terms of detention are comparatively short. Considerable reliance is still placed on variants of probation, that hope of the nineteenth-century child-savers. One genuine innovation was the introduction of semicustodial measures, which require periodic attendance at centers at which work and educational activities are undertaken.

In general, however, at present, the courts and their supporting services cannot be described as innovative. We must turn to the search for alternatives to the courts and the variety of approaches revealed by this search if we wish to identify current practices that hold promise for the future.[11] Perhaps it can be said that the idealism that characterized the nineteenth-century child-saving movement is now entirely focused on the development of informal responses to offending. These responses seek to involve offenders, their families, victims, and members of local communities in procedures that may do no more than ensure that young offenders make reparation or may pursue the loftier goal of restoring social harmony. It is, however, important to be cautious: the conference system may embody a carefully considered reorientation of the juvenile justice system, or it may be no more than the current fashion.

Meanwhile, as recent experience in Western Australia has demonstrated, the dangerous juvenile offender will continue to pose troubling problems for the juvenile justice system. On one hand, the system must endeavor to retain its pursuit of reintegration, reconciliation, and restorative justice. On the other, it must offer realistic and convincing answers to the questions posed by those who express concern about "hard-core" offenders. If answers to these questions cannot be provided, the whole system could be undermined. Ideally, the aim must be to accommodate a very wide range of offenders within the Children's Court structure; as far as possible, we must resist the bleak conclusion that certain categories of juveniles do not belong in that structure. Yet political realities cannot be ignored. The events that occurred in Western Australia in the early 1990s provided a vivid illustration of the fragility of society's commitment to the search for humane, flexible, and imaginative solutions to the problems posed by juvenile offenders.

NOTES

1. These are New South Wales (NSW), Tasmania (Tas), Victoria (Vic), Queensland (Qld), South Australia (SA), Western Australia (WA), the Australian Capital Territory (ACT), and the Northern Territory (NT).

2. *Children's Court Act* 1987 (NSW), *Children (Criminal Proceedings) Act* 1987 (NSW), *Child Welfare Act* 1960 (Tas), *Children and Young Persons Act* 1989 (Vic), *Children's Court Act* 1992 (Qld), *Juvenile Justice Act* 1992 (Qld), *Youth Court Act* 1993 (SA), *Young Offenders Act* 1993 (SA), *Child Welfare Act* 1947 (WA) (soon to be replaced by the *Young Offenders Act* 1994 [WA]), *Children's Court of Western Australia Act (No. 2)* 1988 (WA), *Children's Services Act* 1986 (ACT), *Juvenile Justice Act* 1983 (NT). For

a detailed treatment of the provisions of many of these acts, see Seymour, 1988: Chapters 4–9.

3. For an extended discussion of the history of Australia's procedures for dealing with young offenders, see Seymour, 1988: Chapters 1–3.

4. The name is a puzzling one; it is not clear why the term "children's courts," rather than "juvenile courts" (as in England and the United States), was adopted.

5. The various rules are to be found not only in the relevant statutes but also in police standing orders and instructions.

6. For a concise treatment of current law and practice, see Warner, 1992: 4–12. See also Youth Justice Coalition (NSW), 1990.

7. This is defined as an offense "that should, in the opinion of the police officer in charge of the investigation of the offense, be dealt with as a minor offense because of:

1. the limited extent of the harm caused through the commission of the offense;

2. the character and antecedents of the alleged offender;

3. the improbability of the youth re-offending; and

4. where relevant—the attitude of the youth's parents or guardians."

See *Young Offenders Act* 1993 (SA), s 4.

8. *Young Offenders Act* 1993 (SA), s 8 (1) (c).

9. The jurisdiction of the Family Conferences is limited to "minor offenses." See the explanation, n. 7.

10. See *Crime (Serious and Repeat Offenders) Sentencing Act* 1992 (WA).

11. For a recent review of the issues raised by the move toward informal alternatives to the courts, see Alder and Wundersitz, 1994.

REFERENCES

Alder, Christine, and Joy Wundersitz. *Family Conferencing and Juvenile Justice: The Way Forward or Misplaced Optimism?* Canberra: Australian Institute of Criminology, 1994.

Asher, Geoff. *Custody and Control.* Sydney: Allen and Unwin, 1986.

Bargen, Jenny. "Going to Court Cap in Hand: A Preliminary Evaluation of a Community Aid Panel." *Current Issues in Criminal Justice* 4 (1992): 117–140.

Gale, Fay, Rebecca Bailey-Harris, and Joy Wundersitz. *Aboriginal Youth and the Criminal Justice System. The Injustice of Justice?* Cambridge: Cambridge University Press, 1990.

Harding, Richard (ed.). *Repeat Juvenile Offenders: The Failure of Selective Incapacitation in Western Australia.* Perth: Crime Research Centre, University of Western Australia, 1993.

Higgins, Wendy. "Cautioning of Juvenile Offenders: A Study of the Victoria Police Cautioning Program." M.A. thesis, University of Melbourne, 1982.

Morris, Alison, and Gabrielle Maxwell. "Juvenile Justice in New Zealand: A New Paradigm." *Australian and New Zealand Journal of Criminology* 26 (1993): 72–90.

Rees, Neil. "The Rules Governing Police Interrogation of Children." In *The Criminal*

Injustice System, edited by John Basten, Mark Richardson, Chris Ronalds, and George Zdenkowski. Sydney: Australian Legal Workers Group (NSW), 1982.

Seymour, John. *Dealing with Young Offenders.* Sydney: Law Book, 1988.

South Australia. *Interim Report of the Select Committee on the Juvenile Justice System.* Adelaide: Department of Family and Community Services, 1992.

Victoria, Department of Community Welfare Services. *Characteristics of Young People in Youth Training Centers: Results of the Youth Training Center Census 1982 and Trends over the Previous Decades.* Melbourne: Department of Community Welfare Services, 1982.

Warner, Kate. "Legislative and Policy Overview." In *Perceptions of the Treatment of Juveniles in the Legal System,* edited by John Basten, Christine Alder, Ian O'Connor, Kate Warner, and Rob White. Hobart: National Clearinghouse for Youth Studies, 1992.

Western Australia. *Laws for People: The Report of the Legislative Review.* Perth: Department for Community Services, 1991.

Western Australia, Department for Community Services. *An Initial and Supplementary Report on a Study of Children Who Enter the Care of the Department for Community Services and Are Subsequently Admitted to an Adult Penal Facility before the Ages of 20 and 22 Years.* Perth: Department for Community Services, 1982.

Youth Justice Coalition (NSW). *Kids in Justice: A Blueprint for the 90s.* Sydney: Youth Justice Coalition, 1990.

APPENDIX: KEY AGENCIES

Family Services ACT
Juvenile Justice
RMB Mugga Lane
SYMONSTON ACT 2609
(06) 2951600

Family & Community Services
Young Offenders Unit
10th Floor City Center Bldg.
11 Hindmarsh Square
ADELAIDE SA 5000
(08) 2267000

Ministry of Justice
Juvenile Justice Division
5 Allen Court
BENTLEY WA 6102
(09) 4703966

Protective Services & Juvenile Justice
Department of Family Services & Aboriginal & Islander Affairs
Juvenile Justice Branch
Charlotte Chambers
35 Charlotte Street
BRISBANE QLD 4000
(07) 2242111

Health & Community Services
Juvenile Justice Unit
Ethos House
270 Trower Road
CASUARINA NT 0811
(089) 892400

Community & Health Services
Youth Justice Services
12 Murry Street
HOBART TAS 7000
(002) 332209

Health & Community Services
Juvenile Justice Section
19th Floor 555 Collins Street
MELBOURNE VIC 3001
(03) 4127777

Department of Juvenile Justice
Level 5 Roden Cutler House
24 Campbell Street
SYDNEY NSW 2000
(02) 2893333

2

BRAZIL

César Barros Leal

INTRODUCTION

According to some authors, the protective role of the Brazilian legislation in regard to minors started in the Royal Bill, dated from 1693, that ordered the governor of the captainship of Rio de Janeiro to place rejected and abandoned children under the care of the chamber and the council. This was the first disposition in behalf of helpless infants in Brazil, and it set the stage for a great number of norms essentially concerned with the defense and protection of abandoned minors in a hazardous situation as well as victims of aggression or perpetrators of a crime.

Reference to minors was present in the Philippine Ordinances that were in force during the colonial period from 1603 to 1830 and that stated in Article 134 of Book V:

In regard to minors, they will be punished in accordance with their offenses. If he is more than seventeen years old and not older than twenty, it is up to the judge to apply a punishment, and if he deems the minor deserves total punishment, he will say so, even if it means death. If the minor is not seventeen yet, even if he deserves to die for his crime, the judge will not apply such punishment.

In 1830, the Criminal Code of the Empire attended only to minors' penal responsibility, fixed at age 14, and it adopted, taking as model the Penal Code of France of 1810, the criterion of discernment without an inferior limit:

If they perform with discernment, they will be taken to a reform house for the time the judge considers adequate, provided that the seclusion will not go beyond seventeen years old.

Discernment—that is, the capacity to understand the illegal nature of the act and to determine oneself in accordance with that understanding—was accepted as a criterion by laws of many countries in the world. Their laws intended to replace the chronological criterion under the reasoning that the evolution of the personality is not always the same and that merely taking age into consideration is neither scientific nor fair.

The previous criterion was included in the first Penal Code of the Republic in 1890, which established the age of 9 for penal responsibility. However, minors from 9 to 14 years old were not held responsible if it became evident they performed crimes without discernment.

The federal government, by means of an uncommon instrument, Budget Law 4242 of January 5, 1921, authorized the organization of assistance and protection to abandoned and delinquent children, raised to 14 years the age of penal responsibility, and put an end to the discernment criterion. Until then, one did not think of codifying the laws regarding minors, an idea that led the first judge of minors of Latin America, José Cândido de Albuquerque Mello Mattos, to present to the Senate a project of his own, which was approved and promulgated (Decree 17.943-A, October 12, 1927) and had the merit of consolidating the sparse, existent laws at the time and instituting a system of protection and assistance to minors, divided into two groups: abandoned and delinquent.

THE FORMAL SYSTEM

Infractional Act, Individual Rights, and Procedural Guarantees

In the penal system in force in Brazil, one makes a distinction between crime and misdemeanor, the latter qualified as a less important or less serious crime, to which a softer penalty is applied (a fine or simple imprisonment).

In the wake of the Penal Code of 1940, and the reform of its General Part of 1984 as well as of the federal constitution, the Statute of the Child and Adolescent establishes that minors under 18 are not imputable penally, though subjected to the measures in it. It also adds that the law must consider the age of the adolescent at the time that the offense happened.

Like the Minor's Code of 1979, the statute shelters this dichotomous classification when it registers that the infractional act is the behavior depicted as crime or misdemeanor.

This law also distinguishes the measures applicable to the child from those applicable to the adolescent for committing an infractional act.

Article 105 stipulates that children are entitled to protection measures expressed in article 101, namely:

I. transfer to the parents or guardian, by means of a statement of responsibility;

II. temporary guidance, support, and monitoring;

III. obligatory enrollment and assistance in official basic education school;

IV. inclusion in government or community programs of family, child, and adolescent assistance;

V. requisition of medical, psychological, or psychiatric treatment in a hospital or outpatient regimen;

VI. inclusion in an official or community program of assistance, guidance, and treatment to alcoholic and drug addicts;

VII. shelter in an institution;

VIII. placement in a foster family.

The Protective Council, a permanent municipal agency, autonomous, nonjurisdictional, made up of five members, and chosen by the community, will take care of the children who commit an infractional act, applying the measures of Article 101, I to VIII. When the council is not in session, its provisions will be put in action by a judicial authority (a judge of infancy and youth or a judge who performs this function according to the law of local judicial organization).

If the perpetrator is an adolescent, the competent authority can apply to him or her measures that the legislator considers social-educational and that are expressed in Article 112, besides any of the protection measures in items I to VI of Article 101.

In accordance with the fifth article, item LXI, of the federal constitution, the statute establishes that no adolescent will be deprived of his or her freedom save (1) "in flagrante delicto" or (2) by a written and well-founded order of the competent judicial authority. According to the contents of Article 302 of the Code of Penal Proceeding, a person in flagrante delicto is one who:

I. is committing the penal infraction;

II. has just committed it;

III. is persecuted shortly after, by the authority, by the offended party, or by any person in the situation in which he is supposed to be the perpetrator of an infraction;

IV. is found, shortly after, with instruments, weapons, objects, or papers that make us presume he or she is the perpetrator of the infraction.

With the aim of protecting the adolescents' physical and moral integrity, not only do they have the guarantee of access to the identification of those who are responsible for an apprehension, but also the adolescents must be informed about rights (to be assisted either by the family or by a lawyer; to remain silent), and the apprehension and place of custody must be reported at once to the competent judicial authority and to the family or to the person pointed out by the juvenile.

If the parents or guardian show up, the law recommends the immediate release of the adolescent under a statement of commitment and responsibility presented to the prosecutor the same day or the first immediate workday. A release, however, must not take place if the infractional act is grave; because of the act's social repercussion, the adolescent must remain in custody either to guarantee personal safety or to maintain the public order.

If one deems necessary temporary internment (preventive custody) before the sentence, internment is for a maximum term of 45 days, and this decision must be well founded and supported in sufficient proofs of authorship and materiality of the infraction. The constitution states that nobody (including the 18-year-old minor) will be deprived of freedom without due process of law. According to Article 111, adolescents have the following guarantees:

I. full and formal knowledge of the imputation of an infraction by arraignment or equivalent means;

II. equality in the procedural relationship, with the right to confront victims and witnesses and produce all the proofs necessary to his or her defense;

III. technical defense by a lawyer;

IV. free and full legal assistance to those in need, according to the law;

V. the right to be personally heard by the competent authority;

VI. the right to request the presence of his or her parents or guardian in any phase of the proceedings.

These guarantees represent an extraordinary advance of the right of Infancy and Youth, in order to offer the adolescent the full jurisdictional protection of the state.

Social-Educational Measures

Addressed to the adolescent perpetrator of the infractional act, the social-educational measures aim, first of all, at reintegration in both the family and community, and one must take into account the capacity of the individual to follow the measures, as well as the circumstances and the gravity of the infraction.

The Statute of the Child and Adolescent enumerates in Article 112:

I. admonition;

II. obligation to repair the damage;

III. rendering of services to the community;

IV. assisted freedom;

V. insertion in a system of semiliberty;

VI. internment in an educational establishment;

VII. any of the forms foreseen in Article 101, from I to VI.

Applicable both singly and cumulatively, these measures can be replaced at any time by the competent authority, if it is deemed necessary.

Admonition

A milder measure recommended to first offenders or perpetrators of light infractional acts and applied in the presence of the parents or guardian (since it refers to them, too), the admonition, with pronounced preventive character, consists of verbal reproof, expressed in writing and signed.

Obligation to Repair the Damage

Of punishing and pedagogic content, this measure can be applied by the authority when the infractional act has patrimonial effects. The adolescent can be obligated to return the stolen item, to promote the reimbursement of the damage, or to compensate the victim's loss. However, the obligation to repair the damage does not require forced labor, which is forbidden by the federal constitution.

Rendering of Services to the Community

Not considered by the Code of 1979 but present in the penal legislation as a restrictive punishment of right, the rendering of services is an alternative measure to internment and consists of the accomplishment of free tasks, of general interest, for a period not more than six months, at hospitals, schools, and other congenerous agencies as well as in programs developed by the community or by the government.

The tasks, assigned in accordance with the abilities of the adolescent (and with his or her agreement, in the opinion of some authors, for, otherwise the tasks would be forced labor), must be accomplished during a maximum period of eight hours per week, on Saturdays, Sundays, and holidays or on workdays, so as not to hamper attendance at school or normal work hours.

Assisted Freedom

An improved form of supervised freedom and unanimously considered the most important, the most efficient of all social-educational measures, is assisted freedom. As foreseen in the Code of 1979 for minor infraction or deviation of behavior, it is adopted, in the terms of the Statute of the Child and Adolescent, whenever it seems the most convenient for the purpose of monitoring, aiding, and guiding an adolescent who has committed an infractional act. Clearly of educational and preventive character, its application is to those who habitually commit infractional acts, and it must be fixed for a minimum term of six months, subject to postponement or revocation and replacement by another measure.

The counselor, a person who is likely to follow the case, will be entrusted, supported, and supervised by a competent authority with the task of socially helping the adolescent, as well as the family, supervising attendance and school

achievement, and taking the steps to assure vocational training as well as placement in the work market, besides presenting a report of the case.

Here is Sotto Mayor's testimony (1992:340):

[W]e have no doubt to affirm that from the list of social educational measures, the one
which shows the best conditions of success is the assisted freedom on account of being
developed to interfere in the reality both familiar and social of the adolescent, intending
to release, by means of technical support, his potentialities.

System of Semiliberty

The adolescents to whom one applies semiliberty, identified in the adult plane
with a work-release facility, may carry out external activities during the day
(work or school attendance) but must be taken at night to a treatment institution.

The system, which demands technical monitoring, can be accomplished in
two ways:

1. since the start;
2. as a way of transition from internment to the open system.

Making use, when possible, of community resources for schooling and vocational training, the measure does not have a set term, although the law authorizes that the dispositions in regard to internment should be applied to it,
when it is adequate.

Internment

As defined by the statute, internment deprives the adolescent of his or her
freedom. Applicable by a judicial authority in a well-founded decision, it is
based on three essential principles:

1. brevity (without a set time, its maintenance is reevaluated at least each six months;
   and it will never exceed three years);
2. exceptionality (of residual character, the internment will be applied only as a last
   resort, that is, if the other measures are unviable or fail. It is admitted in three cases
   only: an infractional act committed by means of serious threat or violence to the
   person; reiteration in the commitment of other grave infractions; and repeated and
   unjustifiable nonfulfillment of the measure previously imposed. When the maximum
   limit is reached, the adolescent must be released and put in a system of semiliberty
   or assisted freedom, the release being obligatory at 21 years of age);
3. respect for the developmental stage of the person (it is incumbent on the state to
   watch over physical and moral integrity, adopting to this purpose proper measures of
   restraint and safety).

If the accomplishment of external activities is allowed, the internment must
be carried out in an institution only for adolescents, where pedagogic activities

are obligatory, and separation is based on three criteria: age, physical constitution, and gravity of the infraction. Also, adolescents deprived of freedom are guaranteed the rights expressed in Article 124.

Investigation of the Infractional Act

The statute covers only the form of investigation of the infractional act imputed to the adolescent; when it is a child, it is in the sphere of the Protective Council, and if the council is not available, the judicial authority can, in the terms of Article 153, investigate the facts and order, officially, the necessary measures, having previously heard the prosecutor.

Procedure in the Police Phase

According to the form of apprehension of the adolescent to whom is attributed the authorship of the infractional act, the law establishes a clear difference in the proceedings to be adopted:

1. if the investigation comes from judicial order, it will be, as soon as possible, forwarded to the judicial authority;
2. if it occurs in flagrante delicto, it will be shortly after taken to the competent police authority.

In case there is a specialized police office to attend the adolescent, different from the Minor's Code, if the infractional act has been committed with the aid of an adult, both will be sent, initially, to the specialized office, and only after the proper measures have been taken will the adult be sent to the adequate police office. The adolescent cannot be taken, together with the adult, to the common police station and later transferred to a specialized office.

However, if there is not a specialized office, which is the rule in hinterland regions, the adolescent will be transported to a common police station to await presentation in facilities separated from those meant for adults, but the stay, in any case, cannot exceed 24 hours.

In case of flagrante delicto, one must take into consideration these two procedures:

1. if the infractional act is committed by means of violent or serious threat to the person (e.g., robbery, rape), the police authority must register the record of apprehension, listen to the witnesses as well as to the adolescent; seize the product and the instruments of the infraction; and request examinations or expert investigations needed to prove the materiality and authorship of infraction;
2. in the other cases, a detailed report of occurrences can replace the registering.

If immediate release is not admissible, the possibility of which is examined right away, once the gravity of the infractional act ("grave" means an act punishable by the penal law with reclusion) and its social repercussion indicate the need for the adolescent to remain confined to guarantee personal safety or the maintenance of the public order, the police authority will take the youth, at once, to the prosecutor, together with a copy of the record of apprehension or the bulletin of occurrence.

If it is not possible to present a child to the prosecutor at once, the police authority will send the adolescent to the institution of assistance or treatment (it is forbidden to conduct or transport one in a closed compartment of a police car in conditions that hurt one's dignity or imply risk to physical or mental integrity), and its director, in 24 hours, will present the youth to the prosecutor.

If there is not an entity of assistance, the presentation will be carried out by the police authority, under the warning, as has already been stressed, that the eventual stay of the adolescent in a common police station must be in facilities separated from the ones for adults.

If the release is admissible, the police authority will send at once a copy of the record of apprehension or bulletin of occurrence to the prosecutor.

Finally, if the adolescent has not been caught in the practice of the infractional act, but there is evidence of participation, the police authority will send a report of the investigations and other documents to the prosecutor.

Procedure of the Prosecutor

The adolescent, previously released or kept in custody, in the terms of the statute law, will be presented to the prosecutor, who has the duty, on the same day, to take the necessary steps at once, to hear the youth and, if possible, the parents or guardian, victims, and witnesses.

The prosecutor, having in hand the record of apprehension, the bulletin of occurrence, or the police report, duly recorded in a Register Office (judicial) and with information about the past activities of the adolescent, will have, as *dominis litis,* the following options:

1. to promote the permanent filing of the records;
2. to grant the remission (which can eventually include the application of any measure, except the placement in a system of semiliberty and the internment);
3. to present the case to the judicial authority to apply a social-educational measure.

In the first two options, which demand well-founded justification, with a summary of the facts, the records will be remitted to the judicial authority for confirmation. This may or may not occur. If it occurs, the judicial authority will determine the execution of the measure. If it does not, that is, if there is disagreement, the judicial authority will send the records to the chief prosecutor of

010931७

the state, the superior authority of the Prosecutor's Office, by means of well-founded dispatch, who will take one of the following measures:

1. offer representation;
2. assign another prosecutor to present it;
3. ratify the permanent filing or the remission, which the judicial authority must confirm.

In the third option, which does not depend on preconstituted proof of authorship and of the materiality and which will propose the beginning of proceedings to apply the social-educational measure that seems to be the most convenient, the prosecutor's representation will be put forward with a brief summary of the facts as well as with the classification of the infractional act and, when needed, the list of witnesses. This can be done orally, in a daily session (innovation of the Statute of the Child and Adolescent) installed by the judicial authority. In it, the prosecutor should not specify the measure to be applied, as only after the presentation of the report of the interprofessional team, will it be known which is the most adequate measure to be taken as regards the adolescent.

Proceeding in the Judicial Phase

After the offer of representation by the prosecutor, the judicial authority will assign a hearing for the presentation of the adolescent ("of essential importance in order that the judge may check the characteristics of the personality of the adolescent, his familial as well as social situation, the extension and gravity of the practiced infractional act," according to Liberati, 1993:162), deciding, as soon as possible, about the decreeing or maintenance of temporary internment, which cannot exceed 45 days, the maximum term, which cannot be postponed and that one admits, in this case, for the conclusion of the proceedings and of which the nonobservation represents an illegal constraint that can cause reparation by means of habeas corpus.

The Statute of the Child and Adolescent stipulates that the adolescent and parents or guardian will be informed of the contents of the representation, as well as notified about showing up at the hearing, accompanied by a lawyer (the presence of the parents or guardian is a recommendation of the Rules of Beijing and of the Convention on the Rights of the Child). It foresees, equally, not only the indication of a special guardian to the adolescent, if the parents or guardian are not located, as well as if the adolescent cannot be located, the judicial authority will issue a warrant of search and apprehension, determining the suspension of the proceedings until effective presentation. If the youth is interned, one will request a presentation with no prejudice to the notification of the parents or guardian.

In the countryside, an internment unit may not exist in the form stipulated by the law (Article 123). Then, transfer to the nearest town will be arranged right away. If, however, this transfer is impossible, the adolescent will wait for removal in a police station, provided that this is done in a section separated from the one for adults and with proper installations, not to exceed the deadline of five days under the penalty of responsibility (subject to the sanctions of Article 235 of the Statute of the Child and Adolescent).

Nogueira's annotation (1991:244) reads:

The term of twenty-four hours, foreseen in the article 175, the 1st. paragraph, to present the adolescent to the prosecutor seems to conflict with the term of five days in the article 185, the 2nd. paragraph, which refers to the stay of the adolescent in a police office, in the absence of another, after his internment is maintained or decreed by the judicial authority.

However, the term of 24 hours concerns the presentation of the adolescent, apprehended in flagrante delicto, to the prosecutor, which must be on the same day or the next. The deadline of five days refers to the stay in a police office, after internment is decreed or maintained, until the juvenile is transferred to an adequate establishment.

With the adolescent appearing, and the parents or guardian also showing up, the judicial authority proceeds to a hearing, and the youth may ask for the opinion of a qualified professional (who may or may not be part of the inter-professional team). If the adolescent does not show up, without any just cause, a new date will be assigned, determining that the adolescent be presented by force.

At this moment, the judicial authority will judge whether the remission is adequate. If the remission seems adequate, the judge will listen to the prosecutor and will make a decision. If she or he understands differently, and the fact is grave, subject to application of the measure of internment or placing in an establishment of semiliberty, the judicial authority, after making sure the adolescent has no formal lawyer, will appoint one to defend the juvenile, assigning, as soon as possible, a hearing in continuity. The judge may also order the investigations, as well as the study of the case.

The formal lawyer or the designated defender will have three days, counted from the hearing of presentation, to present the previous defense and the list of witnesses.

After hearing the witnesses inscribed in the presentation, as well as in the previous defense, the investigations being completed and added to the report of the interdisciplinary team, the prosecutor will speak, along with the defense, 20 minutes each, and that time can be extended for 10 minutes, according to the judicial authority, who then will issue a decision.

Before the passing of the sentence, in any phase of the procedure, the judicial authority can choose in favor of the remission, as a form of extinction or suspension of the proceedings. The application of the measure will not be accomplished if in the sentence it is recognized that the infraction did not exist; if there is not any proof that the fact existed; or if it did not constitute an infractional act, or there are no proofs that the adolescent helped to commit the infractional act.

If the adolescent is interned, she or he will be released at once. If the judicial authority decides for the internment or semiliberty system, the legal notice of the sentence that applies these two measures is sent to the adolescent as well as to the defense; when the adolescent is not found, it is sent to parents or guardian with no prejudice to the defense.

If the application of any other measure is decided, the legal notice will be sent only to the defense. Should the legal notice be sent to the adolescent, she or he will decide whether to appeal the sentence.

THE INFORMAL SYSTEM

In the last few years, a movement has been growing in behalf of reducing to 16 years the age limit for penal responsibility, described in Article 104 of the Statute of the Child and Adolescent, under the justification that at that age one reaches biopsychosocial maturity and that lowering the age limit, owing to its intimidating force, would limit the high incidence of violence practiced by adolescents, mainly in urban areas.

Many people believe that a great number of young people become delinquents on account of impunity and that the procedural guarantees admitted by the statute make them practically unreachable, leaving them immune to the sanctions provided in it, which contributes to increased infant-juvenile delinquency.

The truth is that many policemen, badly guided, pretend that they have not seen the delinquent actions of these young people (when they do not take part, at the other extreme, in extermination groups), with the approval of a great segment of the population that opposes any repressive attitude as regards adolescent infractors, under the pretext that these youth are victims of society, as though victimization always justified criminality.

On the other hand, the lack of resources, in spite of "the privileged destination of public resources in areas related to the protection of infancy and youth" (Statute of the Child and Adolescent, Article 4, paragraph, subheading d), makes the numerous advancements of the new law unworkable.

It has been said that in many cities of the country, above all, in the hinterland, there are no specialized police stations to attend infractor adolescents. This is a reality that will hardly change in the near future.

Outside the sphere of the capitals, there are few units of internment, and they usually present deep deficiencies and are usually identified, in certain aspects, with prisons for adults. In them, as usual, are fragile measures of custody as well as safety (facilitating frequent escapes) and improper to the conditions of life of the adolescents that, deprived of freedom, without the separation among adolescents established by the law (by criteria of age, physical constitution, and gravity of the infraction), certainly do not believe in the rights related to Article

124 of the Statute of the Child and Adolescent (including to be treated with respect and dignity; to dwell in lodgings in adequate conditions of hygiene and health; to go to school and to receive vocational training; and to achieve cultural activities, sports as well as leisure).

Included among the social-educational measures, the rendering of services to the community has been little imposed by judges, who point out, among the inhibiting reasons, the insufficiency of both community and government support.

Likewise, assisted freedom, in spite of its virtues, recognized by all, has not even been adopted in some states, while, in others, it is clearly falling into disuse or has been terminated for lack of resources.

On account of these and other factors, internment, with all its defects, is apt to lose its residual character and is being used, against the law, with a regularity absolutely damnable.

Investigation of infractional acts attributed to adolescents has also been damaged by the lack of qualifications of a good number of professionals who operate in this field and who are insufficiently familiar with the law (this is explained, in part, by the fact that many academies, either of civil or military police, and courses of law, at the level of graduation and postgraduation, do not include in their curricula a course on Law of Infancy and Youth).

Added to this unpreparedness are the lack of interprofessional teams (which raises difficulties in the study of the cases and supporting the definition of the social-educational measures) and the scarcity of public defenders to take charge of rendering juridical assistance to them.

Among the various attributions of Protective Councils is one of attending children and adolescents, applying the measures in Article 101, from I to VII, as well as making arrangements for the application of the measure established by the judicial authority to the adolescent infractor. However, these councils have not been installed in the majority of counties of Brazil, although the law has been in force since 1990.

The lack of interest of the rulers (who effectively never gave priority to infancy and youth, which resulted in keeping millions of children apart from society and increasing the infant-juvenile delinquency), the apathy of the community (an accomplice in its indifference), and the alienation of prosecutors, judges, and lawyers (many of whom are tied to norms and principles that inform the Minor's Code, and are opponents of the changes established by the statute) strongly combine to widen the gap between legal text and practice.

SUMMARY

Born of the Penal Law, the Infancy and Youth Law came from a main worry: replacing the penalties previously imposed on minors that were of essentially retributive nature, with preventive and pedagogic measures that would aim to return minors to society.

The Introduction showed this gradual separation of the penal legislation, as well as the consolidation of a humanist current that takes into account the peculiar condition of boys and girls as persons in development and gives emphasis to measures that strengthen their familial and community links.

In this historic evolution, the Minor's Code of 1979 had a relevant role for the changes it promoted in the treatment of the minor infractor, demanding, for example, that one consider, in its application, the social, economic, and cultural context in which the minor was found, as well as parents or guardians, besides the study of each case, brought about by a team in which technical personnel takes part, whenever possible, even signaling the importance of the interests of the minor over any other value or interest juridically protected.

The code was definite in disciplining the measures applicable to minors, perpetrators of penal infraction, substituting a watched freedom, foreseen in the Mello Mattos Code, with the assisted freedom and determining that internment would be carried out only if the other measures were unviable or failed.

It is absolutely certain, from a delayed analysis of the Law 6.697, that, in spite of its imperfections, it represented, at its time, a remarkable advance in coping with the problem of minors.

The Statute of the Child and Adolescent, however, took an important step when it defined a new policy of assistance, with the participation of the community, and adopted the doctrine of integral protection, calling attention to the entitlement of both children and adolescents to rights and perceiving them as objects of absolute priority.

In dispositions for infractional acts, one has to stress the establishment of different measures for both children and adolescents as well as the guarantee that no adolescent, like the adult, will be deprived of freedom unless she or he is caught in flagrante delicto or by written and well-founded order of the competent judicial authority.

About the social-educational measures, it is suitable to repeat:

1. the demand to consider the capacity of the adolescent to fulfill them, as well as the circumstances and the gravity of the infraction;

2. the prohibition of forced labor;

3. the presupposition of sufficient proofs of the authorship as well as of the materiality of the infraction, except the hypothesis of remission;

4. the inclusion of the measure of rendering services to the community for a period of not more than six months.

Mindful of the defects of internment, one of the main challenges of the statute, legislators subjected it to the principles of brevity and exceptionality and with respect to the peculiar condition of people in development; established the re-evaluation of its maintenance every six months at most; fixed a maximum period of three years for internment, with compulsory release at 21; and listed the rights of the adolescent deprived of freedom, reaffirming the duty of the state to watch over his or her physical and moral integrity.

Looking at the regulating norms of the investigation of the penal infraction, the need to prevent police interference from becoming traumatic is evident, but it is also important, according to Article 111, to determine the full and formal knowledge of the attribution of the act, equality in the procedure, and technical defense by a lawyer.

On the other hand, the power of the prosecutor, an indispensable instrument to the juridical function of the state, was strengthened in the statute, making it a duty to promote and supervise the investigation of the infractions attributed to adolescents, and to grant the remission as a form of exclusion from the proceedings.

Besides its positive points, the Statute of the Child and Adolescent presents, however, some mistakes that must be corrected, for example, the ambiguity of certain dispositions and the adoption of the appeal system of the Code of Civil Proceedings for the procedures of penal nature. Therefore, one cannot fail to recognize, concerning future alterations of the law, the critical reflections that have been made, with profoundness as well as objectivity, by famous jurists like Alyrio Cavallieri and Wilson Barreira.

REFERENCES

Liberati, Wilson Donizetti. *Commentaries on the Statute of the Child and Adolescent.* São Paulo: Malheiros, 1993.

Nogueira, Paulo Lúcio. *The Statute of the Child and Adolescent.* São Paulo: Malheiros, 1991.

Sotto Mayor, Olympio. "On the Social Educational Measures." In *The Statute of the Child and Adolescent, Commented: Juridical and Social Commentaries,* edited by Munyr Cury. São Paulo: Malheiros, 1992.

APPENDIX: AGENCIES IN BRAZIL THAT HANDLE JUVENILE OFFENDERS

Fundação Centro Brasileiro para a Infância e a Adolescência
Setor de Autarquias Sul "SAS"
Quadra 5, Bloco H, Lote 5—2º andar
Brasília—DF.   CEP: 70.070.000
Fax: 550617745869

UNICEF
SEPN—Quadra 510, Bloco A—Edifício do INAM
Brasília—DF.   CEP: 70.750.530

Direct assistance to the juvenile offenders is given, in each state, by public welfare foundations.

3

CANADA*

Raymond R. Corrado and Alan Markwart

INTRODUCTION AND HISTORICAL BACKGROUND

Juvenile justice in Canada is more controversial than it has ever been in its nearly century-old existence. The contemporary debate is focused on the issue of youth violence. For the first time in Canadian history, politicians at the municipal, provincial, and federal levels of government are responding in earnest and in trepidation to the growing public and media clamor to ''get tough'' with youth criminals in general and violent youths in particular. There are daily media accounts of horrific and senseless violent acts committed by young offenders (ages 12 to 17 inclusive) that are largely unprecedented: youth gangs and ''wanna-be'' youth gangs operating in suburbs; drive-by shootings; home invasions in wealthy neighborhoods; jewelry store ''smash and grabs'' in large shopping malls involving semiautomatic guns being fired into the ceilings and terrorizing shoppers; several children under 12 years old committing serious crimes who can neither be arrested nor charged; and vicious murders by young offenders that often result in failed efforts to transfer to adult courts and therefore a maximum three-year youth detention sentence. While the homicide rate by young offenders in Canada has remained stable over the past 20 years (Silverman and Kennedy, 1993), charges for violent offenses have more than doubled since 1986 (Corrado and Markwart, 1994).

While most Canadians appear to blame the provincial youth justice systems and especially the federal law, the Young Offenders Act (YOA), for not protecting the public and adequately punishing and deterring young offenders, many scholars claim that the fear of youth crime is the unwarranted result of a media-induced ''moral panic.'' They argue that the media sensationalize the few violent

*Excluding the Province of Quebec

acts by a handful of young offenders, which greatly exaggerates the (minimal) real threat to the public. They maintain further that, due to the tremendous spillover of news and entertainment media from the United States, the public projects media images of endemic youth violence in major American cities onto the Canadian context, which results in erroneous views of Canadian young offenders, who have only superficial parallels with their American counterparts. In effect, it is argued that Canadian youth gangs have little in common with American youth gangs, yet the media depict a trend, for example, in Vancouver, British Columbia, that is based on projections from youth gang violence in Chicago and Los Angeles. Finally, these academics dismiss the official increase in youth violence statistics as artifacts of inappropriate changes in police charging practices; that is, minor assaults, once processed informally, are now supposedly being subjected to formal charges.[1]

The debate over youth justice in Canada reflects, to some degree, the disillusionment of the public and politicians—along with many criminal justice professionals and many academics—with the various models of youth justice that have been utilized during the twentieth century. Like other common-law jurisdictions, prior to 1908, Canada did not have a separate or distinctive youth justice system. Young persons were processed in the same criminal court system as adults, albeit with certain special common-law principles such as *doli incapax*, or the inability to form criminal intent, being available as a substantive defense for children due to immaturity by age.

Similarly, by the early nineteenth century, houses of refuge had evolved to provide separate custodial facilities to avoid the harmful impact of mixing youth with adults. By the late nineteenth century, however, the "child-saving" movement had matured, largely in the province of Ontario, and its leading proponent, J. J. Kelso, succeeded in convincing provincial and federal politicians that the neoclassical theory of crime was invalid in explaining why youth committed crime and, therefore, that the philosophically related justice model-based criminal justice system was inappropriate for children. This system emphasized due process, procedurally, and the severity of offense and extent of prior record for sentencing principles.

The child-savers in Canada and the United States simultaneously argued that youths engaged in deviant behavior were incorrectly labeled criminal, because they lacked willful intent. Instead, such behavior, it was argued, was the result of predetermined social and economic influences involving inadequate parenting, peers, schooling, and housing, all usually associated with poverty and/or immigrant cultural norms. Justice model principles such as due process (or fair procedures, in the Canadian context), proportionality of punishment and severity of offense, and prior record did not deter deviant youth from evolving into criminals as adults because these youth needed to be rehabilitated, not punished. Positivist theories had become increasingly popular in Canada, and the child-savers were convinced that, with "scientifically" based rehabilitation programs, a separate and distinct juvenile justice system was required.

Since all criminal law and justice legislation in Canada is constitutionally under federal parliamentary jurisdiction, the Juvenile Delinquents Act (JDA) was passed in 1908 as a federal law applicable to all 10 provinces and the two territories. The respective provincial governments—which are constitutionally responsible for the administration of federal criminal law—passed their own laws to create the administrative policies, structures, and programs to implement the philosophical and legal principles stipulated in the JDA. With the exception of one minor adjustment, this law remained in effect in its original form until 1984. It was virtually identical to the juvenile justice laws that were being passed in the United States, beginning in Illinois in 1899; that is, the JDA embodied all the principles of a welfare-based juvenile justice model, including informal court proceedings, the diagnosis of delinquents, and rehabilitating them in their best interests in the case of a wide range of status and criminal offenses.

The movement to reform the JDA began in 1961, in response to concerns expressed in the federal Department of Justice about the apparent increase in adult prison populations. The assumption was that this increase was somehow potentially associated with problems in the provincial juvenile justice systems. Most critically, the question was raised about whether rehabilitation was actually taking place, since it seemed that many, if not most, adult criminals had been juvenile delinquents. An advisory committee was appointed to investigate these principal issues and provide recommendations for reforming the JDA. Committee members received briefs from a wide range of interest groups and organizations, as well as information from similar inquiries and scholars in England, Scotland, and the United States.

In its 1965 report, *Juvenile Delinquency in Canada,* the committee, while critical of the arbitrariness of decision making related to the absence of due process, did not object, in principle, to the welfare model basis of the JDA. Instead, the committee's reform recommendations reflected the goal of curbing abuses and excesses arising from informal procedures, while reaffirming the focus on rehabilitation. This report set the stage for the first bill to reform the JDA in 1968, which failed because of provincial objections to unconstitutional federal incursions into provincial jurisdiction contained in certain sections of the proposed law. The next attempt, in 1970, was defeated largely by opposition from welfare model advocates who were critical of what they believed was a drift away from rehabilitation to legalistic processing and justice model principles. Nonetheless, this feared trend provided the philosophical basis for the subsequent reform bill, introduced in 1975, which emphasized justice model principles. Again, provincial objections involving jurisdictional concerns resulted in the postponement of legal reform.

During the second half of the 1970s, however, some provinces, such as Quebec and British Columbia, initiated their own administrative reforms, which were tantamount to fundamental changes in their provincial youth justice systems. Finally, after several more aborted attempts to replace the JDA, the federal Parliament unanimously passed the YOA in 1982. By the end of the 20-year period of attempts to reform juvenile justice in Canada, the youth justice law that eventually emerged was a product of a broad consensus among politicians and bureaucrats, but juvenile justice was also largely ignored by the media and the public. The initial consensus and lack of controversy reflected the philosophical eclecticism of the YOA and the invisibility of youth crime as an issue in Canada.

The Young Offenders Act

Passed by Parliament in 1982, the YOA was not proclaimed into force until 1984 in order to allow the provinces to pass their own complementary laws and adjust their administrative procedures and programs to the new federal law. The new uniform maximum age provision of 18 years was delayed until 1985 since its implementation for those provinces with previous lower maximum ages required considerable restructuring of youth correctional programs and facilities to accommodate the older young offenders (see note 1).

As mentioned before, several provinces already had adjusted their laws and juvenile justice systems in anticipation of the YOA, and, consequently, only minor adjustments took place while, for the others, fundamental restructuring was required, especially in nonmetropolitan youth courts. Outside major metropolitan juvenile courts, the JDA's welfare model philosophy was deeply entrenched. Informal procedures, the absence of defense counsel, the strong influence of local mores regarding appropriate sentences, and the limited availability of programs in these nonmetropolitan courts were juxtaposed with most metropolitan juvenile courts where due process was common, especially since legal aid programs provided defense counsel (usually identified as duty counsel) not only at the initial intake or first appearance but also for subsequent appearances, including trials. In effect, the much more formalized legal procedures mandated by YOA were already reasonably well established in advance of their proclamation into law in metropolitan centers.

The act's "Declaration of Principle" structures its administrative interpretation and implementation by the provinces and territories and legal interpretation by all the relevant courts, including the Supreme Court of Canada. Eight principles are set out in this declaration, with the first three principles establishing the basis for characterizing this law as representative of a modified justice model approach to juvenile justice: young persons are to be responsible and accountable for their criminal acts, yet not to the same extent as adults; all the rights and safeguards provided to adults are available to youth, along with certain additional rights; and the special needs and circumstances of adolescents must be considered in any decisions about young offenders. The last principle, in particular, modifies the classic justice model approach to criminal justice because it requires that the typical criteria for decision making found in the adult criminal justice system, such as the proportionality of the sentence to the severity of offense and prior record, are to be adjusted according to the special needs of each young offender. In effect, the rehabilitative needs of adolescents still play a crucial, though less prominent, role in the youth justice system. In practice, this principle usually translates into less punitive decisions for young offenders in order to meet their distinctive youthful needs and circumstances. The modified justice model, therefore, generally characterizes the various provincial and territorial youth justice systems because the emphasis in the key principles is on essential justice model principles (i.e., fair procedure, accountability) modified by the main welfare model principle of rehabilitation (Corrado, 1992).

Several of the drafters of the YOA and its subsequent proponents have argued that the YOA is not a mere replication of the laws governing the adult criminal justice system, vehemently denying the interpretation by Marxist and conflict theorists that the YOA is simply a punitive "kiddies' criminal code" (Archambault, 1986; Bala, 1992; West, 1984). Given its long gestation in becoming law, the YOA's supporters assert that its strength is found in the deliberate plan to amalgamate principles from various models of juvenile justice in a manner to best meet the complex demands and rights of both the public and young offenders (Bala, 1992). The protection of society through deterrent sentences is viewed as appropriate in cases where there is a more immediate need to prevent additional crimes. Again, given the "special needs" principle, even when incapacitating or deterrent sentences are imposed, young offenders are supposed to be provided resources to deal with their various personal problems, including physical or mental illness, psychological disorders, and learning disabilities. Yet, despite such needs, the YOA requires the consent of the young offender before a "treatment order" placement in a hospital or other similar institution can take place. In effect, there are to be no explicitly coercive treatment sentences to institutional or residential treatment programs.

The concern with avoiding labeling young offenders for isolated and nonserious criminal behavior, has resulted in the YOA's banning the publication of the identity of all young offenders and restricting access to records. Similarly, these minor offenses are the major rationale for the principle of "minimum interference" in processing and sentencing. Diversion options, known as "alternative measures," and taking no measures (e.g., police caution) are mandated but are not mandatory considerations under the YOA; that is, each province may establish explicit policy and programs that constitute alternatives to a formal processing through youth court. In practice, every province has established such diversionary programs, though there is considerable variation in the extent of diversion; for example, Ontario has a per capita rate of youth court cases that is four times higher than that of neighboring Quebec (Corrado and Markwart, 1994).

Finally, the YOA is heralded by its proponents for providing youth with extensive rights. The police must inform youths of their right to consult a parent or lawyer and to remain silent, and a written statement consenting to waive these rights is required before any admission or incriminating statement is made. As well, youth are provided an absolute right to government-paid counsel, independent of their parents, at every stage of formal youth court proceedings. In essence, youths are accorded a more complete set of rights than adults, and case law since 1984 has effectively confirmed and even expanded these rights. For example, not only must police inform the youths of their rights, but the onus is on the police to ensure that youths comprehend these rights beyond a mere verbal acknowledgment. Similarly, while parents are to be notified quickly about their children upon arrest and detention, parents cannot coerce or induce them into disclosing incriminating evidence.

Transfer to adult court can occur only if a youth 14 years and older has been charged with an indictable (felony) offense. The youth court judge employs the following criteria in making this decision: the severity of the alleged offense; the age and character of the youth; prior record; the adequacy of the youth justice system versus the adult criminal justice system for dealing with the case; the adequacy of youth treatment or correctional resources; and any other factors deemed relevant. In practice, transfers are much less frequent under the YOA than the JDA and have declined since the advent of the YOA to the point where they are now very uncommon—there were only 32 cases in the entire country transferred to adult court in 1992–1993 (Corrado and Markwart, 1994). In effect, transfer is now usually reserved for very serious, violent offenses where the youth court judge considers it necessary to incapacitate the alleged young offender both to protect society and to express sufficient moral condemnation and punishment for those few youths who show little potential for rehabilitation.

Aside from the maximum three-year custodial sentence for murder (which can include an additional two-year conditional supervision period), judges can impose an absolute discharge, a fine up to $1,000, restitution or compensation, up to 240 hours of community service, up to two years' probation, or detention for the purposes of treatment for up to two years (if the younger offender consents to treatment). For offenses other than murder, judges can impose custodial dispositions up to a maximum of three years, two years, or six months, depending on the type of offense. Judges also decide the type of custody, that is, open versus secure, and review their own fixed-length dispositions to ascertain the progress of the young offender and determine whether a mitigation of the disposition (e.g., early release) is justified. Automatic annual court reviews of custodial sentences are required by law, with the youth also having the right to apply for earlier reviews. In effect, judges have considerable power over youth correctional authorities to guard against abuses or arbitrary decisions, which were seen to have occurred far too often under the JDA welfare model approach to indefinite sentencing.

The mixture of principles from the various models of juvenile justice, again, was a conscious attempt to balance the complex needs of young people and their due process rights with public perceptions of justice and protection. The emphasis, while subject to considerable ongoing debate and controversy, has been on due process and other justice model principles, yet the reform trends are clearly toward crime control model principles of punitiveness, retribution, incapacitation, and deterrence (Corrado and Markwart, 1992, 1994).

Although only 10 years old, the YOA has already been amended in two separate parliamentary bills. While these changes were hardly draconian, they have focused almost exclusively on law enforcement concerns, for example, enforcement of court orders and penalties for murder. In 1994, a bill was introduced into Parliament that will, among other things, provide for a presumption of transfer to adult court of 16- and 17-year-olds charged with homicide, attempted murder, aggravated assault, and aggravated sexual assault. In effect, there has been a shift in the modified justice model YOA along the continuum of juvenile justice models toward the crime control model and away from the welfare model. However, not all provinces have responded to the YOA and the subsequent reforms and controversies in the same manner. Since several provinces had initiated changes in their youth justice systems as early as the middle of the 1970s, institutions, programs, and procedures have become quite entrenched. This process is most visible in Quebec, where a corporatist model (Pratt, 1989) approach was adopted, and, despite the YOA, it has remained essentially intact. The emphasis in Quebec is on administrative (diversionary) processing of most cases, with the youth court acting as a residual option for the most serious offenses or offenders. Diversion and multidisciplinary integrated intervention plans characterize the typical assessment and processing of youths, which is not unlike the recent trends in other jurisdictions, such as England and Wales (Corrado and Turnbull, 1992).

British Columbia, in contrast, initiated justice model reforms in the late 1970s. The emphasis was on fair procedures, the protection of the public, the seriousness of offense and prior record, and decriminalizing status offenses. Crown counsel quickly became the pivotal decision maker at the intake stage and an important role player during the trial and sentencing hearings. When the YOA took effect, the British Columbia youth justice system, in principle, had few major adjustments, other than resource requirements required by the influx of 17-year-olds arising from the rise in maximum age jurisdiction to 18 from the previous age of 17 years. Other provinces, however, had to undertake fundamental changes in their provincial laws, policies, institutions, programs, and roles.

THE FORMAL SYSTEM

Keeping in mind that Quebec is entirely different, the remaining nine provinces have drawn closer in institutions and programs over the decade that the YOA has been in effect. The initial most common and major structural change occurred in the organization and delivery of youth correctional services. Given the welfare model JDA emphasis on rehabilitation, it was not surprising that in all the provinces, except British Columbia and New Brunswick, organizational responsibility for dispositional or correctional services rested with departments of social services (child welfare). Mixing juvenile delinquents and child welfare wards was common in most provinces under the JDA; however, since the YOA strictly limits youth justice jurisdiction to criminal offenses and has a much stronger justice model/criminal law orientation, seven provinces shifted dispositional services entirely to correctional departments, which also administered adult correctional services and fell under the auspices of a justice ministry. Ontario has retained a split departmental jurisdiction, with the Ministry of Community and Social Services (child welfare) responsible for young offenders under 16 years and correctional services responsible for the older youth; a similar approach is taken in Nova Scotia.

With respect to court systems, Ontario and Nova Scotia established "two-tiered" or "split jurisdiction" court systems, with the former family courts hearing cases for youths under 16 years and provincial criminal courts dealing with the older youths. In recent years, Ontario has begun to rely on the senior provincial court for the processing of YOA cases. In the remaining provinces, the court systems have remained intact, with the established provincial courts being responsible for processing cases.

Finally, because of the principle of alternative measures (diversion), several provinces had to develop new diversion programs. British Columbia, Quebec, and Manitoba, in varying degrees, already had institutionalized these programs before the YOA. While these organizational/structural changes were, in total, substantial, especially for those provinces that adhered to welfare model principles more strictly, the more substantial impact in the way that youths are processed under the YOA involved the changing roles of key actors in the youth justice system.

There is little doubt that, for much of the history of the JDA, probation officers and (in certain provinces such as Ontario) the police played the key intake roles. As well, probation officers had considerable influence in assisting the court in the remaining key decision-making stages, including sentencing. As stated before, most provinces had already begun to enhance the role of prosecutors and defense counsel (usually in major cities), especially at the expense of probation officers, but the YOA entrenched and accelerated this trend. As well, the role of judges, again at the expense of probation officers and correctional authorities, expanded under the YOA since they were accorded the capacity to impose definite sentences, determine level of custodial placement (open or secure), and review (mitigate) and enforce their own sentencing decisions.

Crown Counsel (Prosecution)

Crown counsel's enhanced role is most complete in British Columbia, Quebec, and New Brunswick, where all intake decisions, including diversion and the decision to proceed with a charge (and what type of charge), rest exclusively with them, albeit in consultation with the police and probation officers for some cases. Even in the remaining provinces, where police still directly lay charges,

Crown counsel can stay or withdraw the charge or refer it for diversion, thereby effectively ending any further proceedings. Crown counsel's function is to review all cases regarding the sufficiency of evidence to determine both the appropriateness of a specific charge and the likelihood of a conviction. The latter assessment has been remarkably impressive since the average guilty rate (across 10 provinces) is 94 percent (Corrado and Markwart, 1992).

While there are currently no jury trials under the YOA, recent proposed reforms will require jury trials in murder cases that are not transferred to adult court.[2] Crown counsel conduct the prosecution of trials. However, given the enormously high rate of guilty outcomes (including negotiated or plea-bargained guilty pleas), they also can play important roles in bail/detention and the disposition stages of proceedings. With respect to detention before trial, the onus is on Crown counsel to "show cause" as to why the accused must be detained, usually on the grounds of the need for public protection or a likelihood of failure to appear.

At the dispositional stage, Crown counsel will usually make submissions, based on their own personal view of the young offender, the seriousness of the offense and offense history, and the predisposition report (PDR) prepared by a probation officer. The PDR provides a detailed review of social history, including possible mitigating and aggravating factors, and sentencing options. There is evidence to suggest that Crown counsel's input is strongly desired by judges, which is not surprising, given the principles of accountability and protection of the public of the YOA (Hanscomb, 1988). At the dispositional stage, it is considered appropriate for Crown counsel to play a key role regarding the application of these principles to the particular case.

Another key function for Crown counsel involves the decision in more serious, usually violent, offenses to seek a transfer to the adult criminal court. Only Crown counsel or the young person may apply for a transfer, but the latter rarely occurs. In these applications, Crown counsel will typically argue the position that the alleged young offender is likely not to benefit from the unique treatment resources available in the youth correctional system and that the protection of public and the severity of the offense justify the need to employ the much longer custodial sentences available in the adult justice system.

Finally, Crown counsel solely decide whether to appeal the (perceived) unfavorable decisions of youth court judges involving transfer to the adult court, procedural issues, verdicts, bail, or sentences. Unlike the JDA, appeals are no longer uncommon, given the confusing mix of legal principles from the various youth justice models that are incorporated into the YOA and the much greater procedural complexity of the new act. Crown counsel, along with all other decision makers, are faced with ambivalent, conflicting, and vague criteria. Transfer hearings, in particular, have been a major area of appeals because, in almost every province, Crown counsel will seek transfer in cases involving extremely violent offenses, especially murder, committed by alleged older offenders. Given that the highest appellate courts in the different provinces varied in their emphasis on the different YOA principles, yet the constitutionally entrenched federal *Charter of Rights and Freedoms* guarantees equal treatment under the law, it remained for the Supreme Court of Canada to decide which principles should hold sway in transfer applications. The Supreme Court, in various decisions, has leaned heavily toward the special needs principle and against transfer, despite widespread public anger about lenient youth court sentences for extremely violent young offenders. Despite the Supreme Court precedents, Crown counsel in most provinces still routinely seek the transfer of all older youths charged with murder and, more sporadically, in cases involving other vicious, violent offenses.

Crown counsel are also involved in the sentencing appeal process, where similar problems have arisen regarding which of the often conflicting principles of the YOA have precedence. Crown counsel, as expected, have argued in support of more punitive or "just deserts" sentences. There also have been frequent appeals respecting the admissibility of evidence, given the stringent and technical constraints on the admissibility of such evidence.

The Police

Crown counsel, while making the critical intake and prosecutorial decisions, nonetheless remain dependent on the police and probation officers in various ways. To begin, the police retain their traditional function of reacting to, and investigating, youth crime. The police report begins the process of "swearing an information" or the laying of a criminal charge. The initial decision concerning the specific charge, for example, murder versus manslaughter, is based on the investigating police officer's interpretation of the evidence. Before an information is sworn in British Columbia, New Brunswick, and Quebec, Crown counsel must first approve the charge. In all other provinces, however, Crown counsel must approve of a case's moving beyond the initial charge stage.

Since the advent of the YOA, the police have to follow strict procedures in investigating cases, especially once any contact is made with a youth. If a police officer asks any questions of a youth that are potentially self-incriminating, they are inadmissible in court without prior warnings by the police about the right to remain silent and the right to have and contact a defense counsel or other adults before questioning. Equally critical, the youth must sign a written waiver that acknowledges any statements as voluntary and that they are aware of these YOA rights. The appellate court decisions, to date, have been strict in their interpretation of police investigative procedures, which, as expected, has resulted in considerable resentment by the police about the ensuing difficulties they face in investigating and charging youths, whom they see as "hiding" behind their rights or "playing the technicality game" to avoid criminal responsibility. This issue has become particularly troublesome for the police investigating property offenses since they have traditionally relied on confessions and related interview techniques to extract incriminating evidence in the absence of either direct victims, stolen property, catching them in the act, or eyewitnesses.

More recently, the police have expressed considerable frustration with violent young offenders, especially those belonging to either informal groups, "wannabe" gangs, or hybrid adult/youth gangs that engage in more systematic property and violent crimes, yet avoid being charged and/or successfully prosecuted because they have learned how to utilize their due process rights to prevent the police from gathering the necessary evidence. In this regard, the police, not infrequently and derisively, refer to the YOA as the "Youth Protection Act."

Further, the police often criticize Crown counsel for being too technical and timid in their decisions not to proceed with a case. They are equally frustrated with judges who, from a police perspective, do not appreciate the importance of incapacitory custodial sentences and the need for sufficiently punitive sentences for both general and specific deterrence purposes. In effect, the consensus among the police is that the YOA is weighted far too much in favor of young offenders' rights at the expense of the police's primary function to protect the public. They watch, with growing alarm, the increase in both the amount of youth violence and its viciousness. The YOA is seen not as direct cause of this increase but rather as a facilitating factor. This cynicism and frustration have reached the level in some provinces, such as British Columbia, Alberta, and Manitoba, where there appears to be a fundamental crisis of confidence among many police forces about youth justice.

Probation Officer

The triad of interdependent roles is completed with probation officers. As mentioned before, probation officers deal directly with Crown counsel in their investigations of the social backgrounds of young offenders, and, similarly, they can interview investigating police officers as well in preparing precourt inquiries (submitted to Crown counsel to assist in their decision to proceed with a charge or to divert) and predisposition reports. As well, probation officers coordinate with the police in supervising probation orders. Young offenders on probation have their status registered on a national police computer information network, which the police check routinely when they suspect a youth is involved in a criminal incident, or they know the individual is, or likely is, on probation. The police and case probation officer coordinate information in dealing with youth on probation since any breach of a condition of probation can result in a new charge.

Since the YOA, the role of the probation officer also appears directly affected by the modified justice model principle of due process. In an Ontario survey of youth court judges, for example, judges indicated that they preferred that probation officers play a neutral role in their court functions, in contrast to acting according to the welfare model principle of "the best interests" of the youth (Hanscomb, 1988). This more neutral role is reinforced by other provisions of the YOA that restrict the probation officer's former option of recommending direct placement of a youth as a "ward" of the child welfare department. Similarly, a recommendation for a treatment order that mandates that a youth be placed in a hospital or residential treatment center is no longer available. Only if a youth consents to treatment can such an order be recommended in a predisposition report and included in a sentence. Not unexpectedly, few young offenders have been willing to consent to treatment: these orders have declined dramatically since the YOA despite the assertion by several prominent clinicians that many of these youths have serious "special needs" for such services (Leschied et al., 1992).

Beyond limiting the role of probation officers in their former advocacy function of acting in the "best interests" of the youth, the YOA has also restricted their enforcement powers. Under the JDA, probation officers had the rather blunt option of returning a delinquent to court by simply asserting that a breach of probation had occurred, which could then result in a more severe sentence as punishment. This procedure was typically fairly perfunctory in nature. Crown counsel, who prosecute breach charges laid by probation officers, now must convince the court that a breach was intended, and, as well, they face the technical obstacles raised by defense counsel in satisfying the burden of proof beyond a reasonable doubt. Further, in the absence of proof of a breach, new or additional conditions of probation cannot be imposed without the consent of the youth.

Defense Counsel

The routine presence of defense counsel at potentially every stage of processing is the most dramatic role change in youth justice in Canada. While this change was evident in most major cities well in advance of the YOA, its uniform impact on court proceedings was activated by the passage of the act and the broader institutionalization of the role of the defense counsel in the new and far more adversarial proceedings created by the new law. As previously mentioned, youth must be made aware immediately at the outset of a police investigation of their right to counsel before questioning may proceed. Upon arrest and detention, a youth must make a first appearance in the youth court within 24 hours (or within 72 hours on a weekend). Duty counsel are available for these appearances to advise and represent youth about the legal issues, including bail and plea. Upon first appearance in court, a youth is accorded an absolute right to government-funded counsel; that is, if the youth requests counsel, the court is required to order the appointment of counsel, even if the youth or parents have the ability to pay for their own counsel. Youths can typically choose their own lawyer, who will usually receive remuneration on a tariff fee for specific services from a provincially funded legal aid agency. Adjournments are common since youths often require additional time to choose lawyers, and the latter usually need preparation time and coordination of scheduling with the court for future appearances.

The relationship between youth and defense counsel is somewhat ambiguous because, while the YOA requires strict procedural regularity in the proceedings and an absolute right to counsel, the philosophical principle of "special needs" implies that immaturity due to age mitigates against defense counsel's simply acting upon the direction of their client. This ambiguity was evident in research that identified that lawyers adopt a variety of approaches to their client relationships along a continuum between strict advocate to parentlike guardian (Milne, Linden, and Kueneman, 1992). In effect, some lawyers play a purely adversarial role, where the primary objective is to challenge the prosecutor at every proceeding in order to avoid any adverse decisions for their client. At the other extreme, some lawyers maintain that some clients are so troubled with personal and social problems that they serve their clients better by cooperating with youth court officials to work out arrangements that best address these problems, rather than simply addressing the narrow legal issues. For example, to rely on a technical legality to have a case dismissed for a client who is a 13-year-old drug-addicted prostitute with a history of familial and "pimp" abuse is seen as an immoral disservice, given that the youth, upon release, will return directly to the streets, with possibly tragic results.

There is no evidence that the presence of defense counsel has resulted in advantages to young offenders in sentencing hearings. Indeed, there is evidence that significant increases in the use of custody after the advent of the YOA paralleled increases in representation by defense counsel (Corrado and Markwart, 1988). Their presence has also resulted in more and longer hearings and greater court delay (Corrado and Markwart, 1988).

However, there is the widely held view among the police that defense counsel have reduced their ability to assist in the successful prosecution and incapacitation of what they claim are serious young offenders. The police, especially gang specialists, assert that repeat young offenders know the adversarial "tricks of the game" and regard the youth justice system as a joke. Even if convicted and sentenced to custody, gang members or other violent young offenders are seen as unafraid and undeterred by youth custody because they do "easy time" in contrast to what they would have experienced in adult prisons (Corrado, 1994). Yet, there are criticisms from judges who maintain the opposite about the impact of defense counsel, that is, that they too often are unprepared and do not adequately assist their clients, especially at the disposition stage (Hanscomb, 1988). Despite these competing views, there is little doubt that defense counsel have become increasingly central to youth justice since the YOA, and, to date, there is no issue of reforming (either enhancing or diminishing) their role. This is not surprising, given that the major impetus for the YOA, historically, has been the concern that youth be assured of due process safeguards.

Judges

Judges, like probation officers, experienced a fundamental restructuring of their role in youth justice. Under the welfare model JDA, they had enormous individual discretion in defining their approaches to delinquent youth. While more formal procedures became evident among urban judges by the late 1970s, the YOA clearly narrows their authority at the preadjudication stage. They, for example, can no longer transfer young offenders to adult court on their own initiative, and they do not have the latitude to intervene in the same informal manner by making inquiries at initial appearances. The more adversarial process has resulted in youth court judges' (again, more so in the metropolitan courts) adopting a role not dissimilar from that in adult court criminal proceedings.

At the adjudication stage, youth court judges have experienced both an increase in authority and a decrease. They no longer can directly commit a young offender to the care of child welfare officials. Youth court judges, however, now exercise direct control over the administration of custodial dispositions, not only in terms of imposing definite sentencing lengths but also in terms of the level of custody (open or secure), transfers between levels of custody, and early releases from custody.

During the summer of 1994, the federal Parliament introduced an amendment to the YOA that substantially enhances judges' sentencing authority, since it allows youth court judges to sentence young offenders to up to 10 years for first-degree murder and up to 7 years for second-degree murder. Also, the onus will be on 16- and 17-year-olds charged with serious, violent crimes to persuade youth court judges why they should not be tried in adult courts. The political message being sent to youth court judges from the public and politicians is unmistakably clear—serious youth violence is to be punished far more severely. It remains to be seen whether the more punitive custodial trends witnessed since the YOA will be intensified; youth court judges still are subject to appellate court decisions, which, to date, have consistently upheld the ambivalent sentencing principles of the YOA. In effect, the individual sentencing ideology of a youth court judge likely will be the most decisive factor, rather than any automatic response to the public, media, and politicians.

Youth Correctional Services

Youth correctional authorities have also been affected by the due process focus of the YOA. As mentioned before, correctional officials no longer have the authority, at their own discretion, to place, move, and release young offenders in custody. As well, young offenders have various resources available to challenge unfavorable decisions made by correctional officials, including contacting their defense counsel, judicial custodial reviews, and, in several provinces, the politically independent office of the ombudsman. Arbitrary and/or abusive treatment in correctional facilities and programs, therefore, is much more likely to be identified than in the past, and, consequently, it is rarely reported in the media.

Most provinces have retained a wide mixture of youth community correctional programs and custodial facilities. Supervision remains the key function of probation officers, who also play a key role in referring youth to other community-based programs such as community service, intensive supervision, and counseling services. Privately contracted programs such as "wilderness challenge" camps and programs offered by other child-serving departments, such as foster home placement, alternate schools, and community-based substance abuse treatment, add to the variety of program options. Typically, far more extensive resources are available in metropolitan areas, while the more remote communities, especially Native Indian bands, have few immediately accessible resources.

While Ontario and Saskatchewan have taken some steps toward more integration of the delivery of their youth correctional services with child welfare and mental health programs, most provinces have been reluctant to take the extreme move of establishing an integrated youth services department. The YOA is seen as an impediment to such integration, at least philosophically, because its principles direct policymakers away from the traditional dangers of the welfare model's more integrated and treatment-oriented approach. Yet, a major criticism of the current youth correctional service delivery systems (outside Quebec) is that too many serious multiproblem youth "fall between the cracks" of the various departmental programs and receive little, if any, systematic and effective services. In effect, because of the myriad of differing access criteria for the various departmental programs and because of budget restrictions, it is exceedingly difficult for probation officers to develop comprehensive case plans, given that the needed services are spread among so many different government departments.

Custodial institutions vary substantially across the provinces for several reasons. Most important, there is no common operational definition for open and secure facilities. Generally, the degree of physical security distinguishes the two types, but the exact criteria for identifying the level, such as wire-fenced perimeters versus just locked doors, differs considerably by province (Markwart, 1992). As well, the availability of service and treatment programs and resources differs. Typically, the primary program focus in youth custody centers is the provision of security, health, education, and recreational services, whereas treatment services are usually available on an ad hoc demand basis, provided either by private contractors or by arrangement with noncorrectional government agencies. In most provinces, youth correctional services are separate from child welfare and mental health services. In contrast, Quebec policy, since the passage of their provincial Youth Protection Act of 1977, has been to emphasize treatment programs within institutions, while mixing their populations of young offenders and child welfare wards. The rationale in Quebec is that multiproblem youth need extensive treatment resources, regardless of whether they enter these institutions through the youth justice or child welfare systems.

INFORMAL PRACTICES

Given the due process emphasis of the YOA, informal practices are not nearly as evident as they were under the JDA. Defense counsel, in the interest of seeking technical defenses, are likely to keenly scrutinize the police and court processing of their clients. Crown counsel, as well, closely review police processing because they know any inappropriate behavior could be detrimental to the Crown's case, once brought to the attention of a judge. Further, judges are mandated by the YOA and an ever growing body of case law to scrupulously adhere to due process. Nonetheless, informal practices exist in all formal youth justice systems, some of which are controversial.

One controversial issue in Canada involves police charging practices. The current debate is between the police, on one hand, who claim that charging practices have not changed since the YOA in a manner that artificially increases violent offense charge rates, and, on the other hand, government officials and some academics who argue that the police are charging far more youths for minor violent incidents that were informally dealt with or diverted under the JDA (e.g., schoolyard fights). The increased charge rates, the critics claim further, contribute to the media-induced ''moral panic'' among the public, which, in turn, promotes calls for crime control model reforms from politicians (Corrado and Markwart, 1994).

The contrary view is that the more than doubling of charges for violent offenses since the YOA went into effect accurately reflects what the police are confronting. In recent studies in British Columbia, interviews with the police and other youth justice personnel, as well as school officials, revealed that the police are reluctant to charge youths for minor violent incidents because of the extensive and time-consuming paperwork required to initiate the charge process and their fear that, if Crown counsel do not reject the case because it is trivial, then a youth court judge will effectively let the young offender off with a lenient ''slap on the wrist.'' As well, it is argued that fear of retaliation, especially from informal youth groups, wanna-be gangs, and formal adult/youth gangs, inhibits victims from either reporting to the police or testifying. In effect, according to this view, official charge statistics may underrepresent the actual increases in youth violence (Corrado, 1994).

Another issue is the disproportionate number of Native Indian youth committed to youth correctional facilities. In British Columbia, for example, Native Indians are overprosecuted by as much as four times, whereas in other provinces such as Saskatchewan, where there are greater concentrations of Native Indians, more than half of the youth custody population is native. It is not, however, clear whether the arrest and sentencing to custody of Native Indian youth in far greater numbers than non-Native Indian youth are the result of informal discriminatory practices within the youth justice system. An in-depth interview survey of Native Indian youth in all the custodial facilities in British Columbia during a period in 1993 revealed that, in their view, discrimination was not a substantial factor in their experience within the youth justice system (MacDonald, 1994). However, official government inquiries in the provinces of Alberta and Manitoba have reported systematic discriminatory practices against Native Indian youth, which, it was claimed, resulted in more punitive official responses. This issue has intensified the political momentum to establish Native Indian-operated youth justice programs, beyond just hiring Native Indian constables to police primarily rural reservation and ''band'' communities.

The processing of ''street kids'' has become another concern over the last decade. Runaway youths appear to be increasing, and they are congregating in major urban downtown core areas, often engaging in prostitution and drug and alcohol abuse; they, therefore, are far more susceptible to being victimized by pimps, johns, and sexually transmitted diseases. The youth justice system is perceived as being ineffective in protecting society from the (usually minor) criminal acts of street kids and in protecting them from being victimized. The police maintain that the YOA drastically inhibits their ability to arrest street kids unless they are caught committing a criminal act, not only because of due process protections but also because prostitution per se is not illegal (only public solicitation is illegal). Probation officers are also frustrated, since they claim they lack both the authority to control street kids effectively and appropriate access to treatment and support programs that these youths desperately need. Judges similarly claim that under the YOA they cannot force treatment on street kids and that their social service needs do not fall under the jurisdiction of the youth court.

The street kids issue is part of a larger concern with ''youth at risk.'' This label is being applied increasingly by youth justice officials, social workers, teachers, psychologists/psychiatrists, and researchers to those youths who, from early childhood, appear likely to eventually be processed through youth justice as teenagers. They characteristically have a multiproblem profile consisting of family dysfunctionality, alcohol and/or drug abuse, low income, poor educational performance, early aggressive and violent behavior, delinquent peers, and early-age onset of criminal acts. These youths are seen as most likely to join the informal youth groups, wanna-be gangs, and hybrid adult/youth gangs. How to better address youth at risk is a current controversial policy issue, given the restrictions imposed by the YOA minimum age jurisdiction of 12 years and the compartmentalization of child-serving agencies. The fear of youth justice officials is that, by the time youth at risk become delinquent teenagers, the ability to help these youths amounts to ''too little, too late.'' In response, informal processing of youth at risk has become more widespread as the various departments responsible for youth services attempt to coordinate their services in the interest of decreasing the likelihood that these youths will end up as career criminals and/or extremely violent.

SUMMARY

The shift in 1984 from legislation deeply rooted in the welfare model tradition of juvenile justice to the modified justice model approach of the new Young

Offenders Act has resulted in dramatic changes in the administration of juvenile justice in Canada. Although key elements of a justice model approach to the processing of juvenile court cases had already been administratively fairly well established in many major urban centers, the proclamation of the new act considerably strengthened and extended the emphasis on due process and rigorous legal procedure, thereby significantly altering the roles of key players in the Canadian juvenile justice system.

With its considerable emphasis on the rights of young persons, due process, and a right to counsel—including an absolute right to state-funded counsel, independent of parents—the role of defense counsel has been greatly enhanced in all stages of juvenile justice processing. This, in turn, necessitated an enhancement of the role of Crown counsel (prosecutors) to ensure that the procedural safeguards entrenched in the act are, indeed, followed and to argue against the many technical defenses that can arise as a result of these new procedures. The role of youth court judges has, in large part, also been enhanced insofar as they (rather than administrators) now determine a fixed length of sentence and the level of custody (open or secure) and review their own sentencing decisions.

The enhancement of the role and authority of this triumvirate of legally trained professionals has come at the expense of the police, probation officers, and youth correctional administrators. The police role is now more tightly circumscribed by the strictures of due process, especially with respect to statement (confession) evidence. While probation officers still play a key role in influencing many sentencing decisions, they now take more of a back seat to the legal disputations between defense and Crown counsel and have less discretion to administer and enforce court sentences. Similarly, with the provisions for definite sentencing, judicial determination of level of custody, and judicial review of sentencing decisions, youth correctional administrators have reduced authority. As well, because of the greater "justice" orientation of the new act, most provincial governments have separated the delivery of youth correctional and child welfare services, thereby prompting many youth to "fall between the cracks" in service delivery systems.

While the YOA adopts a strict justice model approach in the preadjudication stage of processing, it is in sentencing where the modified justice model principally emerges, insofar as different and competing principles from the justice, welfare, and crime control models all play a key role and are expected to be balanced. This "mixed" model approach has been the subject of considerable criticism and debate (Markwart, 1992) and can lead to considerable variability in sentencing (Doob, 1989).

The evolution of the YOA was largely invisible to the public and essentially was the product of debates among federal and provincial politicians and bureaucrats and some key interest groups, as well as being influenced by academic theory and research. Since the YOA, however, the debate about the direction of juvenile justice in Canada has become much more public and political, principally in response to concerns about increasing youth violence. As a result, in its short life span the act has already been amended twice to strengthen crime control functions, and, as we write, an amending bill is before Parliament to lengthen sentences for juvenile murderers and to increase the certainty of transfer to adult court for other serious offenders. Given this, Canada seems to be following the trend toward tougher sentences and more frequent transfers to adult court that many American states have adopted in recent years (Schwartz, 1991).

NOTES

1. At age 18 an alleged offender is dealt with as an adult; prior to the YOA, the provinces were allowed to set their own maximum ages at 16, 17, or 18 years, and most chose 16 years.

2. The Canadian *Charter of Rights and Freedoms* accords a right to a jury trial only for an offense that carries a maximum penalty of 5 years. At present, 5 years (less one day) is the maximum penalty for murder in youth court, but proposed reforms would increase this to 10 years.

REFERENCES

Archambault, O. "Young Offenders Act: Philosophy and Principles." In *Crime and Canadian Society,* 3d ed., edited by R. A. Silverman and J. J. Teevan, Jr. Toronto: Butterworths, 1986.

Bala, Nicholas. "The Young Offenders Act: The Legal Structure." In *Juvenile Justice in Canada: A Theoretical and Analytical Assessment,* edited by Raymond R. Corrado, Nicholas Bala, Rick Linden, and Marc LeBlanc. Toronto: Butterworths, 1992.

Corrado, Raymond R. "Introduction." In *Juvenile Justice in Canada: A Theoretical and Analytical Assessment,* edited by Raymond R. Corrado, Nicholas Bala, Rick Linden, and Marc LeBlanc. Toronto: Butterworths, 1992.

———. "An Examination of Issues Related to the Policing of Young Offenders." Research paper completed for the Policing in British Columbia Commission of Inquiry, 1994.

Corrado, Raymond R., and Alan Markwart. "The Prices of Rights and Responsibilities: An Examination of the Impacts of the Young Offenders Act in British Columbia." *Canadian Journal of Family Life* 7 (1988): 93–115.

———. "The Evolution and Implementation of a New Era of Juvenile Justice in Canada." In *Juvenile Justice in Canada: A Theoretical and Analytical Assessment,* edited by Raymond R. Corrado, Nicholas Bala, Rick Linden, and Marc LeBlanc. Toronto: Butterworths, 1992.

———. "The Need to Reform the YOA in Response to Violent Young Offenders: Confusion, Reality or Myth?" *Canadian Journal of Criminology* 36 (1994): 343–378.

Corrado, Raymond R., and Susan D. Turnbull. "A Comparative Examination of the Modified Justice Model in the United Kingdom and the United States." In *Juvenile Justice in Canada: A Theoretical and Analytical Assessment,* edited by Raymond R. Corrado, Nicholas Bala, Rick Linden, and Marc LeBlanc. Toronto: Butterworths, 1992.

Department of Justice Canada. *Juvenile Delinquency in Canada: The Report of the Department of Justice Committee.* Ottawa: Queen's Printer, 1965.

Doob, Anthony W. "Dispositions under the Young Offenders Act: Issues without Answers?" In *Young Offender Dispositions: Perspectives on Principles and Prac-*

tice, edited by Lucien A. Beaulieu. Toronto: Wall and Thompson, 1989.

Hanscomb, D. K. "The Dynamics of Disposition in Youth Court: A Report on a Survey of Youth Court Matters Affecting Disposition." Master of Laws thesis, University of Toronto, 1988.

Leschied, Alan W., Peter G. Jaffe, Dan Andrews, and Paul Gendreau. "Treatment Issues and Young Offenders: An Empirically Derived Vision of Juvenile Justice Policy." In *Juvenile Justice in Canada: A Theoretical and Analytical Assessment,* edited by Raymond R. Corrado, Nicholas Bala, Rick Linden, and Marc LeBlanc. Toronto: Butterworths, 1992.

MacDonald, M. P. "Incarcerated Native Youth in British Columbia: Senior Management and Offender Perceptions of the Impact of Custody." M.A. thesis, Simon Fraser University, School of Criminology, 1994.

Markwart, Alan. "Custodial Dispositions under the Young Offenders Act." In *Juvenile Justice in Canada: A Theoretical and Analytical Assessment,* edited by Raymond R. Corrado, Nicholas Bala, Rick Linden, and Marc LeBlanc. Toronto: Butterworths, 1992.

Markwart, Alan, and Raymond R. Corrado. "Is the Young Offenders Act More Punitive?" In *Young Offender Dispositions: Perspectives on Principles and Practice,* edited by Lucien A. Beaulieu. Toronto: Wall and Thompson, 1989.

Milne, Heather A., Rick Linden, and Rod Kueneman. "Advocate or Guardian: The Role of Defense Counsel in Youth Justice." In *Juvenile Justice in Canada: A Theoretical and Analytical Assessment,* edited by Raymond R. Corrado, Nicholas Bala, Rick Linden, and Marc LeBlanc. Toronto: Butterworths, 1992.

Pratt, J. "Corporatism: The Third Model of Juvenile Justice." *British Journal of Criminology* 29 (1989): 236–253.

Schwartz, Ira M. "The Death of the Parens Patriae Model." In the *Young Offenders Act: A Revolution in Canadian Juvenile Justice,* edited by Alan W. Leschied, Peter G. Jaffe, and Wayne Willis. Toronto: University of Toronto Press, 1991.

Silverman, R., and L. Kennedy. *Deadly Deeds: Murder in Canada.* Scarborough, Ontario: Nelson Canada, 1993.

West, W. G. *Young Offenders and the State: A Canadian Perspective on Delinquency.* Toronto: Butterworths, 1984.

APPENDIX: KEY AGENCIES

Canadian Federal Government

Deputy Minister of Justice and Deputy Attorney General of Canada
Justice Canada
239 Wellington Street
Ottawa, Ontario
K1A 0H8

Canadian Centre for Justice Statistics
19th Floor, Section "F"
R. H. Coats Building
Tunney's Pasture
Ottawa, Ontario
K1A 0T6

Provincial Governments

	Justice	Youth Correctional Services
British Columbia	Deputy Attorney General Ministry of Attorney General Room 504, 910 Government Street Victoria, British Columbia V8V 1X4	Assistant Deputy Minister Corrections Branch Ministry of Attorney General 400-910 Government Street Victoria, British Columbia V8V 1X4
Alberta	Deputy Minister of Justice and Deputy Attorney General Alberta Justice 2nd Floor, Bowker Building 9833-109th Street N.W. Edmonton, Alberta T5K 2E8	Assistant Deputy Minister Correctional Service 10th Floor John E. Brownlee Building 10365-97th Street Edmonton, Alberta T5J 3W7
Saskatchewan	Deputy Minister of Justice and Deputy Attorney General Saskatchewan Justice 10th Floor 1874 Scarth Street Regina, Saskatchewan S4P 3V6	Deputy Minister of Social Services Saskatchewan Social Services 12th Floor, Chateau Tower 1920 Broad Street Regina, Saskatchewan S4P 3V6
Manitoba	Deputy Minister of Justice and Deputy Attorney General Manitoba Justice Room 110, Legislative Building 450 Broadway Avenue Winnipeg, Manitoba R3C 0V8	Assistant Deputy Minister Corrections Department of Justice 8th Floor, 405 Broadway Avenue Winnipeg, Manitoba R3C 3L6
Ontario	Deputy Attorney General of Ontario Ministry of the Attorney General 11th Floor 720 Bay Street Toronto, Ontario M5G 2K1	Assistant Deputy Minister Correctional Services Division 101 Bloor Street West 7th Floor Toronto, Ontario M5S 2Z7 Deputy Minister Ministry of Community and Social Services 6th Floor, Hepburn Block Grosvenor Street Toronto, Ontario M7A 1E9

Provincial Governments cont.

	Justice	**Youth Correctional Services**
New Brunswick	Deputy Solicitor General of New Brunswick Department of Solicitor General Room 671, Centennial Building 670 King Street P.O. Box 6000 Fredericton, New Brunswick E3B 5H1	Executive Director Correctional Services Division Department of the Solicitor General 2nd Floor, 15 Carleton Street Fredericton, New Brunswick E3B 5T1
Nova Scotia	Deputy Minister of Justice Nova Scotia Justice 4th Floor Terminal Road Building 5151 Terminal Road P.O. Box 7 Halifax, Nova Scotia B3J 1A1	Executive Director Correctional Services Department of Justice 3rd Floor-1690 Hollis Street Joseph Howe Building Halifax, Nova Scotia B3J 2V9
Prince Edward Island	Deputy Minister and Deputy Attorney General Department of Provincial Affairs and Attorney General 4th Floor, Jones Building 11 Kent Street P.O. Box 2000 Charlottetown, P.E.I. C1A 7N8	Director Community and Correctional Services Department of Health and Community Service 42 Great George Street Charlottetown, P.E.I. C1A 4J9
Newfoundland	Deputy Minister of Justice and Deputy Attorney General Department of Justice 5th Floor East Block Confederation Building St. John's, Newfoundland A1B 4J6	Deputy Minister Department of Social Services 3rd Floor, Confederation Building Prince Philip Drive St. John's, Newfoundland A1B 4J6
Yukon	Deputy Minister Department of Justice 2134-Second Avenue P.O. Box 2703 Whitehorse, Yukon Y1A 2C6	Deputy Minister Department of Health and Social Services Yukon Government Administration Building 2071-2nd Avenue P.O. Box 2703 Whitehorse, Yukon Y1A 2C6

Provincial Governments cont.

	Justice	Youth Correctional Services
Northwest Territories	Deputy Minister of Justice and Public Services Government of Northwest Territories 4th Floor, Courthouse P.O. Box 1320 Yellowknife Northwest Territories X1A 2L9	Director Corrections Service Division Department of Justice Precambrian Building 7th Floor P.O. Box 1320 Yellowknife Northwest Territories X1A 2L9

4

PEOPLE'S REPUBLIC OF CHINA

Xin Ren

INTRODUCTION

China, with a population of nearly 1.2 billion and a size equivalent to that of the United States, has nearly 300 million people, a quarter of the total population, under age 18 (Li and Qian, 1992; Zhao, 1991:13). Protecting the rights of children and handling juvenile misbehavior thus involve enormous work for the society and the criminal justice system in China. Although China, since the founding day of the People's Republic in 1949, has endured many years of political and social turbulence that resulted in millions of deaths and massive social destruction, juvenile misbehavior has always existed side by side with China's social turmoil and has rapidly increased in the post-Mao era.

Unlike the Western countries, where juvenile delinquency has been handled by officially administered institutions in accordance with formally established law and legal procedures since the early 1800s, control of antisocial behavior of adolescents in China has largely been the function of families, schools, and other nonjustice institutions. The institutional formation of the juvenile justice system and official intervention in handling juvenile transgressors started mainly in the early 1980s, when economic modernization and legal formalization were under way in China.

History of Juvenile Justice

The history of juvenile justice in China can be divided into three periods: the rise of juvenile reform schools and the child welfare system (1949–1965); the void of juvenile justice during the Cultural Revolution (1966–1978); and the emergency of juvenile crime and the formalization of the juvenile justice system (1979–1994).

The Rise of Juvenile Justice and Welfare Services for Children

From 1949 to 1965, the major official concern over the juvenile population was not their mischief and antisocial behavior but the plights of millions of children who were the victims of neglect and abuse during the Nationalist regime[1] and their needs for state-sponsored welfare services and institutions for neglected and troubled children. Although China did not promulgate its Criminal Law and Criminal Procedure Law until 1979, numerous statutes or decrees, either carried over from the Soviet Republic era (1927–1934) or enacted after 1949, encompassed ramifications on the protection and treatment of minors.

After the military triumph over the Nationalists, the communist government immediately began its efforts to restore the social order and national production. The vast problem of homeless orphans, juvenile transients, child laborers, human trade and sex exploitation against children, and juvenile street runners controlled by criminal gangs was viewed both as a threat to the social stability of the newly established political power and as desperately in need of help. Rescue of these children from devastating conditions was the overriding goal of the central government. The central government launched a social crusade at several fronts, including abolishing the practice of child labor,[2] mandating public education,[3] eradicating violence and cruelty against minors, and housing homeless children and transgressive juveniles.

While the government was making efforts to eliminate child labor practice in the cities and transfer children from homes, streets, and factories to the school system for mandatory education, the justice and civil services agencies were also mobilized to rescue children from inhumanitarian conditions. For example, before the official crackdown on the sex industry was launched at full scale in major cities in the 1950s, the government took immediate steps to ban the employment of minors under age 18 at brothels (Ren, 1993:87–107) and imposed life sentences or the death penalty on sex crimes against minors. At the same time, human trafficking, that is, selling children and women, was illegalized; for the first time in Chinese history, this thousand-year-old practice was eradicated. The Marriage Law of the People's Republic of China (PRC), promulgated in 1950, also abolished the traditional practice of child bride,[4] infanticide, and discrimination against illegitimate children. Subsequently, 100,000 children were rescued and placed in emergency shelters for medical treatment of malnutrition, diseases, drug addiction, and physical disability and for literacy education. Orphanages and Child Welfare Houses were also set up to help the children make the transition to adoption, foster homes, or reunion with their families (Guo and Ma, 1981:365).

During this period, juvenile transgressors[5] held low priority for the justice authority, since they counted for less than 20 percent of the criminal population, and the youth crime rates were only 20 per 100,000 population under the age of 25 (Yang, 1989a).[6] Those young transgressors were normally regarded not as criminals but as victims of unfortunate circumstances who were in need of help. The welfare approach to deal with juvenile misbehavior prevailed in all jurisdictions. The children's needs, their vulnerability, and dependence on others' support were the central foci for the juvenile justice policy. This policy can been seen in a number of the statutes explicitly addressing the responsibility of parents in raising their children and being liable for their children's misdeeds. For instance, the Marriage Law in 1950 provided that parents have rights and obligations to discipline and protect their children who are under age 18 and are liable to provide compensation if their child has done harm to the public or a private citizen.[7] With the same philosophy, the official concern was that young transgressors could be tempted either by the seduction and instigation of adults or by pornographic and superstitious materials. The law also provided severe punishment for adults who had instigated minors to commit illegal activities (Guo and Ma, 1981:357).[8] In 1954, the Reform through Labor Statute of the PRC provided legal parameters for children's criminal liability and initiated the early formation of penal institutions for juvenile offenders.

The Void of the Juvenile Justice System

From 1966 to 1978, the intensified political power struggle within the Communist Party brought China to the state of lawlessness. The judicial system and criminal justice agencies, including the juvenile institutions, were suspended or dismissed. The society was politically divided into the proletariate and the class enemies. The fates of children were largely determined by their parents' fates in the class struggle. To the public, there was no difference between a criminal misdeed and a political wrong. Millions of people, including innocent children, were subject to political persecution and social and economic discrimination, along with the common practice of the people's justice, lynch mobs, and kangaroo courts in China. The class enemies were the number one concern of the people's revolutionary justice. The youth transgressors of proletariat parents were usually ignored or rendered for mercy based on the political view that crime committed by the children of the working class was a nonadversary conflict within the people themselves.

The Emergency of Juvenile Crime and Restoration of Juvenile Justice

When the Cultural Revolution ended with Mao's death and the downfall of the Gang of Four in 1976, the Chinese took a hard look at what was left from 10 years of political madness and massive social destruction. Shortly after the political recession, the criminal justice authority was suddenly overwhelmed by a sharp increase in crime. The crime rates more than doubled from 28 per 100,000 population before the Cultural Revolution to 65 per 100,000 in 1979 (Yang, 1989b:65–68). The youth offense rates climbed from 14.9 per 1,000 persons under the age of 25 in 1980 to 27.4 in 1989 (Table 4.1). The youth offenders under age 25 in the criminal population also soared from 30 percent in the 1960s to 75 percent in the 1980s (Table 4.2; Yang, 1989a:25).[9] Of these

Table 4.1
Youth Offense Rates (1980–1989) per 1,000 Persons under Age 25

Year	Offense Rate	Year	Offense Rate
1980	14.9	1985	11.6
1981	15.9	1986	12.2
1982	18.1	1987	13.6
1983	17.5	1988	18.7
1984	10.6	1989	27.4

Source: Zhao (1991): 13–16.

youth offenders, 85.2 percent were between 18 to 25 years of age and 14.8 percent were under age 18, which remained consistent for juvenile offense rates since the 1960s. The substantial increase in juvenile offenses occurred in the 1980s (Table 4.3). The authorities suddenly discovered that newly restored penal institutions were no longer filled by the class enemies, but by the sons and daughters of the proletariat class.

In 1979, the People's Congress, China's legislative body, quickly passed the first criminal law and criminal procedure law that defined the age limits in criminal responsibility and the procedure in adjudication of juvenile offenders. The penal institutions, such as education camps through labor and reformatory camps through labor, *shaonianfan guanjiao suo* (SGS—Institutions of Management and Education for Juvenile Offenders), resumed operation at full scale. In 1987, the first juvenile court was opened in Zhe Jiang province exclusively for adjudicating minors under the age of 18, and soon 26 provinces and autonomous regions followed the same step. Subsequently, the Juvenile Protection Law was passed by the People's Congress in 1991, to mark the establishment of the formal juvenile justice system.

FORMAL JUVENILE JUSTICE SYSTEM

Compared to the industrialized nations, the formal system of juvenile justice in China is still at an infantile stage that began to gain legal ground about 10 years ago, when Tianning District Court of Shanghai pioneered the first special juvenile court in 1984 (*Law Yearbook of China,* 1991:875). Within a short period of time, the juvenile courts and juvenile reformatory system were quickly developed throughout the country. Inspired by the United Nations Standard Minimum Rules for the Administration of Juvenile Justice (the Beijing Rules) in 1985 and the United Nations Convention on the Rights of the Child in 1989, China concurred with the international standard by designating the age of 18 to

Table 4.2
Youth Offenders under Age 25 in the Total Criminal Population

Year	Percentage	Year	Percentage
1980	61.2	1985	71.3
1981	64.0	1986	72.5
1982	65.9	1987	74.4
1983	67.0	1988	75.7
1984	63.3	1989	74.1

Source: Zhao (1991): 13–16.

distinguish minors from adults and subsequently defined the jurisdiction of juvenile justice authority (Guo, 1993:22–24).

Legal Culpability and the Juvenile Protection Law

The term "delinquent" has a number of different meanings that appear both in official statutes and criminological literature in China. On one hand, Chinese criminologists frequently use the term to refer to those under age 25 who committed a crime or displayed antisocial behavior; on the other hand, the judicial authority strictly recognizes only those under age 18 as juvenile delinquents in criminal proceedings. The word "delinquency" has never appeared in the official statutes.

China's earliest attempt to clarify the criminal liability of minors derived from a referendum, "On Legal Culpability," issued by the Department of Justice of the Southwest Region in 1950. According to the referendum, legal culpability is applicable only to those 14 years or older (Institute of Juveniles and Youth, 1981:128–130). The People's Supreme Court later confirmed this clarification by declaring that minors between 14 and 18 years of age shall be held culpable for crimes. This nonstatutory definition of legal age for juvenile culpability became the basis for the criminal justice system, handling juvenile offenders for more than three decades, until the criminal law of the PRC was promulgated in 1979.

Article 14 of the Chinese criminal law provides the statutory age limitation for criminal liability as the following:

A person who had reached the age of 16 and committed a crime shall bear criminal responsibility. . . . A person who is between age of 14 and 16 and committed crime of murder, aggravated assault, robbery, arson, or habitual theft shall be criminally liable.

Table 4.3
Juvenile Offenders Age 14–18

Year	Percentage
1986	22.3
1987	21.6
1988	21.0
1989	19.1

Source: Zhao (1991): 13–16.

... Culprits between age of 14 and 18 shall be given a lenient or mitigated penalty. (*The Criminal Law and Criminal Procedure Law of China,* 1984:73–74)

Article 44 of the penal code also prohibits the imposition of the death penalty against offenders under age 18, except in the case of a serious crime, where the death penalty could be imposed against the juvenile offender, with a two-year suspension.

The statutory provision indicates that, although minors between 14 and 18 years of age could be held criminally liable for their crime, age is, nevertheless, an acceptable mitigating factor for sentencing leniency. Apparently, the criminal law does recognize the existence of juvenile offenders because of their age at the time the crime was committed, but not delinquency. In other words, under the Chinese law, no act is criminal in nature if and only if it is committed by a person under age of 18, namely, the status offense as it exists in the United States. "Delinquency" is a meaningful term for Chinese criminologists and sociologists only in etiological research, but it is not valid in the legal statutes.

This is also evident in China's Juvenile Protection Law. Without creating any new category of delinquent acts, the 1991 Juvenile Protection Law further elucidates juvenile offenders' rights, such as the confidentiality of juvenile cases, private court proceedings, and separate pretrial detention for juvenile offenders. The most remarkable feature of this law is that it has defined more legal obligations for adults to be accountable in caring, supervising, educating, or instigating and corrupting minors than it has defined the juvenile's legal culpability. Following the same tone that was set up more than a half century ago during the Soviet Republic regime, the law reaffirmed parents' responsibility in providing basic care and necessity for children's needs, conforming with the mandatory 9-year education rule up to 18 years of age, preventing behavioral problems such as smoking, drinking, running away from home, gambling, drugs, and prostituting. Unlike its counterparts in the West that hold minors accountable for these behavioral problems, Chinese authority upholds the responsibility of parents for their children's misconduct due to their negligence and failure in supervision and persuasion of their children.[10]

Today, China still does not have status offenses that exclusively refer to the concept that an act is deemed illegal if and only if its actor's age status is minor. It is quite obvious that the Western notion of *parens patriae,* or the state as parent, a precedent from the English Chancery Court to intervene into the lives of children, has gained very limited acceptance in the codified laws in China. The statutes not only view juvenile misbehavior as the parents' failure in supervision and control but also legally hold the parents accountable for compensation and rehabilitation of their youngsters. This approach in dealing with youth misbehavior has its roots in Confucius' philosophy that the virtue of fatherhood is to teach children good behavior. If a child misbehaves, the parents, especially the father, should be held accountable.

Police and Juvenile Offenders

The police play an important role in dealing with juvenile misbehavior. However, it is important to note that much of police work with juveniles involves either order maintenance or service activities, rather than law enforcement. Police work in Chinese society is informal and primarily oriented toward crime prevention and services. Normally, police precincts assign their officers to different neighborhoods or a large dwelling complex to work closely with the neighborhood committees and schools to oversee the safety and welfare of those neighborhoods. Children's behavioral problems are often dealt with at the first sign of trouble by an informally organized coalition consisting of parents, schoolteachers, police officers, and neighborhood committee volunteers. Relatively lower expectation for family privacy in the Chinese cultural tradition allows police officers to penetrate the community and family lives. It is not unusual for police officers to casually visit families in which children have been adjudicated by the court for a misdemeanor and have been placed under the parents' custody or in which juveniles have been released from a juvenile institution for postrelease supervision.

Since most police officers in China carry neither a gun nor a baton, they appear more like social workers rather than police officers. As a matter of fact, police usually devote 90 to 95 percent of their time and resources to serving the community's various social and human needs. To individual officers, social work skills, such as counseling, mediation, negotiation, or conciliation, are essential for successful police work. Exercising police discretion to arrest juvenile offenders is rare and considered a last resort. Only when a juvenile commits a serious crime would she or he be taken into police custody and be adjudicated by the court. Otherwise, police normally work with parents, schools, or neighborhood committees to counsel youngsters.

In recent years, police agencies in large cities have either designated juvenile intake officers or set up a specialized juvenile division within the police agency for juvenile intake and investigation. Such a process is minimal and less frequent because the majority of cases are handled at the community, school, or family level, and only a very small number of cases actually require formal police investigation and arrest.

When a juvenile is arrested, the police are responsible for interrogating the detainee in the presence of his or her legal guardian(s) within 24 hours and turning the case to the procurator's office for adjudication within four days. The criminal procedure law requires that the procurator's office must make a decision of adjudication or dismissal within a month.[11] Since the law does not grant the accused bail for pretrial release, the police are responsible for detaining the accused for the entire period of adjudication. Article 41 of the Juvenile Protection Law provides that juvenile offenders should be detained in a facility separate from that for adult offenders. However, the implementation of this law largely depends on the availability of the facility at a given jurisdiction. The law also prohibits police from disclosing a juvenile offender's name, address, or photo to the media before disposition.

Juvenile Court System

The first juvenile court was formed in Tianning District Court of Shanghai in 1984. It handles primarily two types of cases involving minors under the age of 18: protection cases for children's welfare or property rights and criminal cases involving juvenile offenders between the ages of 14 and 18 (Jiangsu Provincial Supreme Court Research Division, 1992:47–50). Occasionally, the juvenile court also handles adult offenders who have committed crimes against minors such as child molestation, selling or distributing pornographic materials to juveniles, or instigating children to commit illegal activities. While the Tianning model of juvenile court represented the first official juvenile court, a variety of jurisdictions experimented with the same reform by either creating separate court dockets or appointing judges exclusively for cases involving minors. By the end of 1992, more than 2,300 juvenile courts in 80 percent of the jurisdictions had been established throughout the country (Li, 1993:19–22).

For the juvenile court system, protection and rehabilitation are the overriding missions. For the protection of juveniles, the Chinese juvenile court, unlike its American counterpart, which primarily deals with persons under 18 who need assistance or supervision, had jurisdiction over a much wider range of cases. It not only handles cases involving juvenile victims or offenders but also deals with cases that involve adults who have committed crimes against, or corrupted, minors. For example, adults who instigate minors to commit crime or sexually abuse or molest children could be tried by the juvenile court. Parents who abuse, neglect, or abandon their children also fall under the jurisdiction of the juvenile court to determine their guilt or innocence, except those cases that result in death or severe bodily injury. In addition, the juvenile courts receive the cases

Table 4.4
Adjudication of Juvenile and Youth Crime (1990–1991)

Year	Age	Total	Crime	Violation of PSR
1990		580,272	271,529	308,743
	Under 18	42,033	17,791	24,241
	18-25	441,397	290,495	140,902
1991		507,238	262,805	244,433
	Under 18	33,392	13,571	19,823
	18-25	234,814	113,890	20, 924

Source: Adopted from *Law Yearbook of China*, 1991, Table 4, p. 934, and 1992, Table 4, p. 853.

of parental custody rights in divorce proceedings, inherent rights of children, adoption, and dissolving or transferring guardianship.

For criminal cases involving minors, the juvenile court system adjudicates two kinds of law violators: those who commit a crime against the criminal law and those who violate the Public Security Regulation. In 1990, the juvenile courts adjudicated a total of 42,033 cases, including 17,791 of the criminal law violations and 24,241 of the public security violations (Table 4.4).[12] The number of cases adjudicated by the courts in 1991 declined 21 percent (33,392) from the previous year. Noticeably, although the official rule claims that the juvenile courts do not adjudicate offenders older than 19 years of age at the time of the adjudication, the court system continues to group both juvenile offenders and those between 18 and 25 years old in the same category. Presumably, in many jurisdictions, juvenile offenders might have been tried in the adult courts due to lack of juvenile tribunals, or perhaps the juvenile courts had adjudicated offenders older than 19 years of age. This practice reflects the official view that because of the similar age of juvenile and youthful offenders, the same etiological explanation of their transgressions may apply.

Similar to the criminal procedure for adults, the intake procurator must first determine whether there is sufficient evidence to warrant a petition. Keeping in mind the principle of greater leniency toward youthful offenders, procurators exercise greater discretion in making the intake decision by frequently consulting with community advising groups for adjudication or community disposition. If there is sufficient evidence, the case will go directly to the hearing before a panel normally consisting of three judges: a judicial judge and two lay judges/ accessors selected from community. Although plea bargaining does not exist in China's criminal proceedings, the juvenile court judges must first determine if there should be an adjudication or waiver of adjudication to place juvenile offenders under the supervision of their parents, community, or Institutions of Juvenile Management and Education for Juvenile Offenders (SGS) if they are under age 16. Unlike the procedure for adults, who may be represented by an attorney during the trial, the law not only requires the presence of the legal guardian of the juvenile offender during the hearing but also mandates that the minor must be represented by an attorney, and if he or she does not have one, the court must appoint an attorney.[13] Pursuant to Article 111 of the Criminal Procedural Law, the hearing of juvenile courts is normally conducted in a private manner for the purpose of protecting a juvenile offender's identity.

For legal comparatists, perhaps, the most frequently asked question about the Chinese criminal procedure is whether it encompasses a presumption of guilt. To a certain degree, the Chinese criminal procedure is inquisitory in nature rather than adversarial, as it is in the United States. Under this inquisitory system, the state has the burden of proof to establish factual guilt rather than legal guilt beyond a reasonable doubt. As pointed out by Richard Myren, "the actual issue is one of the burden of proof" (Myren, 1986:19). Articles 35, 96, 100, 108, 120, and 126 of the Criminal Procedural Law of China repeatedly assert that the state must establish guilt by presenting "clear facts" that constitute "full, conclusive and sufficient" evidence against the accused. Myren believes that the Chinese standard of burden of proof is equivalent to "proof beyond a reasonable doubt" in the United States. This standard of proof for adult offenders is also adopted by the juvenile courts in adjudicating juvenile offenders.

The most notorious trademark of the Tianning model of juvenile court is its educational session for juvenile offenders before disposition. Using this model, all juvenile courts formally hold an educational session normally conducted by the lay judges who represent the community at large. Specifically, the lay judges must conduct a social inquiry outside the courtroom on (1) the juvenile's family background, such as family structure, living arrangement, and child–parent relationship; (2) school performance and possible behavioral problems such as truancy or dropping out of school; (3) association with delinquent gangs or bad peers; (4) personal talent, personality, and psychological weakness; and (5) direct causes of misbehavior. The result of this inquiry is openly discussed during the court session before disposition. The educational session was said to serve the purposes of helping offenders analyze the causes of their crime, understand the detrimental impact of their crime to society, and feel remorse for their criminal wrongdoing (Tianjin People's Supreme Court, First Division, 1988:18–20). Under the Tianning model, the courts also periodically follow up the juveniles sent to juvenile institutions to evaluate the effectiveness of their educational session in court proceedings. This educational function of the Chinese juvenile

Table 4.5

Disposition of Juvenile Offenders in Jiangsu Province (1983–1989) (%)

Penalty	1983	1984	1985	1986	1987	1988	1989
Probation	5.4	10.0	12.0	11.0	8.8	10.4	11.0
5 Years or Less	38.0	43.3	60.0	63.7	64.3	63.5	64.1
5 to 10 Years	35.9	29.5	21.7	21.0	22.0	19.6	18.7
10 or More	17.6	13.3	4.9	3.1	3.3	3.8	3.3
Life	2.0	1.9	1.1	0.5	0.4	0.9	4.0
Death Penalty*	1.0	1.4	0.5	0.5	0.7	0.8	0.7

Source: Dai (1992): 43–47.

*This refers to the death penalty with a two-year suspension for juvenile offenders.

court abundantly reflects the strong moralistic character of the Chinese law and judiciary that routinely engages both formal and informal moralistic persuasion and political education.

The juvenile court system is said to function for rehabilitating, not punishing, juvenile offenders. Article 14 of the Criminal Law provides that offenders between the ages of 14 and 18 shall be given lenient penalty or be entitled to a penalty reduction. The court may even waive the adjudication by placing a juvenile offender under parents' custody, if the juvenile is under 16, or, alternatively, if the youth is in a juvenile institution because the parents are judged unfit to provide such supervision. The death penalty should not be imposed against juvenile offenders, except in case of grave crime, in which a juvenile offender "who has reached the age of 16 but not 18 may be sentenced to death with a two-year suspension of execution."[14]

In recent years, the juvenile courts in many jurisdictions have placed more and more juvenile offenders on probation, especially those who were found culpable of crime and punishable for imprisonment of three years or less. The disposition of juvenile offenders in Jiangsu province clearly indicates the recent shift of juvenile courts from stiff penalty, 56.5 percent for five years or more in 1983, to more lenient treatment for juvenile offenders, 23.1 percent for the same penalty in 1989 (Table 4.5). Beijing reported the same changes, from 59.5 percent of cases receiving five years or more of imprisonment in 1985 to 26.7 percent in 1990. During the same period, probation increased from 5 to 11 percent. It should be pointed out that this said leniency is merely relative, in comparison with the penalty the juveniles received in 1983. Compared to the industrialized nations, the penalty for juvenile offenders in China is still considerably severe and frequent. It is consistent with the Chinese justice model, which strictly controls those who enter the formal proceedings and are found guilty of crime.

Institutional Treatment for Juvenile Offenders

In general, the court adjudicated juvenile population consists of three types of offenders. First are the juvenile offenders who have been placed on probation or released on parole after serving a part of their prison terms. This group of juveniles is usually handled by various community programs and organizations, with supervision from the court or correctional authority. Second are the youngsters between ages 14 and 16 disposed by the court, pursuant to Article 14 of the Criminal Law, for nonadjudication to parental supervision or to institutionalized treatment if their parents were determined to lack the ability to provide adequate supervision. The third group are those juvenile offenders who were disposed after being found culpable of crime and are currently serving their prison terms in juvenile institutions.

Ironically, the second group of juvenile offenders is often incarcerated in the same institutions as the third group of youthful offenders. In addition to these offenders officially disposed by the courts, another category of juvenile offenders is subject to incarceration in Educational Camps through the Labor Department up to three years, under the jurisdiction of police. This group of offenders could face incarceration up to three years without official adjudication. It is commonplace in China for police to refer a juvenile or adult to the Administrative Board of Education through Labor to determine eligibility for institutionalization, if the police cannot provide sufficient evidence to warrant a prosecution or the crime committed by the offender was too trivial to go to court. This system was said to be administrative rather than punitive in nature. However, it bears the same, or even more severe, penalty than the court disposition. The educational camps through labor rarely house children under age 18 because they neither satisfy the educational needs of children nor are suitable for rehabilitating juvenile offenders.

The formal juvenile institutions are basically two types: community-based organizations and *shaonianfan guanjiao suo* (SGS) (Institutions of Management and Education for Juvenile Offenders). As for the adult system, the administration of juvenile institutions is under police jurisdiction, normally, the correctional division of the provincial or municipal public security departments. The correctional authority has widely ranging power in determining eligibility of parole and sentencing reduction. Since China has yet to establish probation departments or parole agencies, such as in the United States, to supervise offenders with suspended sentence or early release, the supervision of these offenders is largely left to the hands of community groups, public safety personnel of trade unions, police community officers, and neighborhood volunteer organizations. Although this segment of correctional services for juvenile offenders is supposed to be formally regulated and administered, it is often conducted in a rather informal and deregulated manner. Presently, only a small group of officially disposed juvenile offenders has been placed in this type of juvenile corrections because of the small number of probations and the scarcity of parole release among juvenile wards. The law provides that prisoners must serve one-half of their prison terms before they become eligible for parole. Nevertheless, implementation of this law for juvenile wards is scanty, largely because 70 percent of wards are between ages 17 and 20, with a sentence of less than three years.[15] According to the official report, parolees constitute less than 3 percent of the total population annually released from China's penal institutions (Dai, 1992: 44).

As part of a reward for the good behavior of prisoners, China's correctional authority frequently provides sentencing reduction. Each year, between 15 and 17 percent of prisoners receive such rewards, ranging from three months to three years.[16] Unlike the time credit granted to inmates in the United States that is solely based on prisoners' good behavior in prison, the sentencing reduction in China is granted on the combination of three evaluating factors: remorse for crime, good behavior, and satisfactory performance in education and work-skill training. Derived from a model of a work-study evaluation score system invented by the correctional facility in Shandong province, prisoners are rewarded with prison time reduction if they have accumulated enough credits from all three areas (Kang, 1986:268–271). Noticeably, prisoners' attitude change toward their crime is ranked the number one criterion for sentence reduction. It has been well documented by many Western observers that Chinese penal institutions routinely conduct an intensive political educational session, such as self-criticism and self-confession as "brainwash,"[17] or thought reform. It is the belief of the Chinese correctional authority that they are responsible not only to ensure good behavior while the prisoners are in prisons but also to produce new persons for society.

Shaonianfan guanjiao suo (SGS) are responsible for providing treatment for two groups of juvenile offenders: (1) juvenile offenders between the ages of 14 and 16 disposed by the courts for nonadjudication but referred for treatment because their parents were deemed lacking ability to provide adequate supervision and (2) juveniles disposed by the courts for prison terms. Among the first group, juveniles are more likely to be institutionalized if they are orphaned, have guardians or curators in prison, have mentally incompetent parents, or are strongly resented by the community. The length of institutionalization varies from one to three years.[18] Since the juvenile institutions usually do not provide separate facilities or programs for those youngsters, a high recidivism rate has been reported among this group of juveniles. A survey sponsored by the Department of Justice in 11 provinces and large cities indicated that reoffense rates within three years for this group of nonadjudicatory offenders were between 50 to 57 percent, compared to 22 percent for those youngsters who were adjudicated by the courts and had served their prison terms (Kang, 1992:46–48). Although the institutionalization of these nonadjudicatory offenders is said to be protective rather than punitive in nature, it may protect them only temporarily from criminogenic elements in the family and community and fail to protect them from bad influences inside prisons and from being eventually returned to the same environment whence they came.

In 1991, the Department of Justice sponsored a survey among 18 juvenile institutions (SGS) nationwide. The survey revealed that between 1981 and 1990, there were 76,131 juvenile wards admitted to the 18 SGS, with the highest admission of 17, 615 in 1983 and the lowest of 3,820 in 1985 (Figure 4.1).[19] Eighty-two percent of the wards entered the SGS between ages 16 and 17, with an average age of 16.8 in 1981 and 17.3 in 1990. In 1990, there were 6,495 adjudicated juvenile offenders and 1, 712 nonadjudicatory offenders, a ratio of 2.8 to 1, incarcerated in the 18 SGS. Their sentences ranged from less than one year to the death penalty with two-year suspension. Reportedly, more than 60 percent of wards received sentences of less than five years (Table 4.6). Proportionate to the one-child family in the general population, the only-child juvenile wards increased from 22 percent in 1979 to 45 percent in 1990. This change demands societal attention to the special needs of the one-child family when their only son or daughter is incarcerated.

In China, rehabilitation is not considered the sole responsibility of the correctional system. Chinese regard rehabilitation as a mission of the entire criminal justice system and the obligation of communities. The unique feature of China's juvenile correction is its "three-extension" program: extensions to preinstitutionalization education, to community resources outside prison, and to the postrelease care programs (Wang and Ma, 1988; Fu, 1992). The first extension can be seen in every stage of adjudication in that police, procurators, and judges are required to provide moral persuasion and political education on the causes and impact of juvenile crime on victims, society, and their own family to ensure that youthful offenders not only know what they have done is wrong but also understand why it is wrong. The second extension mobilizes the correctional officers to go to the wards' home communities to learn the background information on the wards' childhood experience and their relationships with the family, school, and community. This information enables correctional officers to individually design a rehabilitative program for each ward in custody. The third process emphasizes the juveniles' transition from the penal institution to the community. The postrelease care program was inspired by the idea that correctional agencies have the responsibility to deliver their products to the community with a promised result—productive and law-abiding citizens. Frequently, correctional officers must conduct social inquiry on the possible living arrangement, employment, or resumption of school for each ward before release.

Within the institutions, juvenile wards are usually provided with a half day of regular school education and a half day of light labor, such as cooking, janitor work at the facility, or working at the skill-training workshop. Since the majority of wards are close to the age of leaving school for employment by the time of their release, the program is mainly designed to certify them with special work

Figure 4.1
Juvenile Intake at 18 Selected SGS (1981–1990)

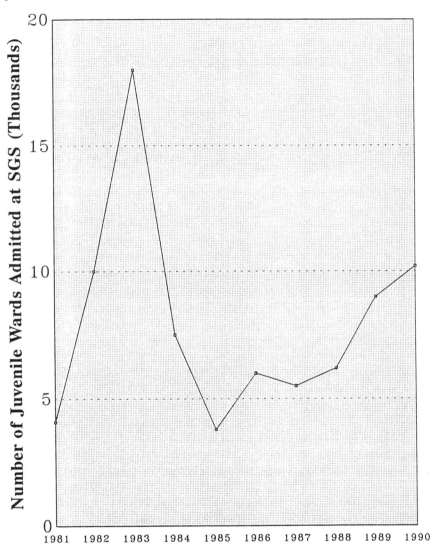

Source: Feng and Lu (1994): 491.

skills or license so they can transfer smoothly from study to employment. Some juvenile institutions also provide job placement services for wards who are ready to be released back to the community.

To set higher work morale for the correctional officers in juvenile institutions, the authority issued a general guideline of "three likes" and three "words" to

Table 4.6
Sentence Length of Juvenile Offenders in 18 SGS (1981–1990)

Sentence Length	Percentage
2 Years or less	13.0
2 to 4 Years	47.2
5 to 9 years	31.1
10 or 15 years	7.3
15 to Life	2.2
Death Penalty*	0.6

Source: Feng and Lu (1994): 490–496.

*This refers to the death penalty with a two-year suspension for juvenile offenders.

those who work at the SGS. The three likes refer to "treating juvenile wards like parents to their children, like school teachers to their students, and like doctors to their patients" (Kang, 1986:260–262). The three words, "education, persuasion, and rescue," exemplify the overriding principle for Chinese juvenile institutions, where education and persuasion take precedence over work and production.

INFORMAL PRACTICES

China has been known for its innovative deployment of community resources in preventing juvenile delinquency and rehabilitating youth transgressors. Informality and widely arranged social participation have been the chief features of China's community services for juvenile offenders (Feinerman, 1985:1–13). Despite the recent development in the official juvenile justice system, China continues to rely on community organizations to draw a vast number of citizen and social groups—such as concerned parents and other family members, school-teachers, public relation and safety officers from trade unions, neighborhood committees, Juvenile Scouts, Youth Leagues, the Communist Party, the Women's Federation, and police community officers—into the process of treating juvenile offenders. The programs provided by the community organizations include *bang-jao* (help and education) groups, mediation committees, and *gongdu* (work-study) schools.

The services provided by the *bang-jao* groups usually take three forms: first, to form a family-school-community *bang-jao* team that works with youngsters on a 24-hour basis; second, to contract the treatment with a counselor or agency for projected goals of behavioral changes; and third, to bail out juvenile offenders from SGS for out-institution treatment (Kang and Guo, 1988:251–253; Mok, 1990:5–19). People involved in these groups not only take care of youngsters in their community but also actively seek out those children who have been removed from the community by the juvenile justice system. Mediation committees were initially established in the 1950s to resolve disputes among families and neighbors, including juvenile delinquency and antisocial behavior of children. The program was known as an alternative way to effectively conciliate interpersonal conflict and prevent the escalation to serious crime. Up to 1984, there were 939,561 people's mediation committees established in cities, and 711,557 village mediation committees formed in rural areas (Guo, Xu, and Li, 1986:36–38).

Gongdu (work-study) schools are middle schools especially designed for children between ages 12 and 17 to complete the compulsory nine-year education. Students at the *gongdu* schools are referred by parents, school, community committee, or police for trivial behavioral problems such as truancy, incorrigible behavior at home, or disciplinary problems at schools. The schools, administered by the Ministry of Education, provide separate boarding facilities where boys and girls live for a period of three months to two years. Compared to regular middle schools, *gongdu* schools are smaller, with a faculty–student ratio of one to two and better financing by the state, with fees paid by the parents and profits from students' work. As of 1994, there were more than 100 *gongdu* schools, with fewer than 10,000 students, operating throughout China (Feng and Lu, 1994:508–509). As with other educational institutions, the law requires the *gongdu* schools to provide at least 24 hours of class instruction and 12 hours of work per week. The mission of these schools is to create a healthy environment that will help students reintegrate themselves into community life. Since many students in *gongdu* schools are close to the age of leaving school for employment, the schools provide various vocational training opportunities to help them move smoothly from school to employment. For instance, students are often brought to regular factories where they are given workers' uniforms and allowed to mix freely with adult workers, and their performance is publicly posted for everyone to see (Epstein, 1986:87–100). In addition to providing intensive counseling to students at the schools, counselors also work with parents or guardians and students' former schoolteachers on how to deal with children who display behavioral or antisocial problems. The schools routinely grant parental visitations or holiday/weekend furloughs to students, not as a right but as a privilege that is subject to official determination of good performance at schools.

In addition to these three informally arranged services for juvenile offenders, the community plays an important role in the system, such as providing community representatives to serve as accessors at a juvenile court panel, on the Task Force for Enforcement of Public Security Regulation, or on the Board of Education and Reform through Labor. For children who display delinquent and antisocial behavior, both youngsters and their families are under constant social pressure and stigma. Chinese society still views parents as having the ultimate obligation to raise their children as conforming persons. If they fail to do so, they could be subject to social stigma, community criticism, or even disciplinary action, such as dismissal from work assignment or demotion at their workplace. It is clear that collective responsibility still has a strong hold in linking a child's deviant behavior to the moral character of parenthood.

CONCLUDING REMARKS

Given the sharp increase in youthful crime in Chinese society since the economic reform, China has recently formalized its juvenile justice system by creating a juvenile court system and reorganizing institutional and noninstitutional treatment for youthful offenders. Despite the fascinating progress in legalization and formalization of law and administration of criminal justice, the Chinese juvenile justice system is continuously characterized as being informal and providing widely ranging discretionary power in adjudicating and disposing juvenile offenders. Community participation has been the chief feature of China's juvenile justice system. In recent years, as other countries are desperately seeking alternative resolutions in community-oriented programs to deal with youth crime, China seems to be moving in the opposite direction—formalization of its community services. On one hand, this change may provide communities with needed financial funding and government support to expand the coverage of the programs; on the other hand, it may also eliminate flexible and individualized treatment for juvenile offenders.

Furthermore, China's economic boom has also mobilized labor forces in Chinese society after the central government lifted its ban on free hiring and job search. As a direct result of such population mobility, conventional community ties and structure have been shaken by massive labor transition from rural areas to cities. The absence of parents from the home and frequent relocation as parents constantly move from one place to another have created a huge pool of school dropouts and unsupervised or even homeless children. Traditional community organizations have gradually lost their momentum and cohesion in providing counseling, persuasion, and mediation to children and families who are so mobile.

Recently, as more and more people have raised concern over institutional dispositions under the nonadjudicatory procedure, such as the nonadjudicated juveniles in the SGS and youthful offenders incarcerated in the Educational Camps through the Labor Department, the broad discretionary powers of juvenile justice officials have been seriously scrutinized by the Chinese legal community and human rights advocates. In addition, severe punishment, such as the death penalty for minors, has been criticized. It has been reported that the Legal Reform Commission of the People's Congress is currently reviewing a proposal to abolish the death penalty for offenders under age 18. As China is moving toward modernization and industrialization, changes in family structure and the labor market will further diminish the power of the informal social control mechanism in Chinese society and increase demands for more formal control agencies to regulate human behavior. Inevitably, the Chinese themselves will have to choose between the formally structured official coercion to keep people in line and the informally arranged moral persuasion for social conformity.

NOTES

1. The Nationalist regime refers to the period of 1911 to 1949, when mainland China was ruled by the Guomin Dang, the Nationalist Party. When the Chinese communists seized power in 1949, the Guomin Dang and its government retreated to Taiwan.

2. The Chinese communists had promulgated its labor law in 1934, during the Soviet Republic regime. Under Article 46 of this law, "children under age 14 are prohibited from being employed or working in evening hours. . . . Employers must obtain a permit from the labor department of the Soviet Republic Government if they hire workers between age 14 to 16." This law was in effect until 1955, when the major provisions of this law were incorporated into the first constitution of the People's Republic of China (PRC). For original texts of the 1929, 1933, and 1934 labor laws of the Soviet Republic, see Institute of Juveniles and Youth (1981:104–108). In 1991, the State Council issued an executive order to reaffirm prohibition of employment of child labor (*Law Yearbook of China, 1992*:191–192). See also Guo and Ma (1981) and Epstein (1993).

3. In December 1949, the central government held a first National Education Convocation to set up guidelines for urgently needed reform of the educational system. The Education Reform Act, which defined the scope and contents of mandatory primary and secondary education, was announced in 1951. During the period of 1949–1951, the initial task of educational reform was twofold: eliminating illiteracy for adults and mandating primary and secondary education for minors.

4. The child bride was a traditional practice in Chinese society; a poverty-stricken family arranged for their young daughter to be engaged to a son of an economically better-off family. The young girl, usually 6 to 15 years old, worked as the house servant until she reached 17 or 18, when the marriage commenced. This practice was seen to serve the needs of both sides. On one hand, the poor family could reduce the economic burden of raising a daughter and the subsequent cost for a wedding; on the other hand, the better-off family had free labor in their house. In reality, most child brides lived in horrible conditions and were often subject to physical abuse, starvation, and mental cruelty. Many of them died young or were sold to others.

5. Including young adult offenders up to 25 years old.

6. It is extremely difficult to obtain an accurate assessment of juvenile crime data because, first, China does not have a system of crime statistics and, second, juvenile offenders are often categorized in the same group with adult offenders up to 25 years old in the limited existing data.

7. The Marriage Law of the People's Republic of China, 1950.

8. In April 1956, *The Policy Restriction on Arresting Counter-Revolutionaries and Other Offenders* provided that "any adult who seduced or instigated the minor to commit crime shall be arrested." In May 1957, the People's Supreme Court and the Ministry of Justice jointly issued *Directives on the Criminal Prosecution in the Cities*, which again provided "severe punishment" against those adults who instigated or organized children to commit crime. In July of the same year, the Ministry of Public Security reaffirmed the same policy against instigators of juvenile crime.

9. Although there seemed to be a dramatic increase in crime from the 1950s to the later 1970s, the juvenile crime rate remained consistent over time. For instance, the nationwide court statistics in 1983 showed that while youth were responsible for 51.4 percent of cases convicted at the courts, among them, 85.2 percent were between 18 and 25 years age, and only 14.8 percent were under the age of 18. Therefore, juvenile crime remained at the same level, with only a slight increase from the 1950s. The public outcry about youthful crime in the post-Mao era was largely due to the vast number of baby boomers who had reached the crime-prone age, 18 to 25, in the early 1980s. In 1983, a total of 60 percent of the Chinese population was under age 25.

10. Under the traditional concept of the family in Chinese culture, children are not mere property of their parents but a family asset, partially because of the existence of the extended family structure in Chinese society. In those families, the most senior paternal figure, rather than the biological parents of the child in the family, is the ultimate authority in determining the child's welfare. In modern China, although the extended family structure has gradually vanished among the urban population because of living arrangements and official housing assignments, the traditional living arrangement of the extended family continues to exist in most rural areas, where 80 percent of the Chinese population reside. Therefore, to Chinese, children are still viewed more as family assets rather than as parental property. Perhaps, what sets China apart from the West is that while the former treats children as family assets, the latter regards them as assets of society.

11. *Criminal Law and Criminal Procedure Law of China*, Articles 44, 48, and 97.

12. The Public Security Regulation was issued by the Standing Committee of the People's Congress in 1983 for the purpose of a crackdown on the crimes that severely disturb the social order but are not serious enough for prosecution. It created several new categories of crime, such as using a weapon in the commission of crime, group fighting in public, and firearm trafficking, and amended enhanced penalty for the crimes that were already defined in the penal code. See *Collection of the Laws of the People's Republic of China* (1989:114–115) for original text.

13. See *Criminal Procedure Law of China*, 1979, Articles 10 and 27 and the People's Supreme Court's Memorandum of January 26, 1991, Section 10.

14. *Criminal Law of China*, Articles 14 and 44.

15. Juvenile institutions allow the wards to serve their term in juvenile facilities up to 20 years old. If wards do not complete their term before age 20 and are not eligible for parole or sentence reduction, they will be transferred to adult prison to complete the rest of their term. See Dai (1992:45).

16. The criteria and procedures for granting parole or sentencing reduction are set forth in Chinese People's Supreme Court's Memorandum of October 10, 1991. Parole and sentencing reduction are usually initiated by the correctional administration, with the approval of the court in their jurisdiction. See *Law Yearbook of China* (1992:535–537).

17. For more discussion on the political education session in China's penal institutions, see Rickett and Rickett (1981) and Lifton (1989).

18. See Ministry of Public Security, 1987.

19. The number of admissions in 1983 accounted for 25 percent of the total admissions from 1981 to 1990. This highly unusual number of admissions in 1983 was largely due to the stern penalty during the anticrime campaign. China was known for its politicalization of administration of criminal justice that disposes law violators not according to

the law and due process but based on the priority of the political agenda. See *Harvard Law Review* (1985:1890–1908) for more discussion.

REFERENCES

Cao, Manzhi. *Chinese Juvenile Delinquency (Zhongguo qingshaonian fanzuixue)*. Beijing: Mass Press, 1988.

Cao, Zidan. *Etiological Research of Crime in China (Zhongguo fanzui yuanyin yanjiu zongshu)*. Beijing: Chinese Political Science and Law University Press, 1993.

Cheng, Rongbin, Kangtai Li, and Jiabao Yin. *Issues on Juvenile Delinquency (Guanyu qingshaonian fanzui de jige wenti)*. Beijing: Chinese People's University Press, 1982.

Collection of the Laws of the People's Republic of China (Zhonghua renmin gongheguo falü quanshu). Changchun: Jiling People's Press, 1989.

"Concepts of Law in the Chinese Anti-Crime Campaign." *Harvard Law Review* 98 (1985): 1890–1908.

The Criminal Law and the Criminal Procedure Law of China. Beijing: Foreign Language Press, 1984.

Curran, Daniel J., and Sandra Cook. "Growing Fears, Rising Crime: Juveniles and China's Justice System." *Crime and Delinquency* 39 (1993): 296–315.

Dai, Fukang. "Inquiry of Parole for Juvenile Offenders." *Juvenile Delinquency Research (Qingshaonian fanzui yuanjiu)* 3–4 (1992): 43–47.

Epstein, Irving I. "Reformatory Education in Chinese Society." *International Journal of Offender Therapy and Comparative Criminology* 30 (1986): 87–100.

———. "Child Labor and Basic Education Provision in China." *International Journal of Educational Development* 13 (1993): 227–238.

Feinerman, James V. "The Disposition of Cases Involving Juvenile Delinquents in the People's Republic of China." *UCLA Pacific Basin Law Journal* 4 (1985): 1–13.

Feng, Shuliang, and Qi Lu. *Crime Prevention in China: Strategy and Measures (Zhongguo yufang fanzui fanglue)*. Beijing: Law Press, 1994.

Fu, Hualing. "Juvenile Delinquency in Post-Mao China." *International Journal of Comparative and Applied Criminal Justice* 16 (1992): 263–272.

Guo, Xiang. "The Legal Protection of Children's Rights in China" *(Wuoguo dui ertong quanli de falu baohu)*. *Juvenile Delinquency Research (Qingshaonian fanzui yuanjiu)* 5 (1993): 22–29.

Guo, Xiang, and Jingmiao Ma. "On China's Juvenile Laws" *(Wuoguo youguan qingshaonian fagui gaishu)*. In *Institute of Juveniles and Youth 1981. Collection of Juvenile Law and Regulations (Qingshaonian fagui Zhaibian jiqi yanjiu)*. Beijing: Institute of Juveniles and Youth, 1981.

Guo, Xiang, Qiancheng Xu, and Chunlin Li. *People's Mediation in China (Renmin tiaojie zhai zhongguo)*. Wuhan: Huazhong Normal University Press, 1986.

Institute of Juveniles and Youth. *Collection of Juvenile Law and Regulations (Qingshaonian fagui Zhaibian jiqi yanjiu)*. Beijing: Institute of Juveniles and Youth, 1981.

Jiangsu Provincial Supreme Court Research Division. "An Experiment in the Establishment of Juvenile System in China: Survey of Adjudication of Juvenile Cases in Tianning District Court" *(Wanshan wuoguo shaonian sifa zhidu de youyi changshi)*. *Juvenile Delinquency Research (Qingshaonian fanzui yuanjiu)* 7–8 (1992): 47–50.

Kang, Shuhua. *Juvenile Law (Qingshaonian faxue)*. Beijing: Beijing University Press, 1986.

————. "Several Issues in Studies of Juvenile and Youth Crime." *Juvenile Delinquency Research (Qingshaonian fanzui yuanjiu)* 1 (1992): 45–48.

Kang, Shuhua, and Xiang Guo. *Reference on Juvenile Law (Qingshaonian faxue cankao ziliao)*. Beijing: Chinese Political Science and Law University Press, 1987.

————. *On Juvenile Law (Qingshaonian faxue gailun)*. Beijing: Chinese Political Science and Law University Press, 1988.

Law Yearbook of China. (Zhongguo falü nianjian). Beijing: Press of Law Yearbook of China, 1991, 1992.

Lei, Xun. *Adjudication of Juvenile Offenders in China (Zhongguo xingshi shenpan shijian)*. Beijing: People's Court Press, 1991.

Li, Kangtai, and Jianhua Qian. "Legal Protection of Minors in China" *(Wuoguo weichengnianren de falu baohu)*. *Juvenile Delinquency Research (Qingshaonian fanzui yuanjiu)* 9 (1992): 25–28.

Li, Yingtian. "The Problems in the Juvenile Courts." *Juvenile Delinquency Research (Qingshaonian fanzui yuanjiu)* 5 (1993): 19–22.

Lifton, R. J. *Thought Reform and Psychology of Totalism*. Chapel Hill: University of North Carolina Press, 1989.

Ministry of Public Security. "Notification on the Scope of Detention and Incarceration at Shaonianfan Guanjiao Sue (Institution of Management and Education for Juvenile Offenders), March 23, 1982. In Shuhua Kang and Xiang Guo, *Reference on Juvenile Law (Qingshaonian faxue cankao ziliao)* pp. 71–72. Beijing: Chinese Political Science and Law University Press, 1987.

Mok, Bong-ho. "Community Care for Delinquent Youth: The Chinese Approach of Rehabilitating the Young Offenders." *Journal of Offender Counseling, Services and Rehabilitation* 15 (1990): 5–19.

Myren, Richard A. "The Developing Legal System of China." *Criminal Justice International* 2 (1986): 9–20.

Ren, Xin. "Prostitution in China." In *Prostitution: An International Handbook on Trends, Problems, and Policies,* edited by Nanette J. Davis. Westport, CT: Greenwood Press, 1993.

Rickett, Allyn W., and A. Rickett. *Prisoners of Liberation*. San Francisco: China Books, 1981.

Sheng, Yu, Deyi Wang, and Changzen Wu. "Chinese Law and Status of Children." *Columbia Human Rights Law Review* 13 (1981): 71–99.

Tianjin People's Supreme Court, First Division. "Discussion on the Adjudication of Juvenile Court." *Juvenile Delinquency Research (Qingshaonian fanzui yuanjiu)* 2 (1988): 18–20.

"United Nations Convention on the Rights of the Child." In *Children, Rights and the Law,* edited by Philip Alston, Stephen Parker, and John Seymour. New York: Oxford University Press, 1992.

Wang, Sheng, and Changseng Ma. "Three Extensions in Corrections." *Juvenile Delinquency Research (Qingshaonian fanzui yuanjiu)* 2 (1988): 27–29.

Xu, Jian. "The Principles and Development of Juvenile Justice Administration in the People's Republic of China." *Police Studies* 10 (1987): 181.

Yang, Chunxi. "China's Control Policy on Juvenile Crime." In *Juvenile Delinquency and Its Treatment by Chinese and American Scholars,* edited by Chunxi Yang. Beijing: Mass Press, 1989a.

————. "Juvenile and Youth Crime is an Important Topic in Jurisprudence." In *Juvenile Delinquency and Its Treatment by Chinese and American Scholars,* edited by Chunxi Yang. Beijing: Mass Press, 1989b.

Zhao, Ji-Sheng. "The Trends of Juvenile Crime and Control Policy." In *Crime Trends in the 1990s and Its Countermeasures of Prevention and Control.* Beijing: Chinese People's Public Security University, 1991.

Zhou, Lu, Ruohe Yang, and Ruquan Hu. *Strategy on Comprehensive Prevention and Treatment of Juvenile Delinquency (Qingshaonian fanzui zonghe zili duicexue).* Beijing: Mass Press, 1986.

APPENDIX: JUVENILE JUSTICE AND RELATED SERVICES AGENCIES AND DIRECTORS

Ministry of Public Security
14 Dong Chang An Boulevard
Bejing, China 100741

Li Junren, Director
Institute for Crime Prevention and Reform through Labor
Ministry of Justice
3 Yumin Road
Chaoyang District
Beijing, China 100029

Professor Guo Xiang, Director
Institute of Sociology of Law and Juvenile Delinquency Studies
China University of Political Science and Law
41 Xue Yuan Road
Beijing, China 100088

Professor Kang Shuhua, Director
Center for Crime Problem Studies
Law Department
Beijing University
Beijing, China 100871

Wang Fei, Director
Shanghai Institute of Corrections
Shanghai Bureau of Reform through Labor
111 Changyang Road
Shanghai, China 200082

Zhu Entao, Director
Interpol National Central Bureau China
Ministry of Public Security
14 Dong Chang An Boulevard
Beijing, China 1000741

5

EGYPT

Nagwa A. Hafez

HISTORICAL OVERVIEW

Egypt, like any other country, faces the challenge of crime and delinquency. It is a negative phenomenon that needs attention from the government and citizens and has existed in all stages of historical development.

Before the 1952 revolution, the country was suffering from the negative impact of colonialism. Poverty and illiteracy were major problems that affected juvenile delinquency, which was limited to property offenses; after independence, juvenile delinquency continued to occur within the same limitations.

In the 1970s, different social changes resulted from new political and economical decisions (Gamal El Deen, 1984). The impact of these changes was obvious on juvenile delinquency: some old forms of delinquency disappeared, such as vagrancy, and new kinds appeared, such as violence.

Dealing with juvenile delinquents is mainly a governmental concern, besides some few efforts from the natives. The government is very much concerned with, and aware of, efforts to deal with the problem. The first step in dealing with delinquents is the juvenile police; juvenile police stations are available in different parts of the country, where delinquents are first processed. The next step is the juvenile court, where trials are held and appropriate decisions are taken.

Decisions such as assignment to an educational institute or rehabilitation institute or placement on probation depend on the size and seriousness of the offense.

Currently, juvenile delinquency is considered a serious problem, which has changed greatly in nature and in kind.

JUVENILE DELINQUENCY AS VIEWED BY THE LAW

The legal definition of delinquency is stated by the Egyptian Law of Juveniles, No. 31, 1974, the latest comprehensive, published law for juvenile welfare.

This law tried to take into consideration several goals of social welfare and principles of social defense. The law for juvenile delinquency follows a new criminal policy in dealing with juveniles and is based on two principles (NCSCR Publications, 1965):

1. It is impermissible to impose a criminal punishment on a juvenile less than 15 years old. Instead, an educational or rehabilitational treatment is more suitable.

2. It is permissible to impose any regular criminal judgment on juveniles from 15 to 18 years old, yet allowing them a chance for continuing education, permission for more family visits, and so forth. The principal items of juvenile law that are related to this chapter are as follows:

Item 1 The law defines the juvenile as anyone not more than 18 years old at the time of the commitment of the crime or at the time of being in a predelinquent situation.

Item 2 A predelinquent situation is one of the following:

1. Beggary, including the selling of any unimportant items or anything considered an unsuitable source for living;

2. Collecting any useless items from streets;

3. Practicing work related to indecency, prostitution, or gambling or working for adults practicing these kinds of work;

4. Having no place to live or sleeping in streets or public areas or places;

5. Contacting predelinquents or suspicious people known by their bad behavior;

6. Escaping from educational and training centers;

7. Committing bad behavior or refusing parental supervision;

8. Having no source of suitable living or having no dependable guardian.

Item 7 A juvenile who is less than 15 years old is not subject to criminal judgment; instead, one of the following treatments is more suitable:

1. reprehension—the simplest way of dealing with delinquents, which involves talking to the juvenile and explaining the size and the gravity of the act. This method is used in cases of very minor offenses;

2. submission to parents or guardian;

3. assignment to a vocational training center;

4. assignment to certain vocational works;

5. put under probation supervision;

    6. assignment to an institution for social welfare;

    7. assignment to a specialized clinic.

Item 15   For a juvenile who is more than 15 years old and less than 18 who commits a serious crime punishable by execution or life imprisonment with work, the judgment is reduced to 10 years of imprisonment. If a crime is punishable by short-term imprisonment with work, it is replaced by imprisonment for a period not less than six months, and if by imprisonment only, it is replaced by three months at most. Generally, any judgment for a crime is reducible, for juveniles, to one-third of the original one.

    The court also has the right to assign the juvenile to a social welfare institution, instead of passing the judgment.

Item 16   A juvenile less than 15 years old who commits two or more crimes must be punished by a suitable treatment, depending on the kind of crimes committed.

Item 19   The treatment ends upon reaching the age of 21. The court also has the right to put the juvenile under probation, depending on the social report and on the request of the public prosecutor.

Item 35   In cases of predelinquency, the court must listen to the social worker report about the juvenile to clarify circumstances of predelinquency and to discuss the case. Also, opinions of experienced people are considered helpful in discussing and evaluating the case.

Item 42   The juvenile court is the responsible institution to adjudicate disputes and quarrels, and it has to follow up the execution of decisions. The judge must visit the institutions of social welfare and the vocational training centers and other institutions that cooperate with the court for the interest of the juvenile at least once each three months. The law also states that it is necessary to establish a special court for juveniles in each governorate, to be connected with an office of social work. The country is divided into 26 governorates, which are regional divisions. This court has to examine the cases in closed sessions, with the possibility of exempting the juvenile from attending the session and facing the court.

In general, the core of this law is the care and the welfare of juveniles, to keep them away from the penal law and from criminal legislation as much as possible.

SOCIOECONOMIC AND POLITICAL CHANGES

To understand juvenile delinquency in Egypt in the last few years, it is useful to mention, briefly, the main changes that occurred in Egyptian society, their impact on crime and delinquency, and societal reactions to delinquent behavior.

During the Revolution of 1952, which was a major event in Egypt that changed the country's history, political changes occurred that brought to the country dramatic socioeconomic changes. These changes led to a reformation of the whole of society.

First, the agrarian laws, applied in the 1950s and 1960s, left some impact.

The major success consisted in restricting aristocracy and big landowners. These laws also tried to reduce the wide gap between the social classes. Still, such laws have been unable to help farmers feel they are really free economically (NCSCR, 1965).

In addition, the social meaning of productivity was formalized within the framework of capitalism, including all its value system. The ideology of socialism was successful in establishing a certain direction toward the state, but actually the participation of the people in formalizing decisions could not be realized through the policy of one major party.

Also, the decline of job opportunities during the 1970s, with many good offers of jobs in the Arab countries, especially, after the war of 1973, led the people to seek work in other Arab countries.

All these factors both within and outside Egypt came together to produce what is known as the open-door policy, which opened the door widely to economic and private sectors to work actively in the country. This new policy caused great change in the structure of society, including its value system.

Egyptian capitalism started to flourish again, but toward a fast and easy way of collecting wealth. New projects and industries were established for the sake of consumption, instead of production. The main value that was formalized and appeared clearly was materialism. People supported and favored material values over the moral ones as a pillar for security. This situation opened the door to some nonlegal ways to acquire money and, accordingly, some forms of deviant behavior among adults and also among juveniles, who started to commit new forms of delinquency.

Another important reason for change, especially after the 1973 war, was the great rush to the oil-producing countries, as one fast method to solve personal economic problems, to relieve personal sufferings, and to formalize fast and great fortunes. Great numbers of people from different categories—graduates, workers, and farmers—rushed to work in Arab countries, especially the Gulf countries, to cope with high rates of inflation.

The previous factors led to the following results:

1. The traditional characteristic of the Egyptian people, that is, strong ties to, and strong settlement in, land—to plant it and live in it and sacrifice for it—has changed (El-Saaty, 1982).

2. The traditional family was also subject to change. The extended family has been replaced by the nuclear family, and its strong relations tended to break down. The absence of at least one parent, who worked outside the country, became an observable phenomenon. This situation negatively affected the process of socialization (Abdel Kader, 1967).

3. Increased education and the availability of schools in the villages, as one fruitful result of the 1952 revolution, did not lead to better quality of education.

4. Seasonal chances for work attracted youth and juveniles; numbers of them left school

looking for work, but, unfortunately, most job opportunities for these people were marginal.

5. The number of dropouts from school, particularly at the primary level, increased as a result of the previous two reasons (Hafez, 1988a).

It is apparent that changes in the socioeconomic structure resulted from political decisions that affected the society deeply in all aspects of life, especially in the value system, which left its impact on morals and, accordingly, on behavior, even among juveniles. The new value that clearly prevailed, especially among youngsters, become the value of high aspiration for success, regardless of real capabilities and conditions (El-Sharkawi and Mohamed, 1985).

The dream of a big fortune started to be everyone's dream, again regardless of capabilities and level of education. If it could not be reached and achieved by correct and legal ways, then why not in illegal ways?

Family values were also subject to great change. The old traditional, conservative values were replaced by new ones characterized or labeled as the values of modern life and modern style. Most new values were mainly centralized around achievement and gaining money, by any means. Values of sacrifice, work, and sincerity became old-fashioned values that fitted old generations. Youngsters and juveniles were influenced, to a great extent, by the new way of thinking and the new values.

ASPECTS OF CHANGE IN DELINQUENCY

To give an idea about the changes in patterns of delinquency among juveniles in this period, namely, the last two decades, I refer to some outcomes of a study that I directed, focusing on tracing the patterns of change in types of crimes among juveniles during five years, from 1979 to 1983. The research first applied to three areas in Egypt, to be followed by other areas. The chosen three areas are characterized differently: city type, rural type, and semirural-urban type.

Cairo, the first area of study, is not only the capital but also a governorate, with its surrounding areas. It has 14 million people (according to the last census), in an area of about 200 square kilometers. It is the largest city not only in Egypt but in Africa and the Middle East and is the main social, educational, industrial, economic, and administrative center of the country. The residents of this governorate are of three types: traditional dwellers, rural immigrants, and modernized dwellers.

The city includes all sorts of contradictions in cultural aspects and in ways of life, ranging from palace dwellers to one-room apartment dwellers. The populace also ranges from millionaires to those in poverty. These characteristics have an impact on criminal behavior, especially among immature juveniles. The total number of delinquents in the Cairo governorate during the period of study was 24,886 cases.

In the second area of study, El-Giza, second largest governorate, only two centers were chosen to reflect different standards of living. The first center, Agouza, to the west of Cairo, is considered the middle-class income area, preferred by middle-class people, visitors, and students from Arab countries. The number of delinquents in Agouza during the period of study was 6,651 cases.

Imbada, the second center chosen in El-Giza, and the third area of study, is considered a semirural area, densely populated with people originally from the surrounding rural areas. It combines different styles of living, as it is a mixture of rural and urban dwellers. It also combines the traditional and rural dwellers with the modern, new-style dwellers. Numbers of delinquents in Imbaba reached 533.

The number of delinquents in the Cairo governorate represents 20 percent of all juvenile crimes committed in the republic. When comparing this percentage with that during the period from 1958 to 1962, over half of the juvenile crimes committed at that time (54 percent) occurred in the Cairo governorate (Naiem, 1983).

The type of crime among juveniles has significantly changed in Cairo. During the 1950s the 1960s, the major kind of crime was vagrancy, followed by beggary, which represented half of the total number of juvenile crimes. In the late 1970s and the early 1980s, these offenses were reduced considerably, to only 8.15 percent of the total number (Naiem, 1983). This kind of change could be interpreted according to the following reasons:

1. The establishment of juvenile police in 1963 helped face the problem and activated police in dealing with cases and, hence, led to the decline of vagrancy and beggary (Ewies, 1965).

2. The new policy applied in the 1970s opened some new opportunities for work among juveniles, although most of these opportunities were marginal kinds, but at least these simple kinds of work were able to reduce the need for vagrancy and beggary.

The major kinds of delinquency during the five years of study were stealing, violence (beatings and injuries), and supply crimes (any deviance related to things needed, especially food). These three offenses represented 46 percent of the total number of crimes committed by juveniles.

Stealing is the major crime in Cairo and the second most frequent crime in El-Giza. This crime is related mainly to the materialistic need and also to low capabilities and a high degree of ambition, especially among youngsters. They want to fulfill their materialistic need by any means. Accordingly, the rate of stealing increased, especially stealing from wealthy households and stealing cars.

Violence consists of beatings and injuries and is related to the juvenile age category. Young people get furious very easily and have strong attitudes toward violence and aggression, especially as a result of grieving for the loss of loved ones.

Supply crimes are relatively new, emerging after the 1960s and resulting from two reasons:

1. with more intervention from the state and also because of the sudden rise of prices, new acts were criminalized, aiming to realize social stability and social control;
2. the increasing number of working children.

The data of the Central Statistical Report revealed that the number of working children under the age of 15 is 1,473,600, or 10 percent of the total working population in Egyptian society. Egyptian law prohibits work by children under the age of 15, even though a large number of children from 8 to 13 years of age do work. Cairo registered the highest rate of working children, followed by Alexandria.

Children work for the following reasons:

1. poverty and the desire to improve family income;
2. broken homes and lack of regular salary or income;
3. an increase in dropout rates from schools, especially from primary levels of education, due to some deficiencies in the educational processes (Hafez, 1988b).

Supply crimes are related, one way or another, to this work by children. Children communicate with different kinds of persons, learn from them new experiences, and are used by them for good, as well as for bad, purposes.

When underage children violate the law by working it is not only their responsibility but the employer's and the guardian's responsibility. In many cases, children are victims of their social environment, which urges them to pursue illegal ways.

FELONIES COMMITTED BY JUVENILES

According to the data collected during the period of study (1979–1983), the felony of drug distribution increased among juveniles and appeared to be a major offense. In 1979, there were 16 cases of drug distribution among juveniles. In 1983, the number of cases reached 100.

Other new kinds of felonies committed by delinquents included rape, kidnapping, carrying unregistered weapons, bribery (offering or receiving), driving without a license, and wrong injury (unintentional harm resulting from a fight or attack). Since these felonies emerged among juveniles for the first time during this period, they are considered a clear sign of change in delinquent behavior.

The gravity of the crimes of rape and possessing unregistered weapons is not in their frequency, but in their meaning or in the concept and significance of committing such acts.

The commission of such crimes by juveniles reflects not only violence but also a great challenge to tradition and to conservative values, the prevailing values for centuries. Criminal behavior of this kind is a great threat to public safety and security.

Delinquency among females, although still not too serious, is increasing considerably. Females in the Islamic culture, the prevailing culture in Egyptian society, are generally characterized as quiet and unaggressive. Accordingly, delinquency among females was, for a long time, a limited phenomenon in size and type. But lately, during the period of study, which is considered the period of great change in society, some change has occurred among female delinquents.

Cases of crimes committed by females during the period of study were 1,831, or 7.4 percent of all crimes. The kinds of crimes committed by delinquent females include crimes of supply, attempted crimes of supply, beating and quarreling, and decency crimes, especially prostitution.

Most crimes were committed by juveniles falling in the age category 13–18, which is the most serious category in life, with the characteristics of adolescence and all its complicated troubles, sufferings, frustrations, tensions, and, in many cases, aggression.

Concerning delinquency areas, again a change has occurred. According to traditional theories, delinquency areas are juvenile settlements, or slum areas. This is not the situation any more (El-Sharkawi and Mohamed, 1985). To the contrary, delinquency areas now are areas of upper-class and upper-middle-class residents; they are also areas of tourism and commercial centers. This change occurred to cope with the change in the types of crimes attracting juveniles.

Juveniles are not satisfied anymore with minor stealing or picking up simple items from streets or from grocery stores; they want to steal rich cars or shoplift expensive items.

Interaction and interrelations between classes, as one result of the policy applied in the 1970s, led to great change in values and aspirations of different classes.

One of the situations recently observed is that upper- and upper-middle-class residential areas are surrounded by lower-class residential people. Such situations lead to some advantages, as well as some disadvantages. People from lower classes acquired, to some extent, the behavior and the way of living of upper-class people. But, on the other hand, they tried to fulfill their aspirations by any means, legally or illegally.

Concerning the kinds of penalties applied to juveniles, some changes have occurred. From the data collected through the period of study, the major kinds of judgments on delinquents are the following:

1. imprisonment for a definite period. This judgment affected 246 of the total cases, while it was rarely applicable during the 1960s. It is considered evidence of the seriousness of crimes committed by juveniles.

2. assignment to an institution, applied to 17.3 percent of all cases.

3. payment of a fine (with different amounts), applied to 18 percent of the cases (most fines ranged from 200 to 500 Egyptian Pounds).

Juveniles received various periods of imprisonment, according to the kind of crime. For first convictions of drug distribution, juveniles received ten years of imprisonment.

Judgment of innocence applied to very few cases, not more than 3.3 percent of the total, which is another evidence of change. This kind of judgment used to be the major one during the 1960s and 1970s.

SUMMARY

Delinquent behavior among juveniles has changed as a result of changes in Egyptian society within the last two decades. Crime and delinquency are the mirror of society, reflecting all the society's problems and sufferings. The new trend of delinquency is directed toward a material need, which reflects the change in society as a whole.

The law for juveniles has been set to protect children and to apply the principle of social defense. But trends of social change have affected juveniles and directed their delinquency toward new, more serious forms of crimes, derived from new relations and values. These changes have also affected the enforcement of crimes and acts of deviance committed by juveniles.

REFERENCES

Abdel Kader, Mohamed. "Socialization Methods in Rural Egyptian Areas." *National Review for Social Sciences* 13 (1967): 39–52.
Abul Ghar, Ibrahim. "Household Stealing in Urban Areas." *National Review of Social Sciences* 27 (1978): 43–49.
Criminal Research Section, NCSCR. "Figures of Juvenile Delinquency in Egypt." *National Review of Criminal Sciences* (1985): 179–202.
El-Saaty, Samia. *Crime and the Society.* Cairo: Anglo-American Library, 1982.
El-Sharkawi and A. Mohamed. *Juvenile Delinquency.* Cairo: Anglo-Egyptian Library, 1985.
Ewies, Saied. "Size and Attitudes of Juvenile Delinquency." *National Review of Criminal Sciences* 8 (1965): 194–199.
Gamal El Deen, N. "Socio-Economical Changes in Rural Areas in Egypt during the Seventies." *Current Education Review* (1984): 58–59.
Hafez, Nagwa A. "The Care of Prisoners' Children in View of Modern Preventive Methods." Published paper in the Conference of Prisoners' Welfare, Cairo, 1987.
———. "Social Work in the Egyptian Prisons." in *Public Security Review,* Cairo, 1988a.
———. "Children's Right of Education." Published paper in Children's Rights Conference, Cairo, 1988b.

Mahdi, A. R. *Criminal Responsibility in Comparative Law.* Alexandria: El-Maarf, 1976:
    56.
Naiem, Samir, "Structural Changes Effect on the Egyptian Society," *Social Sciences
    Review* (1983): 115–119.
NCSCR Publications. *Juvenile Vagrancy: A Statistical Study.* Cairo: NCSCR, 1965.
Public Security Reports. Cairo: Publications of the Ministry of Justice, 1979, 1980, 1981,
    1982, 1983.
Salama, M. *Penal Law.* Cairo: Dar El-Nahda, 1981.

APPENDIX: LIST OF AGENCIES DEALING WITH
JUVENILE DELINQUENTS

Juvenile Police: The first agency that deals with delinquents. It arrests delinquents and
    receives claims from complainants. Each governorate has one police station for juve-
    niles.

Juvenile Court: Deals with juvenile cases transferred from police stations. The court
    board consists of a judge, a social worker, and a psychologist. Sessions are usually
    closed to the juveniles and their family. Each governorate has one juvenile court.

Educational Institute in El-Giza: Specified for delinquents transferred by the court. Its
    treatment depends, mainly, on educational processes. It teaches and rehabilitates de-
    linquents according to their capabilities.

6

ENGLAND

William Wakefield and
J. David Hirschel

INTRODUCTION

A 12-year-old boy in Hyde Park, London, attacks a woman and grabs her purse. A 16-year-old boy in Chicago does the same to a woman walking down the street. A 19-year-old young man in Chelsea, London, attacks an elderly woman and takes her purse. The police in London and Chicago arrest all three. Do their ages make a difference in what happens to them? Yes, very definitely. In both societies, age will determine how they are treated, how they will have their cases processed, and what policies will be used to shape their dispositions. Both countries have a dual system: one set of procedures, institutions, and goals govern juveniles, and another governs adults. Although similar in this regard, juvenile justice systems in the United States and England have many differences that serve to make the two unique in spite of their shared heritage.

Multiple strategies to reduce delinquency have been used in England. Although related to, yet independent from, the adult system, the juvenile justice system has been responsible for dealing with youth crime, as well as youth in need of care and protection. The formal goals of the juvenile justice system thus involve the supervision and protection of needy children and the social control of juveniles who commit crimes or otherwise threaten the stability of society. Protecting the rights of the juvenile is also extremely important. In an informal sense, the juvenile justice system in England contains diverse groups whose goals are shaped by work group relationships and the ambitions and attitudes of personnel within particular agencies, as well as political, economic, and social influences from the outside community.

England's juvenile justice system is currently in a state of flux; its fundamental operation and institutions are being reexamined. The English have found it difficult to resolve the dilemma between promoting the welfare of a juvenile and holding the juvenile responsible for his or her actions under the law. Although a major attempt has been made, England has not fully integrated into the juvenile justice system the required consideration for the welfare of the juvenile offender, which was first set down in the Children and Young Persons Act, 1933. On one hand, many authorities support the social welfare of the juvenile standards that are so well integrated in juvenile courts in the United States. They suggest that the juvenile court is a treatment-oriented agency for dispensing personalized, individualized justice to needy children through the guidance and understanding of the court as a "wise parent." Others, however, hold to a law-and-order orientation, suggesting that the concept of *parens patriae* has been neglectful of the victims of crime and delinquency. They believe that serious and chronic offenders should be disciplined and punished severely, as opposed to "treated" and "rehabilitated." Finally, some believe that court processing of juveniles may well have an adverse effect on children, particularly since they have not been extended the full rights they would receive in an adult court. Advocates of this position would have more rights afforded to juveniles. This would complement the shift in emphasis from the 1960s focus on "care" to the 1970s and 1980s movement toward "control."

This chapter reviews the history of juvenile justice in the unified system of England and Wales and discusses the justice system's processing of youthful offenders.

A History of English Juvenile Justice

Only in recent times has there been an emphasis on the special needs of juveniles in the justice system of England. Originally, adults and juveniles who violated the law were processed in the same manner and were subject to the same types of punishments. These punishments included whippings, mutilation, banishment, torture, and death.

Although the notion that it was unfair to hold children responsible for their actions in the same manner as mature adults is of ancient origin, it took a long time for this notion to find expression in the law. Some indication of how young people were treated comes from our knowledge of early Roman law, in particular, the guidelines set down in the Twelve Tables (c. 488–451 B.C.). There was no question about whether youths were to be held criminally responsible for their acts; they were to be handled entirely within the context of the adult system (Nyquist, 1960). The only concession was in the severity of the punishment meted out to youth. For example:

[A]n adult caught in manifest theft was subject to flogging and enslavement to his victim; a young offender would receive corporal punishment only at the magistrate's discretion and was required to make restitution rather than to enter slavery (Ludwig, 1955:12).

For much of Roman history, incapacity to speak was the criterion for determining whether an offender was too young for punishment. In the fifth century A.D., the age was fixed at 7 for exemption from criminal responsibility. With the onset of puberty (at the age of 14 for boys and 12 for girls), youths were held totally responsible for their acts (Nyquist, 1960; Jolowicz, 1957; Buckland, 1963).

Medieval Europe was not too different from Roman times in terms of laws relating to the criminal responsibility of children. During the entire period between 700 and 1500 A.D., children were simply not seen as a distinct social group with unique needs and behaviors. Much of what we know of life in this period comes from accounts of upper-class, landholding families, for whom the nuclear family was the smallest segment of a larger, extended clan. Little is known about the peasant families of the Middle Ages, who devoted most of their time to work and survival. Children were expected to assume adult roles in the family early in life and apprentice in trades or crafts to wealthier families. Thus, we can see that, to some extent, control over children and their welfare was literally placed in the hands of the more powerful landowners of the country, lifting the burden of child care from their parents.

Development of English Common Law: Chancery Courts and *Parens Patriae*

Early medieval traditions and judgments brought about the development of English common law. The term "common law" refers to that body of judge-made law that became "common" throughout the realm as a result of the decisions of the itinerant judges Henry II began to send around the country in the twelfth century. Both the Chancery court, which became the court that provided equity to the citizenry, and the concept of *parens patriae,* which focused on the sovereign as the protector of his or her subjects, played a significant part in the shaping of juvenile justice in England.

During the Middle Ages, the Chancery court became responsible for settling the estate and guardianship problems of the wealthier classes and for overseeing the general welfare of the citizenry. Since children and other incompetents were under the protective control of the sovereign, English kings could easily "justify their interventions in the lives of the children of their vassals—children whose position and property were of direct concern to the monarch" (Besharov, 1974:2).

As time passed, the concept of *parens patriae* was used more and more to justify intervention into the lives of the peasants in the name of their general welfare. As has been pointed out by Rendleman (1971:209), this was primarily a ploy to reinforce the power of the king and continue his control over the structure of families.

As the common-law tradition began to solidify in England, many practices concerning children become commonplace. Although supposedly responsible from birth for their actions, few children under seven actually faced any legal penalties. By 1300, most English courts routinely used a system of convictions and pardons to release children under seven from any legal recrimination from the court. This practice remained a part of juvenile justice in England until the middle of the fifteenth century (Ludwig, 1955).

Older children between 7 and 14 were another matter where the law was concerned. Rather than a conviction and pardon, children accused of crime at this age were adjudged based on other considerations: severity of the crime, maturity, capacity to distinguish between right and wrong, and any evidence of blatant malice. This almost resembles a type of ''conditional responsibility'' where the law was concerned and suggested a form of individualized justice that was later to become a cornerstone of juvenile justice throughout England (Ludwig, 1955). Individualized justice did not, however, necessarily translate into compassionate treatment of the convicted. Convicted juvenile offenders continued to be subjected to the same punishments as adults. A few examples compiled by Wiley Sanders from case records of the Old Bailey Crown Criminal Court illustrate the reality faced by youthful offenders. A 1686 case involved a 10-year-old boy who had stolen 30 yards of satin ribbon and was ordered to be whipped. A 1690 case involved a 10-year-old boy convicted of stealing two gold rings and some money. His punishment: to be ''burnt in the hand.'' These and other types of corporal punishment were the most frequent penalties for young offenders between the ages of 7 and 14 in England at that time (Sanders, 1970:23–26).

During the 1700s, a common penalty for adult offenders was the practice of transportation—usually to America or Australia. An analogous practice used with young offenders was the occasional decision to ''bindout'' a youth to a tradesman as an apprentice. Since this was a common practice with ordinary young people from poor families, it is not surprising that it became commonplace with delinquents as well. However, according to most sources, this was not used as extensively by the courts as corporal punishment was for convicted youthful offenders (Binder, Geis, and Bruce, 1988:205).

Finally, one of the darker clouds over early English juvenile justice is the fact that there were some 160 to 200 capital offenses listed in the statutes for which young offenders could be sentenced to death (Radzinowicz, 1948). The case records are filled with cases of juveniles sentenced to die, though many were subsequently pardoned, and some were transported. Regrettably, however, some children were executed during that time. For example, in 1690, a 14-year-old boy convicted of robbery was hanged. In 1735, a 10-year-old girl who was an apprentice stole some money and was sentenced to die (Radzinowicz, 1948). Radzinowicz (1948:14) notes that 18 of the 20 people executed in London in 1785 were under the age of 18. Although rare, there are recorded instances of older children being executed well into the 1800s (Binder, Geis, and Bruce, 1988:206).

Young offenders under the age of seven could, then, receive lenient treatment. However, older children accused of crime and subsequently prosecuted were subjected to the same procedures as their adult counterparts. If found guilty, they received the same punishments; there was no provision for separate institutional treatment for youths convicted of crime in the England of that period (Radzinowicz, 1948).

Evolution of Juvenile Justice in the Nineteenth and Early Twentieth Centuries

Not until the latter part of the eighteenth century did some concern begin to be shown for the brutal conditions in which children were placed. Eventually, after the turn of the nineteenth century, some private homes began to be used for housing and caring for the less serious juvenile offenders. Not until 1836, however, was a commission established in order to consider summary (lower court nonjury) trials for youth. Finally, the Juvenile Offenders Act, 1847 was passed, allowing for the summary trial of youth under the age of 14 for theft. In 1854, the first Reformatory Schools Act was passed, which allowed for the commitment of youth under 16 to separate reformatories from adults. The Summary Jurisdiction Act, 1879 permitted the summary trial of youth under the age of 16 for most offenses; however, these trials were still carried out in adult courts, often alongside convicted adults (McClean and Wood, 1969:183; Moore, 1982:3). Finally, in 1908, just nine years after the development of the first juvenile court in the United States, the first separate juvenile court was established in England with the passage of the Children Act, 1908. The court had jurisdiction in criminal matters over "children" under 14 and "young persons" between 14 and 16, as well as civil jurisdiction over those in need of care, protection, and control. Although the court's stated purpose was to deal with youth under the age of 16 in a separate manner in order to keep them from associating with hardened criminals, no special provision was made for any new judges specifically trained and assigned to work only with juveniles (Jackson, 1972:253). Indeed, it has been suggested that "the special needs of children and young persons finding themselves in court were only appreciated when the juvenile courts had been operating for some time" (McClean and Wood, 1969: 183).

Along with the establishment of a separate juvenile court, the practice of sending juveniles to adult prisons was all but abolished for youth under 16. The 1908 Prevention of Crime Act established the specialized juvenile "borstal" (reformatory) system of juvenile institutions, which is discussed in more detail in a later section of this chapter. In 1933, another very significant change occurred with the adoption of the Children and Young Persons Act, 1933. This legislation reaffirmed the guiding principle that the court should always act in the best interests of the welfare of the child (Sec. 44(1)). The age of criminal responsibility was raised from 7 to 8 (Sec. 50), and 16-year-olds were placed under the criminal jurisdiction of the juvenile court (Sec. 107(1)). In addition, the act had the desired effect of removing some of the potentially harmful labels, such as "convicted" and "sentenced," from those involved with the court system. Still, even these changes were somewhat "cosmetic," and it was not until passage of the Children and Young Persons Act, 1969 that significant changes began to emerge in the attitude and approach of the juvenile justice system toward young people in trouble.

The Children and Young Persons Act, 1969

The historical era in which the English juvenile justice system emerged provides considerable explanation of the characteristics of the system and its response to youthful offenders. One factor influencing the development of the children's court movement in England was the philosophical shift in the understanding of crime and delinquency. While classical criminological thought, with its emphasis on "free will" and moral responsibility for actions, provides the basis for legal systems for adults in both England and the United States, positivism is at the base of the traditional juvenile justice system. This orientation shapes policies, procedures, and attitudes toward individualized justice for youth. The conflict between welfare-oriented approaches and more punitive ones leads to what Binder, Geis, and Bruce (1988) have called the "tensions" in the English juvenile justice system. The Children and Young Persons Act, 1969 perhaps represents the apex of the welfare-oriented approach in England.

Essentially, the philosophy behind the 1969 act was that young people in trouble with the law were not very different from those in other kinds of trouble and should not experience the full prosecutorial thrust of the system unless all other available avenues had been exhausted (Cavadino and Dignan, 1992:204; Jackson, 1972:263). Under the 1969 act, the civil jurisdiction of the court was to be expanded to include matters that previously were processed under its criminal jurisdiction. Youth were essentially to be handled by civil "care proceedings," with the commission of an offense being but one factor considered in the decision to order care proceedings. Consultation between the police and social service agencies was to be required before a decision was made concerning the disposition of a juvenile. The incarceration of young offenders was to be officially discouraged, and offenders under the age of 17 were not to be sent to borstals or detention centers. Extensive use of supervision by social workers, rather than probation officers, was a further indication of a move toward non-punitive methods of dealing with youthful offenders.

Binder, Geis, and Bruce (1988:394) suggest that, despite the intentions of the 1969 Children and Young Persons Act, the welfare approach was never fully integrated into the juvenile justice system. Indeed, the provisions of the 1969 act, which were to take effect in stages, were never fully implemented because of a change of government in 1970. The new civil care proceedings were introduced, the minimum age of criminal responsibility was raised from 8 to 10 (but not to 14, as originally envisaged), and those processed under the court's criminal jurisdiction could now be subject to care orders placing them in the care of local authorities. However, incarcerative sentences were not discontinued, and the juvenile court "remain[ed] very much as a 'junior criminal court' rather than the welfare tribunal which the CYPA [Children and Young Persons Act] had intended" (Cavadino and Dignan, 1992:205). Indeed, some believe that there is an ironic possibility that the 1969 act actually increased the punitive character of the juvenile justice system, since it increased the amount of discretion given to the police, courts, and other officials, and many of these officials actually used their discretion in a more conservative manner than intended by the act. Citing Home Office figures, Cavadino and Dignan (1992:206) report that "a distinct decline in the use of community-based provision[s]" was accompanied by "a massive rise in the use of custody" between 1970 and 1978.

The Conservative Party assumed political control in England after the 1979 election with a "law and order" platform. Shortly after this election, a White Paper was issued by the government entitled *Young Offenders* (Home Office, 1980). Although it did not recommend the rejection of community treatment for juveniles, it did advocate the return to a "custodial care" system in which more court appearances are required with more institutionalization for those found guilty (Morris and Giller, 1981:81–82; League Leader, 1981). According to Tutt (1981:249), the Conservatives felt that the laws and the system needed to be "toughened up." As examples of this attitude, Tutt cites the disparity in the wording and language used in the White Papers of the 1960s and those of the 1980s. In the former, offenders were referred to as "children" and "youngsters," with all the appropriate connotations of immaturity and lack of responsibility. However, by 1980, these children had now turned into "juveniles," and their offenses were now "juvenile crimes" or "juvenile offending." As Tutt (1981:249) put it: "In the earlier documents, the youngsters were children first and offenders second; now the order has been reversed."

The 1982 Criminal Justice Act that ensued has been characterized as attempting simultaneously to serve two masters: treatment and punishment (Muncie, 1984). It provided magistrates with additional requirements, such as curfews that could be attached to community dispositions and specified criteria that had to be met before a custodial sentence could be imposed, and changed the framework of custodial sentences. The Criminal Justice Act, 1988 continued this reorganization of custodial sentences by creating a new generic sentence of "detention in a young offender institution." Whereas the court had previously determined the type of institution to which a juvenile would be sent (e.g., a borstal or a detention center), this decision was now to be made by the Home Office Prison Department after the court had determined the length of the custodial sentence.

The Children Act, 1989 and the Criminal Justice Act, 1991 and Beyond

The Children Act, 1989 and the Criminal Justice Act, 1991 saw a further reorganization of the juvenile justice system. The Children Act of 1989 endorsed the principle of using prosecution as a last resort and abolished issuance of the care order in criminal proceedings. This care order had been authorized by the Children and Young Persons Act, 1969 but had been rarely issued in the 1980s. The civil care proceedings of the juvenile court were transferred to the Family Proceedings Court.

The Criminal Justice Act, 1991 renamed the juvenile court the youth court; extended the jurisdiction of the youth court to include 17-year-olds; provided new sentencing powers within the overall sentencing framework introduced by the act with its presumption against the imposition of custodial sentences; individualized sentencing based on the "maturity" of the offender; placed additional emphasis on parental responsibility; renewed focus on "action plans" as strategies for dealing with offenders that would encourage interagency cooperation; and instituted procedural changes, such as new guidelines for presentence reports, probation orders, and detention at police stations (National Association for the Care and Resettlement of Offenders [NACRO], 1994c:3). The overall effect of the changes was what Gibson et al. (1994a:28) referred to as a "fresh new ethos" extending to a wider age group.

The 1989 and 1991 acts, with their focus on limiting both the processing of juveniles through the court system and the use of custodial sentences, led to a renewed concern that the nation was being too soft on juvenile crime. Of particular concern were serious and persistent juvenile offenders. A 1993 case in which two 10-year-olds killed a 2-year-old boy, James Bulger, emphasized just how brutal children could be. A series of tougher proposals was introduced, and after some U-turns, the 1994 Criminal Justice and Public Order Act was passed. This act provided, *inter alia*, for longer custodial sentences for juveniles and the introduction of a new "secure training order" for persistent offenders. It remains to be seen what the effect of these changes will be.

The development of juvenile justice in England thus reflects an ongoing conflict between the welfare and punishment/control approaches. At the present time, there is no way of knowing which approach will prevail and just how tied to the "party in power" the juvenile justice philosophy is in practice. Interestingly, there is a paucity of relevant research fully assessing the relative effectiveness of one approach over another (Farrington and Bennett, 1981).

THE POLICE AND JUVENILES

As in the United States, the police in England always have been, and probably always will be, the first line of contact for troubled youth. In many ways, this can be an uncomfortable role. On one hand, the police are the backup for the major institutions of social control in society, providing assistance for those in need. On the other hand, they are assigned the responsibility for protecting society from delinquent youth when these agencies of social control fail. The decisions made by police officers on the street initiate the entire juvenile justice process, and this application of police discretion in dealing with juveniles makes the job of a police officer quite difficult at times. The aforementioned conflict between care and control tends to be uppermost in their minds as they make the decision of what action to take in response to a complaint of juvenile misconduct. In England, as an alternative to processing the case through the juvenile court system, the police have the option of issuing a police "caution."

The Police Cautioning Process

The police cautioning process for juveniles in England is based upon a highly traditional view of what is considered "proper versus improper" behavior for young people (Wakefield, 1983:7). Although the development of precise police guidelines undergoes continual modification, the juvenile cautioning process, as implemented after the Children and Young Persons Act, 1969, is as follows:

When a juvenile is arrested for a crime, he is taken to a police station. The offence is then investigated by the station officer, who must satisfy himself that the charge is supported by credible evidence. The parents or guardians are requested to attend the police station, and in most instances the juvenile is released to their custody. The case is then referred to the juvenile bureau, which collects information about the juvenile from relevant agencies, such as the probation, education and social services. An officer from the bureau usually visits the offender's home and interviews him together with his parents or guardians. Any police records on the juvenile are also checked. On the basis of all the information collected, the Chief Inspector in charge of the bureau decides whether to prosecute the juvenile in court, to issue a formal caution, or to take no further action. *A caution can only be administered if the juvenile admits the offence, if the parents agree that the juvenile should be cautioned, and if the complainant or victim is willing to leave the decision to the police.* A caution is (usually) administered to the juvenile in the presence of his parents or guardian at the police station by a senior officer (e.g., Chief Inspector or Superintendent) in uniform. The juvenile is warned about his future and reminded of the likelihood that he will appear in court if he offends again (Farrington and Bennett, 1981:127; emphasis added).

Although one study (Tweedie, 1982) found an unusually high rate (83 percent) of cautioned juveniles who had not reentered the juvenile system for at least two years, research on the effectiveness of police cautions versus a court appearance generally seems to indicate that there are no significant differences between cautioned juveniles and court referrals when measured by rearrests (see, e.g., Farrington and Bennett, 1981) or by reconvictions (see, e.g., Mott, 1983; Home Office, 1992:7). However, after passage of the Children and Young Persons Act, 1969, there was a "widening of the net," which resulted in a significant increase in the number of "officially processed" juveniles, even though they may not have ended up in court. In fact, as nearly as can be measured, there was a disproportionate increase in the official processing after the introduction of police cautions, when compared to the increase in juvenile delinquency statistics (Farrington and Bennett, 1981:134).

Despite the rhetoric of the times, the 1980s also saw a marked increase in the percentage of cases diverted from the juvenile court by the issuance of cautions. While 50 percent of known indictable offenders were issued cautions in 1979, by 1989 this figure had increased to 71.3 percent, and in 1992 it was 81.6 percent. In addition, this trend was accompanied by a striking decline in the use of custodial sentences for those processed through the courts (Gibson et al., 1994a:36–38).

Myren (1985:11) suggests that research in both England and the United States yields the following conclusions concerning police discretion in determining whether to refer youthful offenders to juvenile court or utilize diversionary methods: (1) younger boys (defined in England as under 12) are less likely to come to the attention of the police and, if they do, are less likely to be prosecuted; (2) girls are less likely to be prosecuted than boys; (3) previous notice and, more certainly, prosecution increase the rate of prosecution in the instant case; and (4) there is a correlation between seriousness of the current offense and prosecution. More recent data published by the Home Office (1990, 1992, 1993, 1994) indicate that this picture has not dramatically changed. Myren (1985:11) concludes, "Police warnings and release in either formal or informal programs do not seem to retard delinquency any more than court processing." Finally, in a three-year study of police cautioning of juveniles, Lee (1994:43–54) raises questions about the extent to which the locus of the power to punish has shifted from the court to the precourt decision makers.

Both England and the United States have established separate police bureaus/divisions for dealing with youthful offenders. In England, these have emerged as a separate branch of Youth Specialization divisions, where the personnel are trained in the sociopsychological dynamics of young people. New policies and practices have been developed concerning cautioning, preventive patrol, and investigation (Gibson et al., 1994a; Tutt and Giller, 1983).

The Juvenile Court in Action[1]

Juvenile courts in England are presided over by at least one, and normally three, lay justices or magistrates. When there is a panel, it must include at least one male and one female and is most often composed of younger magistrates who sit in the adult courts (Carr, 1990:359; Jackson, 1972:254). As set down in the Children Act, 1908, the courts must sit at a different place or at a different time from that of their adult counterparts. Although they are not a separate and distinct body, juvenile magistrates tend to hear mostly juvenile cases, while maintaining some involvement with adult magistrates' courts (Gibson et al., 1994a: 30; Jackson, 1972:257).

Juvenile magistrates are generally selected from those citizens who appear to be "most suitable" and "especially qualified" for work in juvenile courts (Carr, 1990:359; Moore, 1982:6). Special training, consisting of 12 months of courtroom observation, lectures, visits to other courts and juvenile institutions, and discussions with juvenile probation and parole workers, is required for juvenile magistrates (Warburton, 1972:187). A chair is selected by secret ballot from the juvenile court panel members. The chair generally holds office for three years (Ball, 1993:6; Young and Clarke, 1976:46).

Determination to separate juveniles from adult offenders is so strong that it extends to providing separate entrances and waiting areas for juveniles and adults. However, evidence exists suggesting that, although this treatment is required by the Children and Young Persons Acts, 1933 and 1969, it is not always provided in some of the older courts (Burney, 1979:36–37). If no separate facilities exist, adult courtrooms may be used as juvenile courts, but adult cases must not be heard within one hour before and after juvenile hearings (Harrison and Maddox, 1975:123).

Juvenile proceedings are not open to the public. Only members of the court and other directly related court officials may be present. The chair of the panel can allow others, such as law students or social workers, to observe. This proliferation of persons can lead to some instances in which as many as 20 or more individuals have been present during juvenile court cases (Burney, 1979:7).

Although media publicity concerning juveniles is banned by the Children and Young Persons Act, 1969, the press does have a right to be present at proceedings. They are not allowed to publish names or any other revealing information concerning the juveniles. As in the United States, all cases are tried summarily in juvenile court; there is no right to trial by jury, which is a change from the situation prior to the 1969 act, when juveniles possessed a limited right to demand a jury trial (Acred, 1978:339–340, McClean and Wood, 1969:189). Those over age 10 charged with murder or manslaughter or charged jointly with an adult are, however, committed to the Crown court for a jury trial. Those over 14 charged with other "grave" offenses may also be committed to Crown court for trial (Gibson et al., 1994a:62–63, 200).

Juveniles do have a right to bail, either surety or on their own recognizance. In limited circumstances, juveniles can be held overnight in police custody before a court appearance. If pretrial custody is recommended, the child is normally remanded to "local authority accommodation," although serious offenders can be remanded to a prison or remand center (Gibson et al., 1994a:206–213). A yet to be implemented provision of the Criminal Justice Act, 1991 empowers the courts to impose "security requirements" when remanding 15- and 16-year-olds to local authority accommodation. The Criminal Justice and Public Order Bill, 1994 calls for extending this option for those age 12 through 14 (Gibson et al., 1994a:31, 88, 213–214).

Although proceedings in juvenile court are less formal than those in adult court, the juvenile does have a right to counsel, at state expense if indigency criteria are met. This right has come a long way since before 1970, when legal counsel was not often present in juvenile court proceedings. Working-class people apparently trusted the courts and the police to be fair and just in dealing with youthful offenders. According to Lemert (1976) and Moore (1982), the increase in representation by solicitors in juvenile proceedings signals the end of confidence by the people in the British ideals of "fair play" (Lemert, 1976: 66–67; Moore, 1982:7). It may also suggest a lack of confidence in the police to handle juveniles and their problems in a "welfare-oriented" manner versus referring them to the court, thus necessitating an individual present in the court to advocate the rights of the juvenile and to look out for his or her future welfare (Moore, 1982:11).

The court may require the juvenile's parents to appear at all stages of the court process. If the parents disobey the order to appear, a warrant can be issued (Gibson et al., 1994a:242).

Juvenile Court Procedure

As mentioned earlier, actual practice in juvenile courts in England may vary; however, some general procedures appear common to all courts. Usually, the youth is asked to stand in front of the magistrates at a hearing where the charges are read. When the charge is read to the juvenile, every attempt is made to ensure that he or she understands its meaning. The parents or guardians are also included and, if present, are asked if they understand the charge and the implications of an admission to the charges (Home Office, 1970a). As in the United States, the juvenile court has attempted to differentiate its language and terminology from those of the adult court. The child is asked either to "admit" or "not admit" to the charges. This becomes the plea rather than "guilty" or "not guilty." If the magistrate is not certain of a complete understanding on the part of the defendant and the parents, the magistrate may enter a plea of "not admit" for the youth. This action results in the burden of proof being shifted back to the prosecution (Harrison and Maddox, 1975:12).

In England, in both the juvenile and adult magistrates' courts, it was traditionally the responsibility of the police to prosecute a case. In 1986, a new scheme of public prosecution was introduced to adult courts as a result of the 1985 Prosecution of Offences Act. In the juvenile court, after a plea is received, a representative from the Crown Prosecution Service or a police officer will generally set forth the circumstances of the case. Any relevant information will then be brought forward, and the magistrates will ask the defendant if the information is accurate. Counsel (or the youth's parents) may cross-examine the police officer and any other witnesses for the prosecution and may call witnesses for the defense. Rules of evidence are provided and must be adhered to, even though the atmosphere is somewhat more relaxed than in adult hearings. Should the juvenile not have representation and desire it, the court either accepts the responsibility for helping the defendant or provides someone to attend court with the offender (e.g., parent, guardian, a local official, a social worker, or other representative) at no charge (Cooklin, 1989:11; Marshall, 1978:79).

After all the evidence has been submitted, the magistrates retire to discuss the case. If a finding of guilty is returned, a social inquiry report is requested from the juvenile probation service. As in the United States, this predisposition report consists of relevant background information about the juvenile, which can be utilized by the court in determining which course of action would be most beneficial. Social workers, school officials, and probation officers all have an opportunity for input. The report normally contains basic facts about the youth's home life, personality, character, upbringing, and any previous contact with the juvenile justice system, including cautions or other diversionary measures. As in the United States, the juvenile and the parents have the right to call witnesses or attempt to refute any information contained in the social inquiry report (Moore, 1982:13).

Following the receipt of all reports in the social inquiry, the youth and his or her parents are called before the magistrates to hear the "order of the court," which in the United States would be called the disposition or sentence.

The juvenile court has a great many options available in deciding what is in the best interests of a convicted juvenile offender. The general presumption is against imposing a custodial sentence. If a custodial sentence is imposed, reasons must be given (Criminal Justice Act, 1991, Sec. 1). The maximum sentence that can ordinarily be imposed by the magistrates is 6 months per offense. Consecutive sentences can be imposed, up to a maximum of 12 months. However, offenders aged 15 or over can be sent to Crown court to receive longer sentences. Those convicted at Crown court are also eligible for longer sentences. In the case of murder or manslaughter, they may be "detained at Her Majesty's pleasure" (i.e., for life) (Gibson et al., 1994a:21–22, 87).

Prior to the Criminal Justice Act, 1988, magistrates could impose the three-to-six-month detention center order themselves, but had to commit a juvenile to Crown court for the indeterminate six-month to two-year borstal sentence. The new secure training orders introduced by the Criminal Justice and Public Order Act, 1994 provide a maximum sentence of two years, half of which is to be served in custody, for 12- to 14-year-olds who have been convicted of three or more imprisonable offenses and who have reoffended during, or been in breach of, a supervision order. The variety of juvenile institutions that exist will be discussed in the next section.

Noncustodial options available to the magistrates include:[2]

1. *Discharge.* The juvenile may be absolutely or conditionally discharged. Under a conditional discharge, the order may stipulate that the defendant not commit another offense for a specified period of time not exceeding three years. Should an offense occur, the defendant would be held responsible for not only the new charge but the original one as well. This type of disposition requires no supervision of the discharged individual.

2. *Fines.* Although the most frequently used option, the amount may not exceed a set maximum (most often £250 for 10- through 13-year-olds or £1,000 for 14- through 17-year-olds). In some cases the court can require the parents to pay the fine.

3. *Binding Over.* Juveniles convicted of an offense can be bound over to the court with the agreement that they will conduct themselves in a law-abiding manner for at least

a year. In addition, they are required to pay a recognizance of up to £250, if aged 10 through 13, or £1,000, if aged 14 through 17, to be returned to them on successful completion of their binding over. Parents can also be bound over with the stipulation that they attempt to supervise and control their child's behavior during the time required.

4. *Supervision Order.* Juveniles receiving this order are under the court's jurisdiction for up to three years or their 18th birthday, whichever comes first. This disposition is very similar to what is called juvenile probation in the United States. Under supervision of the local probation authority or social services, various rules of conduct are set down, and the youth is expected to abide by them and report regularly to the supervising officer. Breach of supervision orders can bring response from the youth court and include new sanctions imposed upon the juvenile.

5. *Community Service.* This sentence is available for offenders aged 16 or over. A minimum of 40 hours per offense up to a maximum of 240 hours can be ordered.

6. *Compensation Order.* This option can be assigned in addition to any other sentence imposed by the juvenile court. An order of compensation to the victim up to a maximum of £5,000 per offense can be imposed. It is similar to restitution in the United States. Parents can also be ordered to pay compensation; however, they do have the right to appeal.

7. *Deferred Sentence.* Although not a sentence, it is a device used by the court to see whether a youth will behave for a period of up to six months immediately following conviction. Employment and other factors are considered during this deferral time. At the end of the six-month period, a sentence can then be assigned or dropped, depending upon the review of the juvenile's conduct.

An additional noncustodial sentence that can be imposed is the attendance center order. Attendance centers are community centers that are run by the government but are most often housed in the local police station. The stated objective is to restrict the use of leisure time by providing guidance toward solving a juvenile's problems (Gibson et al., 1994a:133; Harrison and Maddox, 1975:88). In practice, most often the young offender, usually male, will be required to show up at the "nick" (the slang term for the police station) and perform some sort of menial task, physical exercise, or craft work while under the watchful eye of police personnel. Many times a Saturday that has some special meaning for the offender will be chosen, such as when the local professional football (soccer) team is playing or when a rock concert featuring one of his or her favorite stars is performing (Gibson et al., 1994b:133; Moore, 1982:17). It is believed that this sentence provides a lesson for the individual, shaking him or her up a little and dissuading him or her from pursuing a life of crime. Total time commitments range from 12 to 36 hours, depending upon the age of the offender. Though this sentence is considered by the authorities less of a punishment than being sentenced to a detention center, it is still a "punishment understood by children" (Acred, 1978:137).

Juvenile Institutions

In line with the legal developments in the treatment of juveniles by the courts, a related development occurred in the postadjudicatory treatment of juveniles. Beginning about 1900 in London, a small group of "lads," as they were then called, was selected as having the potential to respond well to a specialized type of treatment in Bedford prison. This separation from the general adult population emphasized work and adherence to a strong discipline code (Edwards, 1978:5). These young offenders were the initial clients of a new type of institution, the "borstal," which also contained a deep commitment to aftercare. In 1902, in Borstal, later called the Rochester Borstal, this experiment was extended. A Borstal Association was formed to organize and implement the aftercare system more thoroughly (Edwards, 1978:5). This movement was consolidated and strengthened through the passage of the Prevention of Crime Act, 1908, which carried many more penal reforms, including those that took into account the special needs of young offenders. Borstal training consisted of an indeterminate custodial sentence of six months to two years, with aftercare following release. It focused on "remedial and educational treatment . . . designed to achieve recovery from established criminal habits" (Home Office, 1970b:31). The borstal regime existed until the early 1980s, when the 1982 Criminal Justice Act turned the borstals into youth custody centers and made the sentence to the new youth custody centers determinate and shorter than the old borstal sentence.

Although originally called for in a 1938 Criminal Justice Bill, detention centers for youth 14 to 21 were set aside until after the Second World War. In the 1948 Criminal Justice Act, detention centers were established for "the young offender for whom a fine or probation would be inadequate . . . and for whom it seems necessary to give a *short* but *sharp reminder* that he is getting into ways that will inevitably lead him into disaster. [The regime was to] consist of brisk discipline and hard work" (Mr. Ede, secretary of state for the Home Office, Hansard, 1947, Vol. 444, Cols, 2135–39; emphasis added). The focus was to be on deterrence.

The first junior detention center for boys 14 to 17 years of age was opened near Oxford in 1952. The first senior center for those aged 17 to 21 was opened in 1954. The treatment, whether at senior or junior centers, revolved around several basic values, but uppermost in all of them was the emphasis placed on cleanliness and order.

A visitor to these types of institutions would readily perceive the emphasis on cleanliness and order upon entering the centers, through observation of both the physical surroundings and the attitude of the staff. Over the years, however, the regime in the detention centers mellowed, and they, in effect, became short-term borstals. In 1979, the Conservative Party rediscovered the appeal of the "short, sharp shock" philosophy and in 1980 started implementing tougher regimes in selected detention centers. The Criminal Justice Act, 1982, however, reduced the length of the detention center sentence from between three and six months to between 21 days and four months. Perhaps because magistrates considered this period of confinement too short, there was a dramatic shift from the imposition of detention center to borstal/youth custody orders (Cavadino and Dignan, 1992:209). In 1988, as previously mentioned, the choice of type of institution to which a juvenile would be committed was taken away from the court and entrusted to the Home Office Prison Department. Though detention centers officially ceased to exist, offenders with short sentences still "go to institutions bearing a strong resemblance to the toughened DCs [detention centers]" (Cavadino and Dignon, 1992:209).

CONCLUSION

There is growing concern about the rising crime rates of juveniles in England. The history and development of the juvenile court system have displayed a checkered pattern. On one hand, the early development demonstrated a definite move toward welfare and treatment while viewing juveniles as separate from adults in their needs and socialization process. However, as time passed, even the very acts designed to implement widespread change and reform in the juvenile court have had a difficult time being accepted as workable. England has ideals, goals, and priorities for the juvenile justice system, but the policies and practices seem to be in disarray. As always, politics play a major role, and the direction of the juvenile court is inextricably tied to the winds and fortunes of the party in power—sometimes at the expense of the youths involved in the system.

In the early 1980s, some observers felt that if the amendments and specifications of all the acts were fully implemented, the situation could be resolved (Tutt, 1981:254). But as Moore (1982:24) observed, "[S]omehow English juvenile justice muddles through." As England approaches the twenty-first century, many challenges face the criminal justice system, none of which may approach the significance of the challenge from the problems of youth crime, young offenders, and the treatment of these individuals.

NOTES

1. As mentioned previously, in 1991 the juvenile courts were renamed Youth Courts, and many new policies and guidelines were implemented. For a comprehensive examination of the new Youth Courts, see Gibson et al., 1994a.

2. For a complete description of the sentencing options for juveniles, see Gibson et al., 1994a:16–22.

REFERENCES

Acred, C. J. *Magistrates Court Guide*. London: Butterworths, 1978.
Appavo, S. M. *The Magistrate Powers of Sentencing*. London: Shaw and Sons, 1976.

Ball, Caroline. "A Lost Opportunity? Juvenile Court or Youth Court: What's in a Name?" *Criminal Justice Matters* 10 (1993): 6–7.

Besharov, D. *Juvenile Justice Advocacy-Practice in a Unique Court.* New York: Practicing Law Institute, 1974.

Binder, Arnold, Gilbert Geis, and Dickson Bruce. *Juvenile Delinquency: Historical, Cultural, Legal Perspectives.* New York: Macmillan, 1988.

Buckland, William W. *A Textbook of Roman Law from Augustus to Justinian,* 3d ed., rev. by Peter Stein. Cambridge: Cambridge University Press, 1963.

Burney, Elizabeth. *J. P. Magistrates Courts and the Community.* London: Hutchinson, 1979.

Cameron, S. "Children Think They Can Get Away with Crime." *Times Educational Supplement* 16(1974):4.

Carr, A. P., ed. *Anthony and Berryman's Magistrate Court Guide 1991.* London: Butterworths, 1990.

Cavadino, Michael, and James Dignan. *The Penal System.* London: Sage, 1992.

Cavan, Jordan T., and Ruth S. Cavan. *Delinquency and Crime: Cross Cultural Perspectives.* New York: J. B. Lippincott, 1968.

Cavenaugh, W. E. "England and Wales." In *Justice and Troubled Children around the World,* edited by Lorne Stewart. New York: New York University Press, 1981.

Cooklin, Shirley. *From Arrest to Release: The Inside/Outside Survival Guide.* London: Bedford Square Press, 1989.

Ditchfield, J. A. *Police Cautioning in England and Wales.* London: Her Majesty's Stationery Office (HMSO), 1976.

Dunlop, A. B., and Sarah McCabe. *Young Men in Detention Centers.* London: Routledge and Kegan Paul, 1965.

Edwards, Amy. *The Prison System in England and Wales—1878–1978.* London: Her Majesty's Stationery Office, 1978.

Farrington, David P. "La dejudiciarisation des Mineurs en Angleterre." *Deviance et Société* 4(1980):257–277.

Farrington, David P., and Trever Bennett. "Police Cautioning of Juveniles in London." *British Journal of Criminology* 21 (1981):123–135.

Fox, Sanford J. "Juvenile Justice Reform: A Historical Perspective." *Stanford Law Review* 22 (1970):1187–1205.

Gandy, John M. "Juvenile Justice in England and Scotland." In *Youth Crime and Juvenile Justice: International Perspectives,* edited by Paul C. Friday and Lorne Stewart. New York: Praeger, 1977.

Gibson, Bryan, Paul Cavadino, Andrew Rutherford, and John Harding. *The Youth Court: One Year Onwards.* Winchester, England: Waterside Press, 1994a.

———. *Criminal Justice: In Transition.* Winchester, England: Waterside Press, 1994b.

Goodman, L. "English Juvenile Courts: Recent Changes in Legislation." *International Journal of Offender Theory* 14(1970):105–110.

Harrison, B. F., and A. J. Maddox. *The Work of a Magistrate,* 3d ed. London: Shaw and Sons, 1975.

Hirschel, J. David. "The Lessons to be Learned from England's Approach to Victimless Crimes." Presented at the American Society of Criminology Meeting, San Antonio, TX, November 1983.

Home Office. *Children and Young Persons' Rules. Rule #6.* London: HMSO, 1970a.

————. *The Sentence of the Court: A Handbook for Courts on the Treatment of Offenders.* London: HMSO, 1970b.

————. *Young Offenders,* Cmnd. 8045. London, 1980.

————. *Criminal Statistics England and Wales 1989.* London: HMSO, 1990.

————. *Home Office Statistical Bulletin: The Criminal Histories of Those Cautioned in 1985 and 1988.* Croydon, England: Home Office Research and Statistics Department, 1992.

————. *Criminal Statistics England and Wales 1992.* London: HMSO, 1993.

————. *Home Office Statistical Bulletin: The Criminal Histories of Those Cautioned in 1985, 1988, and 1991.* Croydon, England: Home Office Research and Statistics Department, 1994.

Jackson, Richard M. *The Machinery of Justice in England,* 6th ed. Cambridge: Cambridge University Press, 1972.

Jolowicz, H. F. *Roman Foundations of Modern Law.* London: Oxford University Press, 1957.

Klein, Malcolm "England and Wales." In *Western Systems of Juvenile Justice,* edited by Malcolm Klein. Beverly Hills, CA: Sage, 1984.

Landau, Simha F. "Juveniles and the Police." *British Journal of Criminology* 21:1(1981):27–46.

Landau, Simha F., and Gad Nathan. "Selecting Delinquents for Cautioning in the London Metropolitan Area." *British Journal of Criminology* 23(1983):128–149.

League Leader. *Howard Journal of Penology and Crime Prevention,* 20(1981):1–5.

Lee, M. "Police Cautions of Minors: In Whose Best Interests?" *Deviance and Society* 18(1994):43–54.

Lemert, Edwin M. "Choice and Change in Juvenile Justice." *British Journal of Law and Society* (1976):59–75.

Ludwig, Frederick J. *Youth and the Law: Handbook on Laws Affecting Youth.* Brooklyn, NY: Foundation Press, 1955.

Marshall, P. "As the Pendulum Swings in England and Wales." In *The Changing Faces of Juvenile Justice,* edited by V. L. Stewart. New York: New York University Press, 1978.

McClean, J. D., and J. C. Wood. *Criminal Justice and the Treatment of Offenders.* London: Sweet and Maxwell, 1969.

Moore, Richter H., Jr. "Juvenile Justice in England: The Magistrates' Court as a Juvenile Court." Paper presented at the Annual Meeting of the Academy of Criminal Justice Sciences, Louisville, KY, 1982.

Morris, A., and H. Giller. "Young Offenders: Law, Order, and the Child Care System." *Howard Journal of Penology and Crime Prevention* 20(1981):81–89.

Mott, Joy. "Police Decisions for Dealing with Juvenile Offenders." *British Journal of Criminology* 23(1983):249–262.

Muncie, John. *The Trouble with Kids Today: Youth and Crime in Post-War Britain.* London: Hutchinson, 1984.

Myren, Richard A. "Police Handling of Juveniles in England and the United States." *Criminal Justice International* 1(1985):9–17.

National Association for the Care and Resettlement of Offenders. "The Criminal Justice and Public Order Bill and Young Offenders" (May). London: Youth Crime Section, 1994a.

————. *Briefing:* "Section 53 of the 1933 Children and Young Persons Act" (May). London: Youth Crime Section, 1994b.

————. *Briefing #2:* "What Should Be Done about Persistent Young Offenders?" London: Youth Crime Section, 1994c.

Nyquist, Ola. *Juvenile Justice: A Comparative Study with Special Reference to the Swedish Child Welfare Board and the California Juvenile Court System.* London: Macmillan, 1960.

Orrick, David. "A Closer Look: An Examination of Possible Applications from England to America's Criminal Justice Systems." Presented at the National Academy of Criminal Justice Sciences Meeting, San Antonio, March 1983a.

————. "The Lessons to be Learned from England." Presented at the American Society of Criminology Meeting, Denver, November 1983b.

Parsloe, Phyllida. *Juvenile Justice in Britain and the United States: The Balance of Needs and Rights.* London: Routledge and Kegan Paul, 1978.

Radzinowicz, Leon, A. *A History of English Criminal Law and Its Administration from 1750–1833.* London: Stevens and Sons, 1948.

Rendleman, Douglas R. "Parens Patriae: From Chaucer to the Juvenile Court." *South Carolina Law Review* 23(1971):205–229.

Sanders, Wiley, B. ed. *Juvenile Offenders for a Thousand Years: Selected Readings from Anglo-Saxon Times to 1900.* Chapel Hill: University of North Carolina Press, 1970.

Siegel, Larry J., and Joseph J. Senna. *Juvenile Delinquency,* 3d ed. New York: West, 1988.

Stone, Lawrence. *The Family, Sex, and Marriage in England: 1500–1800.* New York: Harper and Row, 1977.

Thorpe, D. H. "Juvenile Justice Reform in England and Wales." Paper presented to the International Seminar of the National Council on Crime and Deliquency (NCCD), San Francisco, 1983.

Tutt, Norman S. "A Decade of Policy." *British Journal of Criminology* 21(1981):246–256.

Tutt, Norman S., and Henri Giller. "Police Cautioning of Juveniles: The Practice of Diversity." *Criminal Law Review* (1983):587–595.

Tweedie, Ian. "Police Cautioning of Juveniles: Two Styles Compared." *Criminal Law Review* (1982):168–174.

Wakefield, William. "Gimme That Ol' Time Religion: Some Observations on Value Systems in British Juvenile Justice." Paper presented at the Annual Academy of Criminal Justice Sciences Meeting, San Antonio, Texas, March 1983.

————. "Attitudes of London Police Officers toward the Prosecutor's New Role." Paper presented at the American Society of Criminology Meeting, Montreal, November 1984.

Wakefield, William, Deborah Caulfield, and James Kane. "Attitudes of London Metropolitan Police Officers toward the Practice of Police Cautioning of Juveniles." Paper presented at the National Academy of Criminal Justice Sciences Meeting, Chicago, March 1984.

Warburton, B. "The Juvenile Courts in England and Wales." *International Journal of Offender Therapy and Comparative Criminology* 16(1972):187–193.

Young, Agnes F., and Kenneth C. Clarke. *Chairmanship in Magistrates' Courts.* London: Barry Rose, 1976.

APPENDIX

For more information on youth crime and treatment of young offenders in England, contact:

National Association for the Care and Resettlement of Offenders
Youth Crime Section
169 Clapham Road
London   SW9   0PU
England

Justice for Children
35 Wellington Street
London   WC2   7BN
England

Children's Legal Centre
20 Compton Terrace
London   N1   2UN
England

National Association of Probation Officers
Home Office
London
England

Central Office of Information
Home Office
Hercules Road
London   SE1   7DU
England

7

FRANCE

Reynald Ottenhof and Jean-Francois Renucci
Translated by Elizabeth Sammann

INTRODUCTION

Penal law regarding juveniles has, for a long time, taken into account the situation of juvenile offenders. Roman law submitted juvenile offenders to a specific kind of treatment, but it did not have specialized courts for such cases. This principle of special treatment was taken from ancient law with few changes, yet this kind of particular protection was not granted when juveniles committed serious offenses. Revolutionary law attempted to unify child law to a certain extent. In criminal matters, the age was fixed at 16, and sanctions could differ according to an assessment of the minor's judgment; for example, the more discerning minor received the same kind of condemnation as an adult, whereas the less discerning minor was given back to parents or placed in a borstal (reformatory). The Penal Code of 1810 settled the principle of educational treatment concerning juveniles because of the evil consequences of imprisonment and the necessity to reeducate in such cases.

In the nineteenth century, new, specific laws contained the germ of the main guidelines of modern penal law. The law promulgated on June 25, 1824, and April 28, 1842, settled, to a certain extent, the privilege of jurisdiction. Although common-law jurisdictions were competent in criminal matters, for juvenile cases, the competence for penalties was incumbent upon courts and not assizes. Following the August 5 and 12, 1850, law, penitentiary institutions concerning juveniles were deeply modified. Protective dispositions were set up, such as the necessity to open specific quarters for juveniles in prisons and also the need to instruct juvenile delinquents. Finally, the April 19, 1898, law enabled the *juge d'instruction* and the jurisdiction of judgment to entrust the juvenile to the care of a parent, an individual, an institution, or the Assistance Publique. That disposition was significant for the future evolution of the rights of juveniles because it took into account the situation of juvenile delinquents, as well as the situation of endangered juveniles. The idea of prevention was also contained in the law, but it was not yet formalized in the texts.

The beginning of the twentieth century was characterized by a strengthening of the special nature of juvenile justice—becoming more open to the idea of protection rather than repression. The April 12, 1906, law established the idea that the importance of repression should be diminished and that education should be enforced. The July 22, 1912, law created a specialized jurisdiction, the court for children and adolescents. Later, the July 27, 1942, law, which eliminated special treatment for the "discerning" child, created a regional and more specialized jurisdiction and planned the creation of a council for the observation of juveniles in every court dealing with juveniles. Yet, this law was never enforced.

The Ordinance (Ord.) of February 2, 1945, marked an important step in the evolution of minority rights. It really appears as the model for dealing with juvenile delinquency. The improvements concerning the protection of minors were made possible by the creation of children's tribunals and the institution of children's judges. The Ordinance of 1945, completed and modified by the May 24, 1951, law, the Ordinance of December 23, 1958, and the law of July 17, 1970, was the most visionary solution inspired by social defense systems. The contents of the motivations for this ordinance underlined the general principles of juvenile penal law, for example, absolute penal irresponsibility for minors aged 13 and relative responsibility for those aged 18, the preeminence, though rarely applied, of education over repression, which remains exceptional, and the specialization of jurisdictions.

THE FORMAL SYSTEM

Jurisdictions

As regards penal law for juveniles, there exist both specialized jurisdictions and common-law jurisdictions, which have specialized to a certain extent.

The specific jurisdictions instituted by the legislature and concerning juveniles are the judge for children and the tribunal for children. The judge for children was created by the Order of February 2, 1945 [art. L. 531 1. and following, *Code de l'organisation judiciaire* (C. org. jud.), art. R. 531-2 C. org. jud.]. This judge is a magistrate from the Grande Instance tribunal, which is itself part of the children's tribunal (art. L. 532-1, C. org. jud.). The legislature wanted the judges dealing with juvenile cases to specialize and, thus, created the judge for children. This specialized magistrate must know juveniles and understand their personality. The judge for children works in the children's tribunal, the territorial competence of which is established by an order (art. 522-1, C. org. jud.). On the territorial level, the rules of penal competence are identical to those of the children's tribunal. The jurisdiction of the children's judge reveals the originality of that institution. The children's judge is in charge of both the investigation and the judgment. The children's judge who represents the investigation jurisdiction conducts the investigations necessary to gather evidence (art. 8, al. 1st, Ord. 1945). Yet, the children's judge does not have jurisdiction in serious criminal matters or even for offenses of any of the first four categories of lesser crimes, which are a matter for the *Tribunal de Police.* The jurisdiction of the children's judge is limited (as it is for the *juge d' instruction,* or investigating judge) to offenses in the least serious category. Inside those limits the *juge des enfants* (children's judge) decides whether to try the juvenile in the council chamber or send the case to the tribunal for children (art. 8, Ord. 1945). The children's judge, being the judging jurisdiction, is not obliged to respect the principle of the separation of judiciary functions but can judge a case she or he has personally investigated.

The Tribunal for Children, which was created by the Ordinance of February 2, 1945, is a collegiate jurisdiction composed of three members, one of whom is a juvenile judge. The other two are nonprofessional assessors. This tribunal specializes in matters concerning juveniles (art. L. 521 and f.; art. R. 522-1 and f., C. org. jud.). The Tribunal for Children was created so as to enable a collegiate jurisdiction to take possible and stronger measures than those taken by the judge for children. The Tribunal for Children is chaired by the judge for children. This judge is assisted by two assessors who are not magistrates and who are chosen according to their interest in matters concerning children and their skill (art. R. 522-4, C. org. jud.). The jurisdictional venue of the Tribunal for Children is determined by Article 3 of the February 2, 1945, Ordinance. According to this article, the jurisdiction lies with the tribunal of the place where the offense was committed, where the juvenile's parents or guardians live or where the minor was found. The Tribunal for Children is also competent in the area where the minor has been placed in foster care, either temporarily or permanently (art. 31-2, Ord. 1945). When urgent and provisional measures have to be taken, jurisdiction lies where the juvenile is located or arrested (art. 31, 2C, al. 2, Ord. 1945).

The attribution of competence to a tribunal for children reveals a concern to ensure the best protection possible for the juvenile. Juvenile matters must exclusively be judged by specialized jurisdictions; this is the privilege of jurisdiction. The Tribunal for Children has the competence to judge offenses or contravention of the least serious class (art. 9, al. 2 and art. 20-1, Ord. 1945; art. L. 521-2, al. 2, C. org. jud.). This jurisdiction has, in this matter, a competing competence with the judge for children; sharing competence depends on the seriousness of the case. Eventually, if the Tribunal for Children and judges for children can take identical decisions concerning a juvenile, only the tribunal can decide to place a youth in a borstal (reformatory) or pronounce a penal condemnation (art. 14 and 15, Ord. 1945 for the measures; art. 2, Ord. 1945 for the condemnations). The competence of the Tribunal for Children is extended to crimes committed by 16-year-old juveniles (art. 9, al. 2-4, Ord. 1945).

The educational board linked to the Tribunal for Children is a recent institution. It reveals a real concern for efficiency. The intervention of this board is obligatory, as soon as the imprisonment of a juvenile is considered. The situation of an imprisoned juvenile is followed by the board both during and after the proceeding. Finally, members of the educational board give priority to probation measures.

Specialized common-law jurisdictions also take part in the processes of investigation and judgment.

Investigative courts are not exactly specialized courts, but the degree of specialization they require, especially in regards to the examining judge, is not to be overlooked. Each departmental or high court which has a children's tribunal must provide at least one examining judge to oversee delinquency courts. This magistrate is nominated by the first president of the Court of Appeal, after recommendation by the public prosecutor (art. 80, al. 1st., Criminal Code of Procedure [CPP]) or sometimes even by the victim, who can become a civil (injured) party (art. 6, Ord. 1945). The examining judge can also be submitted to an order of removal issued by a colleague from a near district, where there exists no children's tribunal, who states that the offense examined was committed by a juvenile (art. 7, al. 3, Ord. 1945). Moreover, the examining judge can be submitted to removal by the children's judge, when the latter has established the seriousness of the case (art. 5 and 8-1, Ord. 1945). The examining judge is competent to examine criminal matters (art. 5, al. 1st, Ord. 1945). For cases which are exceptionally complex and require delicate and extensive investigation, the investigative or examining judge in charge of juvenile matters will have jurisdiction (art. 5, al. 2, Ord. 1945). The situation is the same as regards contravention of the fifth category (art. 20-1, Ord. 1945).

The special nature of the *Chambre d'accusation* (criminal appellate court) is not important. Yet, when this jurisdiction rules on a case in which a minor is involved, a specialized magistrate, the *Conseiller délégué à la protection de l'enfance* (an advisor delegated to protect the minor) is appointed for three receivable terms of court by the minister of justice (art. 6, Ord. 1945). In case of impediment, this person can be replaced by another magistrate especially appointed by the first president of the Court of Appeal. The *Chambre d'accusation* is competent in criminal matters, but only for minors over 16 (the others can be judged only by children's tribunals). When it is submitted by an order of transmission to the public prosecutor (art. 9, al. 2-4 C, Ord. 1945), the *Chambre d'accusation* must consider if there exist satisfactory charges (art. 211, CPP) in order to decide upon arraignment, if this is the case, or, on the contrary, may declare that there is no necessity to prosecute. The *Chamber d'accusation* is also competent in common-law situations as judge of appeal of the orders made by the children's judge, or the examining judge in matters regarding examination (art. 233, Ord. 1945).

The special chamber of the Court of Appeal consists of a *Conseiller délégué à la protection de l'enfance,* (art. 223, C. org. jud.), who is a judge of the Court of Appeal (art. L. 223, al. 2, C. org. jud.). The *Conseiller délégué à la protection de l'enfance* chairs the special chamber of this Court of Appeal or works as a reporter (art. L. 223-2, al. 1st, C. org. jud.).

Moreover, a magistrate who has been appointed by the public prosecutor is in charge, in the Court of Appeal, of juvenile cases (art. L. 223-2, al. 3, C. org. jud.). The special court in the Court of Appeal judges both the decisions of the judge for children and of the children's tribunal (art. L. 223-1, C. org. jud.). The appeal to the decisions taken by the police tribunal is also introduced to this jurisdiction (art. 21, al. 4, Ord. 1945). In the same way, the orders, taken by the judge for children or by the examining judge, according to the 10th article of February 2, 1945 Ordinance, which deals with the temporary placement of a juvenile offender, must be judged by the special court of the Court of Appeal (art. 24, al. 2, Ord. 1945).

The Court of Assizes, a trial court for juveniles, consists of a jury of nine jurors and has no specificity concerning the age of prosecuted persons (art. L. 512-1, C. org. jud.). The president of the Court of Assizes for minors is appointed or replaced in the same manner as in adult proceedings (art. 20, al. 2, Ord. 1945; art. 244 and f. CPP). He is, therefore, the president of a court or a judge of the Court of Appeal. Yet, there exists some specialization in this jurisdiction. When there exists an impediment, the assessors are judges for children (art. 20, al. 2, Ord. 1945). The office of the prosecution is fulfilled by the public prosecutor or by a magistrate from the Public Prosecutor's Department, who is particularly in charge of juvenile cases (art. 20, al. 3, Ord. 1945). Criminal juveniles aged 16 to 18 will be judged by the Court of Assizes for juveniles (art. L. 511-2, C. org. jud.). This jurisdiction can also judge the factors associated with age or crimes committed by juveniles over 16 years of age.

Procedures

The Prosecution

The prosecution is principally reserved for the public prosecutor's office but also, to a lesser measure, for the injured party.

The public prosecutor of the trial court in the jurisdiction in which the juvenile court is seated is in charge of prosecuting infractions committed by minors (art. 7, Ord. 1945). If the facts are insignificant or not sufficiently established, the public prosecutor can dismiss the case. In the contrary case, it is necessary to distinguish the infractions according to their gravity. If the infraction is a crime, a preliminary investigation is necessary (art. 5, al. 1, Ord. 1945), and the prosecutor's office must then appear before a magistrate dealing with juvenile matters (art. L. 522-6, C. org. jud.) by means of an ordinary introductory indictment. If the infraction is a misdemeanor or an infraction of the fifth class, the prosecutor must then appear before a juvenile judge by petition or appear before a magistrate dealing with juvenile matters. If the affair, particularly complex, presents more criminal issues, thus surpassing the educational mission of the juvenile judge (art. 5, al. 2, Ord. 1945), or if adults are involved in the affair, the public prosecutor having territorial jurisdiction must quickly proceed with the investigation so as to immediately give an opinion to the prosecutor of the court in which the juvenile court is located. (art. 7, al. 2, Ord. 1945).

The victim of an infraction committed by a minor may indirectly institute legal proceedings as a civil suit either before the juvenile judge or before the magistrate (art. 6, al. 1, Ord. 1945). The civil action, however, may also be brought before the juvenile court and before the Juvenile Court of Assizes (art. 6, al. 1, Ord. 1945). The civil action must conform to common law, and to obtain damages, the victim must be able to establish direct and personal injury. In terms of Article 6, paragraph 2 of the Ordinance of February 2, 1945, when one or more minors are implicated in the same incident along with one or more adults, the civil action against all the responsible parties may be brought before the correctional court or before the competent Court of Assizes dealing with adult matters.

The Investigation

Since the mental state of the minor is a *sine qua non* to the effectiveness of the judicial intervention, an individualized investigation is instituted. The magistrate handling the investigation of juvenile affairs, the juvenile judge or magistrate, must not only use utmost diligence to reach the truth but also focus on the mental state of the minor. In all cases, the investigation is necessary for crimes (art. 5, al. 1, Ord. 1945), for punishable offenses (art. 5, al. 2, Ord. 1945), and for violations of the fifth class (art. 20-1, Ord. 1945).

The juvenile judge proceeds with an inquest, not only by using the forms established in the Criminal Code of Procedure (CPP) for ordinary preliminary investigations but also by "official license" (art. 8, al. 2, Ord. 1945). One thus sees an important reduction of formalism, because when one acts by official license, one is not held to follow the provisions of the Criminal Code of Procedure but, in reality, follows a more informal procedure than that of the preliminary inquest. The juvenile judge has one important liberty: the single obligation to respect the common-law rules concerning the issuing of orders (art. 8, al. 3, Ord. 1945).

The other rules relating to juvenile investigations are common to presiding magistrates, whether they are acting as a juvenile judge or as a magistrate. The magistrate conducting the investigation of a minor's case must, at the same time, put together the personal file and the case file. Article 10 of the Ordinance of February 2, 1945, mandates that a lawyer be present. The minor or a legal representative appoints the lawyer. By default, the judge will appoint a defense counsel or will have one designated by the president of the bar. The accused minor has the right to a lawyer immediately after the preliminary hearing at the first court appearance. She or he may forgo the presence of council for the entire investigation, but only in special circumstances. If so, the presiding magistrate must advise the known parents, guardians, or person responsible for the care of the minor of such consequences (art. 10, al. 1, Ord. 1945).

Placement is the principal measure taken against the minor. It can be effected through a closed or open setting. A closed setting is set forth by Article 10, paragraph 3 of the Ordinance of February 2, 1945. The judge may temporarily confine the minor to a reception center, to a public or private institution's reception section, to the juvenile assistance services, or to a hospital. The judge may also confine the minor to an educational, professional training, health, or state or public rehabilitation institution. These measures are always revocable. Sometimes the judge may wish to impose a more severe measure. The minor may be temporarily placed in an observation center, instituted or agreed to by the minister of justice. This temporary detainment can eventually be carried out under the system of supervised release (art. 10, al. 5, Ord. 1945). Open placement does not assume a monolithic character. The minor may be temporarily confined under the supervision of parents, guardian, or other person responsible for the youth's care (art. 10, al. 3-1, Ord. 1945). The judge, in this manner, allows the child to remain in natural surroundings. This measure may or may not be combined with supervised release.

Temporary detention is an exceptional measure. The judge may use this measure when it is the only way to conserve material evidence, protect witnesses, or impede fraudulent collusion between the accused and any accomplices (art. 144, CPP). The legislature recently abolished all forms of preliminary detention for minors 13 years old and younger, as well as for 16-year-olds in terms of correctional matters (art. 22, L. 30 déc. 1987). Temporary detainment can be ordered only after searching for an educational placement. Additionally, the minor must be incarcerated in a special quarter of the prison and, if possible, isolated from all others during the night (art. 11, Ord. 1945). Article 12 of the Ordinance of February 2, 1945, mandates that the educational service of the juvenile court be consulted. The law of 1989 further limits the recourse of preliminary detention. It abolished the order of imprisonment that allowed the judge to put a minor in detention who had, by bad conduct or behavior, rendered any educational measures inoperative (art. 18, L. 6 juill. 1989). Moreover, in criminal matters, the duration of the temporary detention was limited to six months, renewable one time for minors over 16 years old. In terms of correctional measures, when the penalty incurred is not over seven years of imprisonment, the preliminary detention of a minor younger than 16 years old cannot exceed one month. If the minor is 16 years or older, the detention is limited to four months, but an extension of four months after the first four months is possible. However, the total duration may not exceed one year. The extension is set forth by a well-justified ordinance.

The judge handling the investigation may order diverse means of observation in order to discern, as best as possible, the personality of the delinquent. Many techniques that permit such observations have been devised. First, there are judicial inquiries and exams (psychological, medical, neuropsychiatric, or other professional exams). The judge may also conduct an observation of the juvenile's behavior, and, in this respect, the sentence of supervised release appears valuable. This measure, like inquests and exams, allows the personality of the accused to be discerned (art. 10, al. 5, Ord. 1945). Article 8, paragraph 6 of the Ordinance of February 2, 1945, states that the judge may, in the interest of the minor, order no measure of observation or prescribe only one of many.

When the magistrate determines that the investigation is terminated, he or she issues an edict (art. 9, al. 2, Ord. 1945) after having passed the case on to the public prosecutor, who must give closing arguments in three days. If the case concerns only minors, the magistrate has many choices. First, the case can be dismissed if the charges are insufficient, or if the case must be closed. Second, the case is sent before the prosecutor's office if the facts constitute a violation of one of the first four classes. Third, the case is ordered before the juvenile judge or the juvenile court if the facts constitute a violation of the fifth class or a misdemeanor. Finally, if the minor has been charged with a crime, the case will be sent before the juvenile court, if the accused is less than 16 years old. If the criminal is between 16 and 18 years old, the magistrate will order the case to be transferred to the general prosecutor so that it can be filed with the criminal Court of Appeals. Unlike the magistrate of juvenile affairs, the juvenile judge does not have to transfer the case to the public prosecutor to obtain a definitive indictment. Such a transfer is an option for the juvenile judge, but not an obligation (art. 8, al. 7, Ord. 1945). At this point, the juvenile judge may also dismiss the case (art. 8, Ord. Feb. 2, 1945, modified by law of Jan. 4, 1993).

The Supervision of the Investigation

At this stage in the proceedings, two courts intervene. The special chamber of the appellate court is uniquely competent to rule on an appeal from the magistrate's or juvenile judge's decision concerning the temporary detention of the minor. The appeal must be filed within 10 days of the order (art. 24, al. 2, Ord. 1945 and art. 498, C. pr. pen.). The court of criminal appeals receives the appeals of any of the magistrate's and juvenile judge's decisions not relating to temporary detention. In conformity with common law, the judges handling the investigation continue their investigations in the case of an appeal (art. 24, al. 2, Ord. 1945). The court of criminal appeals is equally driven, in certain cases, to regulate the procedure, especially when the magistrate submitted a correctional matter to it.

The Judgment

Judgment of juvenile cases has been subject to important developments. The procedural rules are largely intended to protect the minor, and their effectiveness depends precisely on their specificity.

The juvenile judge possesses a very important liberty because, when a verdict is given in the council chambers, no particular form is imposed by the Ordinance of February 2, 1945: the hearings are conducted as desired. The juvenile judge is accompanied by a clerk, and a representative of the prosecution may be present. The minor and the defense attorney are summoned, as well as, if the case arises, representatives from the social services, released supervision services, and observation and educational organizations. The judgment is given in the council chambers.

In the juvenile court, the procedure is a bit more formal, even if the formalities have been reduced. Articles 13 and 14 of the Ordinance of February 2, 1945, set forth rules that are really aimed at protecting the minor. The juvenile court renders its verdict after having heard the minor; the witnesses; the parents, guardians, or other persons responsible for the care of the minor; the prosecution; and the defense. It may also hear, as simple witnesses, the major accomplices or collaborators. The presiding judge of the juvenile court may, in the interest of the minor, excuse the minor from appearing at the hearing. If this is the case, the minor is represented by a lawyer, or the father, or the mother, or a guardian. Additionally, each charge must be ruled on separately in the absence of all others charged. Finally, the presiding judge of the juvenile court may order, at any time, that the minor or the witnesses leave the courtroom after their testimony for all or part of the hearing. Article 14 of the same ordinance establishes that only the witnesses; parents, guardian, or legal representative of the minor; members of the bar; representatives from the youth protection services; juvenile services, or institutions; and delegates from the supervised release program be admitted to the hearing.

Publicity is restricted during the hearings. The reduction of publicity of the court record is also guided by the same concern for protecting the minor. The Ordinance of 1945 contains two provisions: Article 14, paragraph 4 first states that the publication of the court record of the juvenile court hearing is prohibited without exception and, second, allows the judgment given in juvenile cases to be published but prohibits the mention of the minor's name.

The procedure of the Juvenile Court of Assizes is not very different from the other courts. Nevertheless, the judgments must be separate for each charge, just as in the juvenile court (art. 20, al. 8, Ord. 1945). The presence of the accused minor at the hearing is requested, and he or she may be excused only after an examination (art. 20, al. 9, Ord. 1945). The presiding judge of the Juvenile Court of Assizes may allow the minor to be excused only during "all or part" of the hearings. Therefore, it is necessary for the minor to be present as soon as the closure of the hearing is pronounced. The decision must be given in open court in the presence of the minor (art. 14, al. Ord. 1945).

The Sanctions

Sanctions are of varied character. The court of judgment must choose between an educational or a repressive measure. The only exception to this principle of noncumulative sentences concerns the measure of released supervision, which may be ordered, if need be, concurrently with a sentence providing for education (art. 19, al. 1, Ord. 1945). The choice of the court is guided not by the minor's capacity for judgment but by the appropriateness of the punishment with respect to the minor.

Educational measures are principally used because of the highly esteemed value and role of education. Certain measures directly concerning the guardianship of minors are of dual nature because the minor can be confined either with an individual person or to a legal entity. In the first case, the minor receives an admonition in the form of a verbal reprimand and then is placed in the position that existed prior to the infraction (i.e., placement with parents, guardian, or other person responsible for the juvenile's care) or to another trusted person (art. 8, 15 & 16, 20 & 21, Ord. 1945). In the second case, the minor may be confined to a judicial administration, private establishment, or the juvenile social service or, if the case arises, to a medical or medical-educational rehabilitation establishment.

Supervised release is a special measure because, except for the admonition pronounced by the judge, it can be joined with any other sentence whatsoever (art 8-2 C, and 19, Ord. 1945). Thus, any form of temporary guardianship can be carried out under the regime of supervised release (art. 10 in fine, Ord. 1945). Supervised release may also be joined with any sanction ordered by the court of judgment (art. 8, al. 9, 19 & 20, Ord. 1945) and with any penalty pronounced by the juvenile court or by the Juvenile Court of Assizes (art. 19, Ord. 1945). Finally, supervised release may be pronounced with prejudice because the judge may, before rendering a substantive verdict, order temporary supervised release (art. 8 in fine, Ord. 1945).

Educational measures have a temporary character, justified by the necessity to continuously adapt to the minor's situation, which is assumed to be evolving. The reevaluation proceeding thus plays a very important role, and its field of application is very large. The first assumption concerns the point of law that supervised release, if need be, may be modified or adapted (art. 26, Ord. 1945). The second, more general assumption, relating to the modifying hearing, is based on the fact that the drafters of the 1945 ordinance specified that the measures of protection, assistance, supervision, education, or reform ordered for the minor may be revised at any time (art. 27, al. 1, Ord. 1945).

Repressive measures are exceptional in juvenile law. The measures are nevertheless pronounced when the circumstances and personality of the minor seem to require them (art. 2, al. 2, Ord. 1945). The courts may thus order the different punishments provided for by penal law, namely, imprisonment. However, the minor must be specially protected (e.g., separated from the adult inmates, provision of education or training) to assure that she or he is not perverted even further.

Finally, mediation/compensation constitutes an important new measure. Since the law of January 3, 1993, the new Article 12-1 of the Ordinance of February 2, 1945, created the possibility for the public prosecutor of the examining court or the court of judgment to order the minor to aid or compensate the victim or engage in any other type of public service work.

INFORMAL PRACTICES

The procedural rules established since the Ordinance of February 2, 1945, despite their immense value and practical success, currently give rise to some troubling points. This ordinance, which charts the juvenile delinquency laws, is outdated: a good number of its solutions, formerly attractive, may appear un-adaptable, in whole or in part. The different actors who protect the legal rights of minors feel somewhat unequipped in face of the new realities of juvenile delinquency. They hope to update the text and modernize the legislative tool. Moreover, the authorities have heard these claims and in 1990 conducted a study on the reform of criminal law and procedures applicable to minors. Unfortunately, this has not been integrated yet into the real law, even if certain ideas have been incorporated into recent legislative modifications. This is regrettable, for comprehensive reform is essential. All other action, of whatever significance, may not be satisfactory, because a global and coherent response is indispensable.

SUMMARY

The major principles of juvenile penal law in France have been established since the Ordinance of 1945. These principles primarily focused on education, specialization of functions, and the personalization of applicable measures. However, it is important to go further and consider proposed reforms, namely, by the drafters of the 1990 reform project which actually strengthens specialization as the order of the day.

In the reform project, the role of the public prosecutor's office is strengthened. Increasing its preventive action is desired, but its role with respect to the local councils of prevention of delinquency is not clear. The public prosecutor may, in terms of correctional matters and investigation, summon the minor to appear before the juvenile judge. From the time of the inquest, the prosecutor may consult the public educational services entrusted with protecting the legal rights of the minor. These services establish a written report containing all useful information on the minor's situation, as well as a proposal for an education program. The prosecutor's office may also have the minor summoned by an officer of the criminal investigation department or start a preliminary investigation.

The juvenile judge becomes the only judge competent with respect to correctional matters and does not share the domain with the magistrate to conduct the investigation of juvenile affairs. If a crime is committed, the magistrate will have exclusive jurisdiction; but if a misdemeanor is committed, only the juvenile judge can investigate the affair. The sharing of jurisdiction among the juvenile judge, the court of judgment, and the juvenile court is more established, and thus this new division of labor must be approved. The juvenile judge retains jurisdiction to judge the lesser crimes in chambers. She or he can use an increased number of means. The notion of "placed back with the family" being supreme, the juvenile judge may not only have recourse to a range of more extensive measures (warning, legal surveillance in an open setting or as a type of placement, non-monetary restitution or repair of damages) but also have the power to pronounce the exceptional penalty of imprisonment (fines or penalties that restrict one's rights or liberties). The judge may also decide to forgo or adjourn the penalty altogether (art. 42 av.-proj.). On the other hand, for the most serious affairs, namely, voluntary physical attacks, drug trafficking, or aggravated robberies, the juvenile court will have exclusive jurisdiction. In other words, the examining magistrate loses power to direct the proceedings. The introduction of this criterion of nonconcurrent jurisdiction translates certainly to less flexibility, but it offers the uncontestable advantage of judicial soundness.

The juvenile court's award of jurisdiction is extensive because this court will judge henceforth all minor criminals over 16 years old. The Juvenile Court of Assizes is abolished. This abolition must be approved because without juvenile specialization, it gives rise to important criticisms: the joined judgment of juvenile and adult cases often translates into the nonapplication of rules specific to the minor, and the vulnerability of the adolescent criminal forces the magistrates to use rigid recourse to enter upon delicate assumptions, and such would not be the case with the Juvenile Court of Assizes. For the judgment of crimes committed by a minor between 13 and 18 years of age, the juvenile court, composed of two juvenile judges and three assessors, has jurisdiction (art. 54 av.-proj.).

Strengthening of the procedural guarantees is desired by the drafters of the juvenile criminal law reform project. First, the role of the parents or guardians to exercise parental authority will be increased. The reform project anticipates the investigation and eventually the summons of the parents or legal guardians as soon as an important decision concerning the minor is ready to be taken, advising them of decisions such as to placing the minor in detention or under judicial protection. Finally, the drafters of the reform project desired to increase the rights of the defense of the minor. Henceforth, the minor will have the right to have an attorney present at all stages of the hearing: the defender will have to be summoned from the interrogation during the investigation. Moreover, if diverging interests appear between the minor and the legal guardian, the judge will be able to ask the guardians to choose a different attorney. Finally, delays have been addressed in the procedure. No criminal sanction may be pronounced by the juvenile court against the minor if the charge in which he or she was accused was not sent to trial within one year from the time of the charge. This solution is good in principle. Minors' personalities are assumed to be evolving, and because the sanction largely depends on this fact, it would be absurd to impose one too long after the commission of the acts. But as a practical point of view, this rigid procedure can have deplorable consequences because, taking account of the complexity of certain cases and the lack of personnel in the court, it may often be difficult to respect the one-year rule.

The 1990 reform project also envisages sanctions. The rule of not applying penalties with respect to minors 13 years old and applying only educational measures is maintained. But new principles are affirmed. On one hand, the pronouncement of a penalty with respect to a minor is exceptional. Consequently, such a decision must be obligatorily justified. On the other hand, only the punishments set forth by juvenile law are applicable to minors. Consequently, if the text of the penal law introduces a new punishment, this will not be applicable to minors unless otherwise clearly expressed in the text.

With respect to correctional or criminal matters, the juvenile court may pronounce fines and penalties that restrict the minor's rights or liberties (namely, suspending or revoking a driver's license, even immobilizing a vehicle), but it may no longer order a suspension of rights, or loss of rights, so as not to compromise the minor's chance to be reinserted into society upon reaching the age of majority. The punishment of community service work is maintained, and the courts may order imprisonment. But the limitation of incarceration is the order of the day. Not only is imprisonment of minors of 16 years prohibited with respect to correctional matters, but, additionally, there is a ceiling of three years for correctional matters and a ceiling of 10 years for criminal matters.

Educational sanctions have also been subject to modernization. The drafters of the reform project were driven to affirm the primacy of education measures in creating a new measure: judicial protection (art. 56 and s. av. proj.). This measure is imposed because educational methods have changed considerably since 1945. Assumptions about the education of the minor in relation to the family has developed to the point that the criteria used in 1945 to decide between institutional placement and societal release (on conditions) are no longer in touch with reality. From now, the juvenile courts may order protective measures, assistance, surveillance, reparation, or education, all of which will strengthen the judicial framework protecting minors. This measure, of which the means of application are flexible and effective, may be ordered by the juvenile judge in council chambers or at all stages of the proceedings for a maximum of two years. Putting the minor under judicial protection assures the continuity of the educational process because the measure may be modified at any time the minor's behavior changes. The prosecution of juvenile delinquents is characterized by a strong individualism that prohibits, at least partially, the rigidity of the system created by the Ordinance of 1945. It is important to specify that in the case of placement, the court, but also the juvenile judge, will determine the visitation rights and lodging of the parents or legal guardians. Unfortunately, for political reasons, this 1990 draft has not been enacted.

REFERENCES

General Works

Bouloc, Bernard. *Penology.* Paris: Coll. Précis Dalloz, Dalloz, 1991.
Bouzat, Pierre, and Jean Pinatel. *Treatise on Penal Law and Criminology,* Vol. 3. Paris: Dalloz, 1970.
Gassin, Raymond. *Criminology,* 3d ed. Paris: Précis Dalloz, Dalloz, 1994.
Giudicelli-Delage, Geneviève. *Judicial and Jurisdictional Institutions.* Paris: Coll. Droit Fondamental, Presses Universitaires de France, 1987.
Merle, Roger, and André Vitu. *Treatise of Criminal Law; Penal Procedure,* 4th ed. Paris: Cujas, 1990.

Special Works

Ancel, Marc, and Marcel Molines. *The Judicial Protection of the Juvenile and the Evolutions of Law and Judicial Institutions.* Paris: Pedone, 1980.
Chaillou, Philippe. *The Judge and the Child.* Toulouse: Privat, 1987.
Chazal, Jean. *The Juvenile Judge.* Paris: Sirey, 1948.
————. *Juvenile Delinquency.* Paris: Presses Universitaires de France, 1976.
Lazerges-Roth, Christine. *The Juvenile Court of Assizes.* Paris: Librairie Générale de Droit et de Jurisprudence, 1969.
Pandelé, Georges. *Juvenile Protection by the Juvenile Judge.* Paris: Editions Sociales Francaises (ESF), 1977.
Renucci, Jean-Francois. *Penal Rights of Minors.* Paris: Editions du Centre National de la Recherche Scientifique (CNRS), 1990.
————. *Penal Rights of Minors.* Paris: Masson, 1994.
Robert, Philippe. *Treatise on Minor's Rights.* Paris: Cujas, 1969.
Roumajon, Yves. *Lost Children, Punished Children.* Paris: Éditions Lafon, 1989.

APPENDIX: KEY AGENCIES DEALING WITH JUVENILE OFFENDERS

Ministry of Justice, Direction of the Judiciary, Protection of the Youth
13 Place Vendôme
F—75001 PARIS
Tél (1) 44.77.60.60.

Centre National de formation et d'Etudes de la Protection Judiciaire de la Jeunesse
54 Rue de Garches
F—92420 VAUCRESSON.

Institut de l'Enfance et de la Famille (I.D.E.F.)
3 Rue Cog Héron
F—75001 PARIS
Tél. (1) 40.39.90.03.

Association Française de la Sauvegarde de l'Enfance et de l'Adolescence (A.F.S.E.A.)
28 Place St. Georges
F—75009 PARIS
Tél. (1) 48.78.13.73, Fax. (1) 40.23.98.05.

Journal du Droit des Jeunes
16 Passage Gabois
F—75012 PARIS
Tél. (1) 05.90.77.07.

8

GERMANY

Nancy Travis Wolfe

INTRODUCTION

Consonant with other legal systems in the Western world, the Federal Republic of Germany (FRG) has developed differential policies for responding to crime committed by young persons. Although they are subject to the same substantive criminal law as adults, there are special procedures to be followed when prosecuting juveniles. Principles and practices of sanctioning young persons also differ from those pertaining to adults (Flügge, 1991; Kaiser, 1992; Kaiser, Kerner, and Schöch, 1992: Kerner and Weitekamp, 1984; Schobloch, 1992).[1]

History of the Juvenile Justice System

Since the FRG follows the positive law tradition of Roman and Napoleonic jurisprudence, the highest legal authority is the written law itself, rather than court decisions interpreting the law. The earliest German criminal code (*Constitutio Criminalis Carolina*) included clauses specifically pertaining to young offenders, but not until the criminal code of 1871 did a system of juvenile justice begin (Schaffstein, 1983:25). Early in the twentieth century, chambers within criminal courts were created in Frankfurt am Main, and in 1923 separate juvenile courts were established (Kerner and Weitekamp, 1984:155).

Polity of the Federal Republic of Germany

The FRG has a federal polity consisting of the national government (Bund) and 16 states (Länder). Law is primarily determined at the national level and is administered at the state level. The constitution and national federal legislation control virtually all substantive and procedural criminal law (Herrmann 1981: 88). Although there is basic legal and judicial uniformity, there is allowance for some flexibility in implementation (Fiedler, personal communication, 1994).

Unification

In 1990, the former German Democratic Republic (GDR) became an integral part of the FRG. As a socialist system, the GDR had developed, over a 40-year span, a juvenile justice system that differed, in part, in teleology and legal principles (Buchholz, 1988; Luther, 1987; Hoffmann, 1985; Fricke, 1986; Lekschas et al., 1983; Wendland, 1989; Wolfe, 1991; Schmuck, 1991). Because a period of transition was necessary to transmute the GDR system into that of the FRG, the contract of unification and subsequent laws permitted temporary differences. The following discussion pertains to the current juvenile justice system in the FRG.

FORMAL SYSTEM

Goals of the Juvenile Justice System

The leitmotif of the FRG juvenile justice system is "to educate rather than to punish" (§§ 10 JGG; Matzke et al., 1993), but legal scholars differ concerning the exact meaning of the term "education," whether the goal should be a crime-free life or the wider purpose of resocialization of the offender (Streng, 1994: 60). Responsibility for youths is shared by the family and the state. Included in the constitution of the FRG is a section that accords special protection to the family; although parents have a natural right—and a duty—for the care and upbringing of children, the "national community shall watch over their endeavors in this respect" (§ 6 *Grundgesetz*).

Law

Unless otherwise stipulated by the juvenile court act, the clauses of the *substantive* criminal law code are valid, although the consequences can be different (§ 10 StGB). In other words, there are no status offenses; behavior such as truancy, incorrigibility, and running away is, instead, governed by the Youth Welfare Code (*Jugendwohlfahrtsgesetz*) and handled by the Youth Welfare Office (*Jugendamt*) or the Guardianship Court (*Vormundschaftsgericht*) in civil proceedings (Janssen and Plewig, 1986:27). Intervention can be ordered by the Guardianship Court judge for youths under 18 who are socially maladjusted, neglected, or in need of care or protection. In Germany, a clear legal distinction is made, therefore, between "youth at risk," who are handled through civil proceedings, and juvenile delinquents, who fall within the jurisdiction of the criminal justice system.

The Juvenile Court Code (JGG) of 1923, which was modified in 1943 and again in 1953, is the principal body of law governing *procedures* for prosecution of juveniles and adolescents for violation of the criminal law. If a juvenile or adolescent is being prosecuted for acts committed both as a juvenile and an adult, the JGG is to apply if the emphasis is on behavior that falls within jurisdiction of the act (§ 32 JGG).

Rights of Juveniles

It may be that the juvenile in Germany who is handled under the principles of judicial procedure for youth courts has more legal rights than his counterpart in Western countries, in which the paternal principle of civil proceedings involving juveniles has resulted in restriction of some rights enjoyed by adults (Kröger, 1993). In all criminal proceedings in Germany, the accused juvenile has a full panoply of due process protections, including presumption of innocence and fundamental rights, such as inviolability of human dignity and a right to liberty, which are specifically guaranteed by the FRG constitution (*Grundgesetz*). In addition, the procedural law code (StPO: *Strafprozessordnung*) provides protection from violation of these rights.

Age Categories

In regard to culpability, the juvenile court law recognizes four age categories; the designation of criminal responsibility pertains to the person's age at the time of the offense. The time of the act is determined not by the completion of the criminal harm but by the time of the constituent exercise of will to commit the act (Kaiser, 1992:188). Four age categories have been established by law.

- *Child (Kind):* If, at the time of the crime, the individual was not yet 14 years of age, there is a nonrebuttable presumption of nonculpability (§ 19 StGB).
- *Juvenile (Jugendliche):* If, at the time of the act, the individual was at least 14 years of age but not yet 18, he or she is presumed to be responsible but can be held to be immature (§ 1 (2) JGG).
- *Adolescent (Heranwachsend):* In 1953, a third category was added. If, at the time of the act, the individual was at least 18 but not yet 21, he can be adjudicated under the juvenile code (§ 105 JGG).
- *Adult (Erwachsene):* Persons over the age of 21 at the time of the act.

Historically, the age of culpability varied among German states; for example, it was as low as 8 in Bavaria (Schaffstein, 1983:26). In the criminal code of 1871, the age of 12 was established, and finally, in 1923, the Juvenile Court Code raised this limit to 14 (Kerner and Weitekamp, 1984:154). Juveniles can be held criminally responsible if, at the time of the act, their moral and intellectual development was sufficiently mature for them to comprehend the wrongfulness of the act and to act accordingly (§ 3 JGG). A judge who finds a juvenile too immature to be held culpable but nevertheless in need of education can impose the same measures as a guardianship judge.

Adolescents are, in general principle, held to be criminally responsible. If a judge determines, however, that, at the time of the act, an individual in the age category of an adolescent has a moral and mental development still comparable to that of a juvenile or if, according to the manner or circumstances of motivation of the act, it concerned a typically youthful offense, he or she can be handled as a juvenile (§ 105 JGG).

Persons working within the juvenile justice system suggest that most adolescents are, in fact, handled under juvenile justice law (Weber, personal communication, 1994, Fiedler, personal communication, 1994, Kossack, personal communication, 1994). Sessar (n.d.:3) reported a rate of approximately two-thirds, noting that "the more serious the crime the more frequent the juvenile law and not the general criminal law is applied (in Hamburg, more than 90% of the adolescents are treated like minors)."

JUVENILE DELINQUENCY

Incidence of Juvenile Delinquency

The most recent issue of the FRG statistical analysis of crime (Bundeskriminalamt, 1994:71) provides an age breakdown. As noted in the preface to the report, however, the inclusion of data from the "new" states (areas of the former German Democratic Republic) after 1990 introduced factors that affect the reliability of the analyses (Spieß, 1994). The 1993 report, which reflects crimes investigated by police (other than traffic violations), indicates the following rounded percentages of criminal activity:

Children (0–13 Years)	4.3 percent
Juveniles (14–17 Years)	10.1 percent
Adolescents (18–20 Years)	10.1 percent
Adults (21– Years)	75.4 percent

Geographic distribution figures showed the area of highest rate of 1993 crime by persons under 18 to be in areas of the former GDR: the state of Mecklenburg-Vorpommern (21 percent and more) and the states of Sachsen-Anhalt, Thüringen, and Sachsen (17–21 percent). Third in rank came the former GDR areas of Brandenburg and five states of the FRG (Nordhrhein-Westfalen, Niedersachsen, Bremen, Schleswig-Holstein, and Hamburg (13–17 percent)). In the fourth group were the FRG states of Hessen, Rheinland-Pfalz, Saarland, Baden-Württemberg, and Bayern (Bundeskriminalamt, 1993:89). Two generalizations flow from these figures: there is a higher rate in the area of the former GDR, and there is generally a north–south decline in rate.

Analysis of data in regard to German and non-German suspects indicated a lower rate for non-German children and juveniles and a higher rate for adolescents (Bundeskriminalamt, 1994:72). Female German children and female juveniles show a higher percentage than female non-Germans, but in the category of juveniles, female non-Germans have a higher percentage.

Types of Offenses

Statistics indicate that the most frequent crime in 1993 committed by children, juveniles, and adolescents of both genders was theft without aggravating circumstances (Bundeskriminalamt, 1993:85–86). For males in these three age categories, the second most frequent crime was theft with aggravating circumstances; other high percentages for males appear in regard to vandalism and fraud. Of particular concern is the high percentage of young offenders in the realm of extreme violence, especially violence against foreigners (Viehmann, 1993; Wassermann, 1994: Ostendorf, 1993; Matzke et al., 1993). One author indicates that about 70 percent of the offenders are juveniles or adolescents (Ostendorf, 1993:545).

Describing the juveniles incarcerated in the Youth Detention Institution (*Jugendstrafanstalt*) in Plötzensee in Berlin, the director, Marius Fiedler, noted that about 60 percent had committed violent acts, and 30 percent, property crimes (theft). Among his inmate population were those who were convicted of serious offenses or frequent offenses—sometimes an individual had committed both.

The average offender had committed many crimes, had already been adjudicated by the juvenile court 3 or 4 times and sentenced to probation. With the fourth conviction, he might be incarcerated. The property offender usually has committed many crimes; e.g., stolen automobile radios several hundred times or broken into stores fifty times. We could add the investigations by police on charges which were dismissed (perhaps 30–40), each investigation representing several crimes. Pedagogical measures were tried. Only when all of these fail, does he come here (Fiedler, personal communication, 1994).

Trends in Juvenile Delinquency

As in other countries, the public perception of rising juvenile delinquency is not validated by statistics. Discussions in the summer of 1994 with practitioners involved in the juvenile justice system (prosecution, defense, incarceration) indicated a general perception that the rate of juvenile crime was falling, although they frequently mentioned the problem of the "dark figure" (i.e., unreported numbers) of juvenile delinquency or a particular type of crime that was on the increase. This impression is, in general, consonant with percentage statistics reported for the years 1984–1993 (Bundeskriminalamt, 1994:74–75), although the absolute numbers show an increase. All three nonadult age categories show a decline in percent of all crime, with the strongest trend evident in the juvenile category, but the year 1993 reflects a slight upturn in each group.

The decline in youth crime cannot be explained simply by a fall in birthrates. The recent lower birthrate is balanced by higher numbers of young immigrants and asylum seekers (Traulsen, 1994:101).

JUVENILE COURTS

Although Germany has a federal polity, there is a single judicial system (*Grundgesetz,* § 92); cases are tried in state courts and can be appealed through national courts. Juvenile cases fall within the jurisdiction of one of the five hierarchies of the judicial system of the FRG: the courts of "ordinary" jurisdiction (Kreuzer, 1987). Since the end of the nineteenth century, Germany has had separate juvenile tribunals. Today, trial jurisdiction in juvenile delinquency cases can be exercised by three types of state courts (§ 39-42 JGG):

1. A juvenile judge (*Jugendrichter*) sitting alone in the local court (*Amtsgericht*) has jurisdiction over minor offenses committed by juveniles. His or her sentence of incarceration cannot exceed one year.

2. More serious offenses are heard by a mixed tribunal (*Jugendschöffengericht*) of a state court; the bench is composed of one professional juvenile judge (*Jugendrichter*) and two lay judges (*Jugendschöffen*).

3. Major offenses, including capital crimes, can be heard in a mixed tribunal (*Jugendkammer*) consisting of three professional judges and two lay judges. This tribunal can also hear cases appealed from the first two types of courts.

In juvenile matters, the national court of last resort is the Federal Court of Justice (*Bundesgerichtshof*), where decisions are made by a panel of professional judges. If the case raises a question of violation of the German constitution, it can be appealed to the Federal Constitutional Court (*Bundesverfassungsgericht*).

Proceedings in juvenile matters are considered criminal adjudication, even though the courts are designated as juvenile tribunals. The distinction between adult and juvenile proceedings derives from the discretion allowed the prosecutor and judge, as well as the nature of the sanctions that can be imposed.

Before discussing procedures in juvenile adjudication, it must be noted that, in contrast to the adversarial style of Anglo-American jurisprudence, German trial procedure is inquisitorial. It is the responsibility of the judge, not the attorneys, to bring out in court all relevant evidence. In theory, all participants in the trial are to foster truth-finding, and this principle has a direct bearing on the role played by the juvenile prosecutor, the juvenile judge, and the defense attorney.

PERSONNEL

Prosecutor

By law (§ 36 JGG), juvenile cases are to be investigated and prosecuted by persons especially appointed to the role: (*Jugendstaatsansälte*) (Kreuzer, 1987). A juvenile prosecutor is to be "qualified as an educator" and experienced in the education of youth (§ 37 JGG). In actuality, this stipulation is not followed. When asked about selection procedures, a juvenile prosecutor responded as follows:

That's a bad chapter, I must say, because there is absolutely no specialization. The law requires special pedagogic abilities. Where does he get them? He is educated the same as all lawyers. He may have children but there is no education for that. It is so, to the contrary, that the activity of the juvenile prosecutor is not held in especially high esteem within the prosecutorial office. It is a typical position for beginners (Weber, personal communication, 1994).

Within a juvenile prosecutorial office, there may be specialization. In Berlin, for example, one section handles youth gangs, and one concentrates on violence, as well as four sections of general jurisdiction (Weber, 1994). Juvenile prosecutors are also responsible for young victims (Kossack, personal communication, 1994). Like other German prosecutors, they are career officials, under the authority of the state ministries of justice, and are mandated to seek exculpatory as well as inculpatory evidence (§ 160 (2) StPO).

Juvenile Judge

Judges who preside over juvenile hearings are, like prosecutors, supposed to be persons with special qualification in pedagogy and experience in juvenile education (§ 37 JGG). Failure to abide by this admonition is repeatedly noted in the literature (Kreuzer, 1987, fn. 1). Charges of petty offenses can be heard by a single judge, but all other juvenile trails are heard by a mixed tribunal, which includes lay judges called *Schöffen*. Unlike the lay judges of the other FRG criminal courts, who are nominated by community councils, juvenile *Schöffen* are nominated by the Youth Welfare Committees and are to have the qualifications specified for juvenile prosecutors and judges (§ 35 JGG; Kerth, 1994). In the final stage of selection, a juvenile judge heads the Selection Committee. The law further stipulates that there should be a male and a female on the bench with the professional judge (§ 33 (3) JGG).

Defense Attorney

Juveniles have the right to have assistance of legal counsel, as do their legal representative and the persons responsible for their education (§ 137 StPO, §

67 (3) JGG). When the state provides an attorney, a "duty defense attorney" (similar to a public defender in the United States), the rules of implementation specify a person who has educational qualification and experience in juvenile education (Radbruch, 1993:553). The juvenile judge orders appointment of defense counsel in instances when it would be done for an adult or if the persons responsible for the education of the youth or his or her legal representative would be deprived of rights, if the preparation of an expert opinion concerning his or her maturity would involve possible detention in an institution, or if he or she is to be held in pretrial detention (§ 68 JGG).

The role of defense attorneys in juvenile matters is disputed (Radbruch, 1993). Are they (in line with the *parens patriae* theory of juvenile courts) to be partners of the judge and prosecutor in finding effective measures to foster the education of the young person, or are they (as in adult proceedings) to defend vigorously the rights of their clients (Kreuzer, 1987:273)?

Juvenile Court Aide

Significant figures in juvenile proceedings are the youth court aides. Housed in the Youth Welfare Office, they are charged by law to inform the court about educational, social, and welfare aspects (§ 38 JGG; Nicolas, 1994; Sonnen, 1993). They prepare a presentence report and can make suggestions about measures to be ordered. In the posttrial phase, the juvenile court aide can be responsible for seeing that the juvenile fulfills instructions and injunctions. If the juvenile is on probation, the youth court aide works closely with the probation officer. During incarceration, the aide remains in touch with the juvenile inmate and aids in his or her reintegration after release as well as supervising the implementation of judicial orders.

STAGES OF JUVENILE JUSTICE PROCESS

Apprehension by Police

In the initiation and investigation of a case against a juvenile, the police and prosecutor share responsibility. The police of Germany are under the Ministry of Interior, but the federal polity of Germany allocates extensive authority over law enforcement to interior ministers of the individual states. Although the JGG does not stipulate separate police units for juveniles, it has become customary in large cities to establish juvenile sections staffed by specially trained police. In general, German police have little discretion; their records concerning an allegation and subsequent investigation are to be turned over to the prosecutor (Janssen and Plewig, 1986:30).

Prosecutors, who are under the Ministry of Justice, are independent of the courts (§ 150 GVG). They are bound by the principle of "legality," which requires prosecution when there is evidence to support the charge (§ 152 StPO).

Two clauses modify this precept, however (§§ 153, 153a StPO), permitting dismissal of a case if the culpability of the offender is slight or if no public interest is served by prosecution. A prosecutor can instigate and supervise further investigation by detectives (*Kriminalpolizei*).

The Youth Welfare Office is to be informed immediately of the execution of an arrest warrant (§ 72a JGG), and the arrestee is to be brought before a judge "promptly, at the latest on the day after the arrest" (§ 128 StPO). If a youth is held in pretrial detention, the trial is to be carried out with especial speed (§ 72 (5) JGG).

Pretrial Detention

The FRG criminal procedural code permits restriction of individual liberty in the form of pretrial detention only under certain listed circumstances, such as danger to others, risk of flight, criminal activity, or destruction of evidence. These regulations are equally valid for adults and youths.

The detention warrant must state, in addition to information about the act and the suspect, the specific reason for detention, and the document must be made available to the person detained (§ 112-114 StPO). In addition, the Juvenile Court Code limits imposition of pretrial detention only when the purpose cannot be achieved through education or other measures (§ 72 JGG). Nevertheless, Kreuzer reported in 1987 that around 10,000–12,000 juveniles and adolescents were yearly held in pretrial detention (Kreuzer, 1987:275).

Handling and treatment of a youth held in pretrial detention are governed by statute (§ 93 JGG, Nr. 77-85 UVollzO), but there is considerable room for discretion on the local level (Mehner, 1992). On the juvenile's entry into the detention institution, the director of the institution has responsibility for investigating his or her personality. The investigation, in cooperation with the youth court aide, is to determine the mental, intellectual, and physical characteristics of the youth, as well as life history, schooling, vocational education, and personal and social relationships. The results of the investigation are to be forwarded to the judge or prosecutor. Juveniles who are in need of treatment for addiction can be housed in a withdrawal institute (§ 93a JGG).

The law stipulates that, when possible, the youth is to be housed in a special institution or at least in a special section of the detention facility (§ 93 (1) JGG). A young inmate can, however, be temporarily placed with an adult inmate if health reasons urgently require it. According to the JGG (§ 93 (2–3)), pretrial detention should be educationally structured; these programs usually take place during working hours. For educational reasons, the youth is obligated to work during pretrial detention; one-third of his income is to be withheld for his use after release.

Despite the good intention of the legal rules, actual conditions in pretrial detention often fail to achieve the standards set for the youth and may, in fact, be harsher than those of postsentencing incarceration (Gramckow, 1989:2). A specialist in juvenile justice reached a similarly dismal conclusion.

Young inmates are housed—in opposition to the legal separation requirement—mostly in adult institutions. In spite of the similarly legally required educational model (§ 93 JGG) they often remain left to themselves all day, possibly occupied with cell work. The lack of educational offers has a very burdensome effect, because young first-time inmates see themselves suddenly incarcerated in an age of greatest urge for freedom, and, to be sure, in a situation of uncertainty, social isolation and insufficient behavioral competence (Kreuzer, 1987:276).

Difficulty in classifying a detainee can arise from uncertainty concerning birth-date of foreigners from Southern or Eastern European countries; in such cases, the person is usually categorized as an adolescent and housed accordingly, a decision that may worsen the situation for younger inmates (Fiedler, personal communication, 1994). Additionally, housing of young females causes problems because the number of detainees does not warrant separate facilities. In Berlin, girls are detained in the Women's Prison; their cells are in a separate section of the building, but during the day they mix with women inmates.

Participation in Court

The presence of the accused youth in court is expected, and the trial can take place without him or her only under the same conditions that would apply for an adult (§ 50 JGG). Furthermore, the presiding judge should summon the persons who have educational responsibility for the youth. A representative of the youth court aide is to be notified of the place and time of the trial, and he or she has a right to speak.

The judge has authority to exclude accused youths during discussions from which a disadvantage for their education could arise; subsequently, the judge must inform them of what happened in their absence insofar as it is necessary for their defense (§ 51 JGG). The judge can also exclude relatives and other persons, including the legal representative of the accused, if he or she has reservations against their presence.

The general principle of public access to trials and judgments does not pertain in juvenile cases (§ 48 JGG), but in addition to the participants in the trial, the victim and probation officer, the judge can allow the presence of other persons. If adolescents and/or adults are also on trial, the presumption is that the court will be open, but the judge can exclude the public in the interest of the education of the juvenile defendant.

Trial   ·

At the outset of the trial, before taking evidence concerning the alleged crime, the judge seeks information about the relationships of the accused, his or her development, previous behavior, and all other circumstances that can serve to evaluate his or her spiritual, mental, and individual characteristics (§ 43 JGG). The judge can question youths, those responsible for their education, their legal representative, the school, and apprentice program.

Procedure in juvenile hearings differs in significant respects from that of adult tribunals. An accused youth who is not yet 17 is not required to take an oath (§ 60 StPO); nor is one who lacks mature understanding, is mentally ill or spiritually limited, or does not have sufficient understanding of the meaning of an oath. The accelerated judicial procedure allowable in adult court is not permitted in juvenile cases (§ 79 (2) JGG). The JGG also prohibits in juvenile hearings participation of private parties in prosecution (*Privatklage und Nebenklage*) or pursuit of civil remedy during the criminal trial (§ 80 JGG; Schaffstein, 1983:174). In adult cases, the prosecutor can, after investigation, offer a "penal order" (*Strafbefehl*) to the defendant; if accepted by the defendant, it would authorize punishment without formal trial. Issue of a penal order in juvenile cases is prohibited by the JGG (§ 79).

JUDGMENT

An FRG judge must provide an explanation of his or her reasons for imposing specific measures, including consideration of the moral, intellectual, and physical characteristics of the defendant (§ 54 JGG; Ohle, 1993). This explication of the sentence can be withheld from the juvenile if disadvantages for his or her education are feared. Publication of the judgment cannot be ordered (§ 6 JGG). Judgments against juveniles cannot involve loss of right to hold public office or to vote (§ 6 JGG). The judge can apply this clause to adolescents (§ 106 (2) JGG).

Sanctions

Consonant with the rehabilitative goal of the German juvenile justice system, sanctions are to be tailored to the individual offender, rather than to the severity of the offense. A judge who finds the juvenile not mature enough to be held culpable can impose the same measures as a Guardianship Judge (*Vormundschaftsrichter*) (§ 3 JGG). Measures that can be imposed by a juvenile judge are of three types. A judge can order educational measures (*Erziehungsmnaßregeln,* §§ 9-12 JGG) for a juvenile adjudged responsible for a criminal act. If educational measures are not sufficient, the judge can order disciplinary measures (*Zuchtmitteln,* §§ 13-18 JGG) or incarceration (*Jugendstrafe,* §§ 17-18 JGG). The FRG law regarding restitution (§§ 403-406 StPO) is not applied against juveniles (§ 81 JGG).

Educational Measures

Educational sanctions can be in the form of orders or prohibitions concerning residence, training, supervision, association with certain persons, assistance in education, and so on. The requirements cannot exceed a period of two years.

Disciplinary Measures

Disciplinary sanctions can include a warning, imposition of tasks, or temporary custody (*Jugendarrest*). Tasks might require the offender to apologize, to make restitution, to accomplish work, and/or to contribute to a charitable agency. Disciplinary sanctions do not have the effect of a criminal punishment. Temporary custody could mean detention during leisure time (*Freizeitarrest*), single days of detention (*Kurzarrest*), or a period of 1–4 weeks of incarceration (*Dauerarrest*). When assigning detention, the juvenile judge can take into account the amount of time the offender has been held in pretrial detention (§ 52 JGG). The juvenile can be taken immediately into custody after the hearing (Weber, personal communication, 1994).

Incarceration

As a last resort, when the offender evinced "damaging tendencies" in committing the criminal act, when other measures do not suffice, or when the severity of the act or degree of guilt makes it necessary, the judge can order a youth to juvenile prison (Böhm, 1993; Dünkel, 1990; Eickmeier, 1992; Heinz, 1989).

The minimum period of incarceration (*Jugendstrafanstalt*) is no less than six months. The maximum is to be no more than 5 years, but if the possible penalty is more than 10 years under adult law, then a juvenile can be held for 10 years. A prison sentence, unlike the other types of custodial detention previously discussed, can be replaced by probation.

Since juvenile jurisdiction depends on age at time of act, it could happen that a much older person would be assigned incarceration in a juvenile institution, for example, if an 80-year-old man were prosecuted for an act committed when he was 15. A judge could decide, however, that he should serve his sentence in an adult prison.

Although, in adult criminal cases, responsibility for execution of the sentence rests with the prosecutor, in juvenile cases the juvenile judge bears this responsibility (§ 82 JGG). The judge remains in close touch with the offender, sometimes visiting her or him in the prison. Usually, it is a different judge from the one who sentenced the person, but in some states it is the same judge.

Probation

If a juvenile is sentenced to more than one year of prison, the juvenile judge can suspend it to probation if it is expected that the juvenile has already taken the conviction as a warning and if a change toward a law-abiding life will be effected during probation and without incarceration (§ 21 JGG). The imposition of this type of probation cannot be shorter than two years nor longer than three years, but these limits can be subsequently modified. A probation officer (*Bewährungshelfer*) is assigned by the judge; he can be a volunteer. The probation officer reports monthly and must write a report each year to the court.

Probation status can be withdrawn if the juvenile commits a crime, transgresses the instructions, or fails to fulfill task requirements. Approximately 50 percent of probation orders are revoked, a rate that compares favorably to the higher rate of recidivism among those offenders who are incarcerated (Weber, 1994).

Prison

Although the German term for a sentence of incarceration is "juvenile punishment" (*Jugendstrafe*), and the term the prison includes the word "punishment" (*Jugendstrafanstalt*), the stated objective of incarceration is to educate the convicted person to lead a law-abiding and responsible life (§ 91 JGG). The fundamental basis for this purpose is "order, work, instruction, physical exercise and sensible occupation in leisure time." Spiritual care is also guaranteed. Directors of youth prisons usually have university degrees in law, psychology, or sociology. Correctional officers are trained for their educational function, and most of them remain in the career (Rotthaus, 1986).

Both the general principle that administration on the local level is accorded discretionary room to adapt the legal regulations and the statement in the JGG that, in order to achieve the educational goal, the execution of sentence can be relaxed have resulted in a variety of forms of incarceration among the local jurisdictions (Rieger, 1980; Scheschonka, 1991; Eickmeier, 1992; Grunau, 1991; Dünkel, 1993; Meier, 1993; Oleschinski, 1992; Schmuck, 1991).

Intake

Juveniles sentenced to incarceration are taken first to an intake section. There they are given a medical examination and interviewed by a psychologist to determine the best placement and educational program. In the Berlin institution, youths are housed in pavilions and formed into "residence groups." Each group of about 11–14 inmates has either a social worker or a psychologist as a director, and the correctional officers are assigned permanently to the group. An attempt is made to provide continuity of relationships, as in a normal family; if inmates who have been released come back to prison, they will be assigned to the same group.

Increasingly, German institutions are faced with problems generated by delinquent foreigners. Although some foreign juveniles are proficient in German (such as the Turks), others have only a rudimentary knowledge. An effort is made to house foreign juveniles in a group where there is at least one person of their language group, but at the same time there is a policy of dispersing foreigners among different groups in order to avoid stereotyping (Fiedler, personal communication, 1994).

Work

Most occupations in Germany require training or education beyond the level of high school. Prisons provide, therefore, a range of apprenticeship and training programs, and the certificate that the inmate receives does not indicate the location. Typically, inmates can receive training in occupations such as repair of motor vehicles, carpentry, welding, painting, cabinetmaking, cooking, masonry, wallpaper hanging, and computer technology. If inmates leave the institution before completing the program, they can come back on a daily basis.

Release

From the beginning of a sentence of incarceration, inmates are eligible for temporary release. They can go on "vacation" (*Urlaub*), overnight stays, 21 times a year. Toward the end of the sentence, inmates can go out to find a job or place to live and can go on work release. The institution makes a contract with the employers that stipulates that they have no recourse against a delinquent worker and that they are to inform the institution if the inmate does not show up for work. Often, employers find that inmates are exceptionally good workers; they appear on time (even on Mondays) and do not drink since they are subject to examination when returning to the institution (Fiedler, personal communication, 1994).

Decisions concerning early release of incarcerated juveniles lie with the judge who is responsible for the execution of the sentence. There is a hearing, and almost all inmates are given early release, and they then are under the supervision of a probation officer (Fiedler, personal communication, 1994).

Expungement

Because juveniles accused of crime are handled in a criminal court, convicted juveniles have a criminal record, but in an effort to avoid adverse effect on them, the registry law concerning record keeping of juvenile delinquency differs from that of adult records. In the case of a later offense, it is essential that the judge have information about juvenile delinquency. Nevertheless, only the following types of information are registered: sentence to incarceration (§ 17 JGG), measures for betterment or security (§ 6-7 JGG), and a conviction with a sentence of incarceration suspended to probation (§ 27 JGG). Registration of convictions is erased after a specified period in order to further resocialization; the period is five years if the sentence of incarceration is not more than one year, or if a sentence of not more than two years' incarceration was suspended on probation (Schaffstein, 1983:194). The expungement can occur even sooner if the juvenile judge becomes convinced that incarcerated juveniles have shown themselves to be law-abiding persons. He or she can expunge the record on his or her own initiative or on application by the juveniles or the persons responsible for their education, their legal representatives, the prosecutor, or a representative of the Juvenile Court Aide agency (§ 97 JGG). The expungement order can be issued only two years after completion of sentence; it cannot be issued during incarceration or the period of probation.

DIVERSION

Diversion by Prosecutor

FRG prosecutors are bound by the principle of "legality," which requires them to bring a case to court if the evidence supports the charge, but this prescription was narrowed in adult prosecution by addition of § 153a of the criminal procedure code (StPO). The principle of diversion, however, was specifically endorsed in a government statement in support of modification of the Juvenile Court Code: investigations concerning the extent to which avoidance of formal sanctions in favor of informal procedures is significant in terms of criminal policy—at least in the area of minor or moderate juvenile delinquency—have led to the recognition that informal procedures provide less costly, quicker, and more humane responses to juvenile delinquency (Spieß, 1994:111). Juvenile diversion is not limited to first offenders or to those accused of only minor crimes (Spieß, 1994:111). Prosecutorial discretion in diverting juvenile cases is now stipulated in §§ 45 and 47 of the JGG.

In practice, approximately 60 percent of cases against juveniles and young adults are diverted from the formal court procedure (Spieß, 1994:111). The rate at which juvenile prosecutors utilize diversion varies among the FRG states. Research, for example, indicated that in the city-state of Hamburg about 5 of every 6 juvenile cases were diverted, whereas in the state of Baden-Württemberg the ratio of diverted cases to cases carried through to formal judgment was 0.73 to 1 (Ohle, 1993:408). Empirical research of cohorts in West Berlin indicated that for the majority of occasional offenders diversionary measures were sensible and sufficient, since beyond puberty criminal activity ceased or at least decreased (Matzke et al., 1993:5).

CONCLUSION

As indicated in the preceding discussion, juveniles and adult defendants in the FRG are held responsible for the same substantive criminal law, but procedural rules differ significantly. Juvenile cases are heard by special tribunals of the criminal court; however, emphasis is on the character and developmental level of the offender rather than on the offense. Police and prosecutors are permitted a wider range of discretion, and, where plausible, ambulatory measures are utilized instead of incarceration (Kreuzer, 1987:268).

There is a plethora of literature in FRG pertaining to controversial aspects of the juvenile justice system (Sessar, n.d.; Janssen and Plewig, 1986; Gramckow, 1989; Schmuck, 1991; Dünkel, 1994; Begemann, 1991; Pelz, 1991; Wassermann and Weber, 1993). A review of recent books in this field, for example, indicates concern about the diversion process, rights of juveniles, ambulatory measures, qualifications of juvenile judges and prosecutors, juvenile court aides, legal defense in juvenile matters, incarceration, and decision making in juvenile law (Miehe, Schaffstein, and Dölling, 1992).

In the calls for reform, both conservative tendencies toward restricting the leniency shown young people and liberal objectives stressing preventive measures are evident (Dünkel, 1994). Currently, there is discussion concerning alteration of the age categories. On one hand, there are proposals to reduce the upper age limit for adolescents below 21 (Kossack, personal communication, 1994). Others propose to extend the age limit for adolescents upward to 24 (Weber, personal communication, 1994). A third suggestion is to create an additional category between adolescent and adult. Also, efforts have been made to raise the minimum age for incarceration (Kersten, 1986:283).

Since 1980, there have been three major reform proposals, including one from the Federal Ministry of Justice (Kaiser, 1992:339), though none has led to significant change in legislation.

The federal polity of the FRG, however, allows experimentation on a local level, and some states (e.g., Hamburg) have established social-therapeutic institutions that attempt to ameliorate the root causes of juvenile crime. Other jurisdictions have experimented with community service sentences (as in "Project Bridge" in Cologne). Furthermore, there is discussion about resurrecting an approach of the former German Democratic Republic: the social courts, tribunals in which laypersons through a process of mediation assigned sanctions intended to resolve conflicts.

Contrary to these treatment programs are repeated initiatives toward sharpening legal response to juvenile delinquency, including proposals for more rapid processing through the system and more severe sanctions. Ultimately, in a democracy, fundamental policy toward young offenders must be established through the political process. The elections in the fall of 1994, when Germans again chose a chancellor and members of the legislature, indicated that the FRG would continue along the spectrum toward a law-and-order model, rather than toward a treatment model.

NOTE

1. Much of the information in this chapter was derived from site observations and conversations in May and June 1994 with persons in Berlin who are involved in the juvenile justice system, particularly the following individuals: Marius Fiedler, Suzanne L. Kossack, Victor Weber, and Erich Buchholz.

REFERENCES

Law

Grundgesetz (Constitution)

Grundgesetz für die Bundesrepublik Deutschland vom 23. Mai 1949 (BGBl. S. 1: BGBl. III 100-1), zuletzt geändert durch das Vierunddreißigste Änderungsgesetz vom 23. August 1976 (BGBl. I S. 2383).

GVG (Court Structure Act)

Gerichtsverfassungsgesetz in der Fassung vom 9. Mai 1975 (BGBl. I S. 1077), zuletzt geändert durch Ges. vom 11.3.1993 (BGBl. I S. 50).

JGG (Juvenile Court Act)

Jugendgerichtsgesetz (Juvenile Court Law) in der Fassung der Bekanntmachung vom 11. Dezember 1974 (BGBl. I S. 3427). Zuletzt geändert durch Gesetz vom 16.2.1993 (BGBl. I S. 239), (BGBL. III 451-1).

JAVollzO: (Youth Custody Act)

Jugendarrestvollzugsordnung (Verordnung über den Vollzug des Jugendarrestes) in der Fassung der Bekanntmachung vom 30. November 1976 (BGBl. I S. 3270), geändert durch Gesetz vom 26.6.1990 (BGBl. I S. 1163) (BGBl. III 451-1-1).

StGB (Substantive Criminal Code)

Strafgesetzbuch vom 15. Mai 1871 (RGBl. S. 127) in der Fassung der Bekanntmachung vom 10. März 1987 (BGBl. I S. 945, ber S. 1160), geändert durch Gesetz vom 8.6.1989 (BGBl. I S. 1026), 9.6.1989 (BGBl. I S. 1059), 24.4.1990 (BGBl. II S. 326), 13.6.1990 (BGBl. II S. 494), 26.6.1990 (BGBl. I S. 1163), 20.8.1990 (BGBl. I S. 1764) mit Maßgaben für das Gebiet der ehem. DDR durch Anl. I Kap. III Sachgeb. C. Abschn. III Nr. 1 EVertr. vom 31.8.1990 (BGBl. II S. 889), BtG vom 12.9.1990 (BGBl. I S. 2002), ÄndG vom 28.2.1992 (BGBl. I S. 372), 26. StRÄndG vom 14.7.1992 (BGBl. I S. 1255), OrgKG vom 15.7.1992 (BGBl. I S. 1302), G vom 27.7.1992 (BGBl. I S. 1398), 11.1.1993 (BGBl. I S. 50), 23.7.1993 (BGBl. I S. 1346) und 2.8.1993 (BGBl. I S. 1407) (BGBl. III 450-2)

StPO (Criminal Procedural Code)

Strafprozeßordnung in der Fassung der Bekanntmachung vom 7. April 1987 (BGBl. I S. 1074, ber. S. 1319), geändert durch Ges. vom 22. 10, 1987 (BGBl. I S. 2294), 17.5.1988 (BGBl. I S. 606), 8.6.1989 (BGBl. I S. 1026), 9.6.1989 (BGBl. I S. 1059), 15.6.1989 (BGBl. I S. 1082), 7.3.1990 (BGBl. I S. 422), 9.7.1990 (BGBl. I S. 1354), mit Maßgaben für das Gebiet der ehem. DDR durch Anl. I Kap. III Sachgeb. A Abschn. III Nr. 14 und Abschn. IV Nr. 3e) des Einingungsvertrages vom 31.8.1990 (BGBl. II S. 889), durch Ges. vom 12.9.1990 (BGBl. I S. 2002), 5.11.1990 (BGBl. I S. 2428), 17.12.1990 (BGBl. I S. 2847), 28.2.1992 (BGBl. I S. 372), 14.7.1992 (BGBl. I S. 1255), 15.7.1992 (BGBl. I S. 1302), 23.7.1992

(BGBl. I S. 1366), 27.7.1992 (BGBl. I S. 1398) und vom 11.1.1993 (BGBl. I S. 50), BGBl. III 312.2.

StVollzG (Incarceration Act)

Strafvollzugsgesetz (Gesetz über den Vollzug der Freiheitsstrafe und der freiheitsentziehenden Maßregeln der Besserung und Sicherung) vom 16. März 1976 (BGBl. I S. 581, ber. S. 2088 und 1977 S. 436), geändert durch Gesetz vom 18. August 1976 (BGBl. I S. 2181), 22. Dezember 1981 (BGBl. I S. 1523), 20. Januar 1984 (BGBl. I S. 97, 360), 20. Dezember 1984 (BGBl. I S. 1654, ber. 1985. S. 1266), 27. Februar 1985 (BGBl. I S. 461), 27. Januar 1987 (BGBl. I S. 475), 20. Dezember 1988 (BGBl. I S. 2477), vom 18. Dezember 1989 (BGBl. I S. 2261/2387) und Anlage I Kapitel III Sachgebiet C Abschnitt II Nr. 3 mit Maßgaben durch Abschnitt III Nr. 5 des Einigungsvertrages vom 31.8.1990 (BGBl. II S. 889), und vom 17.12.1990 (BGBl. I S. 2847) (BGBl. III 312-9-1).

UVollzO (Pretrial Detention Regulation)

Untersuchungshaftvollzugsordnung vom 12 Februar 1953 in der Fassung vom 15. Dezember 1976.

Literature

Begemann, Helmut. ''Zur Legitimationskrise der Jugendstrafe: Überlegungen zur Umgestaltung des Jugendstrafrechts.'' *Zeitschrift für die gesamte Strafrechtswissenschaft* 24 (1991): 44–48.

Böhm, A. ''Aus der neueren Rechtsprechung zum Jugendstrafrecht.'' *Neue Zeitschrift für Strafrecht* 13 (1993): 527–530.

Buchholz, Irmgard. ''Mitwirkung eines Kollektivvertreters im Jugendstrafverfahren.'' In *Vorbeugung und Bekämpfung der Jugendkriminalität in der DDR,* edited by Erich Buchholz. Part III, Issue 8. Berlin: Druck-kombinant Berlin, 1988.

Bundeskriminalamt (Federal Criminal Office), ed. *Polizeiliche Kriminalstatistik Bundesrepublik Deutschland: Berichtsjahr 1993.* Wiesbaden: Bundesdruckerei, 1994.

Dünkel, Frieder. *Freiheitsentzug für junge Rechtsbrecher, Situation und Reform von Jugendstrafvollzug, Jugendarrest Untersuchungshaft in der Bundesrepublik Deutschland und im internationalen Vergleich.* Bonn: Forumverlag Godesberg, 1990.

———. ''Strafvollzug im Übergang.'' *Neue Kriminalpolitik* 5 (1993): 37–43.

———. ''Verschärfungen abgewehrt.'' *Neue Kriminalpolitik* 6 (1994): 9–10.

Eickmeier, Walter. ''Entwicklung des Strafvollzugs in den neuen Ländern am Beispiel von Mecklenburg-Vorpommern.'' *Zeitschrift für Strafvollzug und Straffälligenhilfe* 5 (1992): 286–291.

Flügge, Christoph. ''Der Anfang der Gemeinsamkeit.'' *Zeitschrift für Strafvollzug und Straffälligenhilfe* 3 (1991): 153–156.

Fricke, Karl Wilhelm. ''Jugendkriminalität hüben und drüben.'' *Deutschland Archiv* 19 (1986): 208–209.

Gramckow, Heike. ''Legal Background and Use of Juvenile Detention in West Germany.'' Paper presented at the American Society of Criminology Annual Meeting in Reno, Nevada, November 10, 1989.

Grunau, Falko. "Die Arbeit der Abendrealschule in der Untersuchungshaft bei der JVA Wuppertal—Erfahrungen aus der Sicht eines Kursleiters." *Zeitschrift für Strafvollzug und Strafälligenhilfe* 3 (1991): 160–161.

Heinz, Wolfgang. "The Problems of Imprisonment, Including Strategies That Might Be Employed to Minimise the Use of Custody." In *Crime and Criminal Policy in Europe: Proceedings of a European Colloquium,* edited by Roger Hood. Oxford: Centre for Criminological Research, University of Oxford, 1989.

Herrmann, Joachim. "The Federal Republic of Germany." In *Major Criminal Justice Systems,* edited by George F. Cole, Stanislaw Frankowski, and Marc G. Gertz. Beverly Hills, CA: Sage, 1981.

Hoffmann, Julius. "Reaktionen der DDR-Jugendhilfe auf abweichendes Verhalten." In *Jugendkriminalität in beiden deutschen Staaten,* edited by Gisela Helwig. Cologne: Verlag Wissenschaft und Politik, 1985.

Janssen, Helmut F., and Hans-Joachim Plewig. "The Juvenile Justice System of the Federal Republic of Germany." In *Jugendgerichtsbarkeit in Europa und Nordamerika—Aspekte und Tendenzen,* edited by Hans-Jürgen Kerner, Burt Galaway, and Helmut Janssen. Munich: Schriftenreihe der Deutschen Vereinigung für Jugendgerichte und Jugendgerichtshilfen, [New Series, Issue 16], 1986.

Kaiser, Günther. "Juvenile Delinquency in the Federal Republic of Germany." *International Journal of Comparative and Applied Criminal Justice* 16 (1992): 185–204.

Kaiser Günther, Hans-Jürgen Kerner, and Heinz Schöch. *Strafvollzug: Ein Lehrbuch.* 4. neubearbeitete und erweiterte Auflage. Heidelberg: C. F. Müller Juristischer Verlag, 1992.

Kerner, Hans-Jürgen, and Elmar Weitekamp. "The Federal Republic of Germany." In *Western Systems of Juvenile Justice,* edited by Malcolm Klein. Beverly Hills, CA: Sage, 1984.

Kersten, Joachim. "Imprisoned Juvenile Delinquents in the German Federal Republic." In *Jugendgerichtsbarkeit in Europa und Nordamerika-Aspekte und Tendenzen,* edited by Hans-Jürgen Kerner, Burt Galaway, and Helmut Janssen. Munich: Schriftenreihe der Deutschen Vereinigung für Jugendgerichte und Jugengerichtshilfen. (Neue Folge, Heft 16.) 1986.

Kerth, J. "Jugendschöffen im Beitrittsgebiet." *Neue Zeitschrift für Strafrecht* 14 (1994): 252.

Kreuzer, Arthur. "Aus- und Fortbildung von Jugendrichtern und Jugendstaatsanwälten: Analyse der mangelhaften Lage und Verbesserungsvorschläge." *Zeitschrift für Rechtspolitik* 20 (1987): 235–238.

———. "Jugendgerichtsbarkeit." In *Drittes deutschsowjetisches Kolloquium über Strafrecht und Kriminologie Baden-Baden,* edited by Albin Eser and Günther Kaiser. Freiburg im Breisgau: Max-Planck Institut für Ausländisches und Internationales Stratfrecht, 1987.

Kröger, Peter. "Sozialdatenschutz im Verhältnis zum Strafverfolgungsinteresse." *Zentralblatt für Jugendrecht und Jugendwohlfahrt* 80 (1993): 21–26.

Lekschas, John, Harri Harrland, Richard Hartmann, and Günter Lehmann. *Kriminologie: theoretische Grundlagen und Analysen.* Berlin: Staatsverlag der Deutschen Demokratischen Republik, 1983.

Luther, Horst. *Strafverfahrensrecht: Lehrbuch.* Berlin: Staatsverlag der Deutschen Demokratischen Republik, 1987.

Matzke, Michael, Claus Czujewicz, Marius Fiedler, Helmut Frenzel, Gerhard Graetz, Peter Reinecke, Winfried Roll, Steffi Ruß, Hans-Georg Schapdick, Martin Schmidt, Anita Spenner, Victor Weber, Eugen Weschke, and Hanni Winkler. *Bericht der Arbeitsgruppe Reaktionen der Jugendstrafrechtspflege auf Gewalt,* Unabhängige Kommission Berlin gegen Gewalt (Domicusstraße 12, 10823 Berlin), 1993.

Mehner, Heinrich. "Aspekte zur Entwicklung des Straf- und Untersuchungshaftvollzugs in der ehemaligen sowjetischen Besatzungszone Deutschlands (SBZ) sowie in den Anfangsjahren der DDR." *Zeitschrift für Strafvollzug und Strafälligenhilfe* 2 (1992): 91–98.

Meier, Astrid. "Zur Rücknahme des staatlichen Strafanspruches im alten und neuen Jugendstrafrecht auf dem Gebiet der ehemaligen DDR—Eine Befragung bei Jugendgerichtshelfern." Diplomarbeit im Aufbaustudium Kriminologie an der Universität Hamburg im Juni, 1993.

Miehe, Olaf, Frederich Schaffstein, and Dieter Dölling. "Literaturbericht: Jugenstrafrecht (Teil IV)." *Zeitschrift für die gesammte Strafrechtswissenschaft* 104 (1992): 132–166.

Nicolas, Bernhard. "Jugendgerichtshilfe als Jugendhilfe für straffällige Jugendliche und junge Volljährige." *Zentralblatt für Jugendrecht* 81 (1994): 159–161.

Ohle, Karlheinz. "Die Härte der Strafrichter." *Zeitschrift für Rechtspolitik* 26 (1993): 408.

Oleschinski, Brigitte. "Die Abteilung Strafvollzug der Deutschen Zentralverwaltung für Justiz in der Sowjetischen Besatzungszone 1945–1949: Ein Einblick in Akten der frühen deutschen Nachkriegsgeschichte." *Zeitschrift für Strafvollzug und Strafälligenhilfe* 2 (1992): 83–90.

Ostendorf, Heribert. "Jugend und Gewalt/Möglichkeiten und Grenzen der Konfliktregelung." *Strafverteidiger* 13 (1993): 545–548.

Pelz, Eckhard. "Ein erster Rückblick mit Ausblick." *Zeitschrift für Strafvollzug und Strafälligenhilfe* 3 (1991): 158–160.

Radbruch, Jochen. "Zur Reform der Verteidigung in Jugendstrafsachen." *Strafverteidiger* 13 (1993): 553–558.

Rieger, Walter. "Probleme der praktischen Erziehungsarbeit im Jugendstrafvollzug." *Zentralblatt für Jugendrecht und Jugendwohlfahrt* 67 (August 1980): 433–438.

Rotthaus, Karl Peter. "Imprisonment of Juvenile Offenders in the F.R.G." In *Jugendgerichtsbarkeit in Europa und Nordamerika—Aspekte und Tendenzen,* edited by Hans-Jürgen Kerner, Burt Galaway, and Helmut Janssen. Munich: Schriftenreihe der Deutschen Vereinigung für Jugendgerichte und Jugendgerichtshilfen, 1986.

Scheschonka, W. "Verfassungwidrigkeit des Jugendstrafvollzuges." *Neue Zeitschrift für Strafrecht* 11 (1991): 255–256.

Schaffstein, Friedrich. *Jugendstrafrecht.* 8. Auflage. Stuttgart: Verlag W. Kohlhammer, 1983.

Schmuck, Rudolf. "Probleme des Justizvollzugs in den neuen Bundesländern am Beispiel Sachsens." Vortrag auf der Tagung der Bundesvereinigung der Anstaltsleiter vom 10.-14.6.91 in Straubing.

Schobloch, Karen. "Jugendkriminalrecht in Theorie und Praxis am Beispiel des Jugendstrafrechts in Deutschland und Frankreich." *Monatsschrift Kriminologie* 75 (1992): 293–296.

Sessar, Klaus. "Alternatives to the Deprivation of Liberty: The German Experience." Typescript, n.d.

Sonnen, Bernd-Rüdiger. "Täter-Opfer-Ausgleich durch freie oder öffentliche Träger der Jugendhilfe?" *Neue Kriminalpolitik* 5 (1993): 44–45.

Spieß, Gerhard. "Junge Wiederholungstäter" *Kriminalistik* 48 (1994): 111–117.

Streng, Franz. "Der Erziehungsgedanke im Jugenstrafrecht." *Zeitschrift für die gesamte Strafrechtswissenschaft* 106 (1994): 60–92.

Swarzenski, Martin. " 'Lassen Sie uns Kollegen werden!' " *Zeitschrift für Strafvollzug und Strafälligenhilfe* (1991): 157–158.

Traulsen, Monika. "Die Entwicklung der Jugendkriminalität: eine quantitative Analyse." *Kriminalistik* 48 (1994): 101–105.

Viehmann, Horst. "Was machen wir mit unseren jugendlichen Gewalttätern?" *Zeitschrift für Rechtspolitik* 26 (1993): 81–84.

Wassermann, Rudolf. "Ist die Justiz auf dem rechten Auge blind?" *Neue Juristische Wochenschrift* 47 (1994): 833–837.

Wassermann, Rudolf, and Victor Weber. "Soll das Jugendstrafrecht verschärft werden?" *Focus* 26 (1993): 199.

Wendland, Günter. "Die Bekämpfung und Verhütung von Straftaten-ein gesamtgesellschaftliches Anliegen." *Neue Justiz* 43 (1989): 262–265.

Wolfe, Nancy. "Socialist Juvenile Justice." In *Official Response to Problem Juveniles: Some International Reflections,* edited by James C. Hackler. Euskadi, Spain: Onati International Institute for the Sociology of Law, 1991.

9

GREECE

Vassiliki Petoussi and Kalliopi Stavrou

INTRODUCTION

The Greek juvenile justice system, a relatively new institution, is concerned primarily with the behavior of minors as offenders. Specific historical circumstances, influences from similar Western European and North American systems, and international and Greek principles of juvenile law and justice gave the Greek juvenile justice system its present form (Spinelli, 1992:90–91; Troianou-Loula, 1982:379).

Law 5098 of 1931 (5098/1931) "On Juvenile Courts," one of the initial legislative attempts to establish a juvenile justice system in Greece, articulated basic principles necessary for the operation of Greek juvenile courts (Spinelli, 1992:90–91). Additional legislative efforts led to the passing of law 2135/1939, "On the Trying of Offenses Committed by Juveniles" (enacted January 1, 1940), and the first public hearing of the Juvenile Court of Athens was held on March 14, 1940. However, the first courts' lack of operational organization and historical circumstances—World War II and the foreign occupation that followed—impeded the efficient operation of juvenile courts (Troianou-Loula, 1982:379). Consecutive legislative efforts, such as the Penal Code (PC) and the Code of Procedural Penal Law (CPPL) of 1950, the Constitutions (C) of 1952, 1968, and 1975–1986, and a number of other laws, established the present system of juvenile justice, distinguished it from the adult justice system, and set the operating principles of the system[1] (Spinelli, 1992:92).

As we analyze the operating principles of the juvenile justice system, we need to note that many of these principles are not explicit in legal codes and documents. They are, however, inferred from the legal literature and theory (Spinelli, 1992:36).

OPERATING PRINCIPLES

The fundamental, most important principle of the Greek juvenile justice system is the principle of the *best interest of the minor.* The implication of this principle is the state's right and obligation to intervene and protect minors and their best interests every time a law is passed, enacted, and enforced (Spinelli, 1992:36–37).

State intervention is guided by the second principle, the principle of *minimum intervention,* which establishes that the state and its agents should regulate, treat, or sanction the behavior of minors only to the extent necessary (Spinelli, 1992: 32). Theoretical legal arguments caution that extended state regulation carries the danger of paternalism and the subsequent potential abuse of children's human rights (Kourakis, 1986:177). Consequently, only minimum state intervention can serve the best interest of minors (Spinelli, 1992:37).

A third principle—explicitly recognized in Articles 122–123 and 126–128 of the PC—is the principle of *preference of treatment over punishment.* What is of importance, according to this principle, is not so much the severity of the reaction to the juvenile offender but, rather, that this reaction is different in principle from the reaction adults receive. That is, juvenile courts impose not penal punishment, but treatment measures (Troianou-Loula, 1982:385).

The best interests of minors are further served by the fourth principle of *special, individualized treatment* of juvenile offenders, which demands that the sociopsychological characteristics, the personality, and special needs of minors, rather than the specifics of the illegal act, should be the basis on which the reaction to lawbreaking behavior of minors should be decided (Dedes, 1976: 248).

The special, individualized treatment of minors is based on the assumption that the personality of minors is not fully developed yet and, as such, can be influenced. Consequently, aiming at changing the personality of the juvenile, the goal of their special treatment is reform (Dedes, 1976:248). Furthermore, because of their young age, minors are considered lacking the ability to fully comprehend the illegality of their behavior and, thus, to formulate intent. De facto, then, minors are presumed as lacking intent. Lack of intent and incomplete personality are the basic reasons justifying the special treatment of minors (Manoledakis, 1984: 478–479). As an implication of the principle of special, individualized treatment, juvenile judges are provided with much discretionary power (Spinelli, 1992:39, 40–41).

Discretionary judicial power, flexibility of rules, and informality of procedures characterize "welfare" justice systems, which allow comprehensive interpretations of the situation. Welfare justice systems have been evaluated as particularly relevant to the treatment of juvenile offenders. On the other hand, "justice" systems that emphasize strict procedural rules are considered to provide better guarantees against abuses of judicial power (Kourakis, 1986:176–177). In order to guarantee individualized treatment of minor offenders and simultaneous protection of their rights, the Greek juvenile justice system established its fifth principle, the principle of the *combination of welfare and justice systems* (Spinelli and Troianou-Loula, 1987:37–38).

The final principle characterizing the Greek juvenile justice system is the *specialization of professionals* (police personnel, judiciary, lawyers, and social workers), which is necessary for a more efficient operation of the juvenile justice system (Spinelli, 1992:44). Based on its operating principles, the Greek juvenile justice system, similarly to other juvenile justice systems, deals with minors in a unique way, guided by the legislator's attempt to treat and protect, rather than punish, the child, adolescent, or young adult who violates the law (Spinelli, 1992:41).

At the heart of the Greek juvenile justice system is the trial of juvenile offenders, during which the application of operating principles and the interaction of the system's agents become more evident. In the following section we address a number of issues related to the organization and the operation of the juvenile justice system and its agents. First, we look at the jurisdiction of the court and address issues such as the composition of the juvenile court, the age of offenders, the kinds of sanctioned behavior, and the kinds of sanctions the juvenile court can impose. Second, the primary agents of the system and the way they interact with one another and with the juvenile offenders in their trial are analyzed. Finally, we address the way the juvenile justice system differs from the adult penal system.

FORMAL PROCEDURES: THE SYSTEM AND ITS AGENTS

Jurisdiction

Court Composition

The CPPL establishes three kinds of juvenile courts. Each court has a different composition and different number and rank of judges and is responsible for trying different offenses. The kind of violations that fall under the jurisdiction of a particular court depends on the sanction each violation carries. The type of sanction further defines the degree of severity of an offense. Furthermore, although the name of each court depends on the number of judges present, necessary for the legal composition of each court are the public prosecutor and the secretary of the court. This is true for all types of Greek penal courts, including juvenile courts (Vougioukas, 1984a:75).

The composition and jurisdiction of juvenile courts, as defined in Articles 7 and 113 CPPL, are as follows:

1. One-judge juvenile court
This court tries primarily petty violations. It can impose reform and therapeutic measures and a penalty of deprivation of freedom up to five years.

2. Three-judge juvenile court
This court tries misdemeanors for which there is a provisioned sanction of deprivation of freedom for over five years.

3. Three-judge juvenile appeals court
This court tries appeals against the decision of the three-judge juvenile court.

Age of Offenders

According to Article 121, paragraph 1 of the Penal Code of 1950, persons between 7 and 18 years of age are considered minors, and their illegal behavior falls under the jurisdiction of the juvenile courts. The PC distinguishes between children (7–12 years of age) and adolescents (12 years of age and one day until 18 years of age) and in Article 126 provides that the penalty of deprivation of freedom cannot be imposed on children. Under certain circumstances adolescents can be deprived of their freedom and sentenced to a correctional institution.

Sanctioned Behavior

The PC in its section on juvenile offenders does not define or regulate status offenses. To this extent, the status of a person as a minor, although decisive for issues such as court procedures, sanctions, and degree of accountability, is not relevant to the legality or illegality of an act (Spinelli, 1992:58). Consequently, according to the Greek PC, juveniles are sanctioned for acts for which adults are sanctioned as well (Dedes, 1976:241).

Broadly defined status offenses, however, are recognized and regulated in a small number of special laws that prohibit juveniles from engaging in the otherwise legal activity these laws regulate. Some of these prohibitions carry sanctions for the juvenile who engages in the prohibited behavior, while others carry sanctions for adults, such as legal guardians or other adults who have the legal responsibility to deter juveniles from the prohibited behavior[2] (Spinelli and Troianou-Loula, 1987:50).

In addition to the preceding two types of sanctioned behavior, law 2724/1940 recognizes a third type of behavior, "moral deviance," which, although not necessarily illegal, may bring about administrative measures depriving juveniles of their freedom. At the suggestion of the juvenile judge, the minister of justice may order minors who exhibit signs of "moral deviance," such as running away from home and dropping out of school, to be sent to a reform school. The legal justification for the regulation of moral deviance is grounded on the principle of state intervention, whose interpretation has recognized the obligation of the state to protect minors against self-destructive behavior (Manoledakis, 1984: 1110).

Legal scholars have criticized the concept of moral deviance as a particularly problematic, broad, and unclear concept whose ideologically biased interpretations, especially in the past, have allowed paternalistic state interventions (Kourakis, 1986:177). Furthermore, in addition to theoretical and practical questions on the extent to which deprivation of freedom positively deters future illegal behavior, the constitutionality of law 2724/1940 has been challenged, although not in court yet, since it transfers some of the authority of the judiciary, such as sentencing, to the executive branch of government, the minister of justice (Spinelli and Troianou-Loula, 1987:217). Overall, then, minors can engage in three types of illegal or prohibited behavior: (1) behavior that is punishable for adults, (2) status offenses regulated by special laws, and (3) moral deviance.

Police and court data show that most of the cases referred to juvenile courts involve traffic violations and property crimes, that is, violations punishable for adults as well. For example, according to the National Statistical Service of Greece in 1988 (most recent available data), 66 percent of all juveniles arrested were involved in some type of traffic violation, while 16 percent were arrested for property crimes, 85 percent of which were simple thefts. Arrests for violent crimes, primarily bodily harm, constituted 0.72 percent of all juvenile arrests. Of those arrested, the majority, approximately 96 percent, were males. Adolescents (13–18 years of age) represented 3 percent of all people arrested.[3]

Articles 122, 123, 127 PC define that the kind of sanctions imposed on minors fall under three categories; reform measures, therapeutic measures, and deprivation of freedom (sentencing to a correctional institution)

Reform Measures

1. *Reprimand* is the most frequent, rather symbolic, type of sanction imposed. The reprimanded minor is usually advised in court by the judge on the negative consequences of deviant and illegal behavior and warned that future illegal behavior may be sanctioned severely (Diminas, 1984:339).

2. A second reform measure that the juvenile court can impose is to *place a minor under the supervision of his or her parents or guardians* (art. 122 PC). This measure is frequently imposed for traffic-law and property-law violations. The purpose of placing a juvenile under the supervision of his or her parents or guardians is to increase the legal responsibilities that parents and guardians already have (Spinelli and Troianou-Loula, 1987:85). However, there is some skepticism concerning the efficiency of this measure since parents are rarely brought to court for failing to meet their increased responsibilities. Even when parents are brought to court, they are usually acquitted for lack of gross negligence or intent (Diminas, 1984:340).

3. *Placing a minor under the supervision of the Service of Supervisors of Minors,* although considered the most effective sanction imposed by the juvenile court (Diminas, 1984:340), is imposed on relatively few cases, approximately 1,000 per year, more frequently on children and less frequently on adolescents (Spinelli and Troianou-Loula, 1987:90). This type of sanction is similar to probation, and, when imposed, a supervisor is entrusted, for an unspecified time, with the supervision and guidance of the sanctioned minor. The numerous responsibilities and the small number of supervisors are probably the basic reason

this type of sanction is not imposed more frequently (Spinelli and Troianou-Loula, 1987:88).

4. *Placing a minor in a reform school* results in deprivation of freedom, is considered the ultimate reform measure, and is automatically revoked after the juvenile's 21st birthday (art. 125 PC). Because of the severity of the sanction, the Penal Code advises the juvenile judge to use extreme caution and reserve this sanction for serious crimes and after other reform measures have failed (Diminas, 1984:342; Troianou-Loula, 1977:65).

Therapeutic Measures

According to Article 123 of the PC, the juvenile court, after consulting a medical doctor, can order therapeutic measures for an adolescent in need of special treatment, especially if he or she is suffering from mental illness or physical or mental handicap or addiction to drugs or alcohol (Papazaharias, 1953:281–282). Therapeutic measures are rarely ordered by juvenile courts, primarily because of lack of facilities appropriate for hosting and treating juveniles with special needs (Diminas, 1984:123), and are automatically revoked after the 21st birthday of the minor (art. 125 PC).

Sentencing to a Correctional Institution

Placing a minor in a correctional institution is the only sanction that, in terms of theoretical legal reasoning, is equivalent to the penal sanctioning of adults. Juveniles who have committed an illegal act that, if committed by an adult, would have been a felony or misdemeanor and who, according to the judge's opinion, will not be deterred by reform measures or have already failed other reform measures may be sent to a correctional institution (art. 127 PC).

Contrary to the sentencing of adults, juveniles are sentenced for an unspecified time. That is, the judge defines the minimum and the maximum length of the sentence, which, in general, is between six months and 10 years, but not the exact duration (art. 54 PC). However, a juvenile who commits an offense punishable for adults with over 10 years of imprisonment can be sentenced to a correctional institution for a minimum of 5, and a maximum of 20 years. This length of sentencing is problematic because of the following provisions. According to the Greek PC (art. 18), juveniles cannot be charged with a felony. Thus, the most severe criminal act juveniles can commit is a misdemeanor. However, misdemeanors are punishable by imprisonment up to 5 years (art. 51-54 PC). Consequently, there is a discrepancy between the type of offense and the length of sentencing. Nevertheless, only rarely are juveniles sent to correctional institutions, and to that extent the problematic nature of this regulation is somewhat reduced.

In terms of the frequency that the previous sanctions are imposed on juveniles, in 1988 there were 5,016 sanctioned juveniles. Of these, 4,898 (approximately 99 percent) were subject to reform measures. There were no therapeutic measures taken, while only 27 people were sentenced to a correctional institution.

Of all juveniles sanctioned, 96 percent were males, and 98 percent were adolescents.

The reform measure most frequently imposed was the measure of reprimand (56 percent). Approximately 26 percent of juveniles who were sanctioned with reform measures were placed under the supervision of their parents or legal guardians, 16 percent were placed under the supervision of a supervisor, and only 35 people (0.8 percent) were sent to a reform school. Males received the majority of reform measures (96 percent), while adolescents (98 percent) tended to be sanctioned more frequently than children.

The Trial Of Juvenile Offenders

A number of people, each with his or her specific role to perform, participate in the trial of juvenile offenders: the juvenile judge, the juvenile public prosecutor, the defense attorney, and the juvenile supervisor. Except for the defense attorney, all other participants in the trial of juveniles are state agents employed by the courts.

The juvenile judge and the public prosecutor are assigned to their position for a period of two years, with the possibility of renewal. The CPPL provides that judges and public prosecutors with specialized knowledge (such as child psychology, sociology, criminology, social sciences in general) should be preferred for this assignment. In practice, however, juvenile judges and juvenile public prosecutors tend to be selected from among the younger members of the courts. Furthermore, the appointment of judges or public prosecutors to the juvenile court does not relieve them of their duties to the adult court. This double responsibility results in heavy workloads and may even restrict the amount of time and energy judges and public prosecutors spend on the trials of juveniles, given that their promotion and advancement depend on their performance in trials of adults (Troianou-Loula, 1982:380).

In terms of their duties, juvenile judges coordinate the activities of other officers of the court, evaluate all evidence, and decide on the treatment of juvenile offenders. Furthermore, juvenile judges are responsible for maintaining the appropriate climate in the courtroom and observing that the whole process does not become antagonistic but remains, to the extent possible, friendly and nonthreatening. Consequently, the role of the juvenile judge is the central role in the trial of juveniles (Troianou-Loula, 1982:380).

The role of the public prosecutor in the trial of juveniles is to conduct the preliminary investigation and, on the basis of the findings, to decide whether to prosecute. In the event of prosecution, public prosecutors make suggestions concerning the treatment of juveniles. Furthermore, the presence of public prosecutors is instrumental during appeals. Because of the importance of the public prosecutor's role, his or her presence in the trial of juveniles is mandated by law. However, the role of public prosecutors in the juvenile court is not without challenges (Troianou-Loula, 1982:81).

Challenges to the role of public prosecutors in the trial of juveniles are summarized in the argument that their presence may give the impression of a formalized and accusatory, rather than informal, process concerned with the best interest of the juvenile and the prevention of future antisocial behavior. Contemporary legal theory, however, describes the role of the public prosecutor as the "discoverer of the truth," not the prosecution of the accused. Thus, after their investigation, public prosecutors may decide not to prosecute and, given additional evidence, may suggest the acquittal of the accused. Consequently, to the extent that the operating principles of the juvenile justice system are followed, the role of public prosecutors may not be as problematic as argued (Troianou-Loula, 1982:381).

Another participant in the trial of juvenile offenders whose role is debatable is the defense attorney. Challengers of the participation of counselors in the trial of juveniles believe that their role tends to be argumentative, and, as a result, the advisory character of the trial is negatively affected. Furthermore, in the trial of minors, the role of counselors is restricted to the presentation of the specifics of the act. However, in the juvenile justice system, the specifics of the act are secondary to the sociopsychological characteristics of the offender, the investigation and presentation of which are the responsibility of juvenile supervisors. Consequently, it is suggested that counselors whose presence in the juvenile court is allowed by law but not mandated may be an additional procedural guarantee during trials of serious offenses (Troianou-Loula, 1982:381–382).

The people whose role is essential not only in the trial of juvenile offenders but also in the function of the whole juvenile justice system are juvenile supervisors, who are state employees with numerous and various responsibilities. The Service of Supervisors of Minors was established in Greece in 1940 and was staffed initially with unpaid social scientists volunteering their services to the juvenile courts. Law 378 of 1976 formalized the organization of the Service of Supervisors of Minors and established it under the authority of the Department of Justice. Supervisors of minors are social scientists employed by the Department of Justice and are assigned to the service of juvenile courts after receiving special training (Vougioukas, 1984a:64; Diminas, 1984:340).

According to Presidential Decree 49 of 1979, there are several responsibilities of supervisors of minors:

1. They conduct the social research on the living conditions and the family and work environment of juvenile offenders or "morally deviant" juveniles (art. 8). Juvenile supervisors consult with juveniles in order to better understand their needs and the causes of their antisocial behavior (art. 8, par. 2). Their research is discrete and restricted to what is absolutely necessary in order to avoid intrusions in the social life of the juvenile (Spinelli and Troianou-Loula, 1987:199). After the social research is concluded, supervisors file a report with the juvenile judge with all relevant information and suggestions on the appropriate treatment of the juvenile (art. 8, par. 2).

2. When the reform measure of supervision is imposed, juvenile supervisors stay in close contact with the juvenile and his or her family in order to provide guidance and support as needed (art. 9, par. 1). Supervisors keep a record of the progress of the juvenile under supervision and every six months file a report with the juvenile judge in which they suggest whether the supervision should be continued or revoked (art. 9, par. 2).

3. During the trial of juvenile offenders, supervisors act as defense for the juvenile to the extent that they are responsible for collecting and presenting information on the juvenile's sociopsychological characteristics on which the decision of the juvenile court is based (Spinelli and Troianou-Loula, 1987:199; Troianou-Loula, 1982:381).

4. Juvenile supervisors further collect statistical information on juvenile delinquency and are responsible for the enforcement of laws concerning status offenses (art. 11).

The multifaceted role of juvenile supervisors is underlined by their primary obligation to gain the trust and respect of juvenile offenders, establish personal relationships with them, and act with their best interest in mind. To facilitate the development and establishment of personal relationships between juveniles and supervisors, embedded in the juvenile justice system are a number of safeguards, such as the classification of information supervisors collect during their research as privileged. Inappropriate disclosure of such information is punishable. For that reason, juvenile supervisors cannot be examined under oath in the juvenile court. Additionally, when the measure of supervision is imposed, the same supervisor who conducts the initial research is assigned the supervision of the juvenile offender (Spinelli and Troianou-Loula, 1987:210).

Through their personal relationship and communication with the juvenile, it is likely that juvenile supervisors are in the position to influence juveniles and contribute to their reform. On the other hand, through their close cooperation with the other agents of the system, juvenile supervisors can contribute to a social, rather than a legal, understanding and treatment of juvenile offenders before, during, and after their trial.

An issue concerning the trial of juveniles that demands particular attention involves situations in which juveniles and adults are accomplices to the same crime. As a rule, the trials of adults and juveniles are separated, and juveniles are tried in the juvenile court. Exceptionally and for the "interest of justice," the trials of adult and juvenile accomplices may be combined. In that case, the trial of both accomplices falls under the jurisdiction of an adult penal court. The juvenile judge participates in the trial if it is possible but does not make the decision for the treatment of the juvenile (130 par. 3 CPPL).

In practice, combined trials tend to become the rule rather than the exception and have attracted much criticism. In combined trials, juveniles receive unequal treatment since they are deprived of their legal judge, the "closed door" procedure, and the special, individualized treatment to which they are entitled. Adult penal courts are not obligated to—and usually do not—notify the Service of Supervisors of Minors, and, as a result, juvenile offenders are deprived of the benefits of "social search" and the support of juvenile supervisors (Troianou-

Loula, 1987:105). Furthermore, adult penal court judges tend to demand the examination of juvenile supervisors under oath. As a result, confidential information becomes public, and oftentimes the relationship of trust established between juvenile supervisors and juveniles is jeopardized (Troianou-Loula, 1982: 383).

The problems present in the combined trials of adults and juveniles have their source in the fact that the unique character of the juvenile trial is lost in the adult penal trial. The unique character of the juvenile trial is based on both the operating principles of the juvenile justice system and a number of regulations that differentiate the juvenile from the adult penal system.

DIFFERENCES BETWEEN THE ADULT AND THE JUVENILE SYSTEM

A number of significant differences exist between the juvenile justice system and the adult system of justice. The first such difference is the provision for the existence of juvenile judges with specialized social and legal knowledge (art. 27, par. 1; 43; 113 CPPL). The existence of special juvenile judges is of primary importance to the extent that their replacement makes the composition of the court illegal (Troianou-Loula, 1982:390).

Second, as a rule, juveniles are not held in custody before the trial. Juveniles may be held in custody before the trial if they committed offenses that, if committed by an adult, would have been punishable by 10 years of imprisonment (art. 282, par. 3 CPPL).

Third, juvenile courts impose reform and therapeutic measures and only rarely the equivalent of penal sanctions, sentencing to a correctional institution. In other words, juvenile courts treat, rather than punish, offenders. Adult courts, on the other hand, administer punishment to those found guilty of the charges (121, 127 PC).

Fourth, although adults have a relatively extended right to appeal, the right to appeal is restricted for juveniles. Juveniles can appeal sentencing to a correctional institution for over a year (489 CPPL). This restriction of the right to appeal contradicts the Beijing Rules and is problematic to the extent that it reduces the legal resources of juveniles (Spinelli, 1992:100).

Fifth, contrary to the principle of public trial (art. 93 C; 329, 371 par. 1 CPPL), the trial of juveniles is conducted behind "closed doors," and only few people are allowed to be present. The "closed door" procedure, which is constitutionally guaranteed (96 par. 1 C), has been in effect since 1955 and was introduced for the overall protection of the reputation and the character of juveniles (Vougioukas, 1984a:125).

Sixth, the treatment of juveniles is decided on the basis of their sociopsychological characteristics and aims to serve their best interests, while the penalties of adults are based on the specifics and the severity of the act they committed (4, 8 Presidential Decree 49/1979; 239 par. 2 CPPL; 79 PC).

Seventh, the measures imposed on juveniles are removed from their criminal record after their 19th birthday (reform measures) or five to eight years after they were imposed (penal sanctions) (578 par. 1 CPPL). Adult penal sentences, as a rule, remain in the criminal record until the 80th birthday or the death of the person (578 par 1 CPPL).

Eighth, the existence and the role of the Service of Supervisors of Minors are unique to the juvenile justice system. Furthermore, there is no equivalent institution in the adult justice system (Troianou-Loula, 1982:390).

Ninth, when an adult is "caught in the commission of a criminal act" or under circumstances that make it plausible, if not certain, that he or she committed the act (usually petty violations and a small number of misdemeanors), a speedy trial with condensed procedural requirements follows. This type of trial, although designed to administer justice immediately after the criminal act, is criticized for its deviations from standard trials. It is argued that such deviations may not fully protect all the rights of the accused, at least to the extent that the right of the accused depends on procedures (Vougioukas, 1984b:126–127).

In the case of juveniles for whom a background search on their sociopsychological characteristics is essential, speedy trials would significantly violate the principles and the goal of the juvenile trial. For that reason, speedy trials are not explicitly allowed for juveniles (Troianou-Loula, 1982:382).

The differences that exist between the adult and the juvenile justice system provide the latter with a unique character. Although not without problems, the Greek juvenile justice system aims, through rather informal procedures, at the reform of juveniles.

CONCLUSION

In this chapter we presented a brief overview of the basic theoretical principles and practical ways the Greek juvenile justice system attempts to deal with juvenile delinquents. This history of the juvenile justice system in this country has shown that, although it is based on a number of principles rather promising for a humane treatment of juveniles, there is much room for improvement both in principle and in practice. The lack of extended and comprehensive research on the causes of delinquency in Greece and the efficiency of the existing measures makes the articulation of suggestions for change difficult at this point.

However, there is increasing interest on the part of the state and legal and social scientists concerning juvenile delinquency and reactions to the lawbreaking behavior of juveniles. Among the issues presently discussed is the changing of terminology concerning juveniles who violate the law (Alexiadis, 1986:113). Legal scholars following the labeling theory have argued that the legal reference to juvenile criminality should be changed to a term that would better express internationally used terms, such as "juvenile delinquency" (Spinelli, 1976:800).

Legal scholars further argue that new regulations to deal with procedural issues, right to appeal, issues concerning the sanctioning of juveniles, length of sentencing to correctional institutions, and types of sanctioned behavior, such as "moral deviance," are much needed for the modernization of the Greek juvenile justice system (Spinelli, 1992:145–152).

The issue, however, that is possibly of primary importance, especially for a system concerned with the reform of juveniles, is the establishment of facilities able to host young people who have violated the law and have special educational, occupational, or other needs. In a country such as Greece, where the welfare of children and young people is among the responsibilities of the state (Petroglou, 1979:667), it is imperative that the juvenile justice system be reformed.

NOTES

The authors wish to thank the following people for their assistance and support: Donald J. Shoemaker, Michael Moutafides, Amalia Tsoukali, and Yiannis Zardis.

1. In Greece, as in other Western European countries, the laws regulating the juvenile justice system do not exist in a singular collection such as a code of juvenile law (Spinelli, 1992:28). There exist, however, collections of juvenile law that assist the work of juvenile court judges, social workers, lawyers, juvenile supervisors, and other agents of the system (Troianou-Loula, 1987:7).

2. The following laws can be seen as examples of the kind of behavior prohibited by special laws and the sanctions they carry. Under the restrictive conditions defined in Royal Decree 29/1971, betting and gambling that occur in specifically designated public places such as casinos or video-game arcades are legal for adults but not for minors. Article 5, paragraph 6 of Royal Decree 29/1971 defines that minors who enter establishments where betting and gambling take place and participate in betting and gambling commit a petty violation and can be sanctioned with reform measures. Additionally, the adult who operates such a place and allows the entrance of a juvenile commits a petty violation and is liable to a fine and imprisonment up to three months.

Another example of a status offense that does not carry sanctions for the juvenile who engages in the behavior but does penalize an adult is police order 10/1980–1981, according to which it is prohibited to persons under the age of 17 to consume alcohol or to enter places where alcohol is served. However, there is no provision for the sanctioning of the juvenile who consumes alcohol or enters places where alcohol is served. Rather, there are sanctions for the parent or legal guardian of the juvenile and the person who operates the establishment and, contrary to his or her legal obligation, did not prohibit the juvenile from entering and consuming alcohol.

3. In order to establish some numerical bases of reference, we note the following. According to official data, the total population (seven years and older) in 1988 was 9,160,250. The absolute number of all penal violations was 311,179, which represents a rate of 3,397 penal violations per 100,000 people.

REFERENCES

Alexiadis, Stergios. "Juvenile Criminality or Delinquency?" *Poinika Xronika* 36 (1986): 113–120.

Dedes, Christos G. "Dogmatic Problems of the Law of Minors." *Nomiko Vima* 24 (1976):241–249.

Diminas, Dimitrios. "The Need for Modernization of the Law of Minors." *Armenopoulos* 38 (1984):339–349.

Kourakis, Nestoras. "Juvenile Offenders and Penal Justice: Thoughts on a Re-examination of the Current Penal Law of Minors." *Nomiko Vima* 34 (1986):175–179.

Manoledakis, Ioannis. "Young Age as an Independent Legal Good in Penal Law." *Nomiko Vima* 32 (1984):1105–1113.

National Statistical Service of Greece. *Statistics of Justice: Civil Justice, Criminology and Corrections of Year 1988.* Athens: National Statistical Service of Greece, 1988.

Papazaharias, Ioannis K. "On Therapeutic Measures Imposed on Juvenile Offenders." *Poinika Xronika* 3 (1953):281–302.

Petroglou, Antonis I. "The Social Protection of the Child in Our Country: Contribution to the 'Year of Child.' " *Epitheorisis Dikaiou Koinonikis Asfaliseos* 11 (1979): 667–673.

Spinelli, Kalliopi D. "Underage Criminals or Young Offenders? The Problem under the Prism of 'Labeling Theory.' " *Poinika Xronika* 26 (1976):785–800.

———. *Greek Law of Minor Offenders and Victims; A Discipline under Development.* Athens/Komotini: Sakkoulas, 1992.

Spinelli, Kalliopi D., and Aglaia Troianou-Loula. *Law of Minors; Penal Regulations and Criminological Expansions.* Athens/Komotini: Sakkoulas, 1987.

Troianou-Loula, Aglaia. *The Service of Supervisors of Juvenile Courts in Greece.* Athens, 1977.

———. "The Juvenile Offender and His Trial." *Nomiko Vima* 30 (1982):378–390.

———. *The Penal Law of Minors.* Athens/Komotini: Sakkoulas, 1987.

Vougioukas, Konstantinos N. *Penal Procedural Law: Introduction and General Part.* Thessaloniki: Sakkoulas 1984a.

———. *Penal Procedural Law: Special Issues.* Thessaloniki: Sakkoulas, 1984b.

APPENDIX: AGENCIES DEALING WITH JUVENILES IN GREECE

Department of Justice
Mesogion 96
Athens
tel. 01-775-9638

Juvenile Courts of Athens
Stadiou 65
Athens

Department of Justice
Service of Juvenile Supervisors (Ipiresia Anilikon)
Mesogion 96
Athens
tel. 01-775-3129, 771-5590

Department of Justice
Department of Prevention and Control of Juvenile Delinquency
Mesogion 96
Athens
tel. 01-771-1777

Department of Justice
Division of Personnel of Juvenile Correctional Institutions
Mesogion 96
Athens
tel. 01-770-3020

Department of Justice
Statistical Service of the Department of Justice
Mesogion 96
Athens
tel. 01-770-5613

Organization of Juvenile Supervisors of Greece
8th floor, office 809
Stadiou 65
Athens
tel. 01-324-7684

10

HONG KONG

Mark S. Gaylord

INTRODUCTION

When Britain acquired Hong Kong at the conclusion of the First Anglo-Chinese War (1839–1842), the small, hilly, and nearly treeless granite island supported no more than 6,000 or 7,000 inhabitants, many of them living on boats (Morris, 1993). Yet, from this humble beginning Hong Kong has grown to become one of Asia's four "Little Dragons," a dynamic and prosperous territory of nearly 6 million people whose per capita income now exceeds that of Britain itself.

But times are changing. On July 1, 1997, sovereignty over Hong Kong will revert to the People's Republic of China (PRC), thus ending more than a century and a half of British rule in the Far East. Juvenile justice in Hong Kong is based on the English system and is therefore quite different from that of the PRC. Nevertheless, the Sino-British Joint Declaration and the PRC-promulgated Basic Law (Hong Kong's post-1977 constitution) provide that Hong Kong's existing legal system shall continue after China assumes authority over Hong Kong. However, while the policy of "one country, two systems" guarantees the future Hong Kong Special Administrative Region (SAR) a high degree of autonomy, it seems unlikely that the legal system will remain unchanged. Hong Kong, after 1997, is undoubtedly destined for a major legal and political transformation (Tai, 1994).

Prior to 1932, juveniles in Hong Kong were not recognized as a distinct legal category. They were tried in adult criminal courts, subject to the same procedures and sentencing options as adults. Juvenile offenders were held with adult offenders in police stations and, when brought before Police Courts, were placed in the dock with adults. Nor were there separate penal institutions for convicted juveniles. Some were reprimanded by the magistrates in court, but those who were sent to prison received sentences varying from 48 hours' detention to 12 months' hard labor (Lee, 1989). For the Chinese, flogging and the shearing of the queue (pigtail) were common punishments. Throughout the nineteenth century, half of all floggings were administered to juveniles (Endacott, 1973).

Hong Kong's juvenile justice system first came into existence in 1932, when the Juvenile Offenders Ordinance established juvenile courts and a probation service to deal with juvenile offenders. In the same year, reformatory and industrial schools were established under separate legislation. Throughout most of Hong Kong's history, certainly in the 1930s, Britain exported Western concepts of crime and justice to the colony without regard for structural or cultural differences. Thus, like so many other legal innovations in Hong Kong, juvenile justice was imported from England with little thought to how well such legal concepts and procedure would be received by Hong Kong's indigenous population (Vagg and Traver, 1991).

Hong Kong's new juvenile court jurisdiction, modeled closely on its English counterpart, separated offenders under 16 years of age from adult offenders. It sought to advance the welfare of children by abolishing the death sentence and by largely removing them from the jurisdiction of the criminal courts and jails.[1] The juvenile court accepted responsibility not only for youthful offenders but also for children who, although not in conflict with the law, required ''care and protection.'' Thus, children coming before the courts were no longer regarded as merely a subset of the adult population but as weak and malleable persons in their own right and entitled to special care. This change in status was accomplished through the introduction of reformatory treatment and also involved the assertion of new powers of state intervention in parent–child relationships (Lee, 1989).

In Hong Kong, as in England, juvenile courts were courts of summary jurisdiction and, as such, were similar to magistrates' courts in general. To emphasize distinctions, however, the first two juvenile courts were to sit either in a different building or room, or on days or at times different from those when ordinary sittings were to be held. Provisions were also made to prevent the mingling of juvenile and adult offenders. The juvenile courts barred public access to proceedings and restricted newspaper reports of court cases. Unlike their English counterparts, Hong Kong's juvenile courts were presided over by stipendiary expatriate magistrates lacking special training or experience in juvenile justice (Lee, 1989).

Prior to 1932, there were no separate training institutions for convicted children. Magistrates were reluctant to commit juveniles to prison except for the most serious offenses; on the other hand, cautions and warnings that were given in court to juveniles and their families went largely unheeded. In this context, new methods to reform delinquent children were developed.

Most laws currently applicable to juvenile offenders (ages 7 to 15 years) and young offenders (ages 16 to 20 years), namely, the Juvenile Offenders Ordinance (Cap 226), the Probation of Offenders Ordinance (Cap 298), the Detention Centers Ordinance (Cap 239), the Training Centers Ordinance (Cap 280), and the Prisons Ordinance (Cap 234), have been on the books in Hong Kong in one form or another since at least the 1950s.

The history of juvenile justice in Hong Kong thus shows some apparent progress. At the same time, there has emerged a dual process that, while retaining the full vigor of the juvenile court for convicted delinquents, has spawned new forms of surveillance, regulation, and intervention for the so-called predelinquent (Lee, 1989). In recent years, there has been a massive expansion in the scope of juvenile misbehavior; policing strategies targeted at youth; and a probable "net widening," resulting in the official processing of juveniles who previously would have been dealt with informally by the community or by the police. In short, much of the apparent increase in recorded juvenile crime in recent years may be due to these factors rather than greater wrongdoing by youth (Gray, 1991).

THE FORMAL SYSTEM

Once an arrest is made, two options are generally available for dealing with a juvenile; he or she either is cautioned by the police or appears before the court. Following trends in England, the legislation and court proceeding in Hong Kong indicate a mixture of justice, welfare, and punishment ideologies. The Juvenile Offenders Ordinance begins by focusing attention on the offense, stating that the purpose of the juvenile court is to hear "any charge against a child or young person." The initial proceedings in juvenile cases are adversarial and similar to those of the adult court. Pleas are taken, and, if a juvenile denies a charge, a trial ensues to establish guilt or innocence. The legislation lays down clear guidelines for the protection of legal rights of juveniles. In addition, the services of the Duty Lawyer and Legal Advice Schemes are available in court.[2] The physical separation of adult and juvenile courts and the exclusion of the press and general public from hearings are intended to safeguard juveniles against adverse criminal influences and publicity (Gray, 1991).

There are eight juvenile courts in Hong Kong. One of the newest, described by Lee Shuk Yi (1989), is housed in part of a purpose-built judicial and administrative complex. The juvenile court's interior fixtures and fittings, raised dais for the magistrate, large government crest, dock and cells, plus the presence of police officers all retain the look and feel of an adult court.

Inside the courtroom, the presiding magistrate sits on a fairly high dais at one end, and the child stands at the other (sometimes in the dock in criminal proceedings). In front of the magistrate, also on a raised platform but slightly lower than the magistrate, sit the clerk and the interpreter.[3] In the first series of rows are the lawyers, prosecutors, and a Social Welfare Department (SWD) probation officer, all of whom are anonymous strangers to the child. In this setting, children are asked to describe details, comment on, or listen to reports on intimate details of their personal lives, details that do not in themselves constitute infractions of the law (e.g., personal hygiene, family relationships, love affairs, and sexual matters,) but that are open to investigation once a child has been brought into the criminal and care jurisdiction.

Paragraph 8 of the Juvenile Offenders Ordinance provides the following guidelines:

Before deciding how to deal with the child or young person, the court shall obtain such information as may be readily available as to his general conduct, home surroundings, school record, and medical history, in order to enable it to deal with the case in the best interest of the child or young person.

The phrase "in the best interest of the child or young person" is open to a number of interpretations. Juvenile justice professionals usually seem to interpret it to mean that the welfare needs of the juvenile should be taken into account before sentencing. Indeed, in the majority of cases, magistrates will call for social inquiry reports before passing sentence, and if probation appears an unsuitable option, they may also call for reformatory school, community service, detention center, or training center suitability reports or a Young Offenders Assessment Panel report. These reports concentrate heavily on the juvenile's social background, gleaned from the individual, parents, teachers, and employers. Typically, only one paragraph discusses the offense itself (Gray, 1991).

Generally, offense factors do not receive high priority in weighing information that leads either to a recommendation or to a sentence. There are exceptions, of course, for example, where the offense is seen as particularly serious, perhaps involving assaults or woundings and substantial injury to the victim. But for the mundane cases of theft, minor robberies, and assaults, welfare, rather than offense, considerations are of paramount importance. Moreover, a particular aspect of the juvenile's welfare is of interest to the court, that is, his disciplinary needs. The chief concern of court personnel is the degree to which the juvenile is "out of the control" of various social systems (Gray, 1991).

Probation

Probation was first introduced in Hong Kong as part of the Juvenile Offenders Ordinance. The Probation of Offenders Ordinance (No. 57 of 1956; now Cap 298) extended eligibility for probation to adult offenders. Despite numerous amendments, the basic outline of the ordinance has remained unchanged over the years.

Probation is provided by approximately 120 probation officers working in 11 offices. All probation officers hold degrees in social work. In contrast to some jurisdictions, there are no permanent probation officers in the Hong Kong Social Welfare Department. Instead, social workers are assigned to work as probation officers for a limited period, usually not over three years, and then transferred to other posts within the SWD.

While Hong Kong's probation service is part of the Youth and Rehabilitation Branch of the SWD, a probation officer is first and foremost an officer of the court. Following a defendant's conviction and prior to sentencing, a magistrate may order a probation officer to prepare a social inquiry report describing the circumstances under which the offense was committed and the offender's social, educational, and employment background. After taking into account all relevant factors, the probation officer may then recommend a suitable treatment option to the court. If the probation officer's recommendation is accepted, a magistrate will make a probation order covering a period of one to three years. The offender must agree to accept the terms and conditions of the probation order (O'Brian, 1994).

In theory, probation incorporated the casework approach. In practice, however, for a variety of reasons, few probationers in Hong Kong receive individualized treatment and supervision. Here, as in many jurisdictions, the major obstacles are heavy workloads, relatively inexperienced staff, and high staff turnover.

While both adults and juveniles are eligible, approximately 75 percent of those on probation in Hong Kong are below the age of 21. Yet, this age group accounted for only 28 percent of all offenders prosecuted in 1990. In other words, despite the statutory provision for adult offenders, probation, in practice, is still largely limited to juvenile and young offenders.

Community Service

Under a community service order, an offender is required to perform unpaid work (up to 240 hours, to be completed within 12 months) of benefit to the community under the supervision of a probation officer. Thus, the aims of community service are both punitive and rehabilitative.

Community service began as a pilot scheme in 1987 in three Hong Kong magistracies: Eastern, Kwun Tong, and Tsuen Wan. It is organized and monitored by the Community Service Orders Office in Choi Wan. The service was extended to three more magistracies in April 1992 and to the remaining four magistracies in November of the same year.

Under the Community Service Orders Ordinance (Cap 378), a magistrate may place an order on anyone over the age of 14 convicted of an offense punishable by imprisonment and considered a suitable candidate. In practice, community service orders are not usually given for those convicted of rape, arson, or major drug offenses. Moreover, offenders who are drug addicts or who have extensive criminal records are also deemed unsuitable for placement. If an offender fails to comply with the requirements of the order, he or she may be brought back to court for resentencing. The bulk of community service orders involve persons under the age of 21 years. In 1991–1992, just under 58 percent (75 out of 130 cases) of new community service orders involved persons belonging to this age group.

Individuals serving community service orders are not permitted to be in direct economic competition with free workers in the community. Rather, they are meant to carry out duties usually performed by social welfare volunteers. Typical placements range from activities such as gardening and minor repair work to supervising activities for the disabled. Six to eight offenders may be assigned to work together on a group project, or a single offender may be assigned to an individual placement. In 1991–1992, a total of 33 group projects and 17 individual placements served 25 government departments and nongovernment organizations.

In 1991–1992, the Community Service Orders Office completed 468 social inquiry reports, assessing the suitability of offenders for community service. As with probation, community service has been successful in the sense that 138 of 162 offenders have completed community service orders.

Residential Care and Custody

Social Welfare Department programs include probation, probation homes, and reformatory schools. Probation homes and reformatory schools are referred to as "residential care," and all persons below the age of 16 years are eligible. Correctional Services Department (CSD) programs include detention centers, training centers, drug centers, and prison. These are referred to as "custody," and all persons 14 years old and above are eligible.

The Young Offender Assessment Panel is a program that began in 1987 as a joint venture between the SWD and the CSD. The program provides magistrates with a professional assessment of the personal and social circumstances of convicted offenders between the ages of 14 and 25 prior to sentencing. In 1991–1992, the Young Offender Assessment Panel responded to 318 referrals from 38 magistrates. Most of those assessed were males between 14 and 18 years of age convicted of offenses against property or persons. The magistrates followed the Young Offender Assessment Panel's recommendations just over 81 percent of the time.

In 1991–1992, 131 offenders were placed in programs under supervision of the SWD, and 160 were placed in programs supervised by the CSD. As one might expect, offenders under the jurisdiction of the SWD typically received probation, with or without a period of detention, while those under jurisdiction of the CSD were typically placed in a detention or training center. Only 10 received a fine or suspended sentence or were placed under a care and protection order.

Conflicts over the goals of punishment become most evident with juvenile offenders, rather than adults. Despite rapidly changing social values and rising crime rates, Hong Kong's juvenile court judges continue to believe that most youthful offenders are redeemable; therefore, when discussing sentencing alternatives, judges as well as social welfare personnel often use such terms as "training," "treatment," and "care." Nevertheless, while it may be true that officials hold more lenient attitudes toward them, juveniles and young offenders are frequently incarcerated (O'Brian, 1994).

With the exception of those convicted of manslaughter, attempted murder, or wounding with intent to inflict grievous bodily harm, young offenders may not be sentenced to prison if suitable alternatives are available. These provisions normally restrict imprisonment to offenders who are over 16 years of age. Young offenders sent to prison are not allowed to associate with adult prisoners.

Despite such provisions, there are cases in which a magistrate may decide that some form of detention is appropriate for a juvenile or young offender. In these cases, the court has a number of options. First, the court may make a probation order that includes a period of residence in a probation home. The SWD operates three probation homes: Begonia Road Boys' Home, Ma Tau Wei Girls' Home, and Pui Chi Boys' Home. Second, the court has the option of sending an offender to a place of detention for up to six months. The SWD operates two places of detention: Begonia Road Boys' Home and the Ma Tau Wei Girls' Home. Third, juveniles who, in the judgment of the court, cannot be returned to their families while awaiting court proceedings are placed in a remand home. The SWD operates three remand homes: Pui Yin Juvenile Home, Begonia Road Boys' Home, and Ma Tau Wei Girls' Home. Remand homes provide temporary care, custody, and assessment services for juveniles, illegal immigrants (usually from China) between 7 and 15 years of age, and children between 7 and 17 years of age. Periods of stay may vary from a few hours to a maximum of six months. During 1991–1992, 3,737 admissions to remand homes were processed by SWD.

While the terms "probation home," "place of detention," and "remand home" would seem to imply the existence of a number of facilities designed to accommodate disparate populations, in practice such is not the case. Actually, a mere handful of institutions simultaneously house inmates under orders for care and protection, probation, or remand into single mixed populations.

Not surprisingly, within these facilities, subcultures have developed in which older and more experienced youths dominate younger, more recent arrivals. These subcultures may result from the situation of incarceration, the importation of attitudes formed prior to incarceration, or both. One general observation, however, is that such subcultures are stronger when inmates are treated collectively, as in Hong Kong, rather than individually, and have to adapt not only to confinement but to being part of the incarcerated group (Vagg, 1994).

While SWD staff have control over much inmate behavior, mostly in the form of authority to punish for deviation from institutional rules, such control is negligible compared to that exerted by inmates themselves. Because inmate domination over other inmates is valuable to staff, who are far outnumbered by inmates, it should be expected that power of various kinds will unofficially, perhaps unintentionally, be assigned to inmate elites rather than seized by them. Such is the case in Hong Kong.

The SWD also operates two reformatory schools: O Pui Shan Boys' Home and Castle Peak Boys' Home. Reformatory schools are places of detention for offenders who have committed crimes that would be punishable by a fine or imprisonment were they adults. A reformatory order, usually made on the recommendation of a probation officer, lasts for one to three years or until an offender has reached the age of 18. Although children as young as 14 can be sent to a reformatory school, in actual practice it is rare for such youthful offenders to be so placed. The intent of a reformatory order is to provide educational, prevocational, and character training so that offenders can be returned to the community as law-abiding citizens. While remedial in intent, reformatory schools nonetheless are custodial. Offenders are incarcerated against their will, and statutory penalties for nonconformity with the reformatory regime are punitive. Because sentences are indeterminate, inmates can be released early under license and receive aftercare aimed to aid rehabilitation into society.

The SWD seeks to rehabilitate youthful offenders through a combination of supervision and training in order to instill a sense of personal responsibility and self-discipline. This approach is congruent with traditional Chinese values, but, in the absence of independent criteria, it is impossible to say how successful an approach it has been. Lacking more meaningful indicators, there has been a tendency to rely on compliance with supervision and low recidivism rates following discharge as evidence of success. In the final analysis, success is defined as submission to authority and ''keeping out of trouble.'' Nevertheless, this is actually a common phenomenon in most jurisdictions (O'Brian, 1994).

The SWD provides aftercare services for offenders discharged on license from a reformatory school or released from a place of detention after serving less than six months under a detention order. Offenders who receive early release from a reformatory school are placed under supervision for a specific period or until the expiration of the school order or until the offender reaches 18 years of age. In the case of release from a place of detention, the director of the SWD makes a supervision order for a child or young person that remains in effect until the original detention order comes to an end. Failure to comply with the conditions and requirements of a supervision order may result in the individual's return to a place of detention. Aftercare officers provide counseling, make family visits, and assist in finding employment and accommodations.

In Hong Kong, the Correctional Services Department operates five distinct types of institution: adult prisons, young offenders' training centers, a detention center, drug addiction treatment centers, and a psychiatric center for mentally abnormal offenders. However, the custodial sentences passed on young offenders are usually detention center or training center orders. Sha Tsui Detention Center accepts males aged 14 to 24, and the training centers accept males and females aged 14 to 20 (with separate institutions for the two sexes). Descriptions such as ''prison,'' ''training center,'' and ''detention center'' are poor indicators of what transpires within these institutions. The three pieces of legislation central to CSD, the Prisons Ordinance (Cap 234), the Training Centers Ordinance (Cap 280), and the Detention Centers Ordinance (Cap 239), like the English models they are based on, contain comparatively little direction on the actual operation of penal establishments. As described recently by Jon Vagg (1991), visitors to CSD establishments will usually see a high degree of order and purposeful activity, much higher, in fact, than one sees in North American or European establishments. In centers for young offenders, a visitor may well pass by a group of inmates engaged in military-style parade drill or listening attentively to a lecture on the rules they must observe and the privileges they may enjoy. Vocational training and educational facilities, while variable, are generally good. Accommodations for young offenders are mainly or entirely dormitories. If a visitor is shown a dormitory, it will invariably be spick-and-span, with the blankets folded military-style into "bed boxes" and inmates' possessions neatly arranged in small wooden lockers. Personal belongings are few, often only a toothbrush and toothpaste, a few books, and perhaps a small radio.

Training center regimes are highly regimented, with a strong orientation toward vocational training and education. Inmates spend half the day working and half in educational or vocational classes. The centers follow a "progressive" system, in which inmates can be promoted through several grades, offering successively more opportunities and fewer restrictions. The detention center runs on similar lines but with greater strictness than the training centers. Both training and detention center orders are indeterminate. Detention center sentences run from a minimum of one month to a maximum of six months. Training center sentences range from a minimum of six months to a maximum of three years, with the point of release being determined not by the court but by the senior superintendent on the advice of an institutional review board. In practice, most training center inmates are released after serving about 15 months. On completion of training center and detention center services, there is a period of postcustody supervision (three years for training center, one year for detention center) intended to ensure that the ex-inmate has indeed reformed, with the threat of recall to the institution hanging over his or her head (Vagg, 1991).

INFORMAL PRACTICES

Geographically, Hong Kong is contiguous with mainland China, but, following a century and a half of British rule, it has developed into an increasingly distinctive society. Unlike China, Hong Kong is sophisticated, modern, and urban. The colony's lifestyles, patterns of consumption, cultural tastes, and career aspirations more and more resemble those of Western nations. The Hong Kong ethos thus represents a mixture of traditional Chinese and modern Western cultural traits in which its population is more materialistic, individualistic, and self-reliant and less encumbered by deep-seated inhibitions than its mainland China counterparts (Lau and Kuan, 1988).

Its many similarities to the West notwithstanding, Hong Kong remains predominantly a Chinese society. In this highly competitive milieu, each individual must look to personal resources, rather than to those of the government, in times of need. Consequently, what Lau Siu Kai (1981) calls "utilitarian familism," the tendency for the individual to place familial interests above the interests of others and to structure relationships so as to maximize those interests, has evolved to provide a comforting shelter. In Confucian societies, the family is the primary economic, social, and religious unit. Even now, the concept of filial piety, the obligation of children to show deference and respect toward parents, remains a fundamental social relationship in Hong Kong (Lau and Kuan, 1988).

Yet, under the onslaught of modernization, Hong Kong has seen a marked decline in parental control in recent years. Working mothers have long since become commonplace. From the mid-1970s onward, when free and compulsory education for nine years was introduced by the Hong Kong government, children have spent considerable time in the company of peers that in former days was spent within the family setting. Under such conditions it is not unreasonable to assume that the family has lost much of its former potency as an instrument of social control.

Despite the Confucian emphasis on mediation and social harmony, Hong Kong Chinese exhibit a generally positive attitude toward the law. According to a 1988 social indicators survey, 65 percent of the respondents stated that they "trusted judges and lawyers," and 67 percent agreed that the law was an "efficient means of conflict resolution" (Kuan, Lau, and Wan, 1991:216–218). In this and other surveys, Hong Kong's putative "youth problem" was cited by respondents as one of the colony's most serious and problematic social issues.

The degree of concern shown for youthful misbehavior suggests that, while parental control may have declined in recent years, adults continue to demand from juveniles a standard of conduct more in conformance with traditional Confucian norms than those of Western society. In this regard, Patricia Gray (1991) argues that little doubt should prevail that numerous young persons are in residential care and custody not for the serious nature of the crimes they have committed but because of purportedly questionable behavior at home, school, work, or leisure or because of failure to comply with a probation order.

While perhaps higher than in the past, juvenile crime rates in Hong Kong remain low by international standards (Traver, 1991). Since the late 1970s, however, there has been much publicity about the apparently dramatic upward trend in juvenile crime. Many public figures and committees have claimed to see the roots of this increase in the amount of time spent by juveniles in the streets, video centers, and billiard rooms; in dubious peer associations; in the decaying moral standards of youth increasingly faced with materialist values, Western culture, and pornography; and more widely in the deterioration of Chinese family traditions.[4]

While the evidence is mixed, official crime statistics appear to confirm the widely held community view that there has been a dramatic upsurge in both the amount and the seriousness of juvenile crime. The pertinent question, however, is whether such statistics reflect the real nature of juvenile crime. For several reasons, such statistics can give an unrealistic impression; as social products, they are heavily influenced by the response of juvenile justice professionals to community fears (Fishman, 1978).

First, despite the increase in absolute figures, juvenile crime as a proportion of *all* crime showed only a modest increase throughout the 1980s. Over 70 percent of juvenile prosecutions in 1988, for example, consisted of offenses against property, often of a petty nature, such as minor shoplifting and theft. Second, juveniles commit the types of crime that are most easily detected, and this distorts their representation in overall crime statistics. This is usually the case with offenses against public order, possession of offensive weapons, carrying equipment to aid in stealing, and loitering. Third, it is known from victimization surveys in Hong Kong that there has been a greater propensity for crimes to be reported to the police, and it seems likely that less serious offenses as well as more serious ones are being reported more often. Many of the kinds of offenses committed by juveniles are comparatively trivial and, in the past, may well not have been reported. It is possible that the media and public concern about juvenile crime in recent years have led to a lessened toleration of juvenile crime, with a correspondingly greater likelihood of crime reports being made. Fourth, numerous crime campaigns were launched in the 1980s by the District and Central Fight Crime Committees, drawing both public and police attention to certain categories of crime and specific age groups. It is possible that heightened public awareness resulted in greater likelihood of crimes being reported. Whether or not this actually occurred, the effect of such police deployment may well have been to increase juvenile crime detection rates and therefore the arrest rates.

Why has there been such heightened community interest in juvenile crime in recent years? Fears about juvenile crime are a recurrent theme in many countries, leading several writers to argue that such panics often represent a means by which wider social anxieties and uncertainties are articulated and expressed (Box, 1985; Pearson, 1983; Hall et al., 1978). Concern over juvenile crime can divert attention from prevailing political and economic problems and can provide ample justification for exercise of greater control over young people who are seen as a potential threat to social order during such periods. Over the past two decades, Hong Kong has also had its social, political, and economic problems. At all times, the overriding concern has been to maintain the stability and prosperity of the territory. It may be pure speculation to link these events to panics over juvenile crime, but certainly each surge of such concern has resulted in a tightening of control over the lives of young people, as reflected in a number of juvenile justice policies and in the attitudes of the justice system toward youthful offenders.

Juveniles not subject to SWD or CSD programs generally are dealt with by fines, discharges, or bindovers. In 1978, these methods constituted 82 percent of sentencing disposals, but by 1987 the percentage had dropped to 48 percent. Conversely, probation and residential and custodial sentences increased and became the *major* sentencing disposals. Thus, the chance of a juvenile who appeared in court being put on probation doubled over the period, and the chance of a custodial or residential sentence increased by 73 percent, with particular emphasis on detention center and training center orders, which increased sixfold. If one assumes that, as a result of "net widening," offenders appearing before the juvenile court in the late 1980s are not much different from those of the late 1970s, it could then be argued that the rise in the use of residential care and custody and the subsequent use of probation for less serious offenses have resulted from a hardening of attitudes by juvenile justice professionals, possibly in response to community fears that a breakdown in social discipline among young people has occurred.

SUMMARY

Hong Kong's juvenile justice system has changed little since 1932 in terms of basic institutions and procedures, though major changes have occurred within the society. Even though residents of Hong Kong operate under an English-based legal system, the social structures have been more reminiscent of Asian, than of European, society. For example, it is widely agreed that familial social controls that place a premium on the observance of order have contributed to Hong Kong's historically low crime rates (Ho, 1986). State social control complements what exists at the family and community level. A similar situation exists in the newly industrializing countries of Thailand and Singapore. There, as in Hong Kong, low crime rates are achieved not solely through repression but also by means of the preservation of traditional societal values and family structures (Shelley, 1994). Yet, Hong Kong—dynamic, prosperous, and cosmopolitan in outlook—now stands poised to return to Chinese sovereignty. Britain's Crown Colony thus faces perhaps unprecedented social, economic, and political transformation in its immediate future.

The juvenile justice system, of course, is not impervious to the pressures and demands of society. In Hong Kong, as elsewhere, it is subject to constraints, including ideological and financial ones. In the future, Hong Kong's juvenile courts may choose to adopt a more punitive framework for use in determining "the best interests of the child or young person." Required to answer to a more conservative Chinese outlook, juvenile justice may be forced to reexamine its commitment to a rehabilitative philosophy. Yet, Hong Kong would do well to note the experience of countries such as the United States and Britain whose administrations turned to greater repression throughout the 1980s in response to public calls for "law and order." In both instances, conservative administrations simultaneously emphasized a "get tough" approach to juveniles and curtailed social welfare expenditures. These countries now face record-high juvenile crime rates and institutions overflowing with offenders for whom rehabilitation is but a dim prospect (O'Brian, 1994).

Research in other countries has demonstrated that incarcerating juveniles has had little effect in curtailing delinquency. On the other hand, evidence does exist that community programs based on education and the neutralization of delinquent peer groups can significantly reduce rates of juvenile recidivism. Programs that help parents more effectively supervise their children have also been shown to be successful. Nevertheless, there is little prospect that such programs will be developed in Hong Kong. The acceptance of such a new frame of relevance would require major changes in the attitudes of juvenile justice personnel. It would mean acknowledging the often minor nature of most juvenile crime. It would mean balancing disciplinary needs against the other needs of youth by providing more adequate services for dealing with problems at home, school, work, and leisure. Above all, it would mean replacing a faith in institutionalization with one favoring community-based programs. Only time will tell which approach Hong Kong will choose to follow after 1997.

NOTES

1. The majority of offenders from 7 to 15 years of age are dealt with by the juvenile court. Nevertheless, juveniles may also be tried and sentenced in the District and the High Court.

2. Since 1978, free legal representation has been available to indigent defendants in the juvenile court through the Duty Lawyer Scheme. The Hong Kong Law Society, through an executive committee including representatives from the Hong Kong Bar Association, administers the scheme. Funding is provided by the Hong Kong government. The Law Society also administers the government-funded Legal Advice Scheme, which provides free advice to anyone unwilling or financially unable to consult a private lawyer.

3. In a society in which 97 percent of the population speaks Chinese as the first language, the Hong Kong court system continues primarily to function in English. The need for court interpreters is here more pronounced than in most other societies. In such an environment, the quality of justice depends very much on the competence of the court interpreters' services (Sin and Djung, 1994; Lo, 1991).

4. This and the next four paragraphs are based on Gray, 1991.

REFERENCES

Box, Steven. *Recession, Crime and Punishment.* London: Macmillan, 1985.

Endacott, George B. *A History of Hong Kong,* rev. ed. Hong Kong: Oxford University Press, 1973.

Fishman, Mark. "Crime Waves as Ideology." *Social Problems* 25 (1978):531–543.

Gray, Patricia. "Juvenile Crime and Disciplinary Welfare." In *Crime and Justice in Hong Kong,* edited by Harold Traver and Jon Vagg. Hong Kong: Oxford University Press, 1991.

Hall, Stuart, Chas Pritcher, Tony Jefferson, and Brian Roberts. *Policing the Crisis.* London: Macmillan, 1978.

Ho, David Y. F. "Chinese Patterns of Socialization: A Critical Review." In *The Psychology of the Chinese People,* edited by Michael Harris Bond. Hong Kong: Oxford University Press, 1986.

Kuan, Hsin Chi, Lau Siu Kai, and Wan Po San. "Legal Attitudes." In *Indicators of Social Development: Hong Kong 1988,* edited by Lau Siu Kai, Lee Ming Kwan, Wan Po San, and Wong Siu Lun. Hong Kong: Hong Kong Institute of Asia-Pacific Studies, Chinese University of Hong Kong, 1991.

Lau, Siu Kai. "Utilitarian Familism: The Basis of Political Stability." In *Social Life and Development in Hong Kong,* edited by Ambrose Y. C. King and Rance P. L. Lee. Hong Kong: Chinese University Press, 1981.

Lau, Siu Kai, and Kuan Hsin Chi. *The Ethos of the Hong Kong Chinese.* Hong Kong: Chinese University Press, 1988.

Lee, Shuk Yi. "Care and Control of Juvenile Delinquents in Hong Kong." Master's thesis, Department of Sociology, University of Hong Kong, 1989.

Lo, Man Chiu. "The Courts and the Judiciary." In *Crime and Justice in Hong Kong,* edited by Harold Traver and Jon Vagg. Hong Kong: Oxford University Press, 1991.

Morris, Jan. *Hong Kong: Epilogue to an Empire.* Harmondsworth, England: Penguin, 1993.

O'Brian, Charles. "The Social Welfare Department." In *Introduction to the Hong Kong Criminal Justice System,* edited by Mark S. Gaylord and Harold Traver. Hong Kong: Hong Kong University Press, 1994.

Pearson, Geoffrey. *Hooligan: A History of Respectable Fears.* London: Macmillan, 1983.

Shelley, Louise I. "Foreword." In *Introduction to the Hong Kong Criminal Justice System,* edited by Mark S. Gaylord and Harold Traver. Hong Kong: Hong Kong University Press, 1994.

Sin, King Kui, and Joseph S. H. Djung. "The Court Interpreter's Office." In *Introduction to the Hong Kong Criminal Justice System,* edited by Mark S. Gaylord and Harold Traver. Hong Kong: Hong Kong University Press, 1994.

Tai, Benny Yiu Ting. "The Basic Law: Hong Kong's Post-1997 Constitutional Framework." In *Introduction to the Hong Kong Criminal Justice System,* edited by Mark S. Gaylord and Harold Traver. Hong Kong: Hong Kong University Press, 1994.

Traver, Harold. "Crime Trends." In *Crime and Justice in Hong Kong,* edited by Harold Traver and Jon Vagg. Hong Kong: Oxford University Press, 1991.

Vagg, Jon. "Corrections." In *Crime and Justice in Hong Kong,* edited by Harold Traver and Jon Vagg. Hong Kong: Oxford University Press, 1991.

———. "The Correctional Services Department." In *Introduction to the Hong Kong Criminal Justice System,* edited by Mark S. Gaylord and Harold Traver. Hong Kong: Hong Kong University Press, 1994.

Vagg, Jon, and Harold Traver. "Introduction: Crime and Punishment in Hong Kong." In *Crime and Justice in Hong Kong,* edited by Harold Traver and Jon Vagg. Hong Kong: Oxford University Press, 1991.

APPENDIX: KEY AGENCIES AND PERSONNEL

Social Welfare Department
Youth and Rehabilitation Branch
19th Floor, World Trade Center
280 Gloucester Road
Causeway Bay
Hong Kong

Social Welfare Department
Community Service Orders Office
Rooms 108 and 109, Choi Wan Estate
Community Center
Kowloon
Hong Kong

Correctional Services Department
Headquarters
23rd & 24th Floors, Wanchai Tower I
12 Harbour Road
Wan Chai
Hong Kong

Judiciary
38 Queensway
Hong Kong

Legal Department
Prosecutions Division
1st-8th Floors, High Block
Queensway Government Offices
66 Queensway
Hong Kong

Royal Hong Kong Police Force
Police Headquarters
Arsenal Street
Wan Chai
Hong Kong

11

INDIA

Clayton A. Hartjen and Sesha Kethineni

INTRODUCTION

The Indian Penal Code (IPC) provides uniform definitions of criminal acts that apply to all persons above age seven throughout India. In addition, a number of national "special" laws (e.g., Arms Act, Customs Act), as well as various "local" laws enacted by individual states, define specific acts as crimes (Local and Special Laws—LSL). Law enforcement, judicial, and correctional activities are largely carried out at the state and local level in India. However, state and local criminal justice agencies are under the supervision and authority of national administrative agencies that supposedly ensure uniformity of standards and procedures throughout the country.

Until 1986, the national/state system of law and justice produced a diverse (and in some places nonexistent) body of law and judicial/correctional procedures for juveniles in the various Indian states and union territories. Passage of the Juvenile Justice Act of 1986, however, radically changes that situation.

The idea that children and young people should receive distinctive recognition in law and justice is not new. Laws regarding juveniles began to emerge in India by the mid-nineteenth century (Central Bureau of Correctional Services, 1970). The first major law recognizing a special status for juveniles was the Apprentice Act of 1850, which allowed judges to sentence petty offenders to a period of apprenticeship of up to seven years. The 1860 Indian Penal Code established age limits for criminal culpability, and the 1861 Code of Criminal Procedure had provisions that allowed for separate trials of persons below age 15, as well as their separate confinement in reformatories or placement on probation. In 1897, the Reformatory Schools Act stipulated that boys below age 15 could be placed in reformatories rather than sentenced to prison or exile for a period of 3–7 years.

The first major legislation establishing separate judicial systems and correctional handling of juveniles occurred in the early 1920s with the passage of Children's Acts by several states (Natt and Malik, 1973; Ranchhoddas and Thakore, 1953). These laws specifically targeted juveniles as a special category of offenders and stipulated that they be processed by separate courts and confined in facilities apart from adults. In addition, most of these laws included provisions regarding "noncriminal" acts for juveniles (the equivalent of "status" offenses in contemporary American laws) as well as procedures to deal with dependent and neglected children. Typically, the Children's Acts sought to emulate the legal developments that were occurring around that time in the United States and several Western European countries. In this regard, the laws were designed to be inclusive and nonpunitive, with a decidedly rehabilitative orientation.

Embracing these ideals, a "national" Children's Act was passed in 1960. That law applied only to union territories (areas governed by the central government), but it was also designed to provide a legislative model for the various states to emulate (*The Children's Act, 1960, 1981*).

By 1986, separate Children's Acts, more or less based on the 1960 law, were in effect in some 55 districts of India. However, some of these laws were either not implemented or, if so, not actually enforced, so that in many parts of India juvenile justice remained a matter of statute rather than practice.

The 1986 Juvenile Justice Act was truly a revolutionary page in Indian legal history. Besides establishing national definitions of "delinquency" and "neglected" juveniles, the law details the procedures to be used in dealing with delinquent or neglected children, the nature and purposes of the housing or correctional facilities into which these youths can be placed, and the composition and qualifications for judicial and correctional persons dealing with juveniles. More important, the passage of the law was a symbolic recognition of the changing status of young people in Indian society. Specifically, the law seeks:

to provide for the care, protection, treatment, development and rehabilitation of neglected or delinquent juveniles and for the adjudication of certain matters relating to, and disposition of, delinquent juveniles. (*Juvenile Justice Act 1986:* 1)

FORMAL SYSTEM

The Juvenile Justice Act of 1986 pertains to juveniles defined as "neglected" or "delinquent" and sets out the procedures to be used in processing such youths and the various dispositions they may receive if a neglected or delinquent determination is made.

Definitions

A "juvenile" is a boy under age 16 and a girl under age 18. A "delinquent" juvenile is any juvenile found to have committed an offense (violation of the Indian Penal Code or special or local law). A "neglected" juvenile is one who is found to be begging, destitute, or homeless, who has an unfit or incapacitated parent/guardian, who lives in a brothel or with a prostitute or any other person who leads an "immoral, drunken, or depraved" life, or who is in danger of being abused or exploited. In addition, juvenile authorities can have jurisdiction over "uncontrollable" youths defined as juveniles whose parent/guardian is not able to exercise proper care and control over the juvenile.

In short, the 1986 Juvenile Justice Act mandates special proceedings regarding juveniles who commit an act that would be a crime if committed by an adult and/or who are neglected, dependent, or uncontrollable. While quite encompassing, the law does not specify so-called status offenses. However, the rather vague definitions of neglected or uncontrollable juveniles, in effect, allow juvenile authorities to have jurisdiction over a broad range of youths not engaged in criminal activity.

Procedures

Juveniles believed to be "neglected" are to be referred to, and processed by, special Juvenile Welfare Boards. Those accused as "delinquents" are to be handled by special Juvenile Courts. Although the law mandates that all states establish such institutions and prescribes the general procedures and standards they are to follow, the exact composition of each board or court and their specific operation and the facilities to which juveniles may be sent are largely left to the discretion of each state.

Composition of Boards or Courts

Juvenile Welfare Boards have exclusive authority over juveniles deemed to be neglected (or uncontrollable). Such boards consist of a "chairman" and such other persons the state government decides to appoint. At least one member of the board must be a woman, and all members are vested with the authority of a magistrate and function as a bench of magistrates.

Delinquent youths are under the jurisdiction of Juvenile Courts. The composition and membership of such courts are determined by individual states. All must consist of metropolitan or judicial magistrates, with one member serving as a principal magistrate. Every court shall be assisted by a panel of two honorary social workers, with at least one being a woman. These persons are appointed by the state government, which also determines their qualifications to serve.

No person can be appointed as a member of either a board or a court unless, in the opinion of the state government, that person has special knowledge of child psychology and child welfare. Both boards and courts have exclusive power in all proceedings relating to juveniles under their jurisdiction. Decisions by boards and courts are ordinarily by majority opinion.

The decisions of either boards or courts can be appealed to the Court of Sessions for reversal, with two exceptions. No appeal is allowed in the case of acquittal or a finding that a juvenile is not neglected. In addition, no second appeal from the Court of Sessions is allowed.

Neglected Juveniles

Neglected juveniles can be brought before a board by any police officer or any person or organization authorized by the state government to do so by simply "taking charge" of the juvenile. In addition, if information is given to the board regarding suspected cases of neglect, the board can order the juvenile's parent/guardian to produce the juvenile before it and to show cause as to why the juvenile should not be dealt with as a neglected juvenile. Any juvenile believed to be neglected must be brought before the board within 24 hours of coming to the board's attention. At its option, the board can release the juvenile to a parent/guardian or place the individual in an observation home or "place of safety" until the case can be resolved.

The inquiry by the board is totally discretionary as to proceedings, substance, and determination, as is its disposition of the case. At its discretion, the board can direct that the juvenile be placed in a juvenile home for a period until the individual ceases to be a juvenile. The board may also extend this stay until age 18 for boys and age 20 for girls, or the board can reduce the stay to whatever period it deems fit.

Also within its total discretion, the board can place the juvenile under the care of a parent/guardian or other "fit" person to be responsible for the good behavior and well-being of the juvenile. Such placement may not exceed three years, unless specifically extended by the board.

Delinquent Juveniles

A person who is apparently a juvenile and arrested for any bailable or non-bailable offense shall be released on bail unless release would expose the juvenile to association with known criminals or moral danger or defeat the ends of justice. Suspected juveniles not so released are to be housed in observation homes (or places of safety) until the case can be resolved by a Juvenile Court. The parents or guardian of any juvenile arrested and/or detained must immediately be informed of the proceedings and detention. In addition, a probation officer must be notified so that a personal investigation report may be compiled. All proceedings before the Juvenile Court are governed by the Code of Criminal Procedure 1973, unless explicitly modified by the act. If a juvenile is accused along with an adult, no joint trial is permitted.

Figure 11.1
Processing of Neglected and Delinquent Juveniles under Indian Juvenile Justice Act, 1986

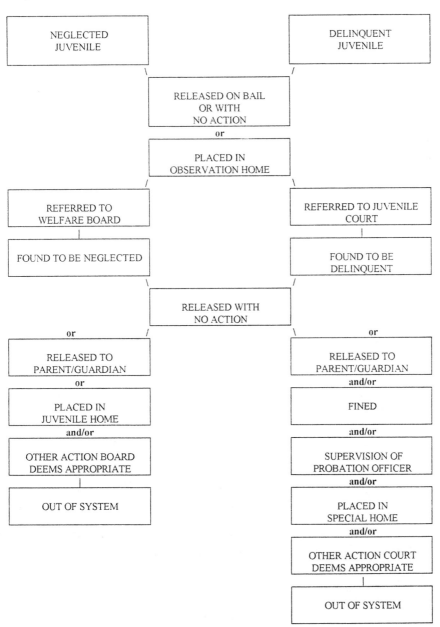

Juveniles found to be "delinquent" can receive one or more of several dispositions at the court's discretion. These include:

1. allow the juvenile to go home after advice or admonition;
2. release the juvenile on "probation" under the care of a parent/guardian, fit person, or fit institution;
3. impose a fine if the juvenile is over 14 and earns money, or;
4. incarcerate the juvenile in a Special Home. In the case of a boy over 14 or a girl over 16 years of age, this placement must be for a period of not less than three years. At its determination, the court can reduce or extend this period. If the latter, the period of stay cannot extend beyond age 18 for boys and age 20 for girls;
5. if released on "probation" or fined, the court can also order that the juvenile be placed under the supervision of a probation officer for up to three years with whatever conditions the court deems necessary, and
6. if on probation, at any time, in the discretion of the court or recommendation of the probation officer, the court could order the juvenile to be placed in a Special Home.

The court is distinctly prohibited from sentencing a juvenile to death or imprisonment. However, if the court deems that a juvenile age 14 or older committed an exceptionally serious offense or cannot be safely housed in a Special Home and that no other means provided by the act offers a suitable disposition, the court can order that the juvenile be kept in "safe custody" as it so determines. This period of detention may not exceed the maximum sentence of imprisonment that could have been imposed on an adult.

Special Procedures for Courts and Boards

Hearings for both courts and boards are to be held in a building or time separate from that used for Civil or Criminal Court proceedings. Proceedings are to be completed within three months unless unusual circumstances dictate otherwise. Both neglect and delinquency proceedings are closed except for the attendance of an officer or competent authority, parties to the inquiry, the juvenile's parent or guardian, others directly concerned with the inquiry, and police officers and legal practitioners (except in neglect cases) as the magistrate directing the procedures considers appropriate. Any person (including the juvenile) could, at the discretion of the hearing officer, be excluded from the proceedings. Any person connected with the juvenile or the case could be required by the board or court to appear. All reports and proceedings before boards or courts are to be treated as confidential. The media are prohibited from reporting any inquiry or in any way identifying the juvenile.

Other Provisions

The 1986 law also gives the court jurisdiction over, and prescribes punishments for, persons committing acts against juveniles. Basically four kinds of punishments are prescribed. (1) A person having actual charge of a juvenile can be sentenced up to six months' imprisonment plus a fine if such person commits, or causes to commit, assault against the juvenile or abandons, exposes, or willfully neglects the juvenile. (2) A three-year maximum sentence plus a fine can be imposed on anyone using a juvenile as a beggar. (3) Similarly, three years and a fine can be the sentence of any unauthorized person who gives a juvenile (or causes to be given) any narcotic drug or intoxicating liquor in a public place. (4) The same sentence applies to any employer of a juvenile guilty of exploiting such juvenile by withholding the juvenile's wages or using such wages for his or her own purposes.

Although the 1986 law is a national law applicable to all states and union territories in India, funds to carry out the provisions of the law must be appropriated by the separate jurisdictions. In addition, the establishment of courts and housing facilities, as well as appointment of magistrates, probation officers, and other personnel, is within the discretion of the various jurisdictions. Not all states in India have as yet complied (or complied fully) with the law, and the degree of adherence to its provisions and the quality of the justice administered under the law undoubtedly vary widely throughout the country (Kumari, 1991; Singh, 1987; Varshney, 1989). As with any comprehensive statute, Supreme Court decisions regarding specific provisions and practices are constantly changing both the scope and character of juvenile justice in India (B. B. Pande, personal communication, 1990).

Arrests and Dispositions

Some sense of the nature of formal juvenile justice practices can be gleaned from data pertaining to the apprehension of persons accused of delinquent acts and the dispositions they receive when processed by Juvenile Courts. Such information is provided in the volume *Crime in India,* published annually by the Indian government. Unfortunately, information on how neglected juveniles are processed and treated since the 1986 law was enacted was not available at the time of this writing, although data from the early 1980s pertaining to such children may shed some light on their numbers and likely treatment after the 1986 law was implemented.

Table 11.1 presents arrest figures for the year 1988 (the first year the law was fully in effect) and the percentages of juveniles that make up all persons arrested in that year. The data in Table 11.1 suggest that either juveniles in India are exceedingly nondelinquent or that the use of formal agencies of control to deal with offenders is rare. Only 22,692 juveniles were arrested in that year for Indian Penal Code offenses, and 15,476 juveniles were arrested for local and special law crimes. A total of only 38,168 juvenile arrests out of a population of over 800 million persons, of whom more than 200 million are juveniles, is dramatic for its small size. This is especially remarkable when compared to the numbers of juveniles arrested in countries (usually Western, economically developed

Table 11.1
Juveniles Arrested for IPC and LSL Offenses, 1988

OFFENSE CATEGORY	NUMBER ARRESTED	% ALL ARRESTS
INDIAN PENAL CODE		
MURDER	491	0.7
ATTEMPT TO COMMIT MURDER	207	0.4
CULPABLE HOMICIDE	38	0.5
RAPE	212	1.6
KIDNAPPING AND ABDUCTION	279	1.3
DACOITY	274	0.8
PREPARATION/ASSEMBLY FOR DACOITY	58	1.5
ROBBERY	346	1.2
BURGLARY	2,215	2.4
THEFT	5,518	2.5
RIOTS	5,250	1.0
CRIMINAL BREACH OF TRUST	115	0.7
CHEATING	67	0.3
COUNTERFEITING	2	0.3
OTHER IPC	7,620	5.9
TOTAL IPC OFFENSES	22,692	0.9
LOCAL & SPECIAL LAW OFFENSES		
ARMS ACT	201	0.4
NARCOTIC DRUGS ACT	49	0.4
GAMBLING ACT	1,780	0.5
EXCISE ACT	925	0.9
PROHIBITION ACT	1,950	0.3
EXPLOSIVES ACT	81	1.8
IMMORAL TRAFFIC ACT	633	3.5
INDIAN RAILWAYS ACT	217	0.6
FOREIGNERS REGISTRATION ACT	3	0.4
PROTECTION OF CIVIL RIGHTS ACT	15	0.2
INDIAN PASSPORT ACT	0	0.0
ESSENTIAL COMMODITIES ACT	41	0.6
TERRORIST & DISRUPT. ACTIV. ACT	11	0.6
ANTIQUITY & ART TREASURE ACT	0	0.0
DOWRY PROHIBITION ACT	58	1.4
OTHER LSL	9,512	0.4
TOTAL LSL OFFENSES	15,476	0.4
TOTAL ALL OFFENSES	38,168	0.6

Source: Crime in India 1988 (New Delhi: National Crime Records Bureau, 1989), 89, 101, 141.

nations) with considerably smaller populations (e.g., compare Federal Bureau of Investigation, 1989). Indeed, where juveniles make up about one-third of all arrests in the United States, in India, juveniles equal only 0.6 percent of all arrests. As measured by arrests, it would seem that juvenile delinquency in India is practically nonexistent and surely not a problem of serious proportions.

Table 11.2
Dispositions Received by Juveniles Arrested and Sent to Court for IPC and LSL Crimes, 1988

DISPOSITION	#	%
SENT HOME AFTER ADMONITION	4,009	17.3
RELEASED ON PROBATION UNDER:		
PARENT/GUARDIAN	7,380	31.8
FIT INSTITUTION	2,229	9.6
SENT TO SPECIAL HOME	920	4.0
FINED	4,841	20.7
ACQUITTED/OTHER	3,849	16.6
TOTAL DISPOSED	23,228	100

Source: *Crime in India 1988* (New Delhi: National Crime Records Bureau, 1989), 149.

Yet, the kinds of activities for which juveniles in India are likely to be arrested seem to be similar to those for which juveniles everywhere come to official attention. Almost one-half of all IPC arrests are for property crimes and gambling, and violations of prohibition laws make up a sizable share of LSL arrests. Few juveniles are arrested for drug-law violations or the more sophisticated crimes such as counterfeiting, cheating (fraud), and other offenses juveniles have little opportunity to commit.

In this regard, Indian youths seem to engage in many of the same kinds of criminality juveniles throughout the world commit. But either they do so infrequently, or, in spite of national legislation specifically targeting them, they are not likely to be subjected to formal control even if they do. The disposition data presented in Table 11.2 imply this latter possibility.

Of the 38,168 juveniles arrested and sent to court in India during 1988, about 61 percent (23,228) had their cases disposed of by the court in that year. Of these, only 4 percent (920) were sent to Special Homes. Almost a quarter were released to parents/guardians directly, were acquitted, or had their cases dismissed. More than 40 percent were released on probation to either parents/guardians or some "fit" person or institution. About 20 percent were fined. Either the offenses for which juveniles are arrested and sent to court in India are relatively mild, and the offenders not noticeably serious delinquents, or the formal juvenile justice system in India takes a decidedly nonpunitive view of their behavior. Undoubtedly, all three factors are involved. But the tendency of Indian authorities to treat juveniles found guilty of criminal acts in a mild, nonpunitive, and informal or semiformal manner is clear.

Information for the early 1980s regarding the handling of juveniles who would be classified as "neglected" under the 1986 law suggests that this "informal" treatment of youths extends beyond reactions to delinquency (*Statistical*

Abstract of India 1989). Indeed, the single most frequent disposition (about 33 percent) by courts for destitute, neglected, victimized, and uncontrollable children is "restored to parent/guardian unconditionally." Relatively few individuals processed under one or another nondelinquent category were sent to any kind of institution, although one might suppose that for neglected and destitute (much less, victimized) youths, this might be a desirable alternative. Indeed, the chances of having one's case discharged or simply being released are typically greater than being sent to a home or placed under some kind of supervision.

When it comes to juveniles, it appears that Indian society has a distinct aversion to dealing with them in a formal, institutional manner—regardless of their behavior or legal status. Instead, release to parents with a stern lecture from the magistrate, the imposition of a fine, or some accommodation resulting in dismissal appears to be the preferred mode of dealing with delinquent or neglected youths. The authors' experiences and observations of Indian society and the limited research on delinquency in India similarly suggest that the social control of delinquency and treatment of needy youths in India are decidedly informal and extralegal in nature. We now turn to this informal system.

INFORMAL PRACTICES

The fact that the Indian Parliament found it necessary to pass a national law regarding delinquent and neglected juveniles suggests that either (1) delinquency has become a problem of major importance in India, or (2) the old patchwork system of state-level juvenile justice systems was undesirable for various reasons. No evidence exists to support the first possibility. Thus, passage of the 1986 legislation undoubtedly represents a creeping formalization of government social control in India. In addition, Indian society appears to be "juvenilizing" its young in a manner similar to what took place in the United States around the turn of the twentieth century (Platt, 1969; Sanders, 1970). The fact that the 1986 law is highly reminiscent in scope and orientation to those enacted in the United States at that time is, thus, not surprising. Indeed, along with the growth of a recognizable middle class in India (now numbering over 200 million people), the formalization of societal reaction to youth problems may very well foreshadow the future development of a delinquency problem of significant proportions.

At present, however, no serious delinquency or youth crime problem seems to exist in India, as measured by official arrest and court statistics. But, on the other hand, self-reported delinquency research carried out by the authors also indicates that while Indian juveniles are considerably less delinquent than their Western counterparts, they are by no means free of misconduct (Hartjen and Kethineni, 1993).

Why, then, the low official rates? The answer to that question, of course, is that the use of official agents of social control, especially when it comes to children, is a last resort in Indian society. For example, a survey carried out by Hartjen and Priyadarsini (1984) asked urban and village adults what actions, if any, they thought were appropriate for a variety of criminal acts committed by juveniles of differing social and economic characteristics. One telling finding from that survey was a distinct reluctance on the part of respondents to call upon the police or other agencies of formal control to deal with (even serious) offenders. Instead, in case after case, respondents felt that either nothing particular should be done about the matter or that intervention should be in the hands of parents, other family members, teachers, village leaders, or various other "respected" persons.

Generally, the police in India are viewed with considerable suspicion and hostility since they symbolize the rule of the former British Raj and are often seen as the muscle behind not always favored political officials today (Bayley, 1969; Shane, 1980). Courts in India are viewed as something to be avoided at all costs. Compared to the degree of intrusion that agencies of government have in the lives of Americans and Western European residents, government intervention into the affairs of most Indians is negligible, although apparently beginning to increase.

About the only quasi-government institution that seems to have a direct and meaningful role in dealing with wayward youths, as well as interpersonal disputes and other such matters, is the *Panchayat*. An ancient institution, after independence, *Panchayats* were reactivated throughout rural India (and to some extent in urban neighborhoods as well) as semiofficial forms of popularly elected village governments. Largely comprising prominent and respected leaders (usually elders) of the community, *Panchayats* often carry out an unofficial judicial/correctional role when called upon to do so by community members. Using such mechanisms as fines, "ex-communication," social boycott, requiring the offender to hold a "grand community feast," and, in some cases, prescribing physical punishment, the *Panchayats* attempt to mediate all manner of disputes and to deal with offenses of almost any kind. Their dispositions do not have the force of law, but they have the backing of custom and community acceptance. As such, many matters that could have become the business of police and courts are simply never brought to official attention and are resolved in an extralegal, nonjudicial manner (Misra and Agnihatri, 1985).

Important as they are, the *Panchayats* are not, however, the main force of social control in India. Instead, the family (and the central meaning that "family" has to the lives of most Indians) provides the major force of social integration and control throughout both rural and urban India. Indeed, only in the absence of a family (or where circumstances are such that the influence or intervention of family relationships breaks down) are other mechanisms to deal with problem or delinquent youths relied on (Karve, 1986; Lannoy, 1971).

To an extent that few Westerners can envision, whatever form it may take in specific cases, the family in Indian society is the central locus of social and economic relations and, consequently, social control throughout most of the society. The family occupies this role (even in the face of the forces of modernization and Westernization), in part, because of its place in the caste (subcaste or *jati*) structure of Indian society and the importance the *jati* has for marriage, social relationships, and the economic/occupational well-being of its members (Caldwell, Reddy, and Caldwell, 1984; Gore, 1968).

For example, marriages in India are still predominantly intra-*jati* affairs. The major function of extensive family relationship is to find appropriate mates within the *jati* for the family's daughters (Caldwell, Reddy, and Caldwell, 1984; Ramu, 1977). This not only relieves the family of the burden of their upkeep but helps to secure their economic future as well. More important from the perspective of social control, the system of intra-*jati*-arranged marriages helps to strengthen the bonds between the members of the *jati*. In turn, these relationships enhance the economic strength of the *jati* for securing jobs, positions in government, admission to university, housing, loans, and the like. In this regard, the *jati* not only forms a social nexus but also provides an economic environment. The dual social/economic importance of the family-*jati* structure of Indian society provides a major source of informal social control.

In modern, economically developed, Western societies, one's deviance is one's own. The sins of the son do not reflect on the father, and those of the sister do not destroy the life chances of a younger sibling. Having others think badly of you may not, of course, be desirable. But that is a personal matter of little consequence to others and even, perhaps, to one's own life chances. In India, the matter is still quite the contrary.

What the members of one's family or *jati* think of one can have serious consequences for the individual in Indian society. Moreover, since one's identity is closely tied to one's family membership and, in turn, *jati* membership, the individual's deviance stigmatizes other family members as well. Not only could the offender suffer the consequences of his or her deviance as such, but others in the family could suffer also. Indeed, in a society where Social Security is nonexistent, pension programs are only beginning to appear and are applicable to only small segments of the society, and most inhabitants live economically marginal lives, the life future of parents is tied to that of their children in much the same way that the economic fate of children was earlier dependent on that of their parents. Both, in turn, are advanced or reduced by their membership in, and status within, the *jati*. In such a system, the consequences of deviance could be profound.

Of equal importance is the central place family/kin (*jati*) relations play in the everyday interactions of Indian youths. In contrast to Western societies, wherein juveniles spend considerable time with one another and apart from the view or control of interested adults, the interpersonal relationships of Indians center primarily around family and kin, especially outside the school environment. Therefore, in light of differential association theory, the closeness of family relationships and the significance they have for the individual reduce the likelihood that young people in India will associate with delinquent peers or, if so, acquire from them delinquent skills, orientations, and attitudes. Nor are they likely to have much opportunity to pursue acts relating to whatever such associations they form.

To Western observers, the rather all-encompassing and confining control that family/kin relationships produce in India would seem oppressive. Indeed, in many ways they are, for they demand a degree of conformity, obedience to elders, and limitation on self-expression that American and Western European youth would find extreme at best. On the other hand, membership (and involvement) in the wider family-*jati* structure of Indian society offers Indian young people a kind of self-identity, security, and set of interpersonal relationships that American and Western European youths might very well envy. Indian juveniles may engage in the mischieflike behavior children everywhere seem to commit. But the major characteristic of those who come to the attention of officials and who wind up in juvenile and special homes is that they lack the bonds of family and kin or are youths for whom such bonds do not, for some reason, seem to function.

Whatever the case, the frequency and seriousness of delinquent behavior in India are comparatively low, and the use of official agencies of control is practically nonexistent because the socioeconomic system of family-*jati* serves as a positive mechanism of control (as envisioned in Hirschi's bond theory) and, at the same time, reduces the situations wherein youths would acquire or be able to carry out delinquent activity in any case (as argued in differential association theory). Oppressive as that system may seem, as it begins to break down and lose its bonding/controlling force in the century ahead, we can expect a greater need for, and increased reliance upon, official mechanisms of control to deal with India's needy and wayward youth (see Hartjen and Priyadarsini, 1984; Shelley, 1981).

CONCLUSION

Under the long influence of British Colonial rule, India developed a sizable body of law pertaining to juveniles and established systems of juvenile justice and corrections throughout most of the country. Following independence, a model national law was enacted, and more recently a national uniform code of juvenile justice binding on all states and regions of the country has been put into place. Nevertheless, relatively few juveniles experience, or are subjected to, formal agencies of control in India, so that, to a considerable extent today, needy and delinquent youths are handled by informal, extralegal mechanisms of control.

To some extent, quasi-official bodies called *Panchyats* administer juvenile justice in villages and urban communities. But the family (kin network) and, in a broader respect, the *jati* in which families are embedded is the primary vehicle of social control in India. This control is exercised in basically two ways. On one hand, the family-*jati* is the principal source of one's identity, social status, economic well-being, and life prospects. As such, it provides a strong institution for social bonding and, consequently, delinquency control. On the other hand, the family and the network of kin relationships it includes provide the most immediate and significant system of interpersonal relationships for Indian youth. Thus, opportunities (or even a need) to associate with delinquent peers are both reduced and impeded. Consequently, the conditions wherein individuals associate with, and acquire, delinquent behaviors and orientations are reduced.

Undoubtedly, the constraint this social arrangement imposes on young people can be described as oppressive (Hartjen and Kethineni, 1993). But, then, the alternative of police and courts seems somehow no more desirable. The winds of change in Indian society, while offering many prospects for the future, also promise to produce an increasing formalization of juvenile justice in the decades ahead. Whether India's youth will be better served as a consequence remains to be seen.

REFERENCES

Bayley, David H. *Police and Political Development in India.* Princeton, NJ: Princeton University Press, 1969.

Caldwell, John C., P. H. Reddy, and Pat Caldwell. "The Determinants of Family Structure in Rural South India." *Journal of Marriage and the Family* (February 1984): 215–229.

Central Bureau of Correctional Services. *Juvenile Delinquency: A Challenge.* New Delhi: Department of Social Welfare, Government of India, 1970.

The Children's Act, 1960. New Delhi: Delhi Law House, 1981.

Federal Bureau of Investigation. *Crime in the United States 1988.* Washington, DC: U.S. Government Printing Office, 1989.

Gore, M. S. *Urbanization and Family Change.* Bombay: Popular Prakashan, 1968.

Hartjen, Clayton A., and S. Priyadarsini. *Delinquency in India: A Comparative Analysis.* New Brunswick, NJ: Rutgers University Press, 1984.

Hartjen, Clayton A., and Sesha Kethineni. "Culture, Gender and Delinquency: A Study of Youths in the United States and India." *Women and Criminal Justice* 5 (1993): 37–70.

The Juvenile Justice Act, 1986. New Delhi: Gazette of India Extraordinary, 1986.

Karve, Irawati. *Kinship Organization in India.* New York: Asia, 1986.

Kumari, Ved. "Constitutionality of Sex-Based Definition of 'Juvenile' under the Juvenile Justice Act, 1986." *Delhi Law Review* 13 (1991):95–108.

Lannoy, Richard. *The Speaking Tree: A Study of Indian Culture and Society.* New York: Oxford University Press, 1971.

Misra, L. A., and V. S. Agnihatri. "The Community Practices of Informal Social Controls." *Indian Journal of Criminology* 13 (1985):96–102.

Mitra, N. L. *Juvenile Delinquency and Indian Justice System.* New Delhi: Deep and Deep, 1988.

Natt, B., and P. C. Malik. *Law and Material on the Code of Criminal Procedure.* Lucknow: Eastern Book, 1973.

Platt, Anthony. *The Child Savers.* Chicago: University of Chicago Press, 1969.

Ramu, G. N. *Family and Caste in Urban India: A Case Study.* New Delhi: Vikas Publishing House, Pvt. Ltd., 1977.

Ranchhoddas, R., and D. K. Thakore. *Law and Crime,* 18th ed. Bombay: Bombay Law Reporter Office, 1953.

Sanders, Wiley. *Juvenile Offenders for a Thousand Years.* Chapel Hill: University of North Carolina Press, 1970.

Shane, Paul G. *Police & People: A Comparison of Five Countries.* St. Louis: C. V. Mosby, 1980.

Shelley, Louise I. *Crime and Modernization: The Impact of Industrialization and Urbanization on Crime.* Carbondale and Edwardsville: Southern Illinois University Press, 1981.

Singh, Hira. "Juvenile Justice Act, 1986." *Social Defense* 23 (1987):1–3.

Statistical Abstract of India 1989. New Delhi: Central Statistical Organization, Ministry of Planning, Government of India, 1989.

Varshney, Anup Kumar. "Juvenile Justice." *Social Defense* 96 (1989):27–30.

APPENDIX: LIST OF AGENCIES DEALING WITH DELINQUENCY IN INDIA

National

National Institute of Social Defense
Ministry of Social Welfare
West Blk. 1 Wing
7 R.K. Puram
New Delhi 110066

Youth Services Division
Ministry of Human Resources Development
Shastri Bhowan
New Delhi 110001

Department of Justice
Ministry of Home Affairs
North Blk.
New Delhi 110001

National Institute of Criminology and Forensic Sciences
Section 3
Main Outer Ring Road
Rohini
New Delhi 110085

Central Vigilance Commissioner
Rm. 3
Jaisaimes Hs.
New Delhi 110011

Social Defence & Child Welfare Wing
Ministry of Welfare
6th floor A Wing
Shastri Bhowan
New Delhi 110066

Central Bureau of Correctional Services
Ministry of Welfare
New Delhi 110022

New Delhi

Directorate of Vigilance, New Delhi
69 B
Old Sectt
New Delhi 110054

Tamil Nadu State

Deputy Director of Approved Schools and Vigilance Services
Tamil Nadu
4 Jagajieevan Ram Street
Shenoy Nagar, Madras 625020

Juvenile Guidance Bureau
153 Purasawalkam High Road
Madras 600100

12

JAPAN

Ichiro Tanioka and Hiroko Goto

HISTORY

Pre–World War II (Juvenile Law, 1922)

The current juvenile justice system in Japan dates from post–World War II. Up to that time, the law in effect was the Juvenile Law of 1922, which had been heavily influenced by the juvenile courts of the United States, and the juvenile justice system of several European countries. The main features of the 1922 Juvenile Law were as follows:

1. The law applied to minors under the age of 18, despite the fact that civil law defined an adult as anyone over the age of 20. If a subject of 18 years committed a criminal act, she or he was put into the adult, criminal justice system rather than the juvenile justice system.

2. The convicted juvenile was subjected to protective disposition, never to a more severe (criminal) punishment. The protective disposition commonly in use before the 1922 law was detention in (juvenile) institutions. In addition to detention at the juvenile institutions and facilities, the 1922 law brought variations of reprimand, including admonition, special admonition by the heads of institutions, submission of oath, and handing over to parents.

3. The Juvenile Adjudication Office was established as the body responsible for judging and issuing the appropriate protective disposition. Before 1922, protective disposition had been grouped along with administrative disposition under the Ministry of Home Affairs. Thus, there had been no specific judicial organization dealing exclusively with juvenile delinquents. The Juvenile Adjudication Office was situated under the Ministry of Justice, shifting juvenile affairs away from the Ministry of Home Affairs.

It was, therefore, regarded as a quasi-judicial organization, and a judge was placed in charge of dispensing the protective disposition.

4. Personalized, case-by-case treatment was a goal of the new law, codified as the "principle of protection." Under this condition, a "personality test" would be conducted on each subject.

5. The prosecutor in charge of the juvenile case was authorized to decide whether the case should be referred to the jurisdiction of the adult criminal court or judged within the juvenile court. If not passed over to the criminal court, the case would then be decided by the Juvenile Adjudication Office. A large percentage of the juvenile subjects were referred to the adult court, as it was a basic rule of decision of the prosecutors that all juveniles of the age of 14 and up were to be punished unless there were special circumstances that suggested otherwise. Though then judged within the adult court systems, juveniles generally received far more lenient punishment than adults.

Although the Juvenile Law of 1922 applied to the entire nation, during its early years there were only two Juvenile Adjudication Offices in the country, located in Tokyo and Osaka. Finally, in 1942, the government decided to expand the offices throughout Japan; but due to the complications of the war, those offices were unable to function as the lawmakers had aimed.

Post–World War II (Juvenile Law, 1948)

In accordance with the new constitution drawn up after the defeat in the war, the entire Japanese system of government, including the criminal justice laws and procedures, underwent redesign and alteration. The Code of Criminal Procedure was renewed, guaranteeing constitutional human rights, including due process under the law. The new juvenile justice laws were established within this context in 1948.

The military government's General Head-Quarters (GHQ) officer in charge of juvenile affairs questioned the custom of deciding the protective disposition as an administrative order. This custom was in conflict with the new Code of Criminal Procedure and the constitution. In 1948, he drafted the new juvenile justice system laws based on the American juvenile court system. The following are the main differences between the new law of 1948 and the earlier law of 1922:

1. The subjects were divided into three subgroups, depending on the factors of age and conduct. The first and primary group consists of "juvenile offenders" between the ages of 14 and 20 who have committed one or more delinquent or criminal acts. As mentioned before, the former law of 1922 regarded anyone age 18 or higher as an adult, which did not agree with the civil law as written at the time. The new law of 1948 removed this irregularity.

   The second subgroup, the "child offenders," comprises those who have committed delinquent or criminal acts but are aged 14 years or younger. Punishment and treatment of these first two groups differed, as shall be detailed later in this chapter. In addition to these first two groups, a third, the "predelinquent juveniles," was defined. This group targeted those juveniles aged 20 and younger who had not yet committed a criminal or delinquent act but who were deemed likely to and, therefore, were in need of treatment. As these juveniles had not committed a criminal act, treatment was a very sensitive area and was handled so that their human rights should not be violated. The new law of 1948 spelled out the definite typology of conduct regarded as "predelinquent" in nature.

In contrast, in the earlier law of 1922 the concept of the "predelinquent" child had been ambiguous, a gray, ill-defined area regarded as dangerous territory by the prosecutors.

2. Under the law of 1922, protective disposition took many forms. The new law of 1948, in contrast, limited it to three options: "probation," "commitment to a juvenile training school," and "commitment to a child education and training home." In addition to these three primary options, there was also treatment under the Child Welfare Law, namely, "commitment to a home for dependent children."

3. The decision of which of the preceding protective disposition options to apply to each case was placed in the hands of the Family Court, which is on a judicial level with the district courts. Thus, as of 1948, "juvenile justice" was for the first time in Japan's history codified as an integral part of the entire judicial system.

4. The power held by the prosecutor under the law of 1922 was severely constricted by the new law. Under the earlier law, this individual had held the preemptive right to dispose of a juvenile offender's case. The new law established the Family Court as the primary decision maker in the disposition of the juvenile offenders.

5. Case investigators, the family court probation officers, were to be assigned by the Family Court, and a new institution, the juvenile classification home, was established. These new developments allowed access to up-to-date psychological evaluations and counseling to determine the optimum handling of each case.

6. Under the new law, subjects could file a "complaint." In the earlier system under the law of 1922, complaints against the administrative disposition were not permitted, as the disposition was not officially "judicial" in nature.

When viewed as a whole, the reforms and reorganization of the juvenile justice system under the new law of 1948 profoundly liberalized the system in favor of the offenders. Later in this chapter, the Juvenile Law of 1948 will be discussed in fuller detail.

Recent Movements toward Further Reform of Juvenile Law

Forty-five years or more have passed since the 1948 law was put into effect. Since then the text of the law has remained virtually as it was originally written. However, during this same span of time, nearly every aspect of the text and articles of the law has come into question, and the necessity for reform has been strenuously argued. We would like to summarize here three important aspects of these arguments.

First, the target age of "less than 20 years old" (in contrast with the law of 1922, which defined juveniles as "less than 18 years old") has come under attack. The critics have grown louder as the delinquent behavior of 18- and 19-year-olds has grown more serious, and events have grown more numerous, most especially during the last 30 years. In 1970, the minister of justice proposed the "Outline of Juvenile Law Reform," in which those aged 18 or 19 would be placed in a category called "youth." Youths would then be processed as adult criminals, dependent on the severity of the crime. For the protection of youths, they were to have the choice of either the adult criminal justice process or protective disposition. In 1977, a progress report of the "Outline of Juvenile Law Reform" was submitted to the government, stating, in reference to the age question, that youth (18 or older) be treated individually and with care. At the time of the writing of this chapter there has yet been no conclusive decision on this issue.

The second point at issue is the due process of law. As stated earlier, the 1948 law borrowed much from the American juvenile justice system, which was heavily based on the *parens patriae* doctrine. Consequently, there may have been occasions when juveniles were processed without guarantee of strict due process of law. The movement in the United States in the 1960s toward a model of strict due process was highly influential in Japan. When the Kent (*Kent v. United States,* 383 U.S. 541, 1966) and the Gault (*In re Gault,* 387 U.S. 1, 1967) cases were introduced, stressing the protection of juvenile rights, many Japanese scholars and law practitioners surfaced, expressing their own strong opinions on this subject. The aforementioned progress report of 1977 stressed, as well, the need for consideration that the right to counsel and other rights accorded to adult criminal defendants be bestowed on juvenile offenders. This issue has not been decided conclusively and is still being argued.

The third point at issue is the personalization of the content of protective disposition. As stated before, only three forms of treatment are approved under the current protective disposition. To resocialize the juveniles under treatment more quickly, it is viewed as necessary to adapt treatment appropriate to the individual juveniles. Although the law has not been reformed on this issue, in reality, adjustment of treatment is already in effect, because of the regulatory order by the Ministry of Justice. For example, traffic incidents are processed differently from other delinquent incidents.

PRINCIPLES OF THE JUVENILE LAW

The first article of the juvenile law states: "The object of this Law is, with the aim of the sound upbringing of juveniles, to carry out the protective dispositions relating to the character correction and environmental adjustment of delinquent juveniles." This purposeful statement, in support of the sound upbringing of juveniles, stresses that the law (or nation) shall undertake to support delinquent juveniles to the end that they may live lawfully as members of society in the future. That is, the nation shall undertake to supplant the role of the juvenile's parents, should the parents prove incapable of correcting their child's behavior. As stated before, the current Japanese juvenile law is based on the *parens patriae* doctrine exported from the United States, which considers the juvenile in need of protection. Under this point of view, limited autonomy of the juvenile is acceptable as the parents/nation bear the role of advising and rearing the juvenile. Thus, through the concept of paternalism, the use of forcible disposition of juveniles is justified.

Of the target groups of the juvenile law, the law focuses primarily on those juveniles older than 14 years who have committed a crime and those who are predelinquent. The "child offenders" are usually processed through the Child Welfare Law. Consequently, the juvenile law deals with juveniles who have infringed on another's rights; the direct result is that the juvenile law closely reflects the criminal justice system. Under this state of affairs, the "harm principle" would be more applicable than the paternalistic principle. Thus, due process must be assured, as the current practice of forcible disposition by the nation can be construed as punishment.

Taken as a whole, the foundation of the Japanese juvenile justice system is the principle of paternalistic responsibility. However, due process rights of the children and parents are also emphasized.

OUTLINE OF THE FORMAL SYSTEM

Figure 12.1 shows the flow model of the juvenile justice system in Japan. This system is applicable to those juveniles who have committed a crime (termed "juvenile offenders"), those who have violated the criminal code but are less than 14 years old ("child offenders"), and those who are deemed likely to violate the law/criminal code in the near future as indicated by their conduct, personality, and living environment ("predelinquent juveniles") (Article 3 of Juvenile Law). The last group, the predelinquent juveniles, would be further subdivided into two groups by age category: those less than 14 and those 14 years or older. The means by which each of these four groups is processed shall be explained individually.

The police, after investigation of the case, should refer the juvenile offenders to either the Family Court, if the violation is trivial or of lesser severity, where the maximum penalty for conduct is a fine or less, or to the public prosecutor, if the violation is of greater severity. It should be noted, however, that upon receipt of the juvenile's file, the public prosecutor is required to pass it to the Family Court. This is obligatory, as the only body with authority to decide the outcome of a juvenile case is the Family Court, not the prosecutor or the police. The prosecutor, therefore, does not carry the authority to decide the fate of the case, whether a suit should be filed or whether it should be dropped entirely.

The policeman or citizen who encounters a child offender or a predelinquent child (under 14 years old) should inform either the Child Guidance Center or

Figure 12.1
Flow Chart of Treatment Proceedings for Juvenile Offenders and Delinquents

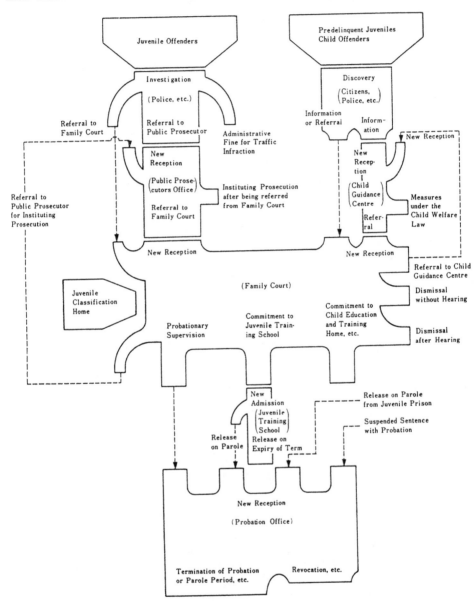

Source: Research and Training Institute, Ministry of Justice. 1993. *Summary of the White Paper on Crime*, p. 136.

prefecture Child Welfare Station of the incident. Should the head of the Child Guidance Center or the governor of the prefecture refer the incident to the Family Court, then the justice procedure may be initiated. In absence of such a referral, the Child Welfare Law bears the authority of the final decision.

In the case where a predelinquent juvenile aged 14 or more is discovered by someone (usually a policeman), the person would then refer the incident directly to the Family Court. Should the predelinquent juvenile be in need of psychiatric treatment or special care, she or he can then be referred to the Child Guidance Center.[1]

Regardless of which of these four processes is observed, the Family Court handles each subject in the same manner as if he or she had been referred directly to the court. The only exception occurs when the juvenile offender has been referred after arrest and detention, in which case there are certain additional procedures.

The Family Court, after receipt of the referral, commences an investigation into the juvenile's case. A Family Court probation officer is assigned to research the life history, home environment, and other aspects of the subject's personal background. Should the Family Court probation officer deem it necessary to obtain further information as to the subject's personality or psychological state, it would be proposed that the subject be sent to the juvenile classification home for testing. The decision whether or not to further test the juvenile is known as the order of "measures for case and custody" and must be decided by a judge of the court.

Upon conclusion of the investigation, the information is reviewed by the judge, who decides whether a Family Court hearing should commence, or if the juvenile should be referred to the Child Guidance Center. Should the judge decide against a hearing, the case is declared "dismissal without hearing." On the other hand, should the judge decide to open a hearing on the case, one of two next steps will be possible. One is a "dismissal after hearing," and the other is to impose a "protective disposition."[2] The protective disposition can be either "probationary supervision" or "commitment to a certain institutional facility for treatment."[3] Yet, as a matter of fact, institutional treatment is rare, occurring in fewer than 10 percent of all the protective dispositions. After the Family Court investigation of the juvenile, the cases for which treatment under the Child Welfare Law are deemed more appropriate would be sent to the head of the Child Guidance Center.

The Family Court may also decide, in exceptional cases, that a referral to the public prosecutor for instituting the process of prosecution may be optional for those juveniles whose committed act is more suited to criminal penalty and who are 16 years of age or older. The resulting process reflects the adult criminal system, with the exception that the penalty accorded may be of lesser severity compared to that of adults (e.g., there is no application of the death penalty for anyone under 18 years of age) or the specific treatment would differ from that of adults (e.g., a juvenile would be incarcerated in a separate juvenile jail, apart from the adult institution). These differences are in accordance with the principles of the juvenile law.

THE ROLE AND FUNCTION OF EACH AUTHORITY WITHIN THE JUVENILE JUSTICE SYSTEM

The Police

Generally, juvenile offenders encounter the police when they are being apprehended after committing a crime or act of delinquency, similar to adult offenders. Police are involved both in trying to prevent juvenile delinquency from occurring and in investigating a crime after its enactment. As such, their role is substantial with regard to juvenile offenders. The Juvenile Law was written specifically for the juvenile offenders, but in the areas where it lacks specific instructions, such as extreme criminal activity, the Code of Criminal Procedure is adapted as applicable to the juvenile cases (Article 40 in the Juvenile Law of 1948).

The police are required to refer juvenile cases to the Family Court directly after completion of investigation in the cases where the police believe the suspected juvenile committed a crime punishable by a fine or lesser penalty (Article 41 in the Juvenile Law of 1948). In the cases where the crime committed demands the maximum punishment, as according to Article 246 of the Code of Criminal Procedure, the cases are referred first to the prosecutor. A juvenile case must be referred either to the Family Court or to the prosecutor, irrespective of the gravity of the crime or the possibility of recidivism. This is the principle that all cases must eventually pass through the Family Court. However, due to the shortage of human and institutional resources, an exception to this principle has been authorized: summary referral. When a case is clearly of a trivial nature, with no possibility of recidivism, and penalty or productive measures deemed unnecessary, the police may authorize a summary referral.[4] This measure is carried out once a month, and often the Family Court adjudicates the dismissal without hearing.

If at all possible, police should avoid officially arresting the juvenile suspect, and, when unavoidable, the police officer should carefully consider the time and manner of the arrest.[5]

Child offenders and predelinquent juveniles aged less than 14 years must in all cases be referred to the Child Guidance Center or to the head of the prefecture's Child Welfare Station. The predelinquent juveniles 14 years of age or older must be referred to the Family Court.

The police occupy the first step of the juvenile justice system, being the body that is first notified of a juvenile's delinquent or criminal conduct and that then apprehends the juvenile and processes the case as appropriate. The police also necessarily participate as investigators of a juvenile case.

Prosecutor

The prosecutor must refer the suspected juveniles to the Family Court should it be determined that the committed crime is punishable by more than a fine (Article 42 of the Juvenile Law). This article specifically limits the principle of discretionary prosecution in suspected juveniles' cases. In the case of a suspected adult, the Code of Criminal Procedure provides: "In case it is unnecessary to prosecute according to the character, age and environment of an offender, the weight and conditions of an offense as well as the circumstances after the offense, the public prosecution may not be instituted." This is the principle of discretionary prosecution, and in adult criminal cases the prosecutor has broad discretion to public prosecution.

However, it is provided that should the Family Court adjudicate that a juvenile's case should be considered for a criminal penalty, it may transfer the juvenile offender case back to the prosecutor, who must then prosecute the case. Thus, the authority to decide whether to prosecute rests with the Family Court and not the prosecutor, and by extension the principle of discretionary prosecution is also limited. Yet, there are certain conditions under which the prosecutor may decide not to prosecute. This may occur when a part of the transferred case bears insufficient suspicion of crime to sustain public prosecution or when new facts related to the circumstances of the crime are revealed or uncovered by the prosecutor (Article 45, item 5 of the Juvenile Law).

In reference to a request of detention, the law states that the "prosecutor shall not request a judge to detain the suspected juvenile unless unavoidable circumstances exist." In lieu of a request of detention, the prosecutor may request a protective detention exacting measures for care and custody of the juvenile. This aspect of the law is realized through the juvenile's detention in a juvenile classification home. This point will be elaborated later in this chapter.

As discussed before, the participation of the prosecutor in the juvenile justice system is clearly delineated and consequently limited.

The Child Welfare Law

The Child Welfare Law was drafted with the aim of promoting the healthy birth and upbringing of each citizen in both mind and body.

The Family Court is the main authority in the treatment of juvenile offenders and predelinquents aged 14 years or older. Child offenders and predelinquents are handled under the stipulations of the Child Welfare Law. Therefore, when such cases arise, the police first inform the Child Guidance Center. The Child Guidance Center then bears the authority to decide whether further judicial treatment is necessary, at which point they then refer the case to the Family Court. Should the results of a case investigation point toward taking measures under the Child Welfare Law, the Family Court then refers the case to the authorities under the law (Article 18 of the Juvenile Law).

As described before, the Juvenile Law and the Child Welfare Law are closely interrelated. This is so especially in the cases of juveniles younger than 14 years, the specified age limit of criminal responsibility. The measures under the Child Welfare Law take precedence after the juvenile is diverted from the juvenile justice system.

The Family Court

The Family Court is an independent body comprising the same number of persons as the District Court of the present criminal justice system. The Family Court as defined in 1949 brought together two separate bodies: the executive institution established in 1922, the Juvenile Court; and the judicial institution established in 1927, the Domestic Relations Court. The Family Court is the primary institution of the juvenile justice system.

At this point, we would like to discuss the role of the Family Court probation officers. This position is unique to the Family Court, not being applicable to the adult judicial system. Probation officers are trained in the disciplines of the human sciences, psychology, pedagogy, and sociology. It is their role to investigate the character of the juvenile's delinquency, determine the necessity of protection (social investigation), and provide tentative probation by the Family Court.

The investigation of the juvenile's conduct and history occurs prior to a hearing. This investigation is divided into two parts: a social investigation conducted by the Family Court probation officers and a legal investigation conducted by the judges. A social investigation must be carried out on each case received by the Family Court: the principle of all investigation. Through the tools of hearing and disposition, the investigation aims to grasp an understanding of the juvenile's "relations with family and parents, circumstances, history, level and situation of education, process of delinquency, character and conduct, case background, mental and physical conditions, and so forth" (Juvenile Hearing Rules, Article 11-1). The factual results of the investigation, along with the investigating officer's opinion, are then submitted to a judge.

Tentative supervision is an intermediate measure pending the decision on supervision of a juvenile's behavior, if any, and its type. This measure reinforces the investigation and places the juvenile under temporary probation.

Moreover, the officer(s) in charge of the case is required to attend the case hearing and to give proper advice to the delinquent based on the confidences shared during the investigation.

The Juvenile Classification Home

The juvenile classification home is the place to which the juvenile is sent from the Family Court to be detained for measures of care and custody and where the officers shall "conduct the classification of the juvenile's nature based on the medicine, psychology, pedagogy, sociology and other technical knowledge that contribute to his/her investigation and hearing in the Family Court, and to the execution of the protective disposition'' (Article 16 of the Reformatory Law).

Measures for care and custody may be exacted if the hearing conditions are satisfactory, a probability of hearing exists, delinquency is highly suspected, and/or it is necessary to the investigation and future hearing that the juvenile be in custody. The period usually set for measure of care and custody is two weeks, with a single renewal permitted, allowing for a maximum detention in custody of four weeks.

The conditions because of which care and custody were recommended must be reported to the Family Court, along with the social investigation report and the opinion of the officers. A judge will seek proper treatment and judgment with reference to this report and opinion.

The Attendant

The attendant assists the juveniles and represents their interests. The role of the attendant is twofold. On one hand, she or he acts as defense counsel for the juvenile, guaranteeing the youth's rights before the judge and speaking for the subject. The other aspect of the attendant's role is to aid the Family Court by clarifying and explaining the judicial procedure and the meaning of the disposition to the juvenile. These roles originate from the hearing system. The Family Court hearing is an inquisitorial system, not an adversarial system.

The attendant is appointed by the juvenile and his or her parents. The juvenile justice system does not provide a public attendant, in direct contrast to the criminal justice system's practice of appointing a public defender. Should the attendant not be a lawyer, she or he should consult with, and receive permission from, the Family Court to aid the client. Despite the recognized importance of the attendant's role in the juvenile judicial process, it is not a common practice to enlist one.

It has been put forward that a public attendant system reflecting the public defender system of the adult criminal court should be introduced to further promote fair delinquent fact-finding in the juvenile cases.

THE HEARING

The hearing is the most important aspect of the juvenile justice system. Based on findings from the investigation report, a judge will determine whether it is appropriate to conduct a hearing (Article 21 of the Juvenile Law).

The hearing is not open to the public (Article 22, Section 2 of the Juvenile Law). During the hearing, personal details bearing on the juvenile's circumstances and family history are likely to be revealed to aid the judge's decision as to whether further protection or probation is necessary. To promote frank communication during the hearing, confidentiality is assured. The Japanese constitution provides that in the case of a trial within the adversary system, the court proceedings must be open to the public. As this is not the case in the juvenile hearing, the closure of the court is not unconstitutional.

Each hearing is rendered individually in support of the "sound upbringing of juveniles," adjusting hearing procedure and disposition decisions on a case-by-case basis. It is also required that the juvenile appear in court for the hearing to provide direct contact with the judging body. The presence of parents, guardians, or attendant is strongly advised to protect the juvenile's rights, but it is not required by law.

Article 22, Section 1 of the Juvenile Law provides: "The hearing must be conducted in a friendly manner and with kind consideration." This means that it is imperative that the hearing be conducted in an educational and protective manner, stressing the juvenile's comprehension of the proceedings, with the use of words and language appropriate to the juvenile's age and level of education. It also means that it is necessary to obtain the juvenile's consent and reliance through speaking fully and clearly.

The primary goal of the hearing is to find and establish the delinquent facts and parameters.[6] However, the procedure is not strictly formalized, and the juvenile law stresses only that in its search, the hearing be "friendly with kind consideration." This informality is based on the concept of *parens patriae,* which emphasizes the protective role of the system. Thus, the inquisitorial and informal procedure is justified. In the past two decades, it has been posited that the protective measures are a disadvantage—promoting a possible violation of the juvenile's rights—and that due process of law should be required in the hearing. It has furthermore entered the current debate that the guarantee of due process of law would align more with the philosophy of juvenile protection under which the juvenile law was drafted.[7] Accordingly, notice of one's right to remain silent and certain rules of evidence (e.g., involuntary confession is not to be considered evidence) should be guaranteed. However, certain aspects of due process conform to the adversary system of the adult court system, and, therefore, their scope is limited in the present inquisitorial system of the juvenile law.

After completion to the satisfaction of the court of the delinquent fact-finding process, the necessity of protection of the juvenile is considered. In this aspect of the hearing, the investigation's classification report and the officer's opinion weigh heavily on the eventual disposition. With these two factors in mind, the final disposition is decided.

INFORMAL PRACTICES

In Japan, once a case is referred to the juvenile justice system, it is very difficult to divert it informally. Therefore, we would like to mention the informal practices that may occur before or just after entrance into the juvenile justice system.

Before the Juvenile Justice System

As an example, take a case where a juvenile shoplifts in a bookstore. When the shopkeeper discovers him or her, the shopkeeper may verbally reprimand and caution the juvenile, report the conduct to the police, or inform the juvenile's schoolteacher or parents. Schools play an important role in preventing juvenile delinquency in Japan. Upon being informed of the delinquent case, the school will take sanctions against the delinquent. Schools take an interest in student activity outside school. Teachers and parents often patrol the neighborhood. It is the tradition in Japan that students wear school uniforms; this has the added benefit of immediately alerting the observing adult to which school a student is enrolled (Tanioka and Glaser, 1991).

Furthermore, a school may have rules concerning a student's behavior outside school. Some high schools have prohibited students from obtaining a motorcycle or driver's license during their school years, even though local traffic law allows citizens to apply for a license after the age of 16 or 18 years.

Students must obey national laws and their own school rules; this twofold curb on students' conduct may contribute to a lessening of their potential for delinquency.

After Entering the Juvenile Justice System

The juvenile law requests that all cases of juvenile delinquency be referred to the Family Court. Nevertheless, in reality some cases never go beyond the confines of the local police stations. Such delinquent conduct as smoking, drinking, and running away from home (conduct by which no other individual or property is injured or damaged) is handled ably by the police without need to refer to the higher level of the Family Court. The police accept their responsibility to protect and guide such delinquents when they come within their sphere; when necessary, the police officer will inform the juvenile's parents or school to enlist their support in observing and correcting the juvenile's behavior.

In 1990, a total of 442,303 juveniles were reported in the official statistics, which is a little less than the year before. It is, however, estimated from self-reported surveys that about 16 times more delinquent acts are committed by high school students (Tanioka and Glaser, 1991). Estimating that not-referred cases by the police are about one-third, roughly speaking, then 20 times more cases, or 8.8 million, might have been committed by juveniles in 1990.

SUMMARY AND CONCLUSION

The particular characteristics of the Japanese juvenile justice system may be summarized as follows:

1. The founding principle of the Japanese juvenile law is to aid in the "sound upbringing of juveniles" through the premise of protection and education.

2. The system is concerned both with delinquents and predelinquents equally, as it emphasizes crime prevention as well as behavior correction.

3. The prosecutor's authority is restricted, and the prosecutor does not attend the hearing.

4. Every juvenile offense case is referred to the Family Court, which alone carries the power of decision whether to prosecute.

5. A specially trained Family Court probation officer carries out a social investigation and reports on each case before it appears in court.

6. The hearing procedure is based on the inquisitorial system. Under these terms, full due process of law is not guaranteed.

7. At every stage of justice process there is a close reliance on national child welfare measures.

The current major controversy surrounding the juvenile justice system is how to go about establishing a guarantee of due process of law. The year 1994 promised to bring the ratification of the Convention on the Rights of the Child, which could bring further weight to bear on the side of changing the system to guarantee due process. In any case, the subject is sure to be a major topic of discussion during the process of ratification. The juvenile justice system was formed, and must continue to be based, on a balance of protection of the juvenile and respect for the juvenile's autonomy and civil rights.

NOTES

1. A Child Guidance Center is an option under the Child Welfare Law. It gives advice to children and their family to solve their domestic problems. If it is necessary, it refers children to child welfare institutions or treats them with child welfare measures.

2. In 1991, the dismissal without hearing was 72.0 percent, and the dismissal after hearing was 17.0 percent, of the number of juveniles adjudicated by Family Courts. (*White Paper on Crime*:366).

3. The "institutions" in Japan are juvenile training school, child education and training home, or home for dependent children.

4. Article 211 in the Code of Conduct on Crime Investigation.

5. Article 205 in the Code of Conduct on Crime Investigation.

6. "Delinquent facts and parameters" include not only criminal acts but also child offense and predelinquent facts.

7. Supreme Court decisions have piled up. See, for example, the "Nagareyama" case, 158 Kasaigeppo 36, 1983.

REFERENCES AND SUGGESTED READINGS

Official Reports

Japanese Only

General Secretariat, Supreme Court. *Annual Report of Judicial Statistics.* Tokyo: Okurasho Printing Office, 1993.
Ministry of Justice. *Annual Report of Statistics on Correction.* Tokyo: Okurasho Printing Office, 1993.
———. *Annual Report of Statistics on Prosecution.* Tokyo: Okurasho Printing Office, 1993.
———. *Annual Report of Statistics on Rehabilitation.* Tokyo: Okurasho Printing Office, 1993.
National Police Agency. *Criminal Statistics.* Tokyo: Okurasho Printing Office, 1993.
———. *White Paper on Police.* Tokyo: Okurasho Printing Office, 1993.
Prime Minister's Office. *White Paper on Youth.* Tokyo: Okurasho Printing Office, 1993.
Research and Training Institute, Ministry of Justice. *White Paper on Crime.* Tokyo: Okurasho Printing Office, 1993.

Available in English

———. *Summary of the White Paper on Crime.* Tokyo: Okurasho Printing Office, 1993.

Books

Dando, Shigemitsu, and Morita, Souichi. 1984. *Shinpan Shonenho,* 2d ed. Tokyo: Yuhikaku.
Hiraba, Yasuharu. *Shonenho (Shinpan).* Tokyo: Yuhikaku.
Hirano, Ryuichi, ed. 1982, 1983, 1985, 1987. *Shonenhogo 1,2,3,4,* Tokyo: Taisei-Shuppansya.
Seki, Chikara. 1987. *Hikoshonen wa Kouatukawareru.* Tokyo: Yushido, 1987.
Tamiya, Hiroshi, ed. *Shonenho (Jobun Kaisetsu).* Tokyo: Yuhikaku, 1986.
Tanioka, Ichiro, and Daniel Glaser. "School Uniforms, Routine Activities, and the Social Control of Delinquency in Japan." *Youth and Society* 23 (1991):50–75.

APPENDIX: KEY AGENCIES

Ministry of Justice
1-1-1 Kasumigaseki Chiyoda-ku, Tokyo 100 Japan
Telephone: (03) 3580-4111

Supreme Court
4-2 Hayabusachou Chiyoda-ku, Tokyo 102 Japan
Telephone: (03) 3264-8111

National Police Agency
2-1-2 Kasumigaseki Chiyoda-ku, Tokyo 100 Japan
Telephone: (03) 3581-0141

13

MEXICO

Ana Josefina Alvarez
Translated by Ivonne Vinay

INTRODUCTION

As a federal republic, Mexico has a variety of judicial instruments concerning juvenile justice. Today, there are 32 different legislations, which correspond to the 31 states and the Federal District (Mexico City). The constitutional foundation for such legislation rests with Article 18 of the 1917 constitution, in force at present.

There are two major trends in justice for the minor in Mexico. This chapter is mainly devoted to discussing the characteristics and differences between those two trends.

Up to 1991, those laws that governed violations by minors had a tutelary character, were local, and belonged to the common court of equity. Yet, a new law regarding this issue was approved: Juvenile Treatment Law for the Federal District within the common court of equity and for the rest of the republic within the federal court of equity. This law was published in the *Federal Official Journal* on December 24, 1991. Such law transforms this situation and provides for its enforcement in the various states of the republic when violations are dealt with in the federal court of equity. At the same time, it grants competence to the juvenile local courts or counsels to hear the case in the jurisdiction where the act or omission was committed.

The new legislation has tried to adapt the Mexican penal justice system for the minor to that established in the articles belonging to such matters found in the Convention on Children's Rights adopted by the United Nations in New York on November 20, 1989. Through the senate, Mexico was one of the first 20 countries to ratify this agreement on July 31, 1990. The president promulgated the law on January 25, 1991; thus, it became a compulsory general rule.

Consequently, in less than a year, an attempt was made to adopt legislation that, at that moment, far from fulfilled the requirements established by the agreement. The new legislation has been adopted only in Mexico City and the state of Morelos.

HISTORY: TUTELARY ASSISTANCE LEGISLATION

Up to now, the legal foundations of the juvenile justice system were in the legislation that created the Juvenile Tutelary Counsel. This was adopted by the Federal District in September 1974 and served as a model for the legislation in the other states of the republic. At present, 30 states still enforce this kind of legislation, which has a fundamentally tutelary character and which implies important prosecution and guarantee limitations, as pointed out later.

The tutelary model replaced the old juvenile courts, which had existed in Mexico since 1929 (Azaola, 1990:52). The greatest improvement achieved with this legislation, at that time, was the definite separation of the juvenile system and imprisonment from the adult system.

The fundamental characteristic of the tutelary approach is that minors are considered not criminals, but offenders. An 18-year-old who commits an act included in the Penal Code is considered nonchargeable as long as, according to the tutelary legislation, there is no penal responsibility, because juveniles, due to their age, are not capable of understanding the penal law. Within this protectionist approach, judges are replaced by counselors, and a sentence is not issued, but instead security or protection measures are taken.

The Counsels generally consist of three people: an attorney, who presides during the prosecution, a doctor, and a professor specialized in juvenile offenders. The hearings are confidential, and the Counsel should refrain from following, insofar as possible, the formalities that characterize prosecution within the justice system for adults.

Despite the fact that the tutelary approach was created with the honest objective of protecting juveniles and submitting them to a less aggressive prosecution than that for adults, it has actually placed them in a situation of defenselessness and vulnerability, for it eliminates the most important constitutional guarantees of the penal process and certain fundamental individual rights.

Limitations of the Tutelary Assistance System

The following are roughly the main limitations in this juvenile justice system (Alvarez, 1990:17).

1. The tutelary system violates the principle of legality and deprives minors of the rights and guarantees that derive from Article 14 of the Mexican constitution, which states "no crime, no sentence without laws," for the juvenile can be confined in a treatment center as a "preventive" measure, without having performed any prohibited act ac-

cording to the penal law or any other rule. This is established in the legislation in Article 2, which points out that the Tutelary Counsel is used when the juvenile violates the penal law "or shows any other behavior which might lead to basically *presume* that he/she is inclined to hurting himself/herself, or a member of his/her family, or society, and consequently, justifies the Counsel's *preventive* action."

2. Another negative aspect of the tutelary legislation is stated in Article 61, which establishes an *undetermined duration* for the measures imposed by the Counsel. Thus, the security measures applied do not directly depend on juveniles' behavior but depend on their "social readaptation." Therefore, juveniles know when they will enter a treatment center but not when they will be released. This measure places the juvenile in a disadvantageous position as compared to the legislation for adults, which imposes fixed terms to the sentence. In Mexico, even in those cases where adults are not held criminally responsible, such as the mentally insane, the Penal Code of the Federal District states that "the treatment cannot surpass the maximum applicable sentence if the actor were to be criminally responsible."

3. The tutelary legislation also eliminates other important rights and guarantees, including the innocence principle and the right to be defended, for juveniles cannot enjoy the help of a counsel for the defense, nor can anybody else play this role, nor do they have the right to call witnesses or present evidence for the defense. Although they have the right to appeal a sentence, the only one who can invoke this right is the "promoter" responsible for each case, who is theoretically independent but who actually is a member of the counsel.

Likewise, the juvenile has no right to invoke the "absence of penal responsibility," which is an integral part of the law for adults. For instance, a juvenile is not allowed to declare innocence on the basis that the violation was committed as legitimate defense or due to necessity. This legislation does not discriminate among the different kinds of participation in criminal acts. That is, it does not consider whether the juvenile was the material actor or an accomplice; nor does it consider the possibility of others having influenced the juvenile's participation or having used him or her to achieve their criminal intentions (Bullen, 1989:10).

DECEMBER 1991 LEGISLATION AND THE PRESENT FORMAL SYSTEM

As stated before, with the new legislation for the Federal District adopted in 1991 for common matters and for the rest of the republic for federal matters, there is an attempt to remedy those situations just mentioned, yet, it is too soon to judge its actual application. It can also be expected that the other states of the republic will begin to adapt their local legislations to that of the Federal District, as usually happens in Mexico, but, for the time being, tutelary legislation still predominates.

Characteristics of the New Legislation

The fundamental objective of the new legislation is summarized in the first article: "The objective of this law is to rule the function of the State in protecting juvenile rights as well as the social adjustment of those whose conduct is typified within the federal laws and those of the Federal District in common courts, and in all the Republic in federal courts."

The most important improvement achieved with the new legislation is to totally banish the possibility of juveniles' being confined in a treatment center without their having violated the law and without having been prosecuted. The "danger" that characterizes the tutelary legislation is thus limited, although not completely, as Article 38 of the new legislation states that a biopsychosocial diagnosis shall be determined for juveniles at the time of the arrest, that is, before knowing whether they are responsible. This diagnosis can influence the decision to be taken, for the "dangerous" degree of the juvenile will be determined, regardless of the severity of the offense.

The main limitation still found in this legislation is that the new ruling body is the Juvenile Counsel, which is an *administrative* organ deconcentrated from the Department of State, like the Juvenile Tutelary Counsel of the former legislation. Therefore, Article 40, iii, of the United Nations Convention is not fulfilled. This article provides for the existence of independent and impartial courts that depend on the judicial system to hear the cases of juvenile offenders. As provided for within the new legislation (and the old one), the president of the Juvenile Counsel is appointed by the president of the republic as proposed by the Department of State (Article 10 of the 1991 law). All the officials who constitute the Juvenile Counsel, as well as those who act as district attorneys and act for their defense, are administrative authorities, not judiciary, and depend on the executive power.

Consequently, "at present, it is the executive power itself which chases and captures the juvenile, the one which gets the evidence to impute him/her with penal responsibility—the Commissioner—the one that prosecutes and decides on the penalty to be served in accordance with the juvenile law—the Unitarian Counsel—and lastly the same administrative organ which decides on the last action because the 'Superior Court of the Juvenile Counsel' is not part of the judicial power . . . nevertheless, its decisions are not appealable before any judicial authority" (Sánchez, 1993:6).

Elements of the Process

The procedure in Articles 36 to 72 establishes that when a juvenile is charged, the case must be immediately transferred to the administrative unit in charge of prevention and treatment, which depends on the Department of State, and turned over to the commissioner on duty, who will integrate the evidence in a 24-hour period, at most, and who will send the minor to the Unitarian Counselor who in 48 hours (which might be extended an additional 48 hours) (Article 36) must issue the initial resolution. As a whole, there is a 120-hour time period, during which juveniles could be arrested, before the decision to free them or continue with the prosecution is taken. To begin with, this seems excessive.

If the Unitarian Counselor decides the juvenile must be prosecuted (initial resolution), the instruction proceeding is opened, then a biopsychosocial diagnosis must be made, which will act as basis for the dictum issued by the Interdisciplinary Technical Committee. This stage will last 15 working days at most, during which the defense and the commissioner may offer the corresponding evidence in writing. The hearing will take place when these 15 days have elapsed and will unfold without interruption in a single day.

The final resolution must be issued within the next five working days, but the bodies of the Counsel may resolve—before they make the final resolution—to make or extend the time for any other probatory action. If the offense has been established, the juvenile will be sent to the internal treatment centers that also depend on the Department of State and that are established by means of the same law mentioned before in Articles 33, 34, 35, 117, and 118.

Article 119 states that outside treatment for the minor can last no more than a year, and internal treatment, or institutionalization, no more than five years.

The resolution established by the Unitarian Counsel could be appealed. Such being the case, it will be heard by the Superior Court of the Counsel, which should resolve the appeal in three to five days, depending on the kind of resolution that was appealed.

To sum up what is established in Article 7 of the legislation, the procedure before the juvenile counsel consists of the following stages:

I. Integration of investigation

II. Initial resolution

III. Instruction and diagnosis

IV. Technical dictum

V. Final resolution

VI. Application of guidance, protective, and treatment measures

VII. Assessment of the application of guidance, protective, and treatment measures

VIII. Treatment conclusion

IX. Further technical follow-up

The bodies of the Counsel for the minor are (Article 8; parentheses are mine):

I. President of the counsel

II. Superior Court (appeal body)

III. General secretary for resolutions from the Superior Court

IV. Unitarian Counselors (judging body)

    V. Interdisciplinary Committee (which issues the diagnosis)
   VI. Resolution secretaries for the Unitarian Counselors
  VII. Actuaries
 VIII. Up to three supernumerary counselors
   IX. Juvenile Defense Unit
    X. The determined technical and administrative units

It should be highlighted that, in addition to the confinement measures, there are guidance and protective measures, which are stated in Articles 97 and 103, respectively. These measures are alternatives to confinement in treatment centers, and their objective is to "prevent the juvenile offender from incurring future violations." Warnings, occupational therapy, ethical formation, recreation, and sports are *guidance* measures. *Protective* measures are promoting family roots (holding parents or those responsible for the juvenile to periodically present him or her in a treatment center and prohibiting him or her from leaving the place of residence without authorization from the counsel); transportation to the family home; encouragement to attend specialized institutions; prohibition to go to certain places and to drive vehicles; and the use of instruments, objects, and products of the offense in terms established by the penal legislation for the cases in which crimes were committed.

These measures, as such, have been hardly applied due to the recent promulgation of this legislation. The most frequent measure is still confinement in treatment centers.

Diagnosis of the Way Juvenile Counsels, Juvenile Tutelary Counsels, and Treatment Centers Work

Up to here, the two legislations for juvenile offenders presently in force in Mexico have been described; the real application of those legislations will be analyzed next. To do so, I will refer to the last and only diagnosis performed as a result of research carried out by the National Human Rights Commission in Mexico, together with United Nations International Children's Emergency Fund (UNICEF)—Mexico. This diagnosis (Comisión Nacional de Derechos Humanos [Human Rights Commission, CNDH], 1993) refers both to the legislation and the way it is applied and to the way treatment centers work and was based, on one hand, on analysis of the two existing legislations in the country and, on the other, on a survey carried out in the 57 centers for juvenile offenders in the country. In each one of these centers, 20 percent of the minors were interviewed. There was a total of 3,045 minors in the centers at the time (CNDH, 1993:10). Some of the main results of this research will be mentioned next.

Juvenile Arrests

In Mexico there is no police corps that is specialized in juveniles or that can arrest a juvenile. It was found in this study that 38.7 percent were arrested by the preventive police, 42.2 percent by the judiciary police, and 19 percent by others (p. 41), frequently without having legal orders (p. 12). Juveniles are almost never told what their situation is, what will happen to them, nor how long their confinement will last. They are generally mistreated, so they confess they are guilty. Among those interviewed, 46 percent said they had been treated well during the arrest process, and 54 percent said they had been mistreated. Among the latter, 34 percent suffered physical mistreatment (blows and torture), 53 percent were insulted, 5 percent suffered theft, 4 percent were threatened, and 3 percent were given no meals (p. 42).

It seems that it is a common practice to take them from one place to another while it is determined whether they are going to be confined or freed, and frequently the oldest are kept in prisons for adults until it is proved they are underage. This is one of the worst experiences to which they can be exposed.

Population Characteristics

According to this research, almost all the juveniles confined in the treatment centers came from low-income, broken families. For example, only 33.5 percent of the juveniles lived with both parents, and 63 percent lived only with their mother (p. 37). However, they generally claimed they had a good relationship with the people they lived with, because 90 percent declared they got along well with them, 89 percent were backed up by them, and 88 percent answered that the people they lived with had a job. These answers suggest that the general belief that juvenile offenders live in an absolutely hostile social environment is false.

Most juveniles had gone to school; only 8 percent declared they had never gone to school, 46 percent had finished grade school, and 20 percent had finished junior high school. Such information, nevertheless, reveals a low level of education, if we consider that most of the juveniles that are confined (72 percent) range between ages 14 and 17. Their distribution is the following: 16 percent were 14, 16 percent were 15, 20 percent were 16, and 20 percent were 17, which shows that the 14–17-year-old age range represents the most delicate period in the formation process of a minor.

The low level of education might be due to the fact that most of the juveniles had a job when they were confined to the centers. Only 15 percent said they were full-time students, while 17 percent worked in the street, 24 percent worked as employees, and 8 percent worked in the fields.

The extreme poverty in which most of the peasant families live leads the underaged to take jobs to plant, cultivate, pick, or carry drugs. Most homicides in which juveniles participate also take place within this drug environment.

Eighty-four percent of the confined juveniles were boys, and 16 percent were girls.

Quality of the Services

In many states there is no adequate separation between boys and girls. Thus, because girls are a minority among confined juveniles, as indicated previously, they receive services of the worst quality, for in many cases they are confined in centers really meant for boys. This situation forces them to be kept within the dormitory all day, where they eat, sleep, attend some classes, participate in workshops, and spend their free time. Frequently, to avoid contact between boys and girls, girls are not given regular access to the rest of the facilities.

There is no adequate classification according to the kind of violation or the age of the juveniles. In some centers, juveniles are confined for very different reasons in a common cell.

Concerning age, the situation is much worse; there are centers in which 7-year-olds live together with teenagers and sometimes even with 20-year-olds.[1] This happens because the minimum and maximum ages according to which they might be considered offenders are different in the various states. The minimum age is not specified in 23 states, theoretically, a four- or five-year-old could be confined as an offender. In the other 9 states, the minimum age varies from 6 to 12. The new legislation approved for the Federal District considers 12 the minimum age.

As regards the maximum age, that is, the age at which they can be penally charged, there is also a difference among states, ranging between 16 and 18. In 15 states, they can be charged at age 16, and in 17 states, at age 18. This tremendous difference in ages, together with the lack of treatment centers, creates an unjustifiable mixture of juveniles within the same institution. This makes the possibility of providing adequate treatment difficult and favors contamination of the younger by the older.

As established in the report we discussed, confinement facilities are almost always in bad condition and are too few. Dormitories are not adequate; they have cement beds, quite frequently without blankets and without privacy. Cases were found in which several juveniles slept in the same bed and some slept on the floor. Facilities are not used, buildings are not appropriate, and minors' well-being suffers so as to provide security, as happens when they are kept in the dormitories all day, and all activities are performed there.

In most of the centers, sanitary installations are not in good condition, endangering inmates' health; in certain cases, toilets were replaced by cans placed within the dormitories, and dining areas were placed close to the bathrooms, which give off very bad smells.

Many of the health problems come from a badly balanced and scant diet. Health services are also deficient, and there is not always a permanent doctor. This situation is more severe when talking about girls because, due to their age, they constantly suffer from gynecological disorders. Some girls had been sexually abused or harassed by the doctors.

Education services and workshops are badly administered, and although in practically every center there is a grade school, not all juveniles have access to it. Those who have a higher education level cannot, very often, continue their education because these levels are not available. Informal education (sex guidance, education, and information about problems related to their age) is practically nonexistent, and facilities, material, and personnel for workshops are deficient, so a professional training cannot be adequately achieved.

Last and closely related to the preceding, personnel are severely deficient, for they do not have adequate training, which becomes worse because basic personnel consist of guards who usually have a low level of education. The guards foster watchfulness and fear among the juveniles and mistreat them. They also practice corruption, sometimes together with the authorities.

Not surprisingly, the greatest number of recommendations given by the National Human Rights Commission for juvenile institutions between 1991 and 1993 had to do with facility conditions, medical service deficiency, service organization, mistreatment of the juveniles, and the lack of training of personnel.

Contact with the Outside

This last issue is most important because confined juveniles must not be isolated from their family, mainly because of their stage of life. Nevertheless, 26 percent of those interviewed stated that they had no possibility of seeing their relatives. It was also found that visitation permits were manipulated—they were used as a pressure tactic—and sometimes juveniles lost those rights.

INFORMAL PRACTICES

The most common informal practices in Mexico are as follows:

1. Police raids and control of homeless children have traditionally been the practices that police follow, more often to control low-income minors, for they live in the poorest zones in the big cities. Although such practices are legally prohibited, they have become a daily practice, mainly in the Federal District, and they are directed against homeless children. Of those indiscriminately arrested, the police frequently manufacture guilty pleas for unsolved crimes; and only 10 percent of those arrested without a judiciary order or without having committed a crime are really offenders (Lazo, 1993:8).

2. Linked to the preceding is an extortion system implemented by the police and mainly directed against homeless children and young prostitutes; in many cases, these minors are not considered within the formal justice system but are illegally controlled by some of its authorities. A good example of this practice was recorded by a nongovernment organization (NGO) working for the defense of juvenile human rights in Mexico. This report states that in July 1993, just in a single day, this NGO received accusations from 39 homeless children who were being extorted by preventive and traffic policemen who demanded 100 pesos a month to let them sleep in a shelter for homeless children (Justicia y Paz, 1993:64).

3. Another example of informal control is raids against minors who violate certain local regulations, such as ones that forbid vendors on streets, especially in tourist areas. It is important to underline this phenomenon because it is estimated that between 6 and 9 million children are involved in this kind of activity (Staelens, 1993:82), due to the extreme poverty in which more than one-fourth of the Mexican population lives.

Because being involved in an activity forbidden by local regulations or by the Federal Labor Law (which does not allow children below 14 to work) is not a crime, these minors are not usually submitted to the juvenile justice system; thus, the wrong application of protective laws allows this repression.

In fact, the police chase and arrest these minors every day and, after taking their merchandise and profits from them, send them to public assistance centers for children in trouble. These centers depend on the National System for Family Integral Development (DIF), which protects and provides assistance to minors and their families. Juveniles are confined in these centers for 15 to 30 days, and they are kept under strict surveillance. While they are there, they do not receive any kind of treatment, and authorities find out where they come from, so they can send them back, only when this term has elapsed. This creates a vicious circle because minors return to their activities because the economic difficulties that originated them still persist, and, therefore, the minors are again exposed to the same kind of repression.

The preceding are examples of the presence of an informal, juvenile control system that is often enforced by the police but that is also influenced by other state units that fall within the formal system itself.

SUMMARY

There are two major trends within the 32 existing juvenile justice legislations that are in force today in Mexico. One trend started in 1974, when the Juvenile Tutelary Counsel gave the juvenile system a protective-assistance character, which, nevertheless, in practice, turned out to be a system by which the minor lost all prosecution guarantees and constitutional rights, among which the most extreme is violation of the constitutional principle that states there is no crime or sentence without law. This kind of legislation, with slight differences, is still in force in 30 of the states of the Mexican republic.

Second, after the approval and ratification by Mexico of the Children's Rights Convention and the commitment that Salinas's administration made in the World Meeting for Children that took place in New York in 1990, such administration was compelled to amend the existing tutelary legislation that violated those rules established by Article 40 in the convention. So, quite hastily approved in 1991, the juvenile law for the Federal District in the common court and for all the republic in the federal court has a more modern approach and provides more guarantees, but it has a fundamental limitation for juvenile prosecution. The fundamental limitation is that both the old Juvenile Tutelary Counsel and the new Juvenile Counsel depend on the State Department, which implies that it still is an administrative organ, whose officials depend on the executive power; thus, there is no real power independence. This means the judging body, the appealing body, and the defense body, as well as the treatment centers to which juveniles will be sent in the event they are found guilty, belong to the same administrative authority.

Most of the population that gets to the counsel and the treatment centers belongs to the most unfavored economic sectors in Mexico, as is true within the adult justice system.

Juvenile inmates in 1993 numbered 3,045 in all the republic; they were distributed in 57 treatment centers. This number is quite low if we consider that the national population was 85 million inhabitants, and more than 50 percent were underage. Most juvenile control is done informally.

Research directed by the National Human Rights Commission and UNICEF–Mexico showed the great deficiencies that still characterize the juvenile justice system and the treatment centers:

- The principles of legality and proportionality are not taken into account, for there may have been no previous offenses, and the intensity and duration of the established measure are not usually proportional to the severity of the offense. Because of this, a juvenile who steals an unimportant object might be deprived of his or her liberty longer than an adult criminal. Loss of liberty is not limited, as it should be, to really severe behavior. This reflects a harder and more unjust criminal policy toward minors than toward adults.

- Essential guarantees and formalities that imply a democratic penal procedure are not contemplated, such as right to defense, free deposition of evidence, separation among the persons who act in the procedure (prosecutor, defense, and judge), possibility of appeal (such possibility is nonexistent in 17 instances), preventive arrest only by a written, founded, and motivated mandate (one of the most violated principles in all the republic), and the benefit of temporary liberty in those cases where the behavior does not merit confinement or liberty under bail (practiced in adult justice).

- In 23 states the minimum age as recommended by Article 40, number 3, paragraph a of the convention for penal law application is not established. It is recommended that, as in the 1991 law, 12 should be the minimum age.

- Time limits for the initial resolution, by which it is established whether the juvenile is to be handed over to the Counsel or not, are not fixed, and in many cases these terms are very long, lasting sometimes up to 72 or 120 hours, during which time the juvenile is really under arrest. As regards the final resolution, 30 days are the usual term, but according to the research, 25 percent of the juveniles waited for such resolution longer than the established term.

- Only four states establish the discontinuance of suit, and only three states provide for indemnity, which is quite beneficial for the other party and allows pardon or suspension of the measure, a procedure that has greatly helped to reintegrate offenders into society.

- The most important problem in the treatment centers, in addition to physical and hygienic conditions, is the absence of a real classification system according to sex, age, and behavior, clearly recommended in Articles 37 and 40 of the convention. In this regard, there are no specific answers, nor are there for those juveniles who become adults while they are in the treatment centers. At present, they are transferred to adult institutions, which is very negative for their reintegration into society.

- In general, the juvenile justice system is not founded on real respect for juveniles' civil and human rights, which is difficult to achieve unless there is the necessary trained personnel to participate in the process from the moment the juvenile gets to the Counsel to the time he or she is released and in a follow-up after leaving the treatment center. In 26 states, there is no such personnel, although Article 18 of the constitution and the convention establish so.

• Last, it can be foreseen that there will be a real conflict of law and jurisdiction when the new legislation is applied in the states of the republic, for there will be an over-lapping of two different judiciary regulations, one belonging to the state under the common court and another under the federal one and because there are two almost opposite procedures and two different administrative bodies in charge of enforcing such regulations.

NOTE

1. I mention 20 years of age because many juveniles are kept within the treatment centers even after they become adults.

REFERENCES

Alvarez, Ana J. "El Consejo Mexicano para Menores Infractores." *Tribuna Internacional de los Derechos del Niño* 7 (1990): 16–18.

Azaola, Elena. *La Institución Correcional en México: Una Mirada Extraviada.* México, D.F.: Siglo XXI/CIESAS, 1990.

Bullen, Marcia. *El Menor Ante el Derecho Penal.* Mexico, D.F.: Ed. Inacipe, 1989.

Comisión Nacional de Derechos Humanos. *Textos de Derechos Humanos sobre la Niñez.* México, D.F.: CNDH Editions, 1992.

———. *Propuesta para el Rescate de los Derechos Humanos de los Menores Infractores en México.* México, D.F.: CNDH Editions, 1993.

Lazo, Pablo. "La Impunidad y la Fabricación de Culpables en los Jóvenes." *Revista Justicia y Paz* 31 (1993): 8–10.

Ley para el Tratamiento de Menores Infractores. México, D.F.: Ediciones Delma, 1994.

Ley que crea el Consejo Tutelar para Menores del D.F. Recopilación de Legislación Sobre Menores. México, D.F.: DIF Organización de las Naciones Unidas. Convención sobre los Derechos del Niño, 1986.

Sánchez, Augusto. "La Ley para el Tratamiento de Menores Viola la Constitución Política y los Derechos Humanos." México, D.F.: Report, Comisión Mexicana de Defensa y Promoción de los Derechos Humanos, 1993.

Staelens, Patrick, comp. *La Problemática del Niño en México.* México, D.F.: UAM-UNICEF-OIT, 1991.

———. *El Trabajo de los Menores.* México, D.F.: UAM-Serie Libro de Textos, 1993.

Tenorio, Fernando. "Entre Definición y Lógica del Sistema: Acerca de la Justicia de Menores, un Análisis Crítico de su Realidad:" *Revista Mexicana de Justicia* 7 (1989): 433–440.

APPENDIX

Agencies Involved in the Juvenile Justice System

Consejo de Menores del Distrito Federal, Obrero Mundial, Distrito Federal.

Centro de Tratamiento para Menores Infractores (varones), San Fernando, Tlalpan, Distrito Federal.

Centro de Tratamiento para Menores Infractores (mujeres), Av. Universidad y Viveros, Coyoacán, Distrito Federal.

Procuraduria de la Defensa del Menor y la Familia, Prolongación Xochicalco 947, Colonia Portales, Distrito Federal.

Agencia Investigadora Especializada en Asuntos del Menor, Niños Héroes 61, planta baja, Colonia Doctores, Distrito Federal.

Comisión Nacional de Derechos Humanos (CNDH), Periférico Sur 3469 esq. Calle Luis Cabrera, Colonia San Jerónimo, D.F.

Consejos Tutelares para Menores de los Estados.

Nongovernment Organizations

Centro de Derechos Humanos Fray Francisco de Vitoria OP, A.C., Odontología 35, Colonia Copilco-Universidad, D.F.

Comisión Mexicana de Defensa y Promoción de los Derechos Humanos.

14

NIGERIA

Sigismund O. A. Akin Bulumo

INTRODUCTION

It seems that the Criminal Code supersedes the customary law in point of penalty, though not of substantive law. The customary law of crime is still valid, even when it recognizes offenses unknown to the Code. Also, customary rules of procedure and evidence . . . may differ from those of English law; they are, however, still valid as long as they are not repugnant to natural justice, equity, and good conscience. (Elias, 1973:37)

The Nigerian juvenile justice system, like the country itself, is a heritage of British colonial rule. Although tendentiously and ignorantly referred to as the "Dark Continent," Africa was for a long time in contact with those who genuinely wanted to know it or who had cause to transact business with it in earlier times, especially the Arabs.

Habituated to their own way of life, men frequently can conceive of no other way and thus regard their own group as the measure of man everywhere. This view constitutes a major obstacle to scientific objectivity (Chinoy, 1967:5). Culture, though relative, has important implications for social interaction and contact between peoples. In the African indigenous setting, kinship and seniority were the two overarching principles that guided human social interaction. The principle of kinship entailed that the training of the young was invariably a communal and cooperative effort, while that of seniority demanded that the young unquestioningly defer to their elders. Any infraction was severely sanctioned by various agents of social control in the community. All this changed precisely at the advent of Europeans.

The baseline of our analysis is, therefore, the triple heritage of indigenous, Western, and Islamic influences, which affect every country on the African continent. In any attempt at reconciling the often conflicting values of Africa's triple heritage, one is inevitably drawn into the dynamics of social change—a ubiquitous phenomenon. It was not Africa's contact with the outside world that was new. For more than 1,000 years, the peoples of Africa (particularly, south of the Sahara) had established contact both with each other and with their neighbors and especially with the Mediterranean culture, through the trans-Saharan trade. But essentially, what was new was the change in both pace and character of the external incursions—particularly from Europe—during the sixteenth century, reaching its depth of social and cultural deprivation in the obnoxious trade in human traffic across the Atlantic Ocean. By far, the most intractable manifestation of this set of circumstances is the weakening of social relations and a strain on the maintenance of social order through traditional democratic institutions as power relations were substituted for reason and consensus.

Assessing whether or not the totality of its triple heritage is to the continent's benefit is beyond the purview of this chapter—the network of human social action together with institutional agencies that identify, categorize, and treat juveniles in trouble. For the purpose of our analysis, however, the relevant question is simply the impact of colonialism on the social life of tropical Africa and the legacies that this has bequeathed in terms of new problems for national management and the painful process of both social and intellectual reconstruction.

The most significant direct impact of colonialism, it is surmised, are the velvet-glove activities of the missionaries on sociocultural life. With their penetration of the land and the consequent evangelizing came the introduction of (West) European culture and values: first, to their individual converts and, then, to the society at large. The missionaries, deliberately or otherwise, sought to impose Western culture on the indigenous cultures of African social structures: monogamy for polygyny, individuality for communality. Because of the close connection between religion and morals (and, by extension, deviant behavior), it is necessary to point out that the outsiders sometimes forcibly imposed new ideas of faith: Christianity and Islam for traditional religions.

Certain other residual features of its legacy need to be underlined in appreciating the magnitude of the problems faced today. First, it created a set of administrative institutions that not only undermined local traditional democratic processes but were eminently unsuited for motivating and mobilizing the community for the real task of massive, sustained development. Second, it accentuated conflict in matters of faith. For example, Islam accepted the African's customary view of crime as sin and punishment as retaliation, while Western missionaries were vehemently opposed to this view, especially in respect of punishment within the ambit of Mosaic law,[1] essentially retaliatory. Emphasizing the new covenant wrought through Jesus' redemptive death on Calvary, the missionaries preached forgiveness: never returning evil for evil.[2] Third, it destroyed an essentially humanistic value system that inherently reconciles material development with moral virtue and social justice. In fact, the loss of this value system constitutes the greatest intellectual obstacle to the search for a meaningful approach to the crime problem in Africa.

In view of the nature of the sociocultural deprivation engendered by Africa's triple heritage as cataloged in the preceding paragraphs, it is of utmost importance to underscore the point that the geopolitical entity referred to as Nigeria is, indeed, a creation of British colonialism. Once merely a convenient description of that area of West Africa through which the Niger River extensively flows, at the amalgamation of the Northern and Southern Protectorates of Nigeria in 1914 by the British, the term became the official designation of the vast area.

Nigeria, with an area of 923,768 square kilometers and a population of 88.5 million, consists of over 300 ethnic and linguistic groups spread over a wide range of ecological zones, from the swamps along the coast through the rain forest and the wetter savannas to the dry Sahel. In this plural society, each culture tends to have a different "cultural landscape." This diversity does not, however, preclude common experiences and similarities in ways of life.

Crime is obviously no great public issue in a simple, small, relatively static, homogeneous, and competition-free community. But it acquires a more serious proportion as the number of people increases, mobility accelerates, and the division of labor subdivides. Indeed, the inexorable spread of industrialization and urbanization implies that these modern ways of living, earning, and producing constitute a "new," pervading, and, at least potentially, criminogenic culture that overlays and dominates local traditions and mores (Clifford, 1974:216). This implicit criminogeny of the new capitalist system, attending evangelization in Nigeria, tends to limit the roles played by the institutions of civil society—the family, the community, religion, and traditional morality—all of which have long ceased to function effectively as social control agents (Odekunle, 1978: 85). Thus, there is little societal support for discipline and good behavior, as the rituals of religion and custom are increasingly questioned and discarded.

When Nigeria—indeed, Africa—is perceived as a "criminological laboratory," whereby its cultural diversity is a challenge to the very meaning of crime (Clifford, 1983:88–90), the background to criminal behavior can be expected to be usually different enough to modify the significance of the act or omission. Moreover, if crime is acknowledged to be directly related to the major institutional and structural problems facing Africa, then it follows that crime in Africa is not a marginal problem confined to only a few deviant members of society. Rather, Kibuka (1980:14) contends that crime in Africa is a major socioeconomic problem that infiltrates whole societies and constitutes a serious impediment to development. But compounding the matter, according to him, is the predominant youthfulness of the population in Africa. This, in effect, makes crime in Africa largely a problem of young people, which thereby adds a note of urgency to the prevention of crime and its treatment (Clifford, 1974:16).

THE FORMAL SYSTEM

Crime is one of the classes of social deviance that follow changes in the qualities of the population, the workings of social institutions, the level of economic development, and the rate of urban growth. It would thus appear that (juvenile) criminology is marked by the qualities of the environment within which it operates. The decades since World War II tend to have generally engendered the spread of conditions that contribute to criminality. In upsetting traditional, social, and cultural systems, these major trends have generated increased crime and new crime patterns (such as the growing involvement of the young) that extend beyond geopolitical boundaries (Johnson, 1983:xiv).

In Nigeria, the most significant consequence of massive social, economic, and political changes since the late 1940s has been the alarming increase in the magnitude of the crime problem. In fact, the high pitch of materialism pervading the society is the major motive driving (mostly) the youth into adopting "innovation" as their basic mode of adaptation[3] in achieving success. Thus, they readily resort to taking shortcuts by getting involved in sharp practices in the ultimate hope of "making it" earlier than otherwise.

When the British took on the administration of Nigeria in 1914, the indigenous judicial system was replaced by customary courts. Although certain aspects of the indigenous system, such as swearing by gods, were retained, it was clear that the indigenous people did not respect the new system (Amadi, 1982:87). It is naive to assume that an alien morality can satisfy the sense of justice of a people when these cultural values are, in essential and fundamental respects, opposed to theirs.

Consequent to colonialism, two penal systems coexist, but with one superimposed on the other. In Nigeria, penal authority was restricted to minor offenses, and the old (indigenous) courts were controlled or gradually assimilated into the English criminal justice system introduced by the colonial masters. Even in many African countries, after (political) independence, the customary laws under the penal code were repealed, while laws and procedures modeled after those of the respective mother country were adopted. According to Szabo (1977: xii), this has resulted in "legal anomie," arising from the administration of a modern official justice—often misunderstood or unrecognized by the people— and the survival of juridicoadministrative structures once well integrated in the rural areas and continuing to function extensively, though informally. Thus, before colonization, there was a very effective "criminal" justice system grounded in community law, with the major goal of maintaining harmony within the community. The maintenance of harmony was more important than the individual. The principal functions of justice, therefore, were to reestablish a relationship of cooperation that was essential to the survival of the group as an entity.

At the dawn of (political) independence on October 1, 1960, the Criminal Code ceased to apply throughout Nigeria. Whereas the criminal code of the southern states[4] has an Anglo-Australian orientation, the Penal Code of the northern states[5] has virtually an Indo-Sudanese orientation. These codes, however, have a common origin in English common law, while identical cultural values have provided the basis for common, broad features between the two codes. The cultural incompatibility of the criminal law with Nigerian cultures thus generated is compounded by the introduction of new laws of criminal procedure[6] and of evidence.[7] Since 1979, customary criminal law in general applies throughout the country.[8]

The Criminal Code was enacted as an instrument of colonial policy, designed to achieve imperial uniformity and to replace "barbarous customs and primitive morality" with the "superior morality" of the common law (Elias, 1963:104). Even in the customary criminal offenses recognized, the code negated what their indigenous concepts stood for, while merely promoting what the imperial government considered to be in the interest of peace and good government. It is thus clear, from the outset, that there is an inherent cultural conflict in the formulation of Nigerian criminal policy. It is needless to dwell upon the differences between the Nigerian cultures and the cultural values on which the English common law is based. Suffice to say, as summation, that the ethical values of a monogamous, monotheistic, and individualistic society are bound to be essentially different in material respects from the values of a polygynous, polytheistic, and collectivistic society (Karibi-Whyte, 1977:10). In short, the formulation of law—rules of conduct—is, to a very large extent, based on ethical considerations whose roots lie in the religious, political, economic, and moral foundations of a society.

With respect to juvenile adjudication in Nigeria, juvenile delinquents are not subject to the same criminal law and formal procedure as adult criminals. Although the Children and Young Persons Act (CYPA) is the main body of legislation, the Criminal Procedure Act (CPA), and the Evidence Act contain special provisions applicable to juveniles. These are also aimed at protecting juveniles and applying a more individualized approach in procedure.

Juvenile delinquency is commonly used to refer to the criminality and misconduct of youth, that is, specifically to punishable acts committed by juveniles in the age group of 7 to 17 years and to juridically nonpunishable misdeeds. Hence, it has insistently dwelt on a restricted range of people and activities. Such offenses include moral danger, sexual misconduct, uncontrollability, petty theft, absconding, truancy, and street trading. But the important point is determining when a youth is in need of care and protection or in moral danger. Since private citizens are also an informal part of the juvenile justice system, detection of juvenile offenders is primarily their responsibility. In this regard, as for adult criminality, the basis of effective crime prevention is the relationship and level of cooperation between the public and the police (Akin Bulumo, forthcoming).

Role of the Police

As in much of crime detection generally, the police role is essentially reactive. In respect of juvenile delinquency, private citizens tend to play a major role in its detection. However, the police exercise wide discretion (both formally and informally) as the gatekeepers of the justice system. In most cases, the police perform welfare services in their handling of youth. The main concern is over the danger of moral contamination, especially by adult criminals. Charged with handling youth differently, the police often mediate informally between juvenile offenders and their identified victims. This mediatory role includes warnings, making arrangements for restitution, and informing parents or guardians. If there is sufficient evidence, and the victim is pressing for charges, the juvenile is detained in the station for a very short period of time or released on bail to parents/guardians for further processing in the juvenile justice system.

Although, in most urban centers in Nigeria, every police station can handle juvenile contraventions, there are only a few stations equipped for handling juveniles in trouble. These ''special'' police stations usually have female police officers in charge and a high-ranking female officer as the public prosecutor in the juvenile court. Juvenile offenders may be detained in police stations overnight, but further detention must be approved by the juvenile court, and offenders are removed to remand homes according to gender. The main purpose of detaining juveniles in special detention centers (and not prisons) is to avoid their moral contamination by adult criminals and thereby prevent or deter later crime.

Nonreporting of delinquency to the police swells the ''dark figure'' of crime, and the double standard widespread in keeping official crime statistics affects their reliability. In Nigeria, statistics of crime are centrally compiled and released annually in a report by the police. They reflect the number of reported offenses, prosecutions, and convictions for a specific period. Sometimes, the available data are for one area or region only; or there have been political upheavals, and older records and files may have been lost or deliberately destroyed. More than that, the older records may have little modern relevance, just as lack of coordination and red tape may render relatively new records obsolete when eventually released at a later date. Juvenile delinquency is a crucial social problem, on the increase vis-à-vis the Westernization process, consequent to the attenuation of indigenous conduct norms. However, as regards official records, this increase may be a reflection of better recording rather than an outright rise in crime (Clifford, 1983:86).

Role of the Juvenile Court

For purposes of adjudication, every high court doubles as a juvenile court except in the then federal capital of Lagos, where there is a statutorily established juvenile magistrate court for the treatment and welfare of juvenile offenders. In accordance with the CYPA,[9] offenses involving children and young persons[10] are referred to the court for adjudication. The juvenile court handles a varying assortment of misdeeds, such as in need of care and protection arising from neglect or exposure to moral danger, theft/larceny, street trading, assault, unlawful possession, and malicious damage.

Over the years, however, offenses handled in the juvenile court can be broadly put into sex-related categories in order of frequency. For boys, the offenses are theft (including car theft), unlawful possession, assault, hawking, attempted felony drug-trafficking, addiction, fraud, and robbery. For girls, they are hawking, theft (including shoplifting), assault, immoral offenses, attempted felony, drug-trafficking, and unlawful damage. The hearing, both in the high court and magistrate's court, is conducted according to certain procedural prescriptions.

Within the framework of the aforementioned relevant legislations, the juvenile court, wherever constituted, has a particular setup and a procedure different from that prevailing in the adult court. The juvenile court is often constituted by a magistrate, presiding, and two lay assessors—one of whom is a woman. Upon every issue or question to be decided by the court, except question of law, the decision of the majority of the members constitutes that of the court. However, where the court is constituted in the high court, the judge sits alone and determines both questions of law and fact. The public is not to attend hearings in the juvenile court, except the parties involved, their counsel (if any), and some auxiliary judicial personnel—the police and social workers. But if the high court is sitting as a juvenile court, the hearing is held in the judge's chambers.

Whereas hearings in the juvenile court are summary, informal, and private, the court has to explain to each juvenile offender in simple language the substance of the alleged offense. Even when admitting the offense in the petition, the juvenile offender has to furnish the court with a full story of the case. If the offense is not admitted, an adjudicatory hearing is conducted to take evidence from the parties in order to determine whether the juvenile is delinquent as alleged. In this respect, the court also allows the offender's parents/guardians or counsel to put questions to the witnesses.

In spite of the court's special procedure, a cardinal principle in the procedure is that the onus of establishing a juvenile's delinquency rests squarely on the party making the allegation. Since the juvenile court is always guided by procedural standards set by the Supreme Court of the federation, a juvenile's delinquency has to be proved beyond reasonable doubt. The action generally taken by the juvenile court is paternalistic, as adjudication is conducted in the juvenile's best interest. For example, if the juvenile admits the offense, or the court is satisfied that the matter has been proved beyond reasonable doubt, the court still asks the offender to say anything that it considers may assist the court in deciding upon a suitable treatment/dispositional measure. Even after a juvenile has been found delinquent by the court, a finding may be entered against the parent/guardian who has contributed to the commission of the offense through the juvenile's neglect or exposure to moral danger as to be in need of care and protection.

However, before a final decision is made as to disposal, the law provides that matters involving juveniles be referred to social welfare officers for a detailed inquiry on the home situation, school record, and offender's medical history (Section 8[7] of the CYPA). To facilitate obtaining such information and for observation, the offender is usually kept in a remand home. The main purpose of the inquiry into an offender's antecedents is to assist the juvenile court to judge the juvenile delinquent as a person and to decide on the best course of action. Despite the implicit humanization of this system, the juvenile court's unfamiliar constitution and procedure have generated disrespect for the court among some members of the public, as some of its orders are confidently disregarded (Oki, 1977:269), compared to those of the more respected adult courts.

Disposition

With regard to the type of offender's treatment needs, the individualization of punishment is of utmost importance. The social report filed by a designated probation officer of the Juvenile Welfare Unit in the Social Welfare Service, as demanded by the court, forms the focus of any dispositional hearing. A variety of treatment measures is open to the court, institutional and noninstitutional. Whereas probation is the most frequently used type of treatment, compensation and restitution are rarely used.

Probation refers to the conditional release of juveniles found delinquent; they are placed under the supervision of a probation officer attached to the court. Thus, it is an important form of community treatment in the juvenile justice system. While on probation, the offender is required to abide by the conditions of the probation order, including reporting to the probation officer at prescribed intervals. Probation is often in the community, especially with the offender residing with parents/guardians for a specified period. In addition, probation is based on the principle that the juvenile offender is not a danger to the community. Therefore, it appears to be most appropriate for offenders who have the greatest chance of successful readjustment to society. Many magistrates and even members of the public still conservatively put retribution for an offense before reformation and rehabilitation. They tend to overlook the punitive element in probation, such as deprivation of complete liberty when on probation. However, this is not to say that probation is an adequate treatment for some categories of offenders. Economically, it costs more to put offenders in institutions than to place them on probation.

With regard to institutionalization, only a very small number of offenders are placed, through "corrective orders," in "congregate care institutions." Empirically, it has been found that more harm than good is done by keeping offenders in institutions during the whole period of the committal order. Thus, for a young person, it is argued that institutionalization is not an effective treatment strategy. These institutions are, in reality, "factories" that produce criminals. Offenders with minor offenses are transformed into hardened criminals. Consequently, when juveniles must be placed in protective custody, recourse is often made to protectories—charitable and public (mostly remand homes)—though they are occasionally allowed home as if parolees.

The aftercare service is an extension of the probation officer's duties in easing the juvenile's reentry into the community. Because of manpower shortage, aftercare is the least functionally developed component of the juvenile justice system. In Nigeria, the extended family system is the most supportive aspect of civil society with regards to the resocialization of juveniles in trouble. There is, therefore, an urgent need for a better understanding of the needs of these young ones by the society.

Disposal measures commonly adopted tend to vary from one juvenile offender to the other. But their frequency along gender lines is as follows: for boys, probation, repatriation (usually to the villages), committal to approved schools, fines, caning, and discharge; for girls, discharge, probation, repatriation, and committal to approved schools. Characteristically, there is still much perceived softness toward female offenders, who mainly appear in the juvenile courts as being in moral danger, probably through exposure, as they are largely picked up by the police for street trading and immoral offenses.

In Nigeria, noninstitutional assistance to juveniles in trouble is woefully inadequate because punishment is generally perceived to be more important than reformation or rehabilitation. Thus, institutional assistance is mostly in the form of penitentiary services, which are essentially places of punishment, since there are no places of early identification, education, and rehabilitation for behaviorally difficult and behaviorally deviant children/juveniles. Even community social agencies and charitable organizations provide no direct services for the prevention of delinquency or the treatment of juvenile offenders as they do for orphans, the handicapped, abondoned children, or gifted children. Just as there is no treatment specifically for behavioral problems, so also is there no community treatment or national prevention program for the welfare of juvenile offenders. In general, therefore, there is no formally established umbrella organization (other than the indigenous institution of the kinship system) striving for crime prevention and rehabilitation among all Nigerian population groups. Admittedly, in Nigeria, there are no nonresidential day treatment programs for juvenile offenders, unlike in many other countries, especially the United States, where Short Term Aid to Youth (STAY), Associated Marine Institutes (AMI), Outward Bound, and other programs play important roles in the welfare of juvenile offenders.

Problems

Currently, problems tend to take many forms as the issue of juvenile delinquency becomes more complex and diverse in an increasingly dynamic society. Juveniles are reeling from today's pressures, and the consequences of massive social, economic, and political changes have been the alarming increase in the

magnitude of juvenile delinquency. Youths are bombarded by powerful influences—television, music, the school, and the peer group—than hitherto. The
assault on families is, therefore, broad in scope and can be devastating. It is
often put that the family accounts for educational success and failure far more
than the school, parents being the most important educators. Since many parents
are not good role models for their children, the family structure has increasingly
lost its primary function of socializing the young into the group's acceptable
standard of behavior. In sum, rapid social change is a catastrophe for children
and youth, who require stability and security for healthy growth and development.

The demise of cherished indigenous values and the increase in moral relativ-
ism, through a Western-type civilization, appear to lend weight to a crisis of
character in human relationships. Nigerian society has moved steadily from self-
control to self-expression, and many people dismiss old and tested values as
repressive. Old values and inconvenient moral restraints are being brushed aside
to clear the way for the fun splurge. But the core of the problem is dissolute
manners, as uncivil behavior appears unbound in modern times. Youths in contemporary Nigerian society appear to have taken their cue from this and to have
tried to overcome the nothingness of life only by "heroic" individualism, dis-
respectfulness, sniffing "coke," smoking "pot," idolizing riches, making love,
seeking personal peace, and indulging in self-worship.

In line with the development in criminology, especially during the latter nineteenth century, an emphasis on humanism and increased respect for human rights
tends to have created a special problem for the juvenile justice system in Nigeria.
But a contrasting endogenous cultural practice is that juveniles' civil rights are
not exercisable until coming of age—marked by a definitive rite de passage.
Consequently, the apparent multiple cultural conflicts appear to have placed
enormous constraints on the handling of juveniles within the juvenile justice
system. The ensuing ambivalence sways between two extremes: more draconian
interventions, such as death by firing squad during Buhari-Idiagbon's military
regime, and the more paternalistic tendencies bordering on sheer neglect of
juveniles in trouble during Shagari's civilian regime.

However, in all, a rising concern over juvenile delinquency and the relentless
public demand that something be done about it have led to an overload on the
system. Thus, in the face of such a burden, the agencies and programs are very
much underfunded and understaffed. In particular, the caliber of the personnel—
especially the judicial auxiliary staff—calls for urgent improvement, as inadequate training seems to be quite rampant among them. Even the functioning of
the main judicial and parajudicial agencies—the police, the courts, penitentiary
services, and aftercare services and agencies—has been severely hampered by
the lack of manpower development. There is still no special training for personnel in the handling of juveniles in trouble, despite the apparent need for this
in the administration of juvenile justice.[11]

In view of juvenile justice's crucial contribution to humanity, Oki (1977:281) has suggested that men of wide experience, trained intellect, and humane temperament should be appointed to dispense justice in juvenile courts, although there may be acute shortages of both competent judicial personnel and adequate facilities. Despite the obviously overtasked adult courts and the attendant delay, they are still charged with handling juvenile matters in most urban areas of Nigeria where courts, correctional centers, and personnel are woefully inadequate. Although juvenile delinquency appears to be more of an urban phenomenon than rural, most governments have paid lip service to attempts at keeping youths off the streets and, therefore, out of trouble.

Prevention and Control

Against the backdrop of any indigenous Nigerian culture, there is a moral breakdown of alarming dimensions in modern society. Thus, to overcome juvenile delinquency, it is necessary to start with educating a youth's emotions, rather than his intellect. The foregoing is predicated upon the view that emotion governs our conduct and that the way we are trained, even if forced at first, influences feelings and tends to change conduct.

The family—the oldest human institution—is the most basic and, in many ways, the most important. But, in recent times, there has been a frontal assault on family life, creating an increase in family distress such as a high divorce rate, massive drug abuse, juvenile delinquency, epidemic incest, and an appalling increase in family violence. In view of the get-rich-quick mania prevailing in the Nigerian society, most parents (particularly in the urban centers) are simply too busy to love their children, with terrible consequences for the future. Children may grow up to become unattached and have no capacity for love, thereby being more predisposed to delinquency and more serious crimes. Disrespect for one's parents and elders, which was a most serious offense under indigenous cultural values and norms, now appears to have no binding force on juvenile conduct, especially in the wake of "modern" urbanization processes. For example, the age-old injunction to honor one's parents and elders ordinarily implies recognizing constituted authority or authority figures. In latter-day experience, however, this injunction is more honored in the breach than in the observance, indiscipline being a significant component of Nigerian behavioral repertoire, reflected in many directive statements of governments and crystallizing in the current policy of War against Indiscipline and Corruption (WAIC).

Certainly, the imported nuclear-type family structure is more of a status symbol than an institution to reckon with in the socialization process. Together with the urban way of life, most parents tend to spoil their children, which may account for much of the increase in juvenile misconduct and criminality. In like measure, whoever the victims of poverty may be, the point remains that it is detrimental to collective social progress. The menace of "children of the streets" in urban centers illumines the criminogenic influence of poverty in families on the causation of juvenile delinquency, moral danger for young females and, generally, street trading being the more important offenses. Thus, an effective prevention approach may very well be the introduction of government policies to constructively bring about substantial improvements in the people's quality of life.

In Nigeria, formal preventive and control programs are vested in large bureaucratic organizations—the police, the judiciary, and the ministry of youth, sports and social welfare (or information and culture)—that are known to exercise formal authoritative and impersonal controls that are too distant to be effective. These programs, though mostly piecemeal and uncoordinated, are carried out within the ambit of the criminal justice system. But, if properly coordinated and formulated, organizational efforts can be used to supplement and assist the widespread familial and community efforts. Although it is widely accepted that there are no proven methods for reducing the incidence of juvenile delinquency and/or criminality through preventive or rehabilitative procedures, something comparable to those government-aided structures put in place in North America and Western Europe need not be done in Nigeria, because of differences in cultural traditions.

However, it is surmised, planning for effective prevention, treatment, and control requires concerned action and systematic research. For the future, it is important to embark on the reorientation of the citizenry toward indigenous norms and values as the directive principle of a national orientation movement in order to accomplish a cooperative and coordinate community-wide effort to deal with delinquency. Moreover, as part of the general concern for the humanization of criminal justice and the protection of human rights—particularly the rights of children, who are the most defenseless section of a society in emergent nations—it is a matter of priority to go beyond duty, on which the welfare system is based, and to embrace love and duty, which nurture the extended family system. If only to avoid the impending crisis over the juvenile justice system, serious efforts must be made toward diversion: the development and greater utilization of binding over, compensation, restitution orders, and community service orders (on weekends, for football hooligans). Above all, there is the urgent need to review the value of some of our informal controls of human behavior. Profiting from Western mistakes in overusing the formal machinery of criminal justice, Clifford (1983:94) claims that it is possible for emergent nations (especially of the Third World) to use their own informal/indigenous approaches more effectively.

INFORMAL PRACTICES

It is important to acknowledge the preeminence of the old institutions of organized indigenous practices of inculcating in the child the acceptable standard of behavior within the human group. There is thus no gainsaying the fact that profound ambivalence appears to be the common response to the conflicting conduct norms attending cultural contact between indigenous cultures and the

Arabo-European cultures. For instance, because of the kinship system, the average Nigerian maintains contact of a more or less intimate character with a much larger circle of blood and affinal relations, neighbors, and friends than does the average European or North American.

Detection

In a typical Nigerian culture, detection of juvenile contravention is a direct responsibility of the whole community. This is predicated upon the notion that, for the solidarity of the group, the full training of the young has to be cooperative effort in which members of each of the more inclusive groups must play a part. Suffice to say, an indigenous Nigerian community is largely ruled by custom in which the element of individual judgment and initiative is very small, while tending toward the stereotyping of attitudes, behavior, practices, and even ways of thinking.

Role of the Extended Family System

Essentially African in origin, the extended family is one of the most powerful social influences in Africa, vibrant in its affections and compelling in its loyalties. As a unit of justice, production, and consumption, it was a multifunctional institution performing various economic, protective, educational, religious, recreational, biological, affectional, and status functions that all contribute to stable personality development. In spite of having been battered by the twin processes of Westernization and urbanization, resulting in increased family mobility and family fragmentation or disorganization, which can give rise to juvenile delinquency and criminality, the successful urbanite of today never disregards considerable influence of the indigenous family system, with particular reference to social control. Also worthy of note is the fact that increased industrialization results in affluence, which actively encourages juvenile delinquency and criminality.

According to Murrell and Lester (1981:27), there is some evidence that broken and/or inadequate family backgrounds are related to delinquency in affluent, industrialized societies which is not the case in societies with the extended family system. Their observation has a halo of truth in it because Nigerian children tend to live surrounded by affection, especially the loving and warm behavior of the many (social) fathers and mothers within the community or group. Indeed, poverty existed in indigenous Nigerian communities, but it was not degrading or dehumanizing as in modern society. Also, there were no demographic isolation and other structural elements predisposing to maladjustment and inferiority, which tend to contribute to criminality and delinquency.

In seeking to account for the relatively low incidence of juvenile delinquency and criminality in indigenous Nigerian social structures, no close observer and student can overlook the principle of kinship, which is complemented by that of seniority. The kinship principle, extended as it is beyond actual relatives, extends the boundary of the group that acknowledges common interests and common loyalties. It is chiefly within the extended family that a child obtains the bulk of his or her education as a member of society. Since the child cannot continuously be under the eyes of parents and older siblings, various members of the extended family take a hand in education at one time or another. By one means or another, the youth has always been made amenable to the opinion of that group through various methods of social control, namely, instruction, persuasion, reward, and punishment.

Just as one learns, under pain of disagreeable consequences, to avoid doing things that will earn the disapproval of the family group, so also does a person learn to respect the opinions and prejudices of the larger society. Respect for authority, inside and outside the household, has been grounded in the superior age of mentors who approve or disapprove of conduct. But owing to the strength of kinship and neighborly solidarity, the members of the extended family, as agents of social control, exercise effective residual powers of control and discipline over juvenile members. These powers range from tongue-lashing (accompanied by an explanation of why conformity to given norms is desirable), to infliction of physical pain, in most cases, or an obligation to report serious improper behavior (likely to cause chaos in society), such as incest and theft, to parents or community leaders for the necessary propitiatory rituals.

According to custom, a young person generally defers to an older person. Thus, in a strictly regulated family life, a younger child is expected to obey orders or instructions from elders once he or she is beyond the infant stage. Some families allow a little laxity in this respect, but, in so doing, they always expose themselves to the reproach of relatives and neighbors. In family life, the practice of handing a whip to the older child and instructing him or her to use it on his or her junior whenever the latter first becomes offensive and insubordinate is constantly being resorted to in order to instill the lesson of respect and obedience into the heart of the rebellious junior. However tolerant a family may be in respect to a child's behavior, very few would condone any insubordination on the part of the child toward another who is three or four years his or her senior. The three years of child spacing through the widely practiced postpartum abstinence is sufficient basis for ordering seniority. Thus, the seniority principle guarantees obedience to authority, which reinforces the concept of leadership.

The principle of seniority also entails classification into exclusive groups based solely on age. These age groups or cohorts perform communal activities relative to their ages, usually set apart by three or four years. More important, however, is that this classification allows one to know one's place in society. This insistence upon younger people keeping or knowing their places in the social order, to which they have been consigned by age, is a significant custom, serving as an effective mechanism of social control. The seniority principle applies in all walks of life and in practically all activities in which men and women are brought together. The custom cuts through distinctions of wealth, rank, and gender. Hence, the principles of kinship and seniority ensure respect for custom, authority, and tradition, upon which the stability of interpersonal relationships rests, especially well defined among the Yoruba of southwest Nigeria.

Role of Religion

Standing out quite prominently in traditional social life is the part played by religion in giving meaning to social experience while enforcing ethical precepts. In Nigeria, indigenous religious practices tend to focus on ancestor worship and polytheism, whereby there is a pantheon of local gods/deities that vary from one community to the other. Generally, they constitute an institutional form of social control as, in totality, they serve to induce compliance with social norms. African traditional religion—the indigenous religion of the African, handed down from generations of Africans—is not a fossil religion but a religion that Africans today have made theirs by living it and practicing it. It is "written" everywhere, particularly in the people's myths and folktales, in their songs and dances, and in their proverbs and pithy sayings (Awolalu, 1976:275). Despite its many forms, it is essentially an integrative mechanism in most groups and communities.

Nowadays, in the wake of secular solutions to the uncertainties and tensions in human life, it is doubtful whether religion, indigenous or imported, can continue to play this significant role for, already, it is apparent that there is a growing problem of the diminishing efficacy of the fear of the gods, which had long served as deterrence to violation of social norms. Though it may be difficult to find a substitute with the same fervor of emotional appeal as in religion, the legal system nonetheless has to be supported by something else. This is predicated upon the widely accepted view in the criminological literature that there would be far more crime if fear of punishment were to be the only deterrent. Conscience and religion, it is surmised, constrain criminal/deviant behavior at least as much as the fear of punishment. Thus, the relationship among religion, morals, and social control has been seriously attenuated with regard to the etiology of criminal/deviant behavior, such that civil society appears to be least relevant in latter-day socialization processes.

Disposition

In an indigenous setting in Nigeria's rural areas, punishment is forceful enough to control children but not to damage them. A child found violating a norm or rule is often whipped or severely rebuked on the spot by the observer of the violation; a relative, neighbor, or even a stranger. In some cases, a report of such violation or any insubordination made to the parents/guardians is swiftly accompanied by a more severe whipping of the child involved. But in serious violations of taboos, for instance, reports are frequently made to both parents and community leaders so as to effect the performance of the required ritual sacrifices to cleanse both the land and the group of the abominations.

Generally, in the category of direct methods, corporal punishment is the most readily resorted to in dealing with any juvenile misconduct. Although regarded as a short-term suppressor of human behavior, physical punishment is generally accepted as a short, sharp shock, especially for first offenders. Other direct methods include fines (mostly in kind), restitution, compensation, ridicule or ostracism, and forbearance from violation through specific information or instruction as to the accepted behavior/activity by seniors or elders.

In respect of the indirect methods of disposition, the most common is benefiting from the experience of others through observing societal reaction to conformists and nonconformists. The most effective indirect method, however, is absorption of the lessons of morality and good manners inculcated in children through the medium of numerous folktales and proverbs in daily use and, generally, employed to drive home some practical truths. Because of the diffusion of Western culture, the least effective indirect method (over time) is instilling fear of the gods in the minds of young persons.

Problems Facing the Informal System

The most telling problem is lack of documentation in view of Nigeria's "oral tradition" whereby ideas, customs, norms, and so on are verbally transmitted from generation to generation. Consequently, in spite of their wider appeal, coordination and implementation of indigenous values and practices in respect of achieving maximum compliance to them have been woefully haphazard. Even the popular drive toward modernity in these transitional societies appears to consign indigenous values and practices of socializing the young into an earlier stage of human and social development. This neglect has given rise to the non-sharpening of indigenous values and practices for relevant adaptation and adoption in the service of the juvenile justice system.

Another major problem is due to cultural diffusion and its conflicting conduct norms, which has been aptly described as "the pillaging of the African culture" (Sofola, 1973:11). Industrialization and urbanization gave rise to the dominance of the nuclear family over the extended family system and, with these processes, diminishing parental authority. Increased industrialization also gave rise to greater affluence, which, in turn, actively encourages criminal/delinquent behavior. In the emergent new environment, values and norms that were cherished, indigenous ways of socialization lost their binding force. The picture, therefore, appears to be that, whereas, in the more settled environments of Europe and North America, the family is in the vanguard in the struggle against delinquency and crime, Africa's triple heritage has severely weighted down the indigenous family system in effectively performing its traditional functions. Although this shift in the family system certainly plays a role in the causation of juvenile delinquency, it is not entirely a direct cause, but one of many in the process of causation.

CONCLUSION AND SUGGESTIONS

Aside from very few material results, colonization has shamelessly and unnecessarily deprived Africans of their customs and indigenous framework. While "science" and the modern way of life may be indispensable for Africa, the "rape" of its kinship classificatory system—the extended family—is agonizingly enduring. As a historical fact, therefore, the establishment of colonial rule in most of Africa changed many of the African's indigenous way of life. Thus, nearly all elements of African society have been unduly affected by Western and/or Arab culture(s). Significantly, the greater affluence generated through contact with the technologically domineering Western culture attenuated family ties. Children become economically active at an early age, which further hampers the disciplining process.

One of the major changes induced by these processes has been an increase in the production and consumption of alcoholic drinks and tobacco. Although traditional alcoholic beverages existed prior to colonization, a major increase in consumption as part of a normal lifestyle started only about 50 years ago. Beer became a popular beverage in Nigeria, especially after World War II. During the oil-boom years of the 1970s, beer (especially, canned beer), in spite of local production since 1949, was imported in large quantities, reaching a peak in 1977. But the consistent rise in its consumption, coupled with indiscriminate importation of canned beer, created a major social problem, as it was widely available to the young. Since there is no age restriction to the purchase of alcoholic drinks in Nigeria, the young are exposed too early to alcohol and its main consequence of lowering inhibitions so as to predispose to criminal/deviant behavior.

Of particular concern in analyzing urbanization in the Third World, however, is "overurbanization," produced by the migration of people from the countryside to the cities. The term, in short, stands for a stream of migration sapping the economic strength of the countryside without correspondingly large benefits to urban production, that is, underemployment and depopulation versus unemployment and overpopulation. This sociostructural and demographic defect is attested to by the many armies of young people living by their wits in most cities in Nigeria. With the growing numbers of unemployed juveniles, the incidence of drug abuse has increased in Nigeria's urban areas. Also of concern is the unique problem of children living in the streets who are alienated from their families, especially in the rural areas. These "street Arabs" are usually the prime agents of destruction during political and religious riots in urban centers. Because of their disordered existence and lack of proper family life, these children become mostly ensnared in the vicious circle of crime/delinquency—activities without which they would not survive because they have nowhere else to turn.

In indigenous Nigerian communities, the use of leisure time revolved around community-based activities, especially collectively in age grades or cohorts. Since most communities were small-scale and homogeneous, leisure activities tended to be small-scale and participatory, utilizing resources that were available within the locality. Hence, if there was any misuse of leisure, it tended to be minimal and was easily controlled. Leisure today has become complex and focused around television, the film and music industries, books, sports, and other mass entertainment activities. Although the causal link between the mass media and crime is not firmly grounded, film, video, computer games, songs, and media presentations of violence tend to promote violence as a reasonable way to solve problems and settle disputes.

By means of television, children see the "violence of the entire planet" and thereby internalize large quantities of violence—characterizing the misuse of leisure by youths today. Because violent behavior is a learned process, parents have a responsibility to be good models and to be their children's advocates. On one hand, parents need to be supportive and to help their children develop self-assurance and build self-esteem to withstand damaging peer pressure or school violence. On the other, parents also need "to give every child a better future," especially the shelter of a loving family in which to learn and mature, but not as the victim of domestic/family violence.

Consequently, to equip youths to function as responsible adults in a competitive, technological, and ideologically multifaceted world, education has to be process-oriented, rather than product-oriented. While education authorities need to take a fresh look at both the school curriculum and the methods used to assess a pupil's progress, the school and the family should be working closer together in the upbringing of children: sharing the responsibility for children's personality development and teaching them standards of behavior. Parents are encouraged to put greater emphasis on the utilitarian motive (general improvement) of education, rather than the instrumental motive (personal gain), as currently practiced. Moreover, government should reintroduce moral instruction into education, but not in the old ineffective manner. Moral instruction and ethical philosophy should be made compulsory subjects in schools and universities, respectively. Teachers of ethics should be dedicated and exemplary men and women whose lives would provide fine moral examples. Neither parents nor teachers can afford to remain "distant" personalities but need to be involved to mutual advantage. Just as problems at home often affect a child's work, so a good home life can help a child to get the best out of school.

As an important aspect in the process of secondary socialization, the age-group system has to be pressingly revisited. The principle of classification involved in this system is not rank or wealth but almost exclusively age. According to Fadipe (1970:253), in precolonial Nigeria, age groups were a convenient way of organizing the people for the performance of most of their civil duties. Government should adapt the age-grade system to modern times by having all juveniles organized into social clubs along the lines of their classification by age. This can be more effective by involving the local governments at the grassroots level in order thereby to encourage a higher stake in conformity in the community concerned. It is surmised that the perennial problems of cultural pluralism dogging criminal/delinquency policy in Nigeria will persist unless adequate consideration and reliance on the relevant operative cultural values of the people are achieved. Hence, in the formulation of criminal policy, nothing but the cherished values of the people should form the substratum. The juvenile justice system in Nigeria, therefore, would perform better by tapping into the reservoir of resources accumulated in indigenous values and practices.

NOTES

Dedicated to Dr. Tai Solarin (1922–1994), a renowned educationist, democrat, and human-rights activist who lived for humanity; and to those truly committed to the establishment of a solid foundation for democracy in Nigeria.

1. For a more comprehensive discussion of Mosaic law, with particular reference to returning evil for evil, see the Pentateuch (especially *Exodus,* Chs. 21 and 22).

2. Jesus Christ, as the mediator of the new covenant/testament, enjoins (absolute) love (1 Cor. 13); but see Mt. 5:38–45, Rom. 12:17–21.

3. For an illuminating discussion of the basic modes of adaptation to the disjunctions between goals and means in a society, see Merton (1957), especially Chapters 3 and 4.

4. Cap. 77; Vol. 5 of the 1990 Laws of the Federation (as amended).

5. Penal Code (northern states) Federal Provisions Act, Cap. 345, Vol. 19, Laws of the Federation, 1990.

6. Cap. 80 and Cap. 81 (re: federal offenses in the northern states), Vol. 5 of the 1990 Laws of the Federation (as amended).

7. Evidence Act, Cap. 112, Vol. 8 of the 1990 Laws of the Federation.

8. While recognizing the diversity in culture, the 1979 Constitution of the Federal Republic of Nigeria established appellate courts in the states to administer either customary or Sharia laws, whichever apply.

9. Cap. 42, Vol. 1, Laws of the Federation of Nigeria and the Federal Territory of Lagos, 1958, and as variously amended thereafter to apply to each state since 1978.

10. "Child" means a person below the age of 14 years. "Young person" means a person who has attained the age of 14 years and is below the age of 17 years, but "young female" refers to any girl between the ages of 14 and 16 years.

11. In fact, many conferences, symposia, and workshops have continuously recommended improved manpower development for the personnel—the police, probation officers, and even magistrates. Being not in the public gaze, because of no media coverage of their activities, juvenile courts are shunned by most personnel who are thirsty for the "juicy" goings-on in the adult courts. Indeed, there is low morale among staff in the juvenile court system.

REFERENCES

Akin Bulumo, Sigi O. A. "Residents' Concern about Crime and Crime Prevention." *Journal of Social Issues* 52 (1996): 62–85.

Amadi, Elechi. *Ethics in Nigerian Culture*. Ibadan: Heinemann, 1982.

Awolalu, J. O. "Sin and Its Removal in African Traditional Religion." *Journal of the American Academy of Religion* 44 (1976): 273–288.

Chinoy, Ely. *Society: An Introduction to Sociology*. New York: Random House, 1967.

Clifford, William. *An Introduction to African Criminology*. Nairobi: Oxford University Press, 1974.

———. "Criminology in Developing Nations—African and Asian Examples." In *International Handbook of Contemporary Criminology: General Issues and the Americas,* edited by Elmer H. Johnson. Westport, CT: Greenwood Press, 1983.

Elias, Taslim O. *British Colonial Law*. London: Butterworths, 1963.

———. *Law in a Developing Society*. Benin: Ethiope, 1973.

Fadipe, Nathaniel A. *The Sociology of the Yoruba,* edited by F. O. Okediji and O. O. Okediji. Ibadan: Ibadan University Press, 1970.

Green, M. M. *Ibo Village Affairs,* 2d. London: Frank Cass, 1964.

Johnson, Elmer H. "Preface" and "Criminology: Its Variety and Patterns throughout the World." In *International Handbook of Contemporary Criminology: General Issues and the Americas,* Part 1, edited by Elmer H. Johnson. Westport, CT: Greenwood Press, 1983.

Karibi-Whyte, Adolphus G. "Cultural Pluralism and the Formulation of Criminal Policy." In *Nigerian Criminal Process,* edited by A. A. Adeyemi. Lagos: University of Lagos Press, 1977.

Kibuka, Eric P. "Crime in African Countries." *International Review of Criminal Policy* 35 (1980): 13–23.

Merton, Robert K. *Social Theory and Social Structure,* rev., enlarged ed. Glencoe, IL: Free Press, 1957.

Murrell, M. E., and Lester, D. *Introduction to Juvenile Delinquency*. New York: Macmillan, 1981.

Nzimiro, Ikenna. *Studies in Igbo Political Systems*. London: Frank Cass, 1972.

Odekunle, Femi. "Capitalist Economy and the Crime Problem in Nigeria." *Contemporary Crises* 2 (1978): 89–96.

Oki, J. O. "The Role of the Social Welfare Service in the Administration of Criminal Justice." In *Nigerian Criminal Process,* edited by A. A. Adeyemi. Lagos: University of Lagos Press, 1977.

Osinbajo, Y., and Kalu, A., eds. *Law Development and Administration in Nigeria*. Ibadan: Intec, 1990.

Shoemaker, Donald J. *Theories of Delinquency: An Examination of Explanations of Delinquent Behavior,* 2d ed. New York: Oxford University Press, 1990.

Sofola, Jafotito A. *African Culture and the African Personality*. Ibadan: African Resources, 1973.

Szabo, Denis. "Preface." In *Nigerian Criminal Process,* edited by A. A. Adeyemi. Lagos: University of Lagos Press, 1977.

Thornton, W. E., Jr., Lydia Voigt, and William G. Doerner. *Delinquency and Justice,* 2d ed. New York: Random House, 1987.

Winslow, R. W. *Juvenile Delinquency in a Free Society*. Encino, CA: Dickenson, 1976.

15

THE REPUBLIC OF THE PHILIPPINES

Donald J. Shoemaker and W. Timothy Austin

INTRODUCTION

The beginning of the juvenile justice system in the Philippines is traced to the turn of the twentieth century. Before this time, juvenile offenders were treated in the same manner as adults. In 1906, a law was passed that provided for the special care and humane treatment of juvenile males aged 8–16 and females aged 8–18 who were found guilty of offenses carrying punishment less than the death penalty or life imprisonment (Esguerra, 1979:48). This law was modified in 1924 and again in 1930, when the ''juvenile delinquency law'' was first established. This law is known as Article 80 of the Revised Penal Code (Esguerra, 1979:49). During the era of martial law, additional amendments to Article 80 were passed, particularly with respect to drug use.

Pursuant to the provisions of Article 80, juvenile courts were established as early as 1955, first in Manila, then in other cities, by local legislation. Currently, these courts are referred to as Juvenile and Domestic Relations Courts (JRDC). Not all of the laws providing for separate juvenile courts are uniform. For example, in Quezon City, the juvenile court has jurisdiction over criminal cases involving youth 16 years of age or younger at the time of the ''trial.'' In other cities, the statutory age of jurisdiction for the JRDC is defined according to when the case was filed. In Dumaguete City, the jurisdiction of the JRDC extends to criminal charges against public officials, including graft and corruption offenses and tax evasion (Esguerra, 1979:50–53). Furthermore, juvenile courts have yet to be established in many metropolitan areas, such as Cagayan de Oro City, on Mindanao Island.

In 1974, Presidential Decree (PD) Number 603, or the Child and Youth Welfare Code, was signed. This document has become the basis for contemporary formal procedures of juvenile justice in the Philippines. This law, along with subsequent amendments, provides that the agency possessing primary responsibility for the welfare of youth ages 9–18 is the Department of Social Welfare and Development (DSWD). PD 603 also details the procedures for the formal processing of youth through the juvenile system, along with provisions for the detainment and/or institutionalization of youthful offenders (Albada-Lim, 1978). These procedures will be discussed in the next section of this chapter.

In 1978, however, another presidential decree was signed into law. This document is PD 1508, commonly referred to as the *Katarungang Pambarangay* Law. The purpose of this law is to establish the jurisdiction of local political units, known as *barangays,* over minor civil and criminal offenses, family disputes, and disagreements among neighbors. In addition, the *barangay* may serve as the first formal setting for hearing cases involving more serious offenses. One of the more significant features of the *barangay* hearing, or court, is the informality of the proceedings. Lawyers are expressly excluded from these hearings. Furthermore, the basic format that is supposed to be followed in conducting these courts is known as ''amicable settlement'' (Orendain, 1978:3).

The person responsible for holding court proceedings at this level is an elected official, known as the *barangay* captain. The captain is a powerful political figure in the community and has considerable latitude in disposing of cases. Records of dispute hearings are recorded by a secretary, appointed by the captain, and eventually sent to a central record-keeping agency in Manila. However, the recordings of *barangay* hearings do not typically indicate the ages of the disputants.

The *barangay* system is virtually mandated for all minor civil and criminal charges (Pe and Tadiar, 1979:Chapter 2). Some feel this system of justice is compatible with basic Filipino values, such as maintaining smooth interpersonal relationships and the importance of the family, although it is recognized that such a system may also facilitate the processing of minor cases and thus relieve the formal court system of dealing with such issues (Orendain, 1978:5–6; Pe and Tadiar, 1979:5–6). For whatever reasons *barangay* justice was created, its importance in the processing of juvenile cases should not be underestimated.[1]

In regard to the settlement of small grievances and disputes, whether of juveniles or adults, the importance of political and geographic subdivisions is substantial. Throughout the Philippines there are over 48,000 *barangays* or distinct village-level communities, with an average size of 900 residents. Even an urban area such as Manila, with millions of inhabitants, is actually an aggregate of over 2,000 individual *barangays.* Thus, in the cities, a youth, for example, benefits from being reared in a setting representing social controls characteristic of small communities generally associated with more rural locales. If youths wander from home, they often come under the watchful attention of *barangay* citizens who likely recognize the youths as members of the local area. A pattern of disciplining children outside the home is even more predictable in the isolated villages and at the sub-*barangay* level, such as the neighborhood *puroks* and *sitios.*

The latitude accorded *barangay* captains and other officials in dealing with juvenile cases, along with the informality of these proceedings, sometimes results in circumventions of established rules and procedures in handling juveniles. Formal rules and policies do exist, however, and these affect the processing of juvenile suspects through the entire system. The next section of this chapter addresses these formal procedures and rules, beginning with the *barangay* level of justice and proceeding through the rest of the system.

FORMAL POLICIES AND PROCEDURES OF THE JUVENILE JUSTICE SYSTEM

Barangay Justice

The *barangay* captain is often the first official representative of government to become aware of juvenile offending in a neighborhood. The captain is supposed to be informed of transgressions committed by youth living in the *barangay*. The decision as to what should be done next is supposed to be a matter of established policy.

Criminal acts may be reported directly to the captain or to members of advisory and watch groups, appointed by the captain. Most *barangay* captains are assisted by a small group known as a *tanod*. Also, all *barangay* captains are assisted by an advisory group known as a *Kagawad*, which, among other functions, helps keep tabs on youth activities and concerns among parents about the youth in the neighborhood. Some *barangays* are divided into smaller geographical units, known as *pooks* (or *puroks*) or *sitios*. In these cases, the practice may be for disputes and complaints to be brought first to a *pook* captain or to a member of the *tanod* for settlement (Tadiar, 1984:43).

When the captain learns of the commission of a criminal act by a juvenile living in the *barangay,* the first thing to be decided is the gravity of the offense. If the act is considered a minor offense, that is, *arresto menor,* then it falls within the jurisdiction of the *barangay.* A minor criminal act carries a jail term of 30 days or less or a fine of 200 pesos or less or, in the case of physical injury, medical attention requiring less than 10 days of treatment (Orendain, 1978:39).

Upon establishing jurisdiction, the captain ideally first schedules a meeting between the juvenile offender and the victim(s). The purpose of this meeting is to attempt to arrive at an agreement between the offender and the victim, and it is usually informal in character. If this effort fails, or if the victim presses for a more formal hearing, a *barangay* court is scheduled. The court hearing is conducted by the captain, who questions disputants and attempts to resolve the disagreement as quickly and amicably as possible. The mediatory nature of these proceedings is underscored by the absence of legal counsel for either side.

If the disputants cannot reach a settlement within a specified time, 15–30 days, the captain is supposed to organize a *Pangkat*, which is a tribunal composed of members of the *barangay*. The purpose of this group is to try to force the disputants to reach some kind of "fair" settlement. If such an agreement still cannot be reached, again within 15 to 30 days, the case is supposed to be referred to the courts for settlement (Orendain, 1978:9–43; Pe and Tadiar, 1979: 30–140).

Police, Prosecutor, and DSWD Procedures

According to the Child and Youth Welfare Code (PD 603), in cases involving more serious offenses, referred to as *arresto mayor,* the formal policy is for the *barangay* captain to refer the matter to the police, the prosecutor (the *fiscal*), or the DSWD. When the police have been informed of a criminal violation, or they have directly observed an offense, their response is supposed to be to arrest the offender and then to refer the case to the *fiscal*'s office. The *fiscal* is supposed to arrange a physical and mental examination of the alleged offender before proceeding with a prosecution of the case. Juveniles who have been found guilty of a criminal act may be placed in a prison, especially if they are repeat offenders. In July 1993, the death penalty was restored in the Philippines. However, capital punishment is not applicable to juveniles below age 18.

A judge may suspend the conviction of a youthful offender upon appeal by the offender and recommendation of a DSWD employee and order the youth to be placed under the supervision of the DSWD until the age of 18, or 21 if the juvenile is considered to be unrehabilitated upon reaching age 18.[2] This policy is particularly likely to happen if the juvenile is a first offender. A youngster placed under the jurisdiction of the DSWD may be placed in a Regional Rehabilitation Center for Youth (RRCY) or any home or facility deemed suitable for the care and custody of juveniles. The DSWD is to submit regular progress reports to the sentencing judge, who holds ultimate dispositional authority in the case.

Before trial, juveniles may be temporarily housed in local detention homes or in separate quarters in local jails. The police have authority to place juveniles in detention, but they may also be sent to these facilities by order of the DSWD. If a person reaches the age of 21 and still has not been released from the supervision of the DSWD, she or he may be retained in the rehabilitation center, sent to a regional prison, or placed on probation. Technically, juveniles are supervised on probationary terms, but formal "probation" is reserved for adult offenders.

Statistical Data

National data on the extent of delinquency in the Philippines are difficult to obtain. *Barangay* reports typically do not indicate the ages of disputants. Furthermore, since the basic purpose of *barangay* justice is to resolve disputes and minor criminal offenses in an amicable and conciliatory process, few such cases end up in formal courts. *Barangay* reports in Cagayan de Oro City, for example, indicated that in the third quarter of 1990, only 3.1 percent of criminal cases had been referred to the court for settlement. A study of *barangays* in Metro Manila concluded that over 85 percent of cases handled in the *barangays* were "successfully" settled (Tadiar, 1984:130). However, this study did not indicate the percentage of criminal cases that were eventually filed in court. Tadiar also concluded that many *barangay* captains were handling criminal cases that lay outside the jurisdiction of *barangay* law, that is, including more serious offenses (p. 106). To the extent such cases are handled by *barangay* officials, information concerning delinquency becomes even more difficult to ascertain.

Figures from the DSWD are more informative relative to delinquency than are other official figures. Even these data, however, are limited. Information supplied by officials with the DSWD, for example, indicates that there are 10 RRCYs located throughout the country. The capacity of each center is 50 juveniles at one time. A total of 1,695 youth were placed in these centers in 1990–1992. An additional 11,103 youth were being treated in noninstitutional settings (undifferentiated).

Of those juveniles placed in an RRCY, 96 percent were males. Forty-five percent of these juveniles were between ages 16 and 18, 38 percent were 13–15, 9 percent were 10–12 years old, and 8 percent were 19 years old or over. No other demographic information on these youth was provided.

The offenses for which the RRCY youth were convicted consisted primarily of property crimes, such as theft and robbery (robbery is classified as a property crime in the Philippines). Over 78 percent of these youth were convicted of a property crime. Person crimes constituted the next largest crime category of RRCY youth, 11.7 percent of the total. The remaining 10 percent of youth were convicted of other kinds of offenses, such as disobeying parents, aggravated violent crimes (such as robbery and rape or homicide), and weapons possession.

Interestingly, no offender placed in an RRCY was convicted of a drug offense. It is unimaginable that drug offenses are not committed by youth in the Philippines. Police and *barangay* officials in Cagayan de Oro City indicated that sometimes youthful drug offenders are handled by military officials. Before 1991, the police were organizationally part of the military of the country. In addition, *barangay* captains in Cagayan de Oro indicated they often handled alcohol and drug offenses in their neighborhoods. DSWD workers in Cagayan also said they sometimes handled cases involving drug and alcohol offenses, but these offenses represented less than 10 percent of total caseloads. From this information, it would appear as if youthful drug offenders are either handled in the community, informally at the *barangay* level or by the DSWD, or they are handled separately, perhaps in military settings or perhaps as convicted criminals not granted suspension who are sent to adult prisons.

INFORMAL REACTIONS TO DELINQUENCY

Financial Considerations

Even though laws permitting juvenile courts and separate detention centers for juveniles have been established for many years, the actual existence of such facilities is problematic. Several years ago, Esguerra noted the lack of funds as an important impediment to the full utilization of the country's legally constructed juvenile justice system and adequate record keeping within the system (1979:62).

Interviews with *barangay* and police officials in Cagayan de Oro City in 1990 indicate Esguerra's concerns still exist. There is no juvenile court system in Cagayan de Oro, which is a major port city of approximately 350,000 people, located at the northern end of Mindanao Island. Records of juvenile offenders are not systematically maintained. In one police precinct, for example, information concerning offenses is kept on matchbook covers. The lack of systematic record keeping for juvenile offenders extends to the *fiscal*'s office. According to the records of this office, 13 juveniles were prosecuted for a crime between March 1988 and July 1990, and none of these cases involved rape or murder. Yet, the *fiscal* indicated that approximately 30–40 juvenile cases were prosecuted each month, and DSWD workers estimated that approximately 10–20 percent of their supervision caseloads involved youth convicted of rape, homicide, or murder.

Motorized vehicles, communications equipment, and other aspects of Western police forces are not routinely available to the police in this city. Even when cars or motorbikes are available, gasoline is rationed. If the police are in pursuit of a suspect and run out of gas, they must abandon the motor pursuit and hope to catch the suspect some other way. This situation occurs throughout the country.

Several police officers who were interviewed in Cagayan de Oro indicated that often suspects would not be arrested because there was no place to put the person, and there were no resources to process the case. One police officer noted that the costs of investigating alleged offenses must be borne by the victim because "[w]e have no budget for this."

One reaction to the lack of funds, facilities, and other resources for formally processing youthful offenders is to exercise informal mechanisms of justice. Often, the police or *barangay* captains in Cagayan de Oro City advise or counsel youthful offenders. Another informal response is to "box" the offender. Boxing involves hitting a person to cause pain and, maybe just as important, shame to the offender. Boxing is also evident in citizen reactions to offenders and is sometimes promoted by the police. Local and Manila newspapers often have photographs of a victim boxing an alleged offender, with the police standing in the background.

A more serious and extreme informal response to crime is to "salvage" the offender. Salvaging someone means simply to kill the person and leave the body for relatives or others to claim. Salvaging is usually reserved for violent and/or repeat offenders, including juveniles. It amounts to an informal exercise of the death penalty, even though capital punishment does not legally exist for juveniles in the Philippines. The police and *barangay* officials are sometimes implicated in the salvaging of offenders or suspects (Ignacio, 1990). Although salvaging is clearly not an official governmental sanction for crime, it is justified by many in the community, including *barangay* and law enforcement personnel, because of the lack of resources for prosecuting and imprisoning violent and repeat offenders.

Sociocultural Factors

While lack of funds, facilities, and basic resources certainly impede the fuller development and utilization of a formal juvenile justice system in the Philippines, social and cultural factors also influence community reactions to youthful offenders. As Austin notes, even when funds are made available to governments, such as for the construction of new *barangay* meeting halls, the money is not always spent on such facilities (1987:246). Several sociocultural values are often cited as basic to Philippine society, and some contend these values undergird the *barangay* system of justice (Orendain, 1978:5; Pe and Tadiar, 1979:5). From the foregoing discussions, it would seem that the majority of juvenile offenders are handled at the local, *barangay,* level of justice, in an informal manner, and with little recorded official information on the characteristics of the offender or the criminal event. This method of handling juvenile offenders not only is less expensive to utilize but also seems more compatible with basic Filipino values and social structures, several of which are discussed next.

The Family System

The family unit is basic to life in the Philippines (Espiritu, 1987; Quisumbing, 1987). The influence of the family is found in social, business, and political relationships. Although many family living arrangements are nuclear, especially in large cities, the *social* significance of the family is in the influence of the extended family. People are socialized to honor and respect their extended relatives, and, for many, family honor is considered more important than personal gain (Quisumbing, 1964; Jocano, 1975). In addition, the family system in the Philippines is augmented by the presence of a compadre system, which places individuals within family relationships, even though they are not blood relatives or related by marriage (Espiritu, 1987). Some contend the extended family and compadre systems extend to the *barangay* (Pido, 1986:19). The *barangay* becomes a further extension of the family, and the captain represents the source of authority within this structure. Thus, when a *barangay* captain exercises discipline on a miscreant youth in the *barangay,* she or he is acting as a parental figure in the neighborhood.

SIR, Reciprocity, and Hiya

The importance of the family and groupings such as *barangays* is connected with certain cultural values that stress social cooperation and order. Lynch (1970:9–10) maintains that one of the more important cultural values in Philippine society is "smooth interpersonal relations," or SIR. SIR basically refers to the importance of getting along with others and not offending one's character or honor. SIR is supported by prescriptions such as promoting social acceptance, the notion that one is to be accepted as a person, rather than for possessions or wealth. In addition, SIR is related to a concept known as *pakikisama,* or "giving in" to the wishes of others. This concept is particularly addressed to children and youth, in their relationships with elder relatives and authority figures (Jocano, 1969:83–95; Lynch, 1970:11).

Another important cultural value in Philippine society is a norm of reciprocity, *utang na loob* (Kaut, 1961). According to this concept, one incurs social debts, such as the debt to one's parents or elders or to a benefactor. This debt is to be repaid with respect and honor, sometimes with political or social loyalty. Hollnsteiner (1970:70) maintains that *utang na loob* was an integral part of earlier *barangay* structures and represented expressions of support and loyalty to *barangay* chiefs.

Utang na loob may also form a type of security net for local residents and may even extend to youth. That is, if people are owed favors by a number of other people, then they may feel secure because they can rely on others to come to their assistance should the need arise (Austin, 1995). Feeling obligated to go to the aid of others appears similar to the obligation that fraternity or gang members may feel toward each other. However, it would be contrary to the admirable trait of *utang na loob* for a Filipino to purposely set up situations where there would be favors owed by others.

Filipino society is also characterized by the importance of avoiding shame and promoting honor. In social relationships, it is important not only to foster SIR but also to display respect for others and not to shame them publicly. The concept of shame is expressed as *hiya* (Bulatao, 1964; Lynch, 1970:15). To act shamelessly or to bring shame on others is considered a major cultural violation in Philippine society. Thus, a juvenile who brings shame on the family or on neighbors by violating laws or by not agreeing to settlements reached by elder relatives or the *barangay* captain courts not only legal sanctions but, perhaps more important, social condemnation.

Voluntary Organizations

A strong tradition of altruism has persisted from earliest years of Philippine history. Assisting others in times of need or danger is prevalent today throughout the islands and impacts on one's daily life, whether young or old. Value orientations that bond citizens together, such as *utang na loob, pakikisama,* and *hiya,* act to set the stage for a variety of community-based voluntary networks or organizations commonly joined by *barangay* youth and adults alike. Volunteering for local service-oriented organizations not only functions to assist the community, as with the *tanod* or *barangay* security force, but also provides considerable pride for the individual member. In several rural *barangays* in the Central Luzon region, local youthful males show great self-esteem by proudly boasting of their membership in the village *tanod*. Many of the young males are unable to find employment but maintain considerable dignity through active work with the local security force. Other older youth volunteer for military or police auxiliary units. With a shortage of professional police or military, towns, especially the isolated villages, rely on voluntary organizations. Many youth participate in the *"Bantay ng Bayan"* (watch of the country), a type of radio net whereby members keep in immediate communications with each other and offer assistance when needed (see Austin, 1988; cf. Austin, 1995).

CONCLUSION

The Philippine government has established a rather elaborate formal system of processing juvenile offenders. This system includes the concept of a juvenile court and separate confinement facilities for juveniles awaiting a hearing and for rehabilitation of those found guilty of a crime. The beginnings of this system appeared in the first third of the twentieth century but were more formalized in 1974.

In 1978, another law was passed that established a conciliatory form of justice within political jurisdictions known as *barangays*. In this system, matters are to be handled more or less informally. Records of proceedings are to be kept and sent to governmental authorities, but lawyers are prohibited from representing disputants, and the atmosphere of the hearings is supposed to avoid the trappings of an adversarial court. Officially, minor criminal cases are to be settled amicably at the *barangay* level, particularly by the elected leader of the *barangay*, the captain. However, studies of *barangay* justice suggest that captains often exceed their jurisdictional boundaries and attempt to settle more serious crimes using the conciliatory framework.

Records of *barangay* hearings do not reflect the ages of disputants. Furthermore, official accounts of juvenile offending in police and court files are inconsistent. The agency primarily responsible for the care and rehabilitation of juvenile offenders is known as the Department of Social Welfare and Development. This agency maintains files and information on youth found guilty of a crime and sent to one of 10 Regional Rehabilitation Centers for Youth, with a suspended conviction, or placed in nonresidential, community-based facilities. However, these juveniles represent only a fraction of all juvenile offenders, and information on even these youth and their offenses is inconsistent and incomplete.

In many areas of the country, the formal system of juvenile justice is nonexistent or underutilized. Lack of funds and resources undoubtedly contributes to this situation. However, it would appear that what has happened in the Philippines is that the law establishing *barangay* justice in 1978 has essentially eclipsed the formal system of juvenile justice, particularly in provincial areas. *Barangay* justice seems more compatible with Philippine values. Coupled with a lack of adequate funds and resources to establish and maintain a more formalized system of juvenile justice, the presence of *barangay* justice seems to be the more common form of handling juvenile offenders. While much of the reaction to delinquency involves advice and counseling, sometimes more physical methods of discipline are utilized, such as boxing or hitting offenders and suspects. In extreme cases, particularly for repeat or violent offenders, the person is salvaged, or killed, even though the death penalty does not officially exist for juveniles.

The Republic of the Philippines comprises a number of distinct cultures, each of which may adhere in varying degrees to the patterns of juvenile justice discussed in these pages. Often separated into isolated island groups, subcultures emerge that occasionally allow for the persistence of people with dissimilar lifeways. In central and southern Mindanao, Filipino Muslims have congregated into an autonomous region and may not totally adhere to the official frameworks of *barangay* justice. It appears that Muslim Filipinos also possess similar value orientations of altruism and volunteerism as seen in other regions. Conflicts that occur between Muslim and Christian citizenry, including occasional fighting or thievery by youth, require a third party "fixer" to intervene and work toward mediation. Generally, such "fixers" are *mestizos,* who were born in one culture and converted to the other but understand and respect each. Full understanding of juvenile justice in the Philippines will eventually have to include more complete discussions of such isolated subcultures (Gowing, 1988; Austin, 1994).

Current conditions of juvenile justice in the Philippines may certainly change as the country modernizes and obtains necessary funds and resources for the fuller utilization of legally established procedures and facilities. This situation should also result in more complete and representative statistical information on the extent and nature of delinquency and the procedures for dealing with this behavior.

NOTES

Data for this paper were gathered from research projects conducted by both authors in Luzon and northern Mindanao and from interviews and documents supplied by officials with the Department of Social Welfare and Development in Metro Manila. These projects were funded, in part, by Fulbright scholarships and grants from the U.S. Peace Institute, Virginia Polytechnic Institute and State University, and Indiana University of Pennsylvania. The conclusions and interpretations of the authors, however, do not necessarily represent the views of these funding agencies. Special acknowledgment is given to Lota Generalao for assistance in data collection and to the faculty and staff of Xavier University in Cagayan de Oro City and the University of the Philippines, Diliman, for logistical and administrative support.

Additional information on the correctional system for juveniles in the Philippines may be found in Donald J. Shoemaker, "Juvenile Corrections in the Philippines: The *Barangay* System," forthcoming in the *Journal of Offender Rehabilitation.*

1. The mediating function of the *barangay* system is similar to the practice of holding family group conferences to deal with juvenile offenders in New Zealand and Australia (Braithwaite and Mugford, 1994). One difference between *barangay* justice and family conferences is the use of a professional coordinator in the family conference, as opposed to an elected leader, the *barangay* captain, in the Philippines. Both settings, however, share an informal format, an emphasis on victim forgiveness, and efforts to handle the reactions to juvenile offending within a wider communal context. Furthermore, these practices would appear to stem from cultural traditions in each country.

2. Juveniles convicted of very serious or "heinous" crimes, such as murder or rape, cannot have their sentence suspended.

REFERENCES

Albada-Lim, Estefania. "Care of the Juvenile Offenders in the Philippines." *International Journal of Offender Therapy and Comparative Criminology* 22 (1978): 239–243.

Austin, W. Timothy. "Conceptual Confusion among Rural Filipinos in Adapting to Modern Procedures of Amicable Settlement." *International Journal of Comparative and Applied Criminal Justice* 11 (1987):241–251.

———. "Fieldnotes on the Vigilante Movement in Mindanao: A Mix of Self-Help and Formal Policing Networks." *International Journal of Comparative and Applied Criminal Justice* 12 (1988):205–217.

———. "Banana Justice in Moroland: Peacemaking in Mixed Muslim-Christian Towns in the Southern Philippines." Report for USIP Project 021 92S (United States Institute of Peace). Washington, DC, 1994.

———. "Filipino Self-Help and Peacemaking Strategies: A View from the Mindanao Hinterland." *Human Organization* 54 (1995):10–19.

Braithwaite, John, and Stephen Mugford. "Conditions of Successful Reintegration Ceremonies: Dealing with Juvenile Offenders." *British Journal of Criminology* 34 (1994):139–171.

Bulatao, Jaime C. "Hiya." *Philippine Studies* 12 (1964):424–438.

Esguerra, Ramon. "The Youthful Offender before the Juvenile Courts." *Philippine Law Journal* 54 (1979):45–62.

Espiritu, Socorro. "The Family." In *Sociology in the Philippines Setting: A Modular Approach,* 4th ed., edited by Chester L. Hunt, Lourdes R. Quisumbing, Socorro Espiritu, Michael L. Costello, and Luis Q. Lacar. Quezon City: Phoenix Publishing House, 1987.

Gowing, Peter G. *Understanding Islam and Muslims in the Philippines.* Quezon City: New Day, 1988.

Hollnsteiner, Mary R. "Reciprocity in the Lowland Philippines." In *Four Readings on Philippine Values,* 3d ed., edited by Frank Lynch and Alfonso de Guzman II. Quezon City: Ateneo de Manila University Press, 1970.

Ignacio, Bert. "Barangay Head, Tanods Chop Up Theft Suspect." *Manila Standard,* December 10, 1990.

Jocano, F. Landa. *Growing Up in a Philippine Barrio.* New York: Holt, Rinehart and Winston, 1969.

————. *Slum as a Way of Life: A Study of Coping Behavior in an Urban Environment.* Quezon City: University of the Philippines Press, 1975.

Kaut, Charles. "*Utang na Loob:* A System of Contractual Obligation." *Southwestern Journal of Anthropology* 17 (1961):256–272.

Lynch, Frank. "Social Acceptance Reconsidered." In *Four Readings on Philippine Values,* 3d ed., edited by Frank Lynch and Alfonso de Guzman II. Quezon City: Ateneo de Manila University Press, 1970.

Orendain, Antonio. *Barangay Justice: The Amicable Settlement of Disputes.* Metro Manila: Alpha Omega, 1978.

Pe, Cecilio L., and Alfredo F. Tadiar. *Katarungang Pambarangay: Dynamics of Compulsory Conciliation.* Manila: UST Press, 1979.

Pido, Antonio J. A. *The Filipinos in America: Macro-Micro Dimension of Immigration.* New York: Center of Migration Studies, 1986.

Quisumbing, Lourdes R. "Child-Rearing Practices in the Cebuano Extended Family." *Philippine Sociological Review* 12 (1964):109–114.

————. "Philippine Values." In *Sociology in the Philippine Setting: A Modular Approach,* 4th ed., edited by Chester L. Hunt, Lourdes R. Quisumbing, Socorro C. Espiritu, Michael L. Costello, and Luis Q. Lacar, 77–100. Quezon City: Phoenix Publishing House, 1987.

Tadiar, Alfredo F. *Research on the Conciliation of Disputes under the Katarungang Pambarangay Law.* Quezon City: University of the Philippines, School of Law, 1984.

APPENDIX: AGENCIES THAT DEAL WITH JUVENILE OFFENDERS AND OTHER YOUTH CONCERNS

Hon. Rafael M. Alunan III, Secretary
Department of Interior and Local Government
Second Floor, PNCC Building
EDSA cor., Reliance Street
Mandaluyong, Metro Manila
Philippines

Ms. Lourdes G. Balanon, Director
Bureau of Child and Youth Welfare
Department of Social Welfare and Development
Constitution Hills, Diliman
Philippines

Ms. Amina Rasul-Bernardo
Chairperson
National Youth Commission
Room 485, Administrative Building
Malacanang, Manila

Hon. Teofisto-Guingona, Secretary
Department of Justice
Padre Faura Street
Ermita, Manila
Philippines

Hon. Ricardo T. Gloria, Secretary
Department of Education, Culture, and Sports
National Sports Academy
Meralco Avenue
Pasig, Metro Manila
Philippines

Mrs. Irene M. Isaac, Director
Institute of Vocational Training and Development
5th Floor, National Manpower and Youth Council
South Super Highway
Taguig, Metro Manila
Philippines

16

POLAND

Dobrochna Wójcik

HISTORICAL BACKGROUND

As in many other countries, the ideas of different regulation of responsibility of juveniles, as opposed to adults, have been formulated for a long time (eighteenth century) in Poland (Groicki, 1953). The ideas were realized when Poland regained independence in 1918, after 123 years of servitude. The first juvenile courts were organized in 1919 in three cities: Lódź, Warsaw, and Lublin. The principles of criminal responsibility[1] of juveniles were regulated in the Penal Code of 1932 and the Code of Criminal Procedure of 1928. The development of Polish juvenile justice was interrupted during World War II and resumed after the war. Two changes in the juvenile justice system are worthy of mention. In 1969, Polish penal legislation was changed; this resulted, among other things, in lowering the age of criminal responsibility to 16 in certain special cases specified in the penal code. Second, in 1978, after several years of experimentation, juvenile courts were transformed into family courts.

THE FORMAL SYSTEM

Introductory Remarks

The legal situation for children who commit an offense or manifest symptoms of demoralization is regulated by the Act of October 26, 1982, on Treatment of Minors.[2] The act contains issues of substantial law, certain procedural regulations,[3] and provisions concerning the carrying out of the educational, medical, and corrective measures applied to juveniles. Thus, in principle, it deals with the whole range of problems related to the treatment of juvenile delinquents.

The institution competent to examine cases of juvenile delinquents is the district court, family and juvenile division, called the family court in the act. The grounds and paramount object of the family court's intervention in a juvenile's life include:

a. prevention of demoralization and juvenile delinquency;

b. creation of conditions for juveniles who have come into conflict with the law or the rules of social conduct to return to normal life;

c. strengthening the care and educational functions of the family and its sense of responsibility for the rearing of children.

The guiding principle of the entire act has been expressed in its Article 3, as the chief consideration to the juveniles' well-being. Stressed explicitly in the treatment of juveniles are ideas of prevention, education, and resocialization, the justice-oriented approach being less marked. It has to be stressed that the juvenile's basic rights have been guaranteed.

Definition of a Juvenile

The act applies to the following categories of persons, whom it defines as juveniles:

a. Persons under 18 years of age who manifest symptoms of demoralization.
    The notion of demoralization has not been defined clearly in the act.
    Article 4 of the Act on Treatment of Minors (ATM) quotes, by way of example, some circumstances that may evidence demoralization: "breaches of social conduct,[4] commission of an unlawful act, systematic evasion of obligatory school or vocational training, use of alcoholic beverages or other means of intoxication, prostitution, vagabondage, association with criminal groups." Meant here is not drinking on a single occasion or playing truant several times, but a relatively systematic and persistent infringement of the fundamental social and moral norms whose observance is required of young persons in the age brackets concerned (Ostrihanska, 1972).

b. Persons who commit an offense or transgression while over aged 13 but under 17 (Article 1, para. 1, ATM). The transgressions include mainly petty offenses against property, public peace and order, safety of persons and property, and safety and order in communications (Article 1, para. 2, point b, ATM).
    Therefore, the act applies both to children and to young persons who commit offenses and to those showing symptoms of demoralization. Children under age 13 who commit an offense are nevertheless treated as showing symptoms of demoralization.

c. Persons under age 21 toward whom educational or corrective measures are administered.

Age Limits of Responsibility of Juveniles before the Family Court

Polish legislation fails to regulate consistently the question of the upper and lower age limits of a juvenile to be brought before the family court because of demoralization or an offense (Kołakowska-Przełomiec and Wójcik, 1992; Rdzanek-Piwowar, 1993).

In the case of demoralization, the upper limit has been set at age 18; the lower limit below which a case for demoralization cannot be instituted has not been specified.

Thus, theoretically (which also happens in practice), even a very small child can be brought before the family court because of the symptoms of demoralization (Kołakowska-Przełomiec and Wójcik, 1990). Other persons falling under the act on treatment of minors are juveniles who commit an offense between the age of 13 and 17. Persons age 17 and over who commit an offense are tried under the penal code (PC) as adults.

In exceptional cases, however, penalty can be imposed on a juvenile even at the age of 16. Article 9, paragraph 2 of the penal code provides that the penalties specified in it can be imposed on a juvenile who, after attaining the age of 16, commits "a serious offense against life, rape, robbery or a serious offense against public safety, or intentionally causes a serious bodily injury or a serious impairment of health." It is stated, however, that such a juvenile may be subject to liability on the basis specified in the code if "the circumstances of the case as well as the traits and personal conditions of the perpetrator warrant it, and especially when previously applied educational or corrective measures have proved ineffective." Therefore, even if a 16-year-old commits a serious offense specified in Article 9 of the penal code, a penalty is not necessarily imposed, as its imposition is decided by the judge in each individual case. It is exceptional for a family judge to apply Article 9, paragraph 2, PC to a juvenile and impose the penalties normally intended for adults (penalties are imposed on 5–12 juveniles a year).

Article 9, paragraph 3, PC also provides for the possibility of applying educational or corrective measures to a person who commits a less serious offense between the ages of 17 and 18, if the circumstances of the case, as well as the traits and personal conditions of the perpetrator, so warrant. A decision is made by the common court that examines the case; having applied a definite measure, the court transfers the records to the family court, which carries out the decision.

The fact that criminal responsibility has been set at the age of 17 and that majority according to civil law has been set at the age of 18 manifests legislators' inconsistency. This incoherence of provisions results in considerable confusion in practice and needs to be removed.

It also has to be stressed that the penal code provides for a category of young adults: persons under 21 at the moment of imposition of penalty by the court (Article 120, para. 4, PC). In the penal code, it is recommended that the court imposing a penalty on a young adult should aim first and foremost to "educate the person sentenced, to teach him a trade and to accustom him to respect the legal order" (Article 51, PC).

Family Courts: Structure, Competences, Jurisdiction, and Venue

Family courts are contained in the organizational structure of common courts. As the first instance, they are positioned at the level of district courts. The appellate authority in cases of juveniles is the voivodship court.

Under the act, the family court (and judge) has very broad competences. It decides in all vital matters relating to a juvenile. Having been notified of an offense, it decides whether the case should be conducted, discontinued, or referred for settlement to the juvenile's school or a social organization (see Figure 16.1). The family judge concentrates all procedural functions, conducts explanatory proceedings and examination of cases, commissions various actions to the police and court-appointed probation officers, orders a diagnostic examination, applies educational, medical, and corrective measures, and carries out the measures applied, which may also be changed in the course of their execution. Competences of the family court include, among other things,[5] examination of cases of demoralization and offenses of juveniles (Article 14, ATM). Therefore, competence of the family court is the rule in cases of juveniles. Yet, the act provides for exceptions to this rule, where a case of a juvenile may be conducted by a common court. These exceptions occur when

a. there are grounds for sentencing a juvenile under the terms of Article 9, paragraph 2 PC (Article 18, point 1, ATM);

b. proceedings have been instituted against a juvenile who has committed an offense, the institution of proceedings having taken place after the juvenile's 18th birthday (Article 18, point 2, ATM);

c. a juvenile has committed an offense together with an adult (Article 16, para. 2, ATM).

In this last case, the act provides that in the case of proceedings instituted against a juvenile and an adult, the public prosecutor diverts the case of the juvenile and refers it to a family judge (Article 16, para. 1, ATM). In particularly justified cases where the juvenile's offense is closely related to that of the adult, and the well-being of the juvenile constitutes no obstacle to a jointly conducted case, the prosecutor proceeds to institute or conduct the inquiry.[6] Upon its completion, the prosecutor may either discontinue the case of the juvenile or refer it to the family court. Should a joint examination of the cases prove indispensable, the indictment is submitted to a common court, which follows provisions of the act in passing judgment on the juvenile (Article 16, para. 2, ATM).

Figure 16.1
Proceedings before the Family Court

Delinquency or
demoralization is
reported by ...

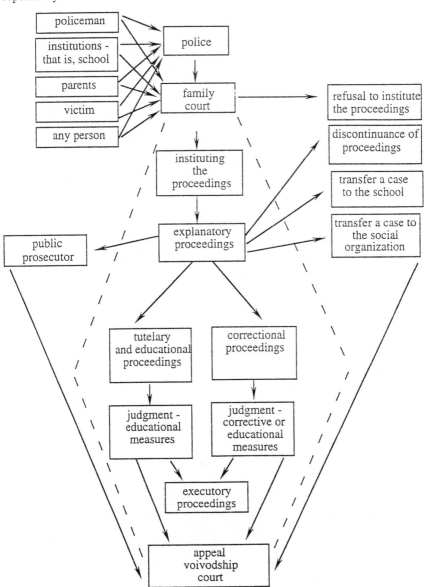

Proceedings before the Family Court

Institution of Proceedings

The agency that most often notifies the family court of the reasons for institution of proceedings is the police; less often, the court is notified by the school, other institutions, the juvenile's parents, the victim, or other persons.

The family judge institutes proceedings if there are reasons to believe that the juvenile manifests symptoms of demoralization or has committed an offense (Article 21, para. 1, ATM). Proceedings are conducted ex officio.

Otherwise, the family judge does not institute proceedings or discontinues the instituted proceedings if the circumstances provide no grounds for further proceedings or if institution of proceedings would be inexpedient.

As follows from Article 21, paragraph 1, ATM, the institution of proceedings in cases of juveniles should be based on the principle of legalism, whose force is much limited, due to the broad powers of discretion granted to family judges (Article 21, para. 2, ATM). In practice, the judges make extensive use of those powers. Up to 40 percent of cases of juveniles referred to family courts result in a refusal to institute proceedings or discontinuance of proceedings as inexpedient (Kołakowska-Przełomiec and Wójcik, 1990:57).

Explanatory Proceedings

The purpose of explanatory proceedings is to find out whether there are circumstances that show the juvenile's demoralization and, in a case of an offense, whether she or he has actually committed it. The judge gathers information about the juvenile's educational, medical, and living conditions, and collects and preserves the evidence. The judge also hears the juvenile, parents, or guardians, as well as other persons, if need arises, and performs other actions aiming at a comprehensive examination of the case. For example, the judge may refer the juvenile to the Center for Diagnosis and Consultation of the Family for psychological, pedagogical, and medical examination. (The examination is obligatory before a juvenile can be placed in any institution.)

The judge commissions the police to gather, secure, and prove the evidence. These are the actions to which the function of the police is limited. In exceptional cases, the judge may commission the police to interrogate the juvenile.

In special situations, if there are reasons to fear that the traces and evidence of an offense might be tampered with, the police may, on their own initiative, apprehend and interrogate the juvenile who has committed the offense and also secure the evidence.

Obligatory participants in an interrogation of a juvenile by the police are the parents, guardians, or counsel; if those persons are absent, a teacher or representative of a social organization must be present.

Having conducted explanatory proceedings, the family judge decides the further course of the case, choosing from the following options:

a. The family judge discontinues explanatory proceedings if the circumstances of the case do not justify such proceedings, or if the ordering of educational or corrective measures is inexpedient, due especially to measures already ordered in another case (Article 21, para. 1, ATM).

b. Having found that educational or medical measures ought to be applied toward the juvenile, the family judge orders examination of the case in tutelary and educational proceedings (Article 42, para. 1, ATM).

c. Having found that the juvenile qualifies to be placed in a house of correction, the family judge orders the case to be examined in correctional proceedings (Article 42, para. 2, ATM).

d. Having found that the juvenile qualifies to have a penalty imposed under Article 9, paragraph 2, PC, the judge decides to refer the case to the prosecutor (Article 42, para. 3, ATM; this concerns only the juveniles over age 16 who have committed a serious offense).

e. The family judge may also refer the case to the juvenile's school or organization if the educational measures at that institution's disposal are sufficient. The school or organization is obliged to notify the family court if the educational measures it has applied prove ineffective (Article 42, para. 4, ATM).

Examination of the Case

The case may be examined in two forms of the proceedings: tutelary and educational or correctional. To the former, provisions of the code of noncontentious civil procedure apply. Cases are examined at a sitting by one family judge. Correctional proceedings are based on provisions of the penal procedure, and the court decides in a bench of one professional and two lay judges.

In both modes, the sessions are closed, as a rule, unless the family judge finds openness of the sitting or trial to be justified for educational reasons (Articles 45 and 53, ATM).

In tutelary and educational proceedings (and also at the earlier stage of explanatory proceedings), the juvenile may be represented by a counsel for defense; involvement of the counsel is obligatory in the case of a conflict of interests between the juvenile and parents (Article 36, para. 1 and 2 ATM); if the juvenile has been placed in a remand home; and in correctional proceedings (Article 49, ATM).

Measures

The family court may apply educational and medical measures to all juveniles and also impose duties on them. Corrective measures (placement in a house of correction) are applied only to juveniles who have committed an offense and meet the additional conditions specified in Article 10, ATM.

Article 6 of the act provides for the following educational, medical, and corrective measures and duties:

a. reprimand;

b. obligation to a specified conduct, particularly to redress the damage, to enter school or take a job, to avoid specific places, or to abstain from alcohol or other intoxicants;

c. accountable supervision by parents or guardians;

d. supervision by a youth or other social organization, the workplace, or a trustworthy person who stands surety for the juvenile;

e. supervision by a probation officer;

f. committing the juvenile to a supervisory child welfare center;

g. ban on driving motor vehicles;

h. forfeiture of objects acquired in connection with the offense;

i. placement of the juvenile in an institution or organization providing vocational training, in a foster family, an educational institution, or another adequate guardianship and educational center;

j. confinement to a house of correction;

k. the family judge may also apply to juveniles the measures specified in the family and guardianship code;

l. with respect to juveniles who require special medical treatment, the family court may order placement at a mental hospital or another medical institution (Article 12, ATM);

m. instead, if the juvenile needs only education and care, the family court may commit the youth to a social welfare institution or an adequate educational center.

The most severe measure that can be applied to a juvenile by the family court is commission to a house of correction. The act limits the possibilities of applying this measure to situations where the juvenile has committed an offense, and the use of this measure is warranted by a high degree of the juvenile's demoralization and by the circumstances and nature of the act, especially if educational measures have proved ineffective or are unlikely to cause the juvenile's resocialization (Article 10, ATM). A juvenile is confined to the house of correction for an unspecified period of time, until the age of 21 (which seldom happens in practice).

Confinement of a juvenile to a house of correction may be conditionally suspended for a probation period of one to three years. The family court may revoke conditional suspension and send the juvenile to a house of correction if the duties that have been imposed are not met or conduct shows an advancing demoralization (Article 11, para. 1, 2, 3, ATM).

Confinement to a house of correction (ordered for a 13–17-year-old) should not be identified with a penalty. The measure aims at education and resocialization of the juvenile, not at a "just revenge." "What speaks against a penal law interpretation of the corrective measure are formal reasons as well as the provisions that regulate the procedure of carrying out of that confinement" (Strzembosz, 1984:50).

Appeal Proceedings

An appeal is examined by the voivodship court sitting in a bench of three judges. The proceedings may follow provisions of either the civil or the criminal procedure, depending on the type of educational versus corrective measure applied to the juvenile and on the request contained in the appeal.

In the appeal proceedings, the educational measure may be replaced with a correctional one or with a penalty, and the correctional measure with a penalty, only if an appeal contains a motion for these sanctions (Article 63, para. 1 and 2, ATM).

Both the parties and the injured persons may lodge complaints against the family court's decisions ending the proceedings in the case (Article 29, para. 1, ATM) and against actions of the family court in explanatory proceedings if such actions have infringed upon the rights of those persons.

Executory Proceedings

Executory proceedings are instituted as soon as a judgment has become effective (Article 64, ATM). Measures ordered under the act and under Article 9, paragraph 3, PC are executed by the family court (penalties, instead, are carried out by the competent common court under the code of execution of penalties). The family judge supervises the execution of decisions. In the case of confinement of the juvenile to all kinds of institutions, this consists in supervising the legality of confinement and the correctness of all educational methods and measures applied, the juvenile's living conditions, and the observance of her or his rights and freedoms. In this connection, the family judge has free access to the institution at all times and to all the records and may demand explanations from the staff and interview inmates in private (Article 77, para. 1 and 2, ATM).

Supervising the supervision by parents or probation officer, the family judge appraises the parents' or officer's reports. For important reasons, the family court may order postponement or interruption of the execution of educational and corrective measures and also recall that decision if the reasons for its original taking have ceased or the juvenile glaringly infringes the legal order. The family court may also change educational measures in the course of their execution (but cannot replace an educational with a corrective measure). Some educational measures cease by force of the law on the juvenile's 18th birthday. Confinement to a house of correction may last until the 21st birthday; also, supervision by a probation officer lasts until that age.

Auxiliary Agencies and Institutions Cooperating with the Family Court (see Figure 16.2)

Probation Officers (Professionals and Volunteers)

A family probation officer has most extensive functions and tasks. In explanatory proceedings, the officer gathers information about the juvenile's person-

Figure 16.2
Cooperation of the Family Court and Principal Agencies

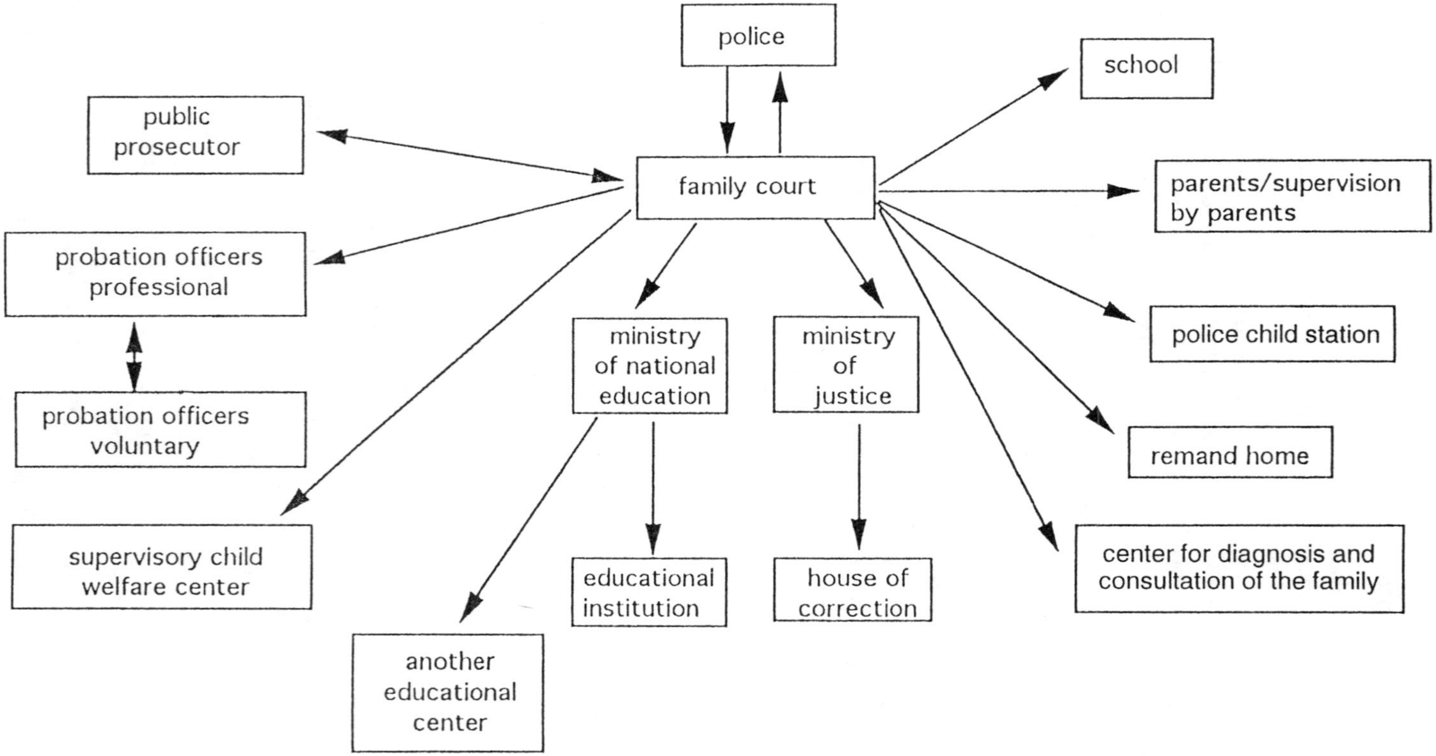

ality and the school and family situation. This person also performs preventive supervision, as well as the supervision ordered by the court as the educational measures in executory proceedings.

Supervisory Child Welfare Centers

The centers are attached to family courts. The juveniles are assisted in doing homework, have their leisure time organized, and get meals at least four times a week. The guiding principle of organization of the centers is education of the juveniles within and through a group.

Centers for Diagnosis and Consultation of the Family

A center is to diagnose the juvenile's personality and situation and to prepare an opinion for the family court and also to help the teachers and tutors of educational institutions and houses of correction properly apply the educational measures and methods.

Remand Homes

These homes are special preventive and diagnostic institutions for juveniles over age 13 and under age 17, referred to the home by an order of the family court, family judge, or public prosecutor, if there are reasons to fear that the juvenile might go into hiding or destroy the evidence, or if identity cannot be ascertained (Article 27, para. 1, ATM).

The Police

Policemen in special juvenile departments deal mainly with prevention of juvenile demoralization and delinquency and also perform acts of investigation ordered by the family judge.

Police Child Stations

The stations are comprehensive care institutions for summary placement of the children and young persons who run away from home, loiter the streets, manifest other symptoms of demoralization, and commit offenses.

Emergency Child Centers

The centers perform the functions of diagnosis, classification, and care. Their inmates are children aged 3–18 who have to be taken away from their family environment because of a lack of care, symptoms of demoralization, or perpetration of offenses.

THE FUNCTIONING OF JUVENILE JUSTICE IN PRACTICE

What shows the actual quality of a system of handling juveniles is not only its main theoretical basis but also, to a large extent, its functioning in practice. A variety of factors that are more or less dependent on that system may, in fact, alter the ideas and legal solutions on which it is founded. The functioning of juvenile justice depends on a great number of factors (on both the macro- and the microscale), such as the social, economic, and cultural situations, the people's views, and so on. Also affecting this functioning are former experiences and tradition in the sphere of handling juveniles, professional qualifications of the staff (e.g., judges and probation officers), their attitudes and opinions on resocialization of juveniles, and the economic, technical, and organizational capacities of criminal justice and other agencies. Another important factor is cooperation and communication between the separate agencies dealing with the problems of prevention of delinquency and education and resocialization of juveniles within and without the juvenile justice system. A lot also depends on the social policy of the state.

In a brief chapter such as the present one, all these conditions can hardly be discussed. Mentioned here will be the major problems only, relating to diversion of juveniles from the administration of justice and the practice of application of the various measures. To begin with, however, a number of general problems have to be stressed:

1. Juvenile justice is uniform on the national scale in Poland. There are no formal differences between regions, and the possible actual differences are rather slight and difficult to discern empirically.

2. Throughout the postwar period and practically till the present day as well, all institutions that handle juvenile delinquents—both within and without the juvenile justice system—have been state institutions, run in accordance with nationally uniform principles of organization, economy, and education. Only recently have the possibilities been opened for a greater differentiation of these institutions, for organization of various forms of juvenile care and resocialization by organizations, private persons, religious unions, and other associations.

3. Polish society is rather uniform with respect to nationality, religion, and culture. There have been, so far in Poland, no great problems with the national minorities (with the possible exception of Gypsies, with their different culture and inability to become wholly integrated with local community). Poland does not have a large number of immigrants with the related social problems, such as a trend in society to perceive and treat such persons differently or a belief as to their greater inclination to delinquency.

One of the major problems involved here is selection of juveniles to be diverted from the juvenile justice system. Related to this concern is a broader issue of the grounds for the family court's intervention in the life of juveniles and their families and of the extent of that intervention (Jasiński, 1976). This problem can hardly be resolved explicitly and should not be subject to strict legal regulations. What arises here is a conflict between a need for the family court's intervention in the juvenile's situation and limitation of excessive and undesirable intervention of the judicial authority. No solution is perfect here. It sometimes happens in practice that the family court's intervention takes place where it is not needed at all. A question might therefore be asked, What factors make some children and young persons become involved in juvenile justice, although this ought never to have happened, while some others do not become involved who actually ought to be supervised by the family court?

Juveniles are selected at various stages of judicial proceedings and also before their case is referred to the family court. What are the related provisions and practices in this respect?

The act imposes on state institutions and social organizations the duty to notify the family court or the police of offenses committed by a juvenile.[7] The need closely to observe this provision—for example, a school's duty to refer to the family court all cases of petty thefts committed by its students—gives rise to obvious doubts. Of course, the statutory obligation is not always observed in practice.

The police, in principle, lack discretionary powers; officers are obliged to notify the family court of all offenses or transgressions committed by juveniles. On the other hand, the duty to refer to that court all juveniles who manifest symptoms of demoralization has not been stated explicitly. Here, the appraisal and decision may indeed belong to the police officer. In practice, the officer may also abstain from referring to the family court a juvenile perpetrator of petty theft. He or she is authorized to take this course by Article 26, PC, which provides that an act that involves a slight social danger should not be treated as an offense. Therefore, the possibility of discretion is inherent in the penal law system itself. Referral to the family court of a juvenile perpetrator of an offense depends on a decision of both the police and other institutions, such as the school. The actual extent of this kind of selection is difficult to appraise and examine empirically.

Only the family judge enjoys full discretionary powers. Once a juvenile's case has been referred to the family court, it may be diverted only by the following decisions of the judge:

1. refusal to institute proceedings, or

2. discontinuance of proceedings.

At the same time, the provisions do not enable the judge to offer certain forms of assistance to such juveniles or to refer them to educational and reso-cializing programs (modeled after diversion programs in other countries). However, the family judge may institute guardianship proceedings if it is found that the child's well-being is threatened.

Criticized in the light of empirical research is the practice of unduly extensive diversion of juveniles from juvenile justice. As many as 30 percent of discretionary decisions of family judges seem unjustified. The judges discontinued cases not only of those juveniles who did not manifest any symptoms of demoralization and whose offense was accidental but also of others who did manifest distinct symptoms of demoralization and lived in negative family environments. Taking the decision in quite a considerable number of cases, the judges had insufficient information about the juvenile concerned and his or her family or were unable properly to use the acquired evidence of the juvenile's advanced demoralization. Of juveniles whose cases had been discontinued, 20 percent had new cases before the family or common court within the next five years (Kołakowska-Przełomiec and Wójcik, 1990: 205).

Other ways of diverting a juvenile from juvenile justice include:

3. referral of the case to the school, or

4. to a social organization.

In practice, such decisions are rarely taken by the family judges, who know from their experience that the schools are unable to provide adequate care and education to such juveniles.

Therefore, provisions of the act grant considerable discretionary powers to family judges, who actually use those powers extensively. At the same time, those provisions oblige institutions and citizens to report cases of offenses committed by juveniles (Hołda and Drwal, 1992). This situation supports the legislators' intention to invest the family judge only with the power to divert a juvenile from juvenile justice; instead, the legislators mistrusted the other institutions and persons in this respect.

Also worth discussing here are the measures applied to juveniles in practice by family judges, the related policy of family courts, and the problems involved in it.

Despite a certain but still unsatisfactory extension in the act of the catalog of measures, family judges still show a rather traditional attitude. Today, as before, the measure ordered most often is supervision by a probation officer or accountable supervision by the parents. Rarely applied, instead, are some other measures introduced by the act, such as referral to the supervisory child welfare center or imposition on the juvenile of specific duties (Wójcik, 1988). According to statements of some family judges, they have doubts as to the efficiency of those measures. Measures involving "isolation" (confinement to an educational institution or house of correction) are rarely ordered. Family judges treat education in a closed environment as the "ultimate" measure and argue that the juveniles confined to such institutions become further demoralized, rather than improved.

Thus, in practice, the family judges have the choice of two measures: supervision by a probation officer and supervision by the parents, applied in about 60 and 20 percent of cases, respectively. The Polish juvenile probation system (combining professionals with volunteers) is based mainly on the work of lay probation officers and urgently requires reorganization. Professional probation officers, whose number should be made much larger, are seriously overburdened with duties, which naturally affects the quality and promptness of their work. During the past two to three years, financial difficulties led to the winding down of about 30 percent of supervisory child welfare centers, which largely limited the actual application of this measure. Educational results of these centers have been found effective (Zieliński, 1979).

On the whole, therefore, various factors (economic, organizational, legislative, or related to the staff) act jointly to limit the family judges in their decisions. Judges are not always free to order the measures they actually find the most appropriate.

PROPOSED CHANGES OF POLISH JUVENILE JUSTICE

From the moment of its introduction, the Act on Treatment of Minors met with considerable criticism (Grześkowiak, 1986; Stanowska, Walczak-Żo-chowska, and Wierzbicki, 1982; Strzembosz, 1984). For several years, the need has been stressed in the professional literature for a radical amendment of that act, although no official draft of the amendment has been prepared.

What is criticized first and foremost is the introduction of two different modes of proceedings (tutelary and educational, correctional treatment) and the need to have two different codes of procedure (Kołakowska-Przełomiec, 1983). It is postulated that uniform provisions on procedure in cases of juveniles should be developed.

Also condemned is the introduction of a legal fiction, the principle (Article 42, ATM) that upon completing the explanatory proceedings, the family judge should already anticipate the degree of punishment to apply toward the juvenile and be prepared to order the juvenile to a tutelary, educational, or correctional institution. In other words, family judges decide about the measure to be applied before they can actually examine the case, while that very examination should normally provide the grounds for such a decision (Kołakowska-Przełomiec and Wójcik, 1992).

It is also argued that the heterogeneous solutions which relate to the age of criminal responsibility (17) and majority under civil law (18) should be standardized, and that the lowest possible age limit should be defined below which a juvenile would not be brought before the family court, even if there were symptoms of demoralization (Kołakowska-Przełomiec and Wójcik, 1992). It is postulated that the age of criminal responsibility should be raised to 18. At the same time, however, some practitioners demand a lowering of that age limit in the face of a general growth in crime, juvenile delinquency included.

What is mentioned as a defect is the unduly small catalog of the measures that can be applied to juveniles. Concerned here is, first of all, an extension of the possibility to apply measures not involving removal of the juvenile from the original educational environment. Also postulated here is that judges should be permitted to order measures increasing the juvenile's sense of responsibility and enabling the redress of damage done to the victim (e.g., mediation and unpaid work for the local community).

It is also suggested that at least a portion of the juveniles who are diverted from juvenile justice should be offered resocialization and therapy programs.

What also deserves to be reformed is the family probation system. The changes should aim at a regular autonomy of probation officers, transition from supervisory to educational probation, and organizing the judge–probation officer relation on a partnership basis (Sawicka, 1985).

Another urgent need is reorganization of educational institutions and houses of correction. Much has to be done in this sphere, from organizational changes (a greater differentiation of the institutions), to staff adjustments, to development and regular implementation of methods and programs of education and therapy.

The family court's cooperation with the juvenile's parents should also be based on different principles. The aim should be the parents' greater involvement in the process of resocialization of their child, as well as closer contacts not only with the probation officer but also with the family judge.

The Polish Act on Treatment of Minors is generally thought to be consistent both with the Convention on the Rights of the Child and the United Nations Standard Minimum Rules for the Administration of Juvenile Justice (Kołakowska-Przełomiec and Wójcik, 1992). What is praised, for example, is granting the juvenile the rights of party in judicial proceedings and recognition of personal dignity and subjectivity. Some authors argue, however, that the provisions should contain a more explicit formulation of certain rights of the juvenile and of such proceedings securities as the right to refuse depositions or an extended requirement that the juvenile's consent should be obtained for some of the court's decisions, such as the decision to refer a case to the school (Grześkowiak, 1986; Czarnecka-Dzialuk, 1993).

The preceding remarks concern issues of varying degrees of importance. Some problems can be solved by means of amendment of the act and other provisions and of "improvement" of their functioning in practice, while some other ones require a more radical reform. For that reform to be launched—as it probably will be quite soon—the attitude has to be revised to matters of a more general nature: the basic conception and philosophy of handling juveniles. This, however, is a separate issue.

NOTES

1. Criminal responsibility has been set at the age of 17. Educational measures were applied to juveniles under 13 and to those aged 13–17 who acted without discernment. To juveniles aged 13–17 who had discernment of the nature of their act, the judge could apply either corrective measures or educational ones.

2. *Journal of Laws,* November 12, 1982, No. 35, item 228. In this chapter, the Act on Treatment of Minors will be referred to as "the act" or abbreviated as "ATM."

3. As for the application of procedure, as will be discussed further on, the act makes reference to provisions of the codes of civil and penal procedure.

4. Criticized is the introduction in Article 4 of the formulation that "a breach of social conduct may manifest demoralization," as this definition unduly extends the notion of demoralization.

5. Family courts deal also with many different matters related to the family; for example, they decide parental authority, issue marriage licenses to minors, and examine cases for adoption.

6. The role of the prosecutor in proceedings in cases of juveniles has been largely limited, both under provisions of the act and in practice. Despite a status as party to proceedings, the prosecutor takes part in proceedings before the family court in exceptional cases only.

7. Under Article 4, paragraph 2, ATM, the duty to inform the family court or police that a juvenile has committed an offense is imposed on any person who has learned of that fact.

REFERENCES

Czarnecka-Dzialuk, Beata. *Nieletni Sprawcy Czynów Karalnych Przed Sadem Rodzinnym. Zagadnienia Procesowe (Juvenile Offenders before Family Courts. Procedural Aspects)*. Warsaw: Scholar Press, 1993.

Groicki, Bartłomiej. *Porzadek Sadów i Spraw Miejskich Prawa Majdeburskiego w Koronie Polskiej (The Order of Courts and Municipal Matters under the Magdeburg Law in the Kingdom of Poland)*. Warsaw: Legal Publishing House, 1953 (reprinted from the 1630 edition).

Grześkowiak, Alicja. *Postepowanie w Sprawach Nieletnich. Polskie Prawo Nieletnich (Procedure in Cases of Juveniles. Polish Juvenile Law)*. Toruń: M. Kopernik University Press, 1986.

Hołda, Zbigniew, and Radosław Drwal. "Pozasadowe Formy Postepowania z Nieletnimi Sprawcami Czynów Kryminalnych" ("Extrajudicial Treatment of Juvenile Offenders"). In *Prawne i Pedagogiczne Aspekty Resocjalizacji Nieletnich (Resocialization of Juveniles: Legal and Educational Problems)* edited by Barbara Kowalska-Ehrlich and Stanisław Walczak. Warsaw: Warsaw University Press, 1992.

Jasiński, Jerzy. "Sadowe Środki Stosowane Wobec Nieletnich Sprawców Przestepstw w Latach 1951–1971" ("Judicial Measures Applied to Juvenile Offenders in the Years 1951–1971"). In *Wybrane Zagadnienia Patologii Rodziny (Pathology of the Family: Selected Issues)*, edited by Maria Jarosz. Warsaw: Main Statistical Office, 1976.

Kołakowska-Przełomiec, Helena. "Postepowanie w Sprawach Nieletnich" ("Proceedings in Cases of Juveniles"). *Państwo i Prawo* No. 6 (1983):46–51.

Kołakowska-Przełomiec, Helena, and Dobrochna Wójcik. *Selekcja Nieletnich Przestepców w Sadach Rodzinnych (Selection of Juvenile Offenders at Family Courts)*. Warsaw: Ossolineum, 1990.

———. "Ustawa z Dnia 26 Października 1982 r. o Postepowaniu s Sprawach Nieletnich a Konwencja Praw Dziecka" ("The Act of 26 October 1992 on Treatment of Minors and the Convention of the Rights of the Child"). *Studia Prawnicze* Nos. 3–4 (1992):3–29.

Ostrihanska, Zofia. "Kryteria Nieprzystosowania Społecznego Dzieci i Młodzieży"

("The Criteria of Social Maladjustment of Children and Young Persons"). *Archiwum Kryminologii* 5 (1972):15–31.

Rdzanek-Piwowar, Grażyna. "Granice Nieletniości w Polskim Prawie Karnym" ("The Age Limits of Juveniles in Polish Penal Law"). *Archiwum Kryminologii* 19 (1993):191–231.

Sawicka, Katarzyna. "Projekt Modelu Organizacyjnego Kurateli Sadowej" ("Draft Model of Organization of Probation"). *Zeszyty Naukowe Instytutu Badania Prawa Sadowego* No. 23 (1985):101–117.

Stanowska, Maria, Anna Walczak-Żochowska, and Krzysztof Wierzbicki. "Uwagi o Profilu Ustawy o Postepowaniu z Nieletnimi. Zagadnienia Materialno-Prawne i Procesowe" ("Remarks on the Act on Treatment of Minors. Material Law and Procedure"). *Państwo i Prawo* No. 6 (1982):52–64.

Strzembosz, Adam. *Postepowanie w Sprawach Nieletnich w Prawie Polskim (Procedure in Cases of Juveniles in Polish Law)*. Lublin: Catholic Lublin University Press, 1984.

Wójcik, Dobrochna. "Praca Kuratora dla Nieletnich w Opinii Sedziów Rodzinnych i Kuratorów Społecznych" ("The Work of a Juvenile Probation Officer as Seen by Family Judges and Lay Probation Officers"). *Archiwum Kryminologii* 15 (1988):203–249.

Zieliński, Antoni. "Kuratorskie Ośrodki Pracy z Młodzieża" ("Supervisory Child Welfare Centers"). *Zeszyty Naukowe Instytutu Badania Prawa Sadowego* No. 11 (1979):181–207.

APPENDIX

State Institutions Handling Juvenile Offenders

Ministry of Justice
00-567 Warszawa, Al. Ujazdowskie 11
(the ministry is in charge of houses of correction, professional and lay probation officers, supervisory child welfare centers, centers for diagnosis and consultation of the family.)
Court Statistics
Part I. Activity of courts and penitentiary institutions (based on the data concerning judicial decisions legally invalid) Part II. Family cases (based on the data concerning judicial decisions valid in law).

Ministry of National Education
00-580 Warszawa, Al. Szucha 25
(Administers educational institutions, emergency child centers, and other centers for care and education.)

Ministry of Health and Social Welfare
00-246 Warszawa, ul. Miodowa 15
(Administers medical institutions.)

Ministry of Labor and Social Policy
00-513 Warszawa, ul. Nowogrodzka ⅓
(Administers welfare homes.)

Nongovernmental Institutions Involved in Prevention of Juvenile Delinquency and Resocialization (Nationwide)

Committee for Protection of the Rights of the Child
00-259 Warszawa, ul. Boleść 2
(Activities toward perfecting the system of protection of the rights of the child.)

Association MONAR
00-528 Warszawa, ul. Hoźa 57
(Assistance to young persons threatened with drug addiction and to their families; assistance to prisoners and inmates of houses of correction; assistance to the homeless and to sexual minorities.)

Society of the Families and Friends of Drug-Addicted Children ''Powrót z U''
00-950 Warszawa, ul. Ordynacka 9
(Assistance to drug addicts and their families.)

Polish Scouting Union
00-491 Warzsawa, ul. Konopnickiej 6
(Organization of scouting for socially maladjusted youth.)

17

RUSSIA

James O. Finckenauer

INTRODUCTION

Before embarking on this examination and description of juvenile justice in Russia—an examination and description that encompass in their scope both the old Soviet Russia of the former USSR as well as contemporary Russia—two key points need to be made. First, the juvenile justice system in both Soviet and post-Soviet Russia is not nearly as well defined and distinct from the adult criminal justice system as it is, for example, in the United States. For instance, there is no separate juvenile or family court. The overall unitary nature of the Russian criminal justice system is illustrated by a remark of the deputy head of the Russian Ministry of Internal Affairs department for the prevention of juvenile crime, who observed that there are really no special juvenile justice agencies in Russia (Kurant, personal interview, March 1994).

The second point to be noted is that the fundamentals of Russian legislation and criminal procedure pertaining to the handling of children and youth have not changed substantially in more than 30 years. There have been administrative and procedural changes, as we will see, but the fundamentals have not changed. So of necessity, any discussions of the history of juvenile justice and of contemporary policy and practices must overlap.

By way of further introduction, let me just briefly outline the sources of information and the methods used to gather the materials from which this chapter is derived. In addition to being generally familiar with the pertinent historical and contemporary literature on crime and criminal justice in Russia, I have visited and observed agencies and institutions and questioned officials and scholars involved with juvenile justice in Russia on numerous occasions over the past 10 years. Most recently, in March 1994, I interviewed persons in the Ministry of Internal Affairs, the Office of the Procuracy, and the procurator's office for the Moscow region, as well as Russian president Boris Yeltsin's legislative liaison to the Russian Parliament. A copy of the president's latest decree concerning juveniles and juvenile offenders was also obtained at that time.

We will consider essentially four sets of questions in the discussion that follows:

- What are the principal agencies that deal with juveniles, and how do these agencies interact with one another?
- What are the procedures prescribed by law for processing juvenile offenders?
- What informal mechanisms or procedures are used to divert juveniles from the formal system? What influences the use of this diversion?
- What changes are occurring or are likely to occur in the handling of juvenile offenders?

BACKGROUND

In the Russian Soviet Federative Socialist Republic—the name by which Russia was known as part of the USSR—during the period 1918 to 1991, two of the primary agencies charged with dealing with juvenile delinquency and juvenile offenders were the *inspectorates on juvenile affairs,* which were (and still are) part of the *militsia* or police, and the *commissions on juvenile affairs,* which operated in local towns, city districts, and regions and which had broad powers of prevention as well as adjudication and correction.

The *militsia* inspectorates are under the state Ministry of Internal Affairs (MVD). The latter is roughly comparable to the U.S. Department of Justice, with the exception that it has much more responsibility for policing throughout the country, including at the local level. It also has responsibility for corrections, detention, prisons, and so on. Courts and prosecutors (called procurators) are, however, separate from the MVD.

The inspectorates on juvenile affairs handle the initial investigations or "inspections" into any offenses of young people. Just as with the juvenile aid bureaus of American police departments, which would be their counterparts, they have wide powers to question and counsel young people, to make referrals, and to deal with parents and schools; but they also have authority to impose and supervise informal dispositions, such as requiring the juvenile to report to the *militsia* on some regular basis for supervision. Beyond that, they have a kind of parole function in that they supervise juveniles who "have served their sentences or were sentenced to conditional punishment or to a type of punishment not involving placement in an educational institution, and with youngsters who were paroled or amnestied" (Yakovlev, 1979:124). The latter practices stand in contrast to those of many other countries where parole and the supervision of juvenile dispositions are correctional functions kept clearly separate from the police.

COMMISSIONS ON JUVENILE AFFAIRS

The Commissions on Juvenile Affairs (CJAs) were first established in 1918. They were very much a "Soviet" idea—formalizing communal or collective responsibility for children and youth around the local soviets of the Communist Party. From the time of their creation and continuing through the end of 1991, they played the primary role in preventing and controlling juvenile delinquency in Russia. Their functions included integrating and directing the efforts of all the various institutions and organizations having responsibility for children and youth. The memberships of the CJAs, which could vary in size from as few as 2 to 12 or more persons, depending on the size of the jurisdiction, were made up of local government officials, trade unionists, the *militsia,* public health workers, social workers, teachers, and youth workers from organizations like the Komsomol or Young Communist League. The CJAs were simultaneously a sort of child welfare and child advocacy body, a probation agency, a family court, an ombudsman, and a kind of inspector general—all rolled into one. Their powers and responsibilities included:

- protecting the rights and interests of juveniles, looking after their social adjustment, and investigating inadequate supervision and neglect (measures could be taken against parents in instances of antisocial behavior by their children);
- supervising the activities of community educational and cultural institutions for youth;
- supervising special educational institutions and the so-called educational-labor colonies (correctional institutions) operated by the Ministry of Internal Affairs;
- preventing recidivism.

SCOPE OF CJA JURISDICTION

The age of criminal responsibility in Russia is 16. For certain serious crimes, however, that age is reduced to 14. Those particular crimes—some 10 in all—include homicide, rape, intentional battery, and assault with intent to rob. For youngsters under 14, although they are not criminally liable, they can be dealt with administratively if they engage in what are called "socially dangerous acts," such as abusing drugs and alcohol. Administrative handling can mean placement in a special residential educational facility.

We will examine the previous procedures at greater length in the subsequent section, but just in the context of our discussion of the CJAs, given this broad area of responsibility, their jurisdiction had to embrace: (1) children under 14 who had committed socially dangerous acts (these included both crimes and what are called in the United States status offenses, such as running away, truancy, and so on); (2) children 14 to 16 who had committed less serious crimes or socially dangerous acts; and (3) 16- to 18-year-olds who likewise had committed socially dangerous but noncriminal acts or even minor criminal acts but who were, in the latter case, in the opinion of the investigator, the procurator, or the court, to be diverted to the supervision of a Commission on Juvenile Affairs.

The CJAs operated very much like a family court in many cases—holding hearings and meting out dispositions. Available dispositions consisted of the following (McClellan, 1987):

- instructing youth to apologize to their victims or reprimanding and warning them;
- ordering them to pay fines and restitution;
- giving them over to the supervision of their parents, social workers, or the collective at a place of work (the latter was a kind of workers' committee or soviet established, in effect, to run the workplace);
- putting them on a kind of probation;
- committing them to special schools for mentally ill or handicapped children or to special technical schools. It should be noted that these latter commitments were made without benefit of a court trial.

THE FORMAL JUSTICE SYSTEM

Beyond the two major players—inspectorates and commissions—the other primary institutions dispensing juvenile justice are the *procurator,* the *court,* and the institutions of correction called *colonies.* The Russian procurator is a kind of superprosecutor, because, in addition to having the normal functions and powers of a prosecutor—to investigate allegations of wrongdoing, to bring charges, to try cases, to recommend sentences, and so forth—he or she has the additional authority to oversee the legality of the actions of all public institutions and to supervise the judicial process as well. In the juvenile realm, the procurator conducts the criminal investigation of a juvenile initially apprehended by the *militsia* to determine if that juvenile should be formally arrested. The procurator also decides if and for how long the juvenile should remain in custodial detention while that investigation is taking place. The procurator then prosecutes the juvenile in court. If the juvenile is convicted, which he or she almost always is once a case proceeds to trial,[1] the procurator then oversees the juvenile's confinement in a correctional colony. All the while, this same official has the responsibility to see that the juvenile's rights are being protected and that a modicum of due process is followed.

As previously indicated, there is no separate juvenile or family court in Russia. All court cases are thus handled in adult courts, which are called people's courts. However, in certain of the largest cities, such as Moscow and St. Petersburg, the volume of cases and the resources are both sufficient that there are de facto juvenile courts operating. That is, some judges have become juvenile specialists, and most, if not all, juvenile cases get referred to their courts. Legislation has been proposed to create new juvenile courts in Russia, but passage of this legislation is not considered likely—largely due to financial and resource constraints (Kurant, 1994). Approximately 30 percent of arrested juveniles are referred by the procurator for formal court processing; the other 70 percent are diverted from court generally to the *militsia* or to a CJA, usually bringing a conditional or suspended sentence.

Again, in order to be liable to arrest, the juvenile must be 16, or at least 14 and charged with a serious crime. There are, incidentally, exceptional cases where 14–15-year-olds who have committed a crime other than the 10 serious ones that are stipulated may also be referred for court processing. This is said to require a special ruling from the procurator. Thus, there seems to be an operating practice that is somewhat analogous to the United States system of waiving serious offenders from the juvenile to the adult court, in that juveniles under 16 who would normally be handled administratively can be waived up to be processed criminally.

After conviction, the court can sentence the juvenile in a variety of ways: to deprivation of liberty in an educational labor colony; to a conditional deprivation of liberty (meaning the juvenile is put on a kind of probation); to corrective work without a deprivation of liberty; or to a fine, restitution, or social censure. It has been estimated in the past that about 60 to 70 percent of the court-convicted delinquents were sentenced to a term in a labor colony (Connor, 1972).

The juvenile colonies—which are the equivalents of juvenile training schools in the United States—are of two types: general and reinforced regimes. General regime colonies are used for male juveniles sentenced to deprivation of liberty for the first time, as well as for all female juveniles. Reinforced regime colonies—those with more security—are reserved for those with previous colony terms or for those who have been convicted of especially dangerous crimes. Sentences to general regime colonies do not exceed 3 years, but those to reinforced regime colonies may range from 3 to 10 years. Most committed juveniles actually serve amounts of time in the lower ranges of these minimums/maximums. It has been estimated that at least half of the committed juveniles are paroled before the expiration of their sentences. In 1992, there were 17,886 male minors in 52 general regime colonies and 664 in four colonies of reinforced regime. There were also 876 female minors in three general regime colonies (King, 1994). As to the success of these colony placements, staff of the Moscow City Procurator's Office indicated (March 1994) that the recidivism rate from the colonies was about 30 percent. This figure, if accurate, would compare very favorably with recidivism rates from juvenile training schools in the United States, which again would be comparable institutions, and where recidivism ranges up to as high as 70 percent. It is not clear, however, exactly how this colony recidivism is defined and measured.

CONTEMPORARY ISSUES AND PROBLEMS

Let us now look further at the current procedures, both formal and informal, in more detail and see if we can discern what and where are the major problems. Beginning with the police, there are presently some 12,000 juvenile officers assigned to the *militsia* inspectorates on juvenile affairs, which are under the MVD. Seventy percent of these juvenile officers are women. This high number of women is in keeping with past practice, when most of the staff of both the inspectorates and the CJAs were women. This fact in itself says something about the operating philosophy and the priority accorded to juvenile matters in the Russian criminal justice system. The philosophy was to use more informal approaches with juveniles and to have male law enforcement officers devoting their attention to "more important" criminal matters. Now, however, this philosophy is becoming a problem because of the increasing brutality and criminal sophistication of juvenile offenders (Kurant, 1994). Sophisticated young criminals or youth gang members—sometimes affiliated with organized criminal networks—are less likely to be appropriate candidates for the traditional social work methods and diversion that have been used in the past. In 1993, for example, some 1,500 young persons were prosecuted for committing felonies as members of organized criminal groups.

In Kurant's judgment, first offenders are not, as a rule, now sentenced to "real" punishment, that is, deprivation of liberty. The courts, he said, generally show too much leniency to juvenile offenders, giving too many suspended sentences and thus stimulating repeat offending.

According to Kurant, who was reflecting his position with the MVD, law enforcement currently stands alone in giving any kind of special emphasis to juveniles. One can, however, argue that this is not so, because there are juvenile specialists in the procuracy, and there are the juvenile colonies in corrections. But there is a general absence of specialization on juvenile delinquency and juvenile justice, and that absence echoes an earlier observation made by Klein and Gatz (1990) to the effect that, although individual juvenile specialists can be found in the *militsia*, courts, and procuracy, "special juvenile units are rare, as is specialized training in juvenile matters" (p. 1). In an interview I had several years ago with a juvenile officer in the Moscow police department, he indicated that juvenile work at that time was considered easy and also that no special training was required—perhaps not unrelated to the presence of large numbers of women in the field. He, likewise, concurred that there was a shortage of specialists in the juvenile justice field.

In recent years conditions have changed, and much of the change has been for the worse. The amount of juvenile crime and the seriousness of juvenile crime are both up, but the resources to combat it are down. It is estimated that over the last 10 years the rate of growth of juvenile delinquency has been 10 times that of adult crime. As a result, in the Moscow police department, for example, the unit for combating juvenile crime recently bemoaned the fact that, despite dramatic increases in the magnitude and seriousness of juvenile crime, they had only 12 staff members, one broken-down van, and a disastrous shortage of equipment (Chelnokov, 1993). It is clear that law enforcement is having a hard time keeping up with what is happening with juvenile crime and delinquency in Russia.

ARREST AND PRETRIAL DETENTION

The processing of a juvenile offender usually begins with apprehension by the *militsia*. The juvenile may be taken to a local police lockup and, by law, detained up to midnight of the day in which the apprehension occurs. I am advised that this midnight rule holds whether the custody begins at six o'clock in the morning or eleven o'clock at night. This apprehension is recorded but is not considered an arrest. The procurator (a lawyer for the state) is duly notified by the *militsia,* and, in turn, following some preliminary investigation, either orders the offender's release or approves further detention beyond midnight. That further detention, usually in a separate section of an adult jail and described as special, isolated custody, may extend for 48 more hours. At that time, formal criminal charges are brought, and the juvenile is arrested or released. After the arrest, pretrial detention may then extend from one month up to nine months (extensions are with special permission of the Office of the Procuracy).

Detention is supposed to be limited to those juveniles who are at least 14 and have been charged with crimes, but there are no figures on exactly who is detained, where, and for how long. A senior researcher from the procurator's office described a problem that has recently arisen regarding the illegal use of detention (Pankratov, personal communication, March 1994). He said that the *militsia* sometimes unnecessarily detain juveniles in order to pressure their parents into retaining a defense lawyer (an *advokat*). The *militsia* do this because they have an arrangement with particular *advokats* in which they receive a kickback for making client referrals. Corruption of this kind has a long and infamous history in the former Soviet Union, and therefore its presence in the current processing of juveniles is not surprising.

The earlier mentioned Moscow police officer pointed out an example of the contradictions that also often plague the system. He said that there was a law that limited detention of juveniles to three hours' duration. There was another law, however, that required juveniles who had to be released from custody at night to be released only into the custody of their parents. If parents could not be found or gotten to the place where the juvenile was being held, the problem for the police became deciding which of these conflicting laws to follow.

DIVERSION

The Commissions on Juvenile Affairs that were described earlier ceased to exist after 1991. Their demise occurred because they were linked to, and had been organized under, the auspices of the Communist Party, which was itself outlawed after the coup attempt against Soviet president Gorbachev in August 1991. Now efforts are being made to restore these agencies, or at least agencies like them, at every governmental level. The disappearence of the CJAs has left a critical vacuum in the capacity to divert juveniles from the formal justice system into informal and community-based programs.

Although there are said to be many opportunities for diversion, my discussion of this issue with officials in Moscow indicated that these were labeled opportunities in the sense of situations in which juveniles should or could be diverted. Candidates for diversion from court or from colony placement include, for instance, those whose convictions are dismissed because the crime is petty or at least nondangerous, those who are convicted of a nondangerous crime, and those whose social circumstances have changed since the time of the offense. The latter might include an improved home environment or family situation.

Religion plays little, if any, role in the informal handling of juveniles in Russia. This is because religion, being officially outlawed, played such a minimal role in Soviet society in general. Politics sometimes does play a part in what is done with juvenile offenders, for instance, when amnesties are granted by the president or the legislature to individuals, to classes of individuals, or to classes of offenses.

Despite numerous candidates for diversion, there are not many placement opportunities or alternatives to which juveniles can be referred. This is largely because there are even fewer of these diversion alternatives—such as the CJAs—than there were before. Pankratov (the research director for the procurator's office) said there is now no effective system in Russia for the diversion of youth to nonsystem agencies. There are, he said, no special schools or foster homes for this purpose, and what is needed is a complex of bodies.

In the United States, there is the notion of *diversion from* the formal system (meaning removal from any further formal system handling), as well as *diversion to* a variety of ancillary agencies and programs that are part of a larger informal system. Until 1992, Russian juvenile justice operated with a similar notion— with a lot more use of diversion to than diversion from. That diversion may be rejuvenated is indicated in the emphasis in the juvenile justice reforms that are currently being considered by the Russian legislature, on diverting juveniles into special schools, as opposed to having them go to colonies.

RESIDENTIAL PLACEMENT

Besides the correctional colonies already described (and which we will take up again shortly), there are other forms of residential placement for juveniles. For example, juveniles who are 11 years old or older who commit socially dangerous acts (but not crimes) that "willfully and habitually violate rules of social behavior" (McClellan, 1987:11) can be given administrative placement in various special technical schools under the Ministry of Education. These youngsters are mostly status offenders. The schools are supposedly for deviant children who are in need of special treatment, for example, handicapped children. Officials from the procurator's office for the Moscow region estimate that the recidivism rate from these schools is only 20 percent. This, of course, is an excellent success rate. Again however, as with the earlier colony rates, it is difficult to assess the validity of this estimate of recidivism. Russian officials admit that commitment to these kinds of schools has been criticized by juvenile justice experts from the West because of the absence of judicial proceedings to govern such placements. Removing youngsters from their homes and placing them in a secure institution without the benefit of due process of law is a procedure that can be justly criticized. This "administrative" handling, in contrast to judicial handling, is, in many ways, a distinction without a difference, when viewed from the perspective of the child. There is even wider use of discretion to deprive children of their liberty, a practice justified on the grounds of what is said to be in the best interests of the child—in other words, a kind of *parens patriae* philosophy. In this administrative processing, evidentiary standards are even less than they are in the case of criminal offenders. This procedure does have the political attractiveness to the state of keeping the juvenile delinquency statistics relatively low, since cases that are handled administratively do not count as juveniles registered for crimes. Combined with the higher minimum age of criminal responsibility, one result is to keep the official rates of juvenile crime down. In the legal reforms proposed so far, there have not been any changes in the law that would reform or prohibit this administrative practice.

In addition to the special technical/vocational schools, there are reception/distribution centers under the Ministry of Internal Affairs that are used for what is said to be the temporary isolation of runaway, neglected, homeless, and abused children. Those youngsters with grave psychiatric problems are supposed to be placed in psychiatric hospitals. The MVD reports that approximately 30 to 40 percent of juvenile crimes are committed by youngsters who have some form of emotional or mental problem. Of those committed to a colony, one in five has a psychiatric disorder. There are, however, no special facilities charged with working with such juveniles—and education and health care agencies and officials are accused of ignoring this problem. This current situation supports the observations of Klein and Gatz (1990) with reference to the emotional and mental problems of Russian youth. They concluded that psychology seemed to have a rather limited role in juvenile justice in the former Soviet Union. "There appears to be relatively little concern with psychiatric diagnosis of offenders," they observed, "and mental retardation seems more legitimated than emotional disturbance as a mitigating factor in criminal behavior" (Klein and Gatz, 1990: 1). Further, they concluded that psychological treatment and referral to mental health clinics appeared to be quite rare.

CORRECTIONAL LABOR COLONIES

The colonies, as pointed out earlier, are presently the principal means of dealing with juvenile offenders who have been convicted of crimes. Given the disappearance of the CJAs, there is reason to believe that these colonies are absorbing even higher numbers (and perhaps different types) of offenders than before. Thus, it is worth looking more closely at the special problems that surround this particular placement. The following discussion draws, in part, upon two documents from the Moscow-based Center for Humanization of the Penal System, which is affiliated with the International Foundation for the Survival and Development of Humanity. Prepared in 1990 by Russian penal reformers, the documents set forth a proposal to study the conditions and consequences of juvenile institutionalization and to lay the foundation for reform. These documents need to be viewed in the context of their preparation by human rights advocates and activists, one of whom had been a prisoner in the Soviet *gulag,* or prison camp system.

Among the numerous conditions in the colony system that are criticized by these reformers is one that, although not unique to Russian correctional institutions, is peculiarly endemic to them. It is akin to what is referred to in American jails and prisons as the inmate subculture system.

The juvenile colonies are condemned for not fulfilling their roles of rehabilitating, socializing, and educating the youth who are placed in them. In fact, quite to the contrary, the system is said to actually lead to the degeneration and destruction of juvenile personalities and to the formation of strongly negative tendencies. This, according to these human rights activists, is because the administration of the penal system does not have any moral authority for the inmate. The absence of moral authority is due mainly to the pervasiveness of the "criminals' law or code." The latter is an informal system of rules developed by the inmates. It is "present and distinct . . . in colonies and other institutions for juvenile delinquents (special schools, special detention centers, etc.)" (Chesnokova, Parfenov, and Andreev, 1990:2). The problem is not limited to the colonies but also extends to the schools and distribution centers just described.

As a result of this situation, a young person, whose personality is as yet undeveloped, or even worse, has already been malformed, is left without any positive educational influences at this crucial stage in [his or her] development. The youth does not relate with the adults in the administration, opposes them, does not trust them, doesn't respect them, and, because he is being punished, is very negatively disposed to them. The inmates who act as informal "authorities" among the prisoners themselves have largely underdeveloped personalities and acquire their status very often by "illegal means." Moreover, the administration often makes use of the juveniles' instability, their psychological inability to refuse privileges or handouts, which are at the administration's disposal, in order to bring them into their system of brigades and group monitors, which is the final source of their authority over the prisoners. But a young person must somehow become socialized, adopt some role models that are more or less generally recognized. In [colonies] the model is the "criminals' law."

Having undergone such socialization, a young person is doomed to return again and again to prison . . . [because] he has become part of the criminal milieu. . . . Socialization in prison binds him to those who recognize and uphold the "criminals' law" as a form of social life and morals (Chesnokova, Parfenov, and Andreev, 1990:3–4).

This kind of prisonization effect, to repeat, is certainly not unique to Russian institutions for juvenile offenders. But, given the traditional emphases of corrections authorities in the former USSR upon building collective, communal responsibility among inmates for discipline, work, and so forth and given their considerable encouragement and exploitation of an inmate hierarchy to enforce rules and maintain order, the inmate subculture with its criminals' code is more highly developed and influential there than it is in other countries.

In addition to this general problem, there is agreement among reformers and observers that the colonies are overly repressive, that they do not give sufficient emphasis to treatment, and that they are too work-oriented. Even the minimum security facilities have double fences, barbed wire, electric wire, guard towers, and dogs. There is no treatment (such as behavior modification, group or individual counseling, and so on), educational and recreational resources are very limited, and there is a great emphasis upon work—up to eight hours a day for six days a week.

The juvenile specialists from the Moscow procurator's office complained that there were only two colonies, with a combined capacity of 1,250 youth, serving the populous Moscow region. Further, there are only two facilities for delinquent girls in the entire country. In general, these specialists said, the system of social rehabilitation so necessary to deal with juvenile delinquency and other juvenile problems—including both a community-based and an institution-based system—is critically weak.

THE OUTLOOK

As the preceding summary has indicated, there are many problems with the contemporary Russian juvenile justice system. The officials with whom I spoke argued that among the things that are needed, both more placements and a system of juvenile courts are priorities. Some believe that any juvenile court system that might be created should not be governed by criminal procedures, but rather, should be empowered to act in the more informal, *parens patriae* tradition. When asked about juvenile justice reform, most specialists were of the opinion that so far there have been no changes, and in the words of one: "It's a pity!" That this somewhat sorry state of affairs has not gone entirely unrecognized, however, is reflected in a decree issued by Russian president Yeltsin in September 1993. That decree (the text of which is in the appendix) is the basis for legal reforms being taken up by the Russian legislature. Unfortunately, according to one observer, juvenile justice reform is not a high legislative priority. What will ultimately emerge from this process is difficult to predict; but whatever the outcome, one thing that is clear is that the directions in which change is being pointed have a rather different practical and philosophical foundation.

Yeltsin's decree, "On the Prevention of Neglect of Juveniles and Juvenile Delinquency, and the Protection of Their Rights," is intended to provide for a single system of treatment for deviant, neglected, and homeless children. So-called special prevention bodies would be created within the Ministry of Education and the Ministry of Social Protection. What is believed to be fundamentally new are the planned treatment and rehabilitation institutions for juveniles to be established under the auspices of the Ministry of Education. Children in need of rehabilitation and children who have psychological or physical handicaps but who are also deviant, for example, would be the responsibility of these two ministries. Whether all or any of these types of placements would be decided by courts is not clear. According to the plan, social workers would work with abandoned children and runaways, both in residential facilities and in the community. They would not, though, be responsible for paroled youth or others who have been sentenced to closed, custodial institutions.

The Ministry of Internal Affairs would retain jurisdiction over any juveniles who have committed crimes. Juvenile specialists in the *militsia* would deal only with youth who have violated the law, such as parolees from colonies and those whose sentence to a colony has been suspended. The police, therefore, would continue to have a parole supervision function.

Given the shifting and often volatile political situation in Moscow, the outlook for these proposals is rather unclear as of this writing. At least one ominous sign can be detected upon close reading of the Yeltsin decree: there is likely to be a shortage of money to pay for any changes that might be adopted.

In the meantime, juvenile crime will certainly continue to increase for the forseeable future, because the ongoing social and political upheavals and the severe economic deprivation will continue the instability that is conducive to criminality. Both the formal and informal social controls in the country have broken down. This is obviously having severe consequences for children and youth. All this will influence the future of juvenile justice in Russia.

NOTE

1. A high rate of convictions after a formal court hearing is not unusual for juvenile offenders. This is mainly because of the options for diversion and other alternative handling available to the juvenile justice system that screen out cases that are unlikely to result in adjudication or for which adjudication is considered unnecessary. There is a high rate of conviction of juveniles who go to court in the United States as well.

REFERENCES

Chelnokov, Aleksei. " 'Problem' Teenagers Experience State's Concern." *Current Digest* 45 (1993):24.

Chesnokova, V., V. Parfenov, and A. Andreev. *Reforming the Soviet Penal System for Juvenile Delinquents.* Moscow: Center for Humanization of the Penal System, International Foundation for the Survival and Development of Humanity, 1990.

Connor, Walter D. *Deviance in Soviet Society.* New York: Columbia University Press, 1972.

King, Roy D. "Russian Prisons after Perestroika." *British Journal of Criminology* 34 (1994):62–82.

Klein, Malcolm W., and Margaret Gatz. "Soviet Psychologists' Role Is Limited in Bleak Juvenile Justice System." *Psychology International* 1 (1990):1, 4–5.

Kurant, Leonid. Personal interview, March 1994.

McClellan, Dorothy Spektorov. "Soviet Youth: A View from the Inside." *Crime and Social Justice* 29 (1987):1–25.

Pankratov, Vladimir, personal communication, March 1994.

Yakovlev, Alexander M. "Criminological Foundation of the Criminal Process." In *The Criminal Justice System of the USSR,* edited by M. Cherif Bassiouni and V. M. Savitski. Springfield, IL: Charles C. Thomas, 1979.

APPENDIX: DECREE BY THE PRESIDENT OF THE RUSSIAN FEDERATION

On the prevention of neglect of juveniles and juvenile delinquency, and the protection of their rights

In order to completely solve the problems of juvenile delinquents and uncared for and homeless children, and in order to secure children's rights and interests, it is decreed:

1. Special committees or institutes are to be set up as the state system of preventive measures against juvenile delinquency and for the protection of their rights. These institutes of care and guardianship shall include commissions on juvenile affairs, and the management and specialized services of social protection, the ministries of education, of public health, of internal affairs, of employment, and others.

2. In order to coordinate the work of the ministries and departments of the Russian Federation against juvenile delinquency, an interdepartmental Commission on Juvenile Affairs under the auspices of the Council of Ministries of the Government of the Russian Federation shall be established.

The mutual cooperation of the State institutes of all members of the Federation is to be carried out by the committees of juvenile affairs in the chief executives' (offices) of Republics which are members of the Russian Federation, and by the chief executive of regions, autonomous regions, large cities and local towns, and district administrations.

3. The Council of Ministers of the Russian Federation:

    a) Shall establish in 1993–1994, together with the combined executives of the Russian Federation, the executives of independent republics, regions, autonomous regions, cities, as well as self-governing agencies:

Specialized institutions (services) for disorderly children who need care and social rehabilitation—within the framework of agencies dealing with the social protection of the population;

Special schools of the open type for juveniles who have committed acts against the law, and special corrective institutions of learning and education for juveniles who have developmental defects and have committed dangerous acts—within the framework of educational institutions;

b) Shall reorganize the reception/distribution facilities for juveniles within the framework of agencies of internal affairs, transforming them into centers for the temporary isolation of juveniles who have committed socially dangerous acts;

c) Shall prepare and introduce within 3 months to the Supreme Soviet of the Russian Federation the following bills:

• On changes and additions to the statute on the Commissions on Juvenile Affairs stated by the decree of the Presidium of the Supreme Soviet of the RSFSR on 3 June 1967;

• On special schools and boarding homes for juvenile delinquents within the framework of agencies dealing with the social protection of the population;

• On the special institutions of learning and education for juveniles within the framework of the agencies of education;

• On the units for the prevention of juvenile delinquency within the militia agencies of public security;

• On the centers of temporary isolation for juvenile delinquents within the militia agencies of public security;

• On amending change 2 of the law of the Supreme Soviet of the RSFSR of April 18, 1991 about the order of introduction of the law of the RSFSR "On the Militia," and the law of the Supreme Soviet of the Russian Federation of February 10, 1993 about the amendments to change 2 of the law pertaining to transferring the reception/distribution centers for juveniles to the jurisdiction of other bodies.

4. The Council of Ministers—the government of the Russian Federation, executive agencies of the republics within the Russian Federation, territories, regions, autonomous regions, and federal cities—shall provide, when drawing up their budgets, for funds to subsidize agencies and institutions for the prevention of neglect of juveniles and juvenile delinquency, established according to this decree.

5. It is recommended to local government agencies to finance in 1993 the specialized institutions (services) for juveniles within the framework of bodies dealing with the social protection of the population in part from the redistribution of funds (for payroll and other appropriations) previously granted for keeping the reception/distribution centers in the Department of Internal Affairs (in view of the resulting decrease in their juvenile populations), and then subsequently from funds from their own budgets.

B. Yeltsin
President of the Russian Federation

Moscow, Kremlin
September 6, 1993
No. 1338

18

THE REPUBLIC OF SOUTH AFRICA

Herman Conradie

INTRODUCTION

The identification of the early signs of criminal behavior in juveniles is of the utmost importance, because only then can criminal behavior be effectively curbed in youngsters. In South Africa, as in other developing countries, there is a marked profile for juvenile offenders. Also, the juvenile courts and children's courts keep a close watch on juvenile perpetrators. Others are kept in places of safety such as clinic schools, child care schools, and industrial schools. In South Africa the crimes committed by juveniles constitute about one-third of all reported crimes.

According to South African law, a juvenile is a person between the ages of 7 and 20 years of age. Under certain circumstances (e.g., mental retardation), this age can be extended to include persons who are 21 years old. These age restrictions are important. Persons under the age of 7 years are rendered *doli incapax,* according to South African law; therefore, they cannot be tried or held responsible for any crimes whatsoever. Between the ages of 7 and 14 years of age, juveniles are evaluated as *doli capax* (refutably accountable). This means that the court will have to be convinced that a child between the ages of 7 and 14 is not criminally accountable. It is the onus of the state to prove that the juvenile is accountable.

Juveniles between the ages of 7 and 14 years are subject to the same criminal law, procedural law, and rules for giving evidence as is the case with adults. However, certain judicial rules make special provision for juvenile delinquents. These are highlighted by four acts: the Children's Act (Act 33 of 1960); the Criminal and Procedures Act (Act 51 of 1977); the Act on Correctional Services

(Act 8 of 1959); and the Child Care Act (Act 74 of 1983). This chapter is primarily based on these acts.

The adjudication of juveniles implies the judicial procedures that are followed if the conduct warrants appearance in a court of law. In this chapter the emphasis will be placed on the juvenile courts, the children's courts, child care schools, and clinic schools. As background, attention will also be given to the criminal profiles of juveniles and the part they play concerning official crime statistics.

HISTORICAL OVERVIEW

Midgley (1975:51) said that before the emergence of the nineteenth-century reformist movement, children convicted of criminal offenses were dealt with no differently than were adults. They were also brutally punished. However, after the British colonization of the Cape in 1806, the Masters and Servants Act of 1856 gave magistrates the power to place juveniles under the guardianship of a suitable person. The first reformatory in South Africa came into being on January 26, 1882. This was afforded by means of a private donation of R40,000 by William Porter. This led to the acceptance of the Reformatory Institutions Act of 1879. On March 30, 1881, a committee was appointed to report on the establishment of a reformatory. On January 26, 1882, Sir Hercules Robinson, the governor, made a proclamation for the erection of a reformatory at Valkenburg. This reformatory was moved to Tokai on June 9, 1890, and named after William Porter. At the end of the nineteenth century, the Porter Reformatory at Tokai was the only one in South Africa. It made provision for the detention and rehabilitation of juveniles of all races under the age of 16 years (Midgley, 1975:51).

Shortly after unification in 1910, Act 13 of 1911 was passed. This act provided for the erection of reformatories in the Union of South Africa. Article 3 made provision for the erection of nine different types of reformatories (Engelbrecht, 1952:19–20). Act 25 of 1911, the Child Protection Act, provided for the implementation of educational principles in the treatment of juveniles in these facilities. These principles were later incorporated in Act 31 of 1937 and in Act 33 of 1960, the Children's Act. However, on November 10, 1911, a section of the Diepkloof Prison was set apart as a reformatory for black children (Engelbrecht, 1952:26).

Based on this history, there exist different institutions like childrens' homes (also named child care schools) and reformatories. They do not differ very much in principle. Of these institutions the reformatory is the strictest and serves as the last resort for rehabilitation of juveniles before prison.

THE CODE LIST OF CRIMES

The Central Statistical Service (1994) publishes the official crime statistics of South Africa every year. This is done according to the so-called Code List of

Crimes, which comprises six classes, each with subclasses. For the purposes of this chapter, only those subclasses relevant to juveniles are listed.

Class A: Government authority and good order

Subclass A1	State security
Subclass A2	Peace and order
Subclass A3	Administration of justice
Subclass A4	Public finance

Class B: Communal life

Subclass B1	Communal life and care of children
Subclass B2	Indecent, sexual and related matters
Subclass B3	Drugs and dependence-producing substances
Subclass B4	Other matters against communal life

Class C: Personal relations

Subclass C1	Life and body of a person
Subclass C2	Reputation and honor of a person
Subclass C3	Liberty and right to possess

Class D: Property

Subclass D1	Burglaries and related matters
Subclass D2	Theft from the person or gaining advantage by means of force or threats
Subclass D3	Theft of livestock and related matters
Subclass D4	Other thefts
Subclass D5	*Falsitas* and related behavior (deceit, fraud, cheating)
Subclass D6	Other matters related to property
Subclass D7	Animals

Class E: Economic affairs

Subclass E1	Economy, general
Subclass E2	Agriculture, animal husbandry, fisheries and water affairs
Subclass E3	Mining and related matters
Subclass E4	Manufacturing and construction
Subclass E5	Commerce and business services
Subclass E8	Other economic affairs

Class F: Social affairs

Subclass F1	Road traffic
Subclass F6	Health services

JUVENILES' PART IN THE CODE LIST

During 1992, juveniles in South Africa were convicted for a total of 404,509 cases of class D crimes (against property). Furthermore, there were convictions of 210,159 offenses of the class C type (personal relations). The third highest category of offenses by juveniles, during the same period, pertained to communal life (class B); there were 130,444 convictions in this area. Next follows class F crimes (relating to social affairs), with 70,729 convictions. Lower down are convictions regarding government authority and good order (class A), with 40,235, and class E (economic affairs), with 2,613 convictions. All these put together amount to a massive 858,689 convictions.

The reasons these types of offenses are in the majority are, of course, linked to the universal lack of skills younger persons have in these fields of human existence. Because they are young, juveniles have not yet acquired property, they are not yet skilled in interhuman relations, and they are not always able to find their proper place in society's communal life. Then they end up in the country's juvenile courts when they contravene the law.

JUVENILE COURTS

Hearings

Juvenile trials are regulated by the Criminal Procedures Act (Act 51 of 1977). This act makes provision for aspects like court appearances by juveniles, court procedures during hearings, and various types of penalties that can be imposed. Furthermore, this act addresses matters of age; for example, persons under 18 years of age are regarded as children (not as adults); this refers to diminished capacity. Depending on the type of offense, juveniles can be tried in magistrates court, regional courts, and even in supreme courts. The term "juvenile court" denotes a magistrates court reserved for trials of juveniles. These courts are not ordinary criminal courts. These courts are established in areas where the number of cases warrants their existence. If, for some reason, juveniles are to stand trial with adults for a particular crime, they can be tried in an "ordinary" magistrates court, a regional court, or the supreme court.

Juveniles can be brought before a juvenile court by means of the following (Act 51 of 1977):

1. arrest;

2. summons;

3. written notice;

4. warning;

5. indictment (relating to cases of the supreme court).

When a juvenile is arrested, the police are obliged to inform the parent or guardian of the trial date. This notification is demanded by section 74(2) (a) of Act 51 of 1977. Parents or guardians who live within the magisterial district are required to attend the trial. If the juvenile is released after an arrest, she or he could be placed in the custody of the parent or guardian. The parent or guardian must then ensure that the juvenile appears in court.

Special Provisions

The act (Act 51 of 1977) makes the following special provisions concerning hearings of juveniles:

1. While entitled to legal representation, a juvenile is also entitled to assistance by a parent or guardian during the proceedings. This assistance may take any form (Act 51 of 1977, section 73(3)).
2. Criminal cases are always heard *in camera.* It is stipulated that nobody, except the parent or guardian, or an individual selected *in loco parentis,* may attend the hearing, except with authorization by the court (Act 51 of 1977, section 153(4)).
3. Juveniles may not be detained in a prison or police cell, unless the court finds such detention necessary and no other suitable place of custody is available (Prisons Act, Act 8 of 1959).
4. No one may publish any information disclosing the identity of an accused juvenile (Act 51 of 1977, section 154(3)).
5. The criminal trial of a juvenile may be converted into a case for the children's court when the juvenile is found to be in need of care (Act 51 of 1977, section 254).

Criminal Accountability

In juvenile court trials in South Africa, the important judicial principle of criminal accountability becomes effective. Children below the age of 7 years are irrefutably presumed to be not criminally accountable by the court. Therefore, they cannot be charged in a criminal court. When children reach the age of 14 years, they are refutably presumed to be criminally accountable. The prosecution has to prove this presumption beyond reasonable doubt, namely, that the child is criminally accountable (Snyman, 1981:141). It is the state's onus to prove that the accused juvenile is capable of comprehending the nature and consequences of actions and the wrongfulness of such deeds and that she or he was acting according to her or his insights (Sonnekus, 1993:50–52).

Presentence Procedures

During the presentence proceedings, the prosecution may, when the juvenile is convicted, prove previous convictions. This is taken into account by the court in determining sentence. The juvenile, a legal representative, and parents or guardians are given the opportunity to plead in mitigation. Furthermore, during the court hearing of a juvenile case, a probation officer is often called upon to present evidence regarding the accused's background, home life, and other individual circumstances. This is done to make sure that the court understands all the accused's problems before sentencing.

Judgment

In terms of the Criminal Procedures Act (Act 51 of 1977), the following sentences may be passed with regard to juveniles:

1. the death penalty (Act 51 of 1977, section 277);
2. imprisonment (Act 51 of 1977, section 276);
3. periodic imprisonment (Act 51 of 1977, section 285);
4. declaring one a habitual criminal (Act 51 of 1977, section 286);
5. a fine (Act 51 of 1977, section 276);
6. corporal punishment (Act 51 of 1977, section 294).

Although these harsh judgments can be passed on juveniles, the Criminal Procedures Act also contains special provisions regarding the judgment of juveniles. For example, in section 290(1), instead of punishment, the court can order that a juvenile be placed under the supervision of a probation officer or correctional official or be placed in the custody of another suitable person, such as a family member. When placed under supervision, a treatment program is devised in consultation with the accused and parents or guardians, the school, and other involved parties. The supervisor monitors progress with the aim of resocializing the offender. This order—placing one under probation—can also be given in place of punishments, such as fines and corporal punishment.

Corporal punishment for juveniles is limited by law. It may not exceed a maximum of seven strokes with a light cane. Corporal punishment can be administered only under the supervision of a medical doctor and in the presence of the parent(s) or guardian of the juvenile (who must by law be informed of their right to be present). The law also prescribes that the cane used for corporal punishment should be three feet (914 centimeters) long and half an inch (9.525 millimeters) in diameter. The caning must always be done on the buttocks only, which must be covered by ordinary clothing. Canings are not allowed to be administered to female offenders. If the medical doctor certifies that the person in question is not healthy enough to undergo corporal punishment (or part of it), the court is free to change the sentence as it pleases.

According to Hiemstra (1981:529), Article 294 of the Criminal Procedures Act was written especially for juveniles. Courts can, according to Article 293, instruct canings for the following crimes: rape, robbery, assault with aggravating circumstances, and an immoral deed with the intention to cause serious injury.

Courts can also impose this sentence when juveniles access a premise forcefully with the purpose of committing a crime, theft of motor vehicles or theft from a motor vehicle, acceptance of stolen goods, and bestiality or committing another type of immoral act by one male with another male person. The recent trend in South Africa is to move away from corporal punishment. Whether this trend will continue in the new South Africa remains to be seen.

The age of the perpetrator, aggravating circumstances, and previous convictions are always taken into account when juveniles are sentenced. When the death penalty is imposed, and the perpetrator was under 18 years of age during the commission of the crime, this is automatically taken as a mitigating circumstance, and the death penalty becomes discretionary. Presently, the death penalty has been suspended in South Africa, due to all the political changes that started in 1990.

CHILDREN'S COURTS

In terms of section 1 of the Children's Act (Act 33 of 1960), children's courts exist for the benefit of children in need of care. Children in need of care are defined by this law as children who (Sonnekus, 1993:54–56):

1. have been abandoned or are without visible means of support;
2. have no parent or guardian or have a parent or guardian who is unfit to exercise proper control over the child;
3. are in the custody of a person who has been convicted of committing an offense against that child;
4. cannot be controlled by parents or guardians;
5. are habitually truant;
6. frequent the company of any immoral or vicious persons or live in circumstances calculated to cause seduction, corruption, or prostitution;
7. beg;
8. engage in any form of street trading;
9. are being cared for apart from parents or guardians in domestic circumstances that are detrimental to their interests and whose caretakers cannot be found or have failed to make proper provision for their care and custody, although they have been called upon to do so;
10. are in a state of physical or mental danger.

Therefore, children's courts (hearing cases of children in need of care) should not be confused with juvenile courts (hearing cases of juvenile delinquents). Children's courts are presided over by a commissioner, but, practically, the work is done by a magistrate. The goal of these courts is to conduct investigations regarding children in need of care. Should it become clear during a criminal trial that the accused is a child in need of care, the court may stop the hearing and convert it into a case for the children's court (Act 51 of 1977, section 254). When this happens, all criminal charges against the accused are dropped. This can be done only if, in the course of the hearing of a criminal case against a juvenile, it becomes apparent that the accused is in need of care. However, Hiemstra (1981:520) states that this provision should not be implemented if the said juvenile exhibits serious criminal tendencies.

Thus, a children's court is not a criminal court. It cannot try juveniles or find them guilty of any crimes. It is only an investigative court. Children are referred to children's courts by means of administrative procedures set into motion by a police officer or a social worker (Child Care Act, Article 13) or by means of diversion of a criminal case (Criminal Procedures Act, Article 254).

COMPARISONS BETWEEN JUVENILE AND CHILDREN'S COURTS

The most marked similarity between the juvenile and children's courts is that the hearings in both are held behind closed doors, for the protection of the juvenile's identity. The most salient differences between the juvenile courts and the children's courts in South Africa can be listed as follows:

1. the juvenile court is a criminal court, whereas the children's court is a court of inquiry;
2. the juvenile court normally refers juveniles to institutions such as reform schools and even to prisons, while a children's court refers them to child care schools;
3. the accused in a juvenile court is a juvenile offender or juvenile criminal, while the child in a children's court is not an offender, but a child in need of care;
4. if convicted, the accused in a juvenile court has a criminal record, while in a children's court the child has no criminal record;
5. the presiding officer of a juvenile court is a magistrate while in the children's court, although also a magistrate, the presiding officer is known as a commissioner of child care.

CHILD CARE SCHOOLS

The Commission of Inquiry into Certain Aspects of Child Care (South Africa, 1982:55) recommended that the name "industrial schools" be abolished and replaced with the term "child care schools." The primary aim of these schools is reeducation, that is, child care by means of reform. Only children in need of care in terms of the Children's Act (Act 33 of 1960) and thus also in terms of the Child Care Act (Act 74 of 1983) are admitted to child care schools. This may happen only immediately after a child has been declared as in need of care. However, children who are not manageable cannot be suspended from a child care school—they may only be transferred (with permission of the minister) to a reform school.

The treatment of pupils in these schools is aimed at modifying behavior with the aim of reintegrating the child back into society. The formal educational program is, as in other official schools, differentiated and caters to pupils in the primary secondary phase (standard 5 to standard 10). In these schools, however, more psychological and educational services available to the pupils in these schools concentrate on reconstruction. Social workers are attached to these schools on a permanent basis.

The advantages of child care schools include the following. They provide residential care (South Africa, 1982:19–21). This ensures that physical care can be optimized. Care is undertaken around the clock by qualified and experienced staff. Homeless children are accommodated. Adverse factors are eliminated. They are placed among their peers and in close contact with caring adults. Stimulating programs compensate for earlier deprivations. They are taught not to distrust love. Ties with parents are reinforced and improved. A sense of stability is ensured by the hostel environment. The pupils experience acceptance instead of rejection.

However, the disadvantages include the following. The pupils come into contact with undesirable company. This can, however, be counteracted with an internal classification system. The child may develop a negative self-image. Family ties are disrupted. The routine is strict and not flexible. Separation of the sexes creates the possibility of unnatural sexual relations. Loss of privacy and personal identity may also result, because all activities are group activities (such as eating and studying). Because of this overcrowding, the pupils are not encouraged to think for themselves. Because of the forced admission, children regard their presence in these schools as confinement.

According to a professional guide for educators of pedagogically neglected children in the Children's Act schools, the aims of the child care schools include the following:

1. to give the child a Christian education based on the Bible;
2. to offer education of a broad national character;
3. to educate the pupil to adopt a sound philosophy of life;
4. to educate and instruct the pupil concerning the needs of the country;
5. to educate the pupil as a complete human being;
6. to stimulate the child in areas where she or he has been deprived;
7. to educate the youth to enable her or him to make independent, responsible choices;
8. to teach a child to utilize leisure time positively;
9. to prepare the pupil for an occupation.

REFORM SCHOOLS

The work of reformatories in South Africa is determined by the Children's Act (Act 33 of 1960). In section 39(2)(a), these schools are described as institutions that admit, care for, and train children in terms of Act 33 of 1960 (or any other act). Therefore, a court of law may commit a juvenile to a reform school or transfer the youth from private custody, a children's home, or a child care school to a reform school. Those who are committed directly to a reform school have usually had previous convictions. When committed after a first offense or with only a few offenses, the crime usually is a serious one, such as serious assault, armed robbery, rape, culpable homicide, or murder. Those juveniles who are transferred from other institutions to reformatories usually display serious behavioral problems and need strict discipline and control.

In these schools the juveniles are treated according to a fixed, organized program starting with admission, working through education and treatment, preparation for discharge, and a follow-up phase. The treatment is individualized in order to meet the specific needs of each pupil. Intense observation is maintained. Depending on abilities, the juvenile offender is trained for a specific occupation. Scholastic career, spiritual care, and moral and cultural education receive continuous attention. These aspects are enhanced, with attention given to juveniles' physical development and leisure-time activities.

Hiemstra (1981:633) is correct in ascertaining that these schools are more concerned with treating, than with punishing, juvenile offenders. This can be deduced from the existence of independent psychological units at these schools. Their activities include the following. They make a thorough study of the individual pupil's personal history and background. They administer scholastic tests for correct academic placement. They also apply psychological group tests to determine leadership abilities. Then a complete psychological evaluation is generated as well. The psychologists try to determine the dynamics of the youth's misconduct. They diagnose and characterize the juvenile to form an overall personality profile. Then each individual is classified, aiming at differential institutional treatment. The pupils are then placed in a suitable hostel on the premises. Finally, guidelines for continued therapeutic treatment are spelled out. Against this background, vocational training is given in the following areas: plumbing; sheet metal work; fitting and turning; carpentry; plastering and building; painting and decorating; and upholstery. Shoemaking, tailoring, panel beating, and coppery are also included. Training is also given for handymen, farm laborers, gardeners, cooks, and office workers. For female offenders, training is extended to include needlework, sewing, laundering, cookery, and home management.

CLINIC SCHOOLS

Pupils are referred to clinic schools when they cannot benefit from the normal tuition of the ordinary educational system. This is done when they appear to need a special kind of reeducation. They are also committed to these schools when their presence in the normal class situation is detrimental for themselves and the other pupils. The most common reasons for commitment are unmanageability, poor or no prognosis in pedotherapy, deteriorating or unfavorable family circumstances, or an infringement of the law.

Thus, regarding clinic schools, there is no court intervention. Children are referred to these schools by arrangement with the Transvaal Education Department. This is the only body with this system. Clinic schools are described as follows by Van Greunen (1992:35). They provide temporary therapeutic accommodation to certain deviant children who cannot be helped in other ways. There are only four of these schools in the Province of Transvaal in South Africa, where this system is implemented. All these schools take children of both sexes from primary to secondary school phases. These pupils are "behaviorally handicapped." This means they have been prevented from developing to their full potential because of their misconduct, which also has a harmful influence on pupils in the ordinary schools. So children are sent to clinic schools because of problematic behavior. The main aim of these schools is rehabilitation and the prevention of future problematic behavior. Therefore, attempts are made to help these pupils to adjust to the demands of society. A unique feature in these schools is that while the children are there, the family also undergoes therapy. This is done to assist the child in eventual social reintegration. The main aim of the clinic school can thus be seen to prevent further deterioration on the road to becoming a criminal.

PRISONS

According to South African law, a juvenile can also be ordered directly to a prison. Prisons in South Africa are administered in terms of Act 8 of 1959, as amended. This act is founded on the Standard Minimum Rules, which were adopted in August 1955 at the first United Nations Congress on Crime Prevention and Treatment of Offenders. The aims of the South African Correctional Services include (1) discipline aimed at developing self-discipline, (2) training aimed at self-development and cultivating sound habits, and (3) inculcating a sense of moral responsibility.

Juveniles sentenced to a term of imprisonment have been convicted by a court of law and sent to prison in terms of the Criminal Procedures Act (Act 51 of 1977). The Children's Act (Act 33 of 1960) also makes provision for a juvenile who shows no signs of improvement or rehabilitation to be transferred from a reform school to a prison. However, before this can happen, one is warned several times. If this has no effect, the youth is summoned before a meeting of the governing body of the school, under the chair of a magistrate. Only the minister can approve this transfer. This commitment can be for a maximum of two years (observing the original discharge date from the reform school).

In prisons, attention is given, according to the Standard Minimum Rules, to the physical care of the inmates. All the necessary sleeping, toilet, and laundry facilities are provided. Toiletries and clothing are supplied. Diets include all essential nutrients and meals (planned in consultation with the Department of

Health) and are served regularly. Medical and dental care is available on a 24-hour basis. Referral to external health facilities is also available. Rehabilitation programs have a high priority. Training in the utilization of leisure time is given special attention. Training is also provided for most technical skills. Furthering of academic study is also made available, even at the university level, by means of correspondence. As an example, Nelson Mandela himself obtained the B.A. and L.L.B., a legal qualification (the recognized qualification for advocates in South Africa) from the University of South Africa (which is a correspondence facility) during his time of imprisonment.

The treatment program for juveniles committed to prisons is the same as for adults. When possible, however, juveniles are detained, trained, and treated separately from adults.

NEW DEVELOPMENTS

Skelton (1994), who was the principal legal drafter of the new proposals for policy and legislative change concerning juvenile justice for South Africa, proposed that alternatives for arrests (such as police officers issuing formal warnings and a written notice to attend a referral meeting), be considered in the new dispensation. Furthermore, the grounds for arresting young persons should be limited to crimes like murder, armed robbery, robbery resulting in serious injury, rape or sexual assault, assault resulting in grievous bodily harm, and arson resulting in serious damage. It is also envisaged that they be taken up by a Reception Process, during which a youth justice worker will oversee each case. A referral meeting will be held within 24 hours after arrests have taken place. Whenever possible, juveniles should be released into the care of parents or guardians. Referral meetings can handle cases in the following ways: referral back to the police for a formal warning, referral to a family conference, referral to a children's court inquiry, or no action can be taken at all.

This new proposed policy also provides for changes concerning the juvenile court rules. It is proposed that court personnel should receive special training to deal with matters involving young persons; that even where parents are able to provide for legal representation, but refuse to do so, the juvenile should be given legal representation; all juvenile cases should receive priority status in the courts and the current provision that hearings should be held *in camera* should also be upheld. This document also gave guidelines to be taken into account when sentencing of juveniles is considered. These include: caution (with or without conditions); postponement of sentencing; referral to a family group conference for recommendations and plans; participation in a number of programs; correctional supervision; and custodial sentences (Skelton 1994:30).

Skelton (1994:32) also proposed that the treatment of juveniles in secure-care facilities be reconsidered to include the following: suitable groupings according to age, size or level of danger; constant supervision; exercise, recreation, and health protection. The protection against assault or abuse, appropriate education, counseling, humane correction, contact with family or supportive network and pre-release programs—under the supervision of an appropriately trained staff—should also be in place. This policy document also made provision for the protection of the identity of juveniles. It proposed a central database of all who go through the family group conference. This database should only be accessible to youth justice workers and public prosecutors. Fingerprints will only be allowed when the juvenile is charged.

CONCLUSION

In South Africa, under the current law, much is done to adjudicate juveniles. Although a highly sophisticated system is in place at the moment, this has not had any noticeable effect regarding the diminishing of juvenile offenses. This may be due to different factors, including the argument that laws alien to the people to whom they are applied are administered by officials who are from a different culture. It may also be due to the normal *Sturm und Drang* (storm and stress) period of the juvenile phase of life.

During the current democratization of the South African society, so-called traditional law (customary law, indigenous law, nonstate law) was also put under the spotlight. According to Ndabandaba (1993:10), some of the principles of traditional law are the following: the people are the first and final source of all power; the rights of the community are superior to those of individuals; kings, chiefs, and elders are leaders, not rulers; government and the people are one and the same; the family is the primary political unit; the elder of each extended family or clan is the chosen representative on the council; decisions on council are made by the elders (the chief or king must remain silent); every member has the right of appeal from a lower to a higher court. Analyzing these principles leads to the conclusion that traditional law as an "informal structure" is still playing an important role in the areas of community development, the administration of justice, the administration of tribal land, and restitution, compensation, and reconciliation (Ndabandaba, 1993:1–2). Therefore, the institution of traditional leadership cannot be ignored in the new South African constitution.

These sentiments were echoed by Hiemstra (Ndabandaba, 1993:15). Judge Hiemstra argued, based on research undertaken by the Human Sciences Research Council (HSRC) during 1985, that the administration of justice is in a crisis of legitimacy. This is so because this research established that the administration of justice was viewed with suspicion by large sections of the nonwhite population. Therefore, if the present adjudication system is retained, then this loss of legitimacy in the eyes of the masses should be addressed as a matter of urgency.

The administration of justice, according to traditional law, is done through the king's courts, family councils, local courts, or district courts. Any adult can participate in the court proceedings. In the 1980s the notion of people's courts came to the fore. These served as forums for dispute settlements and as instruments of the liberation struggle. These courts are popular in the squatter camps, where they reflect the continuance of the values and ideas associated with traditional law justice, that is, the idea of communal well-being rather than individual interests. It should be made clear that future recognition of these structures will depend on many factors. The most important of these is their acceptance by the public as an alternative form of justice (Ndabandaba, 1993: 13–15).

REFERENCES

Central Statistical Service. *Crimes, Persecutions and Convictions with Regard to Certain Offenses.* CSS-Report. No. 00-11-01 (1991/92), 1994.

Engelbrecht, Izak. *Die Interne Organisasie van die Suid-Afrikaanse Verbeteringskool.* M.Ed.-Verhandeling. Potchefstroomse Universiteit vir Christelike Hoër: Onderwys, 1952.

Hiemstra, Victor G. *Suid-Afrikaanse Strafproses. Derde Uitgawe.* Durban: Butterworths, 1981.

Midgley, James. *Children on Trial: A Study of Juvenile Justice.* Kaapstad: Nicro, 1975.

Ndabandaba, Lindumusa B. G. "The Role of Traditional Law in the Future South African Constitutional Development." Paper presented at the 13th meeting of the International Association of Forensic Sciences, Dusseldorf, Germany, August 1993.

Skelton, Ann. *Juvenile Justice for South Africa: Proposals for Policy and Legislative Change.* Cape Town: Allies Printers, 1994.

Snyman, Carel R. *Strafreg (Criminal Law).* Durban: Butterworths, 1981.

Sonnekus, Eon F. "*Jeugkriminologie in die RSA.*" Unpublished D Litt. et Phil, University of South Africa, Pretoria, South Africa (Republic), 1993.

South Africa (Republic). Children's Act, Act 33 of 1960. Pretoria: Government Printer, 1960.

———. Criminal Procedure Act 51 of 1977. Pretoria: Government Printer, 1977.

———. *Departement van Gesondheid en Welsyn. Verslag van die Komitee van Ondersoek na sekere aspekte van Kindersorg* (RP99/1984) (*Department of Health and Welfare. Report of the Committee of Inquiry into Certain Aspects of Child Care*). Pretoria: Staatsdrukker, 1982.

———. Child Care Act, Act 74 of 1983. Pretoria: Government Printer, 1983.

Van Greunen, Eugene. *Die Kliniekskool as 'n Residensiële Ortopedagogiese Inrigting: Ongepubliseerde M.Ed.-Verhandeling.* Pretoria: Universiteit van Pretoria, 1992.

APPENDIX: AGENCIES DEALING WITH YOUTH AND YOUTH OFFENDERS

The Chief Medical Superintendent
Weskoppies Hospital
Attention Dr. De Wet (Child Care Unit)
Private Bag X113
Pretoria
South Africa 0001

The Commander: Child Protection Unit
South African Police
Private Bag X302
Pretoria
South Africa 0001

National Children's Rights Committee
185 Corner Smit/Biccard Streets
Braamfontein
Johannesburg
South Africa

National Council for Family and Child Welfare
PO Box 30990
Braamfontein
South Africa 2017

National Institute for Crime Prevention and the Rehabilitation of Offenders (NICRO)
Pretoria Branch
Corner Andries/Bureaulane
Hamilton House 2nd Floor
PO Box 468
Pretoria
South Africa 0001

The Southern African Society for Prevention of Child Abuse and Neglect
PO Box 16089
Bighton Beach
South Africa 4009

Transvaal Education Department
Private Bag X76
Pretoria
South Africa 0001

19

UNITED STATES

Clemens Bartollas

INTRODUCTION

The mission of the juvenile justice system in the United States is to control and correct the behavior of law-violating juveniles. The juvenile justice system, however, has faced mounting criticism for its ineffectiveness. One of the reasons the juvenile justice system has found it difficult to achieve its mission is that there are complex forces intruding upon any attempt to formulate goals or develop effective programs. These forces include the spread of youth gangs across the nation, the increased use of drugs and alcohol among high-risk juveniles, the conflicting philosophies and strategies for correcting law-violating juveniles, and the social, political, and economic problems facing the United States. Indeed, nearly everyone agrees that the juvenile justice system must change, but there is a variety of opinions about what the new form of the system should be.

Some argue that the *parens patriae* philosophy, in which the juvenile court accepts parental responsibility over wayward children, and its rehabilitative emphasis remain the best approach for society to handle children in trouble (Schramm, 1945). Others argue that the ineffectiveness of the juvenile justice system, in either reducing juvenile recidivism or granting juvenile offenders their due process rights, requires that the basic correctional goal of the juvenile justice system be changed from rehabilitation to ''just desserts'' and that juvenile offenders receive their due process rights (Fogel, 1975). Another position is so dissatisfied with the juvenile justice system that proponents want to dismantle the system. Law-violating juveniles, then, would be handled by the adult court (Feld, 1991).

The purpose of this chapter is to review the development of the juvenile justice system in the United States, to depict the formal and informal procedures that explain how juvenile justice takes place, and to discuss the possibilities of systemic reform.

DEVELOPMENT OF THE JUVENILE JUSTICE SYSTEM

The development of juvenile justice in the United States can be divided into six major periods: colonial, house of refuge, juvenile court, juvenile rights, the reform agenda of the 1970s, and the "get-tough" crime control policies of the 1980s and 1990s.

The Colonial Period (1636–1824)

At the time of the American Revolution, juveniles were treated the same as adults. Juveniles who violated community norms, like adults, received fines, beatings, and floggings; were put in stocks; were driven through towns in carts to be ridiculed; and were even hanged, mutilated, burned, or banished from the community. After punishment, some wayward youth were apprenticed to local craftsmen, and others were sent on whaling voyages (Rothman, 1971:46–53).

The House of Refuge Period (1823–1899)

In the late 1770s and early 1800s, the United States was in a period of extensive disorder, stemming from the rise of cities and the decline of the rural way of life. There was increased concern about what to do with the growing number of juveniles who were abandoned, were running the streets, or had run afoul of community norms. An idea emerged at the time that if institutions could be established for children modeled after the well-adjusted family, this would accomplish two purposes. These institutions, called "house of refuge," would bring the discipline, order, and care of the family into institutional life. They would further enable juveniles to avoid the deplorable conditions of jails and workhouses.

New York started the first house of refuge for female adolescents in 1823 and for male adolescents in 1825. In the next few years, Boston, Philadelphia, Bangor, Richmond, Mobile, Cincinnati, and Chicago established houses of refuge for males. Twenty-three institutions were built in the 1830s and another 30 in the 1840s. The capacity of these houses of refuge, most of which were for males, ranged from 90 at Lancaster, Massachusetts, to 1,000 at the New York House of Refuge (Rothman, 1971).

Reformers agreed by the 1850s that houses of refuge were not dealing adequately with juvenile crime. Many of these houses had grown unwieldy in size, and order and discipline had disappeared from most. In addition, juveniles were still being confined with adults in filthy and dangerous jails and prisons. A movement began in the final decades of the nineteenth century to develop an alternative system for youth in trouble.

The Juvenile Court Period (1899–1967)

First created in Cook County (Chicago), Illinois, in 1899 and soon thereafter in Denver, Colorado, the juvenile court was based on the legal concept of *parens patriae*. This medieval English legal doctrine permitted the right of the Crown, or state, to intervene in family relations whenever a child's welfare was threatened.

The informal setting of the court and the parental nature of the judge, according to proponents of the juvenile court, would enable troubled youth to be "saved" from their lives of crime (Platt, 1969). The children who were referred to the court and were adjudicated delinquent or status offenders were to remain under the court's jurisdiction until they were rehabilitated or were no longer juveniles according to state statutes.

The Juvenile Rights Period (1967–1975)

The popularity of the juvenile court skyrocketed during the first couple decades of the twentieth century. Indeed, by 1920, 21 states had developed juvenile courts. But during the next four decades, the juvenile court continued to face mounting criticism. Critics challenged that the court was falling short of its idealistic goals of rehabilitating youths in an informal, noncriminal, and parental context. They claimed that the juvenile court had not succeeded in its goal of rehabilitating youths, in bringing compassion or justice to them, or in providing them their due process rights (President's Commission on Law Enforcement and Administration of Justice, 1967:79–80). The charge was even made that the court was doing great harm to those appearing before it (Richette, 1969; Murphy, 1974; James, 1971).

These criticisms led to a series of U.S. Supreme Court decisions granting juveniles due process rights that changed the course of juvenile justice: *Kent v. United States* (1966), *In re Gault* (1967), *In re Winship* (1970), *McKeiver v. Pennsylvania* (1971), and *Breed v. Jones* (1975). The landmark case, the *In re Gault* decision, ruled that juveniles have the right to due process safeguards in proceedings where a finding of delinquency could lead to confinement and that juveniles have the rights to notice of charges, to counsel, to confrontation and cross-examination, and to privilege against self-incrimination.

The Reform Agenda of the 1970s

The reform agenda of the 1970s in juvenile justice emphasized reducing the use of juvenile correctional institutions, or a policy of deinstitutionalization, diverting minor offenders and status offenders from the juvenile justice system and decriminalizing status offenses.

This reform agenda seemed to focus on the issue of the system's handling or processing status offenses (those offenses that would not be defined as illegal if committed by adults) more than any other. One reason status offenses were so emphasized is that the federal Juvenile Justice and Delinquency Prevention Act of 1974 required, as a means of continuing funding to the states, the need for the diversion and deinstitutionalization of status offenders.

Juvenile Crime Control Policies of the 1980s and Early 1990s

A serious shortcoming of the reform agenda of the 1970s was its failure to give sufficient attention to violent youth crime and repeat offenders. In the 1980s, with Ronald Reagan in the White House, the muted voices of the "get-tough approach" with hard-core juvenile offenders began to be heard and to influence public policy.

In 1984, the National Advisory Committee for Juvenile Justice and Delinquency Prevention expressed this change of philosophy in this way: "[T]he time has come for a major departure from the existing philosophy and activity of the federal government in the juvenile justice field" (p. 9). This committee recommended that the "federal effort in the area of juvenile delinquency should focus primarily on the serious, violent, or chronic offender" (p. 9).

Thus, the major emphasis of the Reagan administration's crime control policies for juveniles was to get tough on serious and violent youthful offenders and to withdraw from the reform efforts of the 1970s. This new federal mandate, in turn, has encouraged the development of five trends throughout the United States: (1) preventive detention; (2) transfer of violent juveniles to the adult court; (3) mandatory and determinate sentencing for violent juveniles; (4) increased confinement of juveniles; and (5) enforcement of the death penalty for juveniles who commit brutal and senseless murders (Krisberg, Liskey, and Austin, 1986).

In the late 1980s and early 1990s, with the administrations of Presidents George Bush and Bill Clinton, the major concerns of federal, as well as state, crime control policies with juveniles focused on violent predators, on trafficking of drugs, and on participation in street gangs. Juveniles' participation in street gangs, especially, received major attention because their recent spread across the nation has resulted in increased trafficking of drugs and in drive-by shootings.

FORMAL JUVENILE JUSTICE SYSTEM: HOW THE SYSTEM IS SUPPOSED TO WORK

The juvenile justice system is, in some ways, similar to the adult justice system in the United States. Three basic subsystems characterize both justice processes, and the flow of justice in both systems is supposed to follow the same sequence: from law violation to police apprehension, from trial to judicial dispositions, and from sentencing to probation or correctional confinement. The same basic vocabulary is used in both systems, and even when the vocabulary differs, no change of intent is generally intended.

The two justice systems do differ in several ways. The juvenile system places more attention on offender rehabilitation than does the adult system. The due process movement, which has gained support in juvenile justice in recent decades, still does not provide juveniles with as many rights as adults have. The juvenile system must deal with status offenders who would not be treated as criminals if they were adults. Finally, the juvenile system is unable to punish offenders as severely as is the adult system. It does not, for example, have the death penalty available as a punishment as does the adult system.

The Police and the Juvenile

The police are generally the first contact a juvenile has with the juvenile justice system. The police officer has broad discretionary power, which he or she can use to either divert juveniles or refer them to the justice system. Most police contact with juveniles, however, is nonofficial and consists of such orders as "Get off the corner," "Break it up," or "Go home." David Bordua's study of the Detroit police, for example, found only 5,282 official contacts out of 106,000 encounters (Bordua, 1967).

A number of factors influence the police officer's disposition of the juvenile. These include the following:

- Nature of the offense: The more serious the offense, the more likely the juvenile is to be referred to the juvenile court.
- Nature of the interaction between the police officer and the juvenile: The less the deference or politeness and respect shown to a police officer, the more likely the juvenile is to be referred to the juvenile court.
- Socioeconomic status: The lower the social class a juvenile belongs to, the more likely the juvenile is to be referred to the juvenile court.
- Citizen complainants: The more that citizens are present or initiate the complaint against a juvenile, the more likely the juvenile is to be referred to the juvenile court.
- Departmental policy: The more that a department has adopted a professional stance to police work, the more likely the juvenile is to be referred to the juvenile court.
- Individual factors of the offender: The more hard-core a juvenile appears to be, as evident by prior arrest record, previous offense, age, gang membership, and peer relationships, the more likely the juvenile is to be referred to the juvenile court.
- External pressures in the community: The more pressure that is found in a community to "get tough" on juvenile crime, the more likely the juvenile is to be referred to the juvenile court (Bartollas, 1993).

The police officer generally has five options when investigating a complaint against a juvenile or arriving at the scene where illegal behavior has taken place.

First, the police officer can warn and release the youth, who typically has been involved in a minor offense. Second, in what is referred to as a station adjustment, the police officer can take the juvenile to the station, record the contact, give an official reprimand, and then release the juvenile to his or her parents. Third, another option of the police officer is to refer the juvenile to a diversionary agency, such as a youth service bureau (YSB), a runaway center, or a mental health agency. Fourth, the police officer can issue a citation referring the juvenile to the juvenile court and can return the juvenile to his or her parents. The intake counselor of the juvenile court decides whether a formal petition should be filed. Finally, the police officer's most restrictive sanction is to issue a citation, to refer the youth to the juvenile court, and to take him or her to a detention center or the county jail if no juvenile facility is available.

Police departments vary somewhat in granting due process rights to juveniles under arrest or taken into custody, but the majority of them now comply with court decisions in granting the following due process rights for juveniles.

- Search and seizure: Juveniles must be presented with a valid search warrant unless they have either waived that right, have consented to have their person or property searched, or have been apprehended committing the crime.

- Interrogation practices: Juveniles taken into custody are entitled to the rights stated in the 1966 *Miranda v. Arizona* decisions. To protect juveniles against excessive police interrogation, many jurisdictions have a statutory requirement that a parent or counsel be present at that time in order for a confession to be admissible.

- Fingerprinting: Although this practice varies significantly among police departments, the more progressive juvenile court statutes require that a judge approve the taking of fingerprints of juveniles and provide for fingerprint destruction.

- Pretrial identification practices: Another controversial procedure is the photographing and placing of juveniles in lineups. It is generally recommended by court decisions and juvenile court statutes that a photograph not be taken without the written consent of the juvenile judge and that the name or picture of the law-violating juvenile not be made public by the media.

The Juvenile Court

The next stage in juvenile justice processing occurs when a juvenile comes before the juvenile court. The court fulfills its role of controlling and correcting the behavior of law-violating juveniles by holding detention, intake, transfer, adjudicatory, and dispositional hearings.

The Detention Hearing

The decision to detain generally must be made within 48 to 72 hours (excluding weekends and holidays). The criteria for detention have been traditionally based on the need both to protect the child and to ensure public safety. Although 20 states permit the posting of bond by, or on behalf of, a minor, the posting of bond is not widely used in many of these jurisdictions. Florida and Utah are the only states denying the constitutionality of bail for juveniles. Furthermore, the U.S. Supreme Court's decision in the *Schall v. Martin* (1984) case reversed the decision of the appeals court in New York state that preventive decision was unconstitutional for juveniles. There is some evidence that this ruling may lead to a significant expansion of preventive, or secure, detention for law-violating juveniles.

The Intake Hearing

Intake refers to a preliminary screening process to determine what action should be taken on a petition. After a complaint has been filed, and most are filed by the police, the intake officer must decide whether the court has statutory jurisdiction. If the decision is made that the court has such jurisdiction, then the intake officer conducts a preliminary interview to determine whether the case should be adjudicated nonjudicially or sent to the court.

In urban courts, the intake unit may have four options for the disposal of cases. First, the complaint is dismissed when legal jurisdiction does not exist, or the case is so weak that the intake officer is reluctant to refer it to the court. Second, the intake officer may decide to divert the case to a diversionary agency, or the officer may warn the youth and then dismiss the case. This is often referred to as informal adjustment. Third, the juvenile may be placed on informal probation, which involves the supervision of a juvenile by a volunteer or probation officer. If the youth fares well during this informal probation period, the decision is then made not to file a petition. Finally, the intake unit can decide to file the petition to the court.

The Transfer Procedure

The U.S. Supreme Court has ruled on two important cases involving the transfer procedure, *Kent v. United States* (1966) and *Breed v. Jones* (1975). In the *Kent* decision, the juvenile judge waived a youth to the adult court without a hearing. Nor did the judge rule on the motions of Kent's counsel or confer with Kent's mother or his counsel. He also made no findings and entered no reasons for the waiver. On appeal, the Supreme Court overturned this decision of the lower court. The higher court ruled that Kent should have been afforded a hearing on evidence and should have been present when the court decided to waive jurisdiction, his attorney should have been permitted to examine the social worker's investigation of the juvenile that the court used in deciding to waive jurisdiction, and the judge should have recorded a statement of reasons for the transfer.

In the *Breed v. Jones* decision, the question was raised whether a juvenile could be prosecuted as an adult after an adjudicatory hearing in the juvenile court. The Supreme Court ruled that Breed's case constituted double jeopardy, which means that a juvenile court cannot adjudicate a case and then transfer the case over to the criminal court for adult processing on the same offense.

These decisions have resulted in juvenile court law, or statute, in nearly every state, requiring four procedural safeguards for law-violating juveniles: (1) a legitimate transfer hearing; (2) sufficient notice to the youth's family and defense attorney; (3) the right to counsel; and (4) a statement of the court order regarding transfer. Juvenile court judges generally are influenced more by prior record and the seriousness of the present offense than by any other factors in deciding to transfer or bind over the juvenile to the adult court.

In the 1980s, legislation was enacted in nearly half the states, which increased the likelihood of transfer being more frequently used, (1) making it easier to prosecute juvenile offenders in adult courts (California and Florida); (2) lowering the age of judicial waiver (Tennessee, Kentucky, and South Carolina); and (3) excluding certain offenses from juvenile court jurisdiction (Illinois, Indiana, Oklahoma, and Louisiana) (Krisberg, Liskey, and Austin, 1986).

Adjudicatory Stage

This fact-finding stage of the court's proceedings usually includes the following steps: the plea of the juvenile, presentation of evidence by the prosecutor and by the defense, cross-examination of witnesses, and the finding of the judge. The *In re Winship* decision ruled that juveniles are entitled to proof "beyond a reasonable doubt" when charged with an act that would constitute a crime if committed by an adult. Youths are further protected during this hearing because the judge must follow the rules of evidence and dismiss hearsay from the proceedings; hearsay is inadmissible because it cannot be held up for cross-examination.

Prosecutors begin the adjudicatory hearings by presenting the case of the state. The arresting officer and any witnesses at the scene testify, and any other evidence that has been legally obtained is introduced. The defense attorney then cross-examines the witnesses. Defense counsel is also given an opportunity to introduce evidence favorable to his or her client, and the juvenile may testify in his or her own behalf. The prosecutor cross-examines the defense witnesses, and the prosecution and the defense present summaries of the case, following which the judge reaches a finding or a verdict.

The U.S. Supreme Court in *McKeiver v. Pennsylvania* (1971) denied the right of juveniles to have jury trials. Ten states do provide for a jury trial for juveniles, but jury trials are seldom demanded. The right to a speedy trial has been guaranteed by state court decisions and by those statutes that limit the time that can take place between the filing of a complaint and the actual hearing.

The Dispositional Stage

Once a judge has found a juvenile to be delinquent at the adjudicatory stage, some juvenile court codes permit the judge to proceed immediately into the disposition hearing. The present trend, however, is to hold a bifurcated, or split, adjudicatory and disposition hearing so that a social study report can be prepared on the juvenile.

There are fewer constitutional safeguards for the juvenile at this stage than at the adjudicatory stage. Rules of evidence tend to be relaxed, witnesses are not always sworn in, and hearsay testimony may be considered (Rubin, 1979). The social study report prepared by the probation officer is generally the starting point of the disposition hearing. Juveniles are permitted to have legal counsel, and the *Kent* decision assures the right of counsel to challenge the facts of the social study investigation.

The alternatives available for the judge at the disposition hearing vary by the size of the jurisdiction. Large urban courts may have most or all of the following alternatives: dismissal; fine or restitution; psychiatric therapy; probation; day treatment program or placement in a foster home, in a community-based residential program, in a county or city training school, or in a state or private training school.

Community-Based Corrections

Community-based corrections are made up of probation, residential and day treatment programs, and aftercare.

Probation

Probation is a judicial disposition under which juvenile offenders are subject to certain conditions imposed by the juvenile court and are permitted to remain in the community under the supervision of a probation officer. Probation is the most widely used judicial disposition, and about 450,000 juveniles were on probation in 1991 (Bartollas and Miller, 1994:135).

Reduced risk and increased surveillance models have been increasingly used by juvenile probation in the 1980s and 1990s. By 1985, more than 400 jurisdictions were known to have formal restitution programs. Alabama, Georgia, New Jersey, North Carolina, Ohio, Oregon, and Pennsylvania are experimenting with, or have, statewide intensive supervision programs for juveniles (Bartollas and Miller, 1994:135). House arrest, or home confinement, is infrequently called upon in juvenile justice, and electronic monitoring equipment rarely monitors juveniles' presence in their residence (Vaughn, 1989). Boot camps, which emphasize military discipline, physical training, and regimented activity for up to 180 days, are increasingly used in juvenile justice. Juvenile probationers are sometimes given the option of a boot camp rather than the standard training school program (Ratliff, 1988).

Residential and Day Treatment Programs

Foster care, group homes, day treatment programs, and survival programs are the main types of community-based corrections for juveniles. Foster care, day treatment programs, and survival programs are quite different from programs offered in adult justice. In foster care, the juvenile court places the youth in a foster home. Juveniles are sent to a day treatment program during the day and return home in the evening. Outward Bound is the most widely used survival program. In Outward Bound, as well as other survival programs, the program uses "overcoming of a seemingly impossible task" to help program participants gain self-reliance, prove their worth, and define their selfhood (Miner and Boldt, 1981).

Juvenile Aftercare

Juveniles released from training school are placed on aftercare status. In 1988, 48,502 youthful offenders were on aftercare, or parole, in various state jurisdictions (American Correctional Association, 1988).

Aftercare is traditionally the most undeveloped aspect of the juvenile justice system. Intensive supervision programs, as with juvenile probation, are being increasingly used, but in-house detention still is not being used as much as is juvenile probation. Juvenile aftercare commonly requires drug and alcohol urinalyses from juveniles on this status and is turning to boot camps to release juveniles early from training schools.

Juvenile Correctional Institutions

Ranches, forestry camps, farms, and private and public training schools are the main types of juvenile correctional institutions.

Ranches, Forestry Camps, and Farms

These minimum-security facilities are generally reserved for juveniles who have committed minor crimes or status offenses or are committed to the youth authority or youth commission for the first time. Ranches and forestry camps are much more widely used than farms. An increasing number of these facilities are under the auspices of private-for-profit agencies. Residents are much more positive about placement in one of these minimum-security facilities than they are about placement in a training school. They prefer the shorter stays, the greater community contact, the more informal relations with staff, and the more relaxed security.

Training Schools

The physical structure of training schools varies from the homelike atmosphere of small cottages, to open dormitories that provide little privacy for residents, to fortresslike facilities with individual cells. The more security-oriented training schools may have high fences and sometimes even walls around them, but even most training schools without fences find ways to maintain perimeter security because of the constant problem with runaway behavior.

Training schools have programs fewer in number but similar to those offered in adult prisons. Residents typically receive very good medical and dental services. The educational program is frequently accredited by the state and able to grant a high school diploma. A variety of vocational programs, especially in training schools for boys, is offered. The most widely used treatment technologies, or modalities, include transactional analysis (TA), reality therapy, behavior modification, guided group interaction, and positive peer culture. Some training schools also offer home visits, off-campus visits, and work release to responsible residents before release.

The quality of life for residents within training schools has been subjected to wide criticism since the mid-1970s (Bartollas, Miller, and Dinitz, 1976; Polsky, 1963; Lerner, 1986; Feld, 1977; Shichor and Bartollas, 1990; Miller, 1991). It has been documented that in too many training schools a "strong shall survive" inmate culture creates a lawless society, which is characterized by intimidation, force, and victimization.

There is evidence, however, that training schools have improved in some respects. Corporal punishment of residents rarely takes place today. Many of the fortresslike training schools across the nation have been closed or reduced in size. Residents have more grievance procedures in place than in the past, and status offenders are infrequently placed in public training schools.

THE INFORMAL NATURE OF THE JUVENILE
JUSTICE SYSTEM

The informal system is much more in place and accepted in juvenile justice than in adult justice. Informality and decision making based on extralegal factors go back to the beginning of juvenile justice in this nation.

The Hidden System of Juvenile Justice

Ira M. Schwartz, Marilyn Jackson-Beeck, and Roger Anderson have recently charged that the substantial numbers of youths being institutionalized in child welfare and mental health systems lend support to the fact that a "hidden" or private juvenile correctional system has evolved for disruptive youth who are no longer processed by the public justice system (Schwartz, Jackson-Beeck, and Anderson, 1984). This charge was supported by a study of institutionalized juveniles in the mental health and chemical dependency systems in the state of Minnesota. Schwartz, Jackson-Beeck, and Anderson found that the majority of these juveniles were admitted on a "voluntary" basis and were not ordered by the juvenile court. Estimated to be about 60 percent female, these juveniles were usually referred by their parents.

Schwartz's *(In)justice for Juveniles* further documents this expanding policy of committing juveniles to inpatient psychiatric and chemical dependency units in private for-profit and nonprofit hospitals. He charges that "the pressures to fill empty beds, coupled with the availability of third-party health care insurance programs with fiscal incentives that favor inpatient rather than outpatient care,

are contributing to the proliferation of services that are largely inappropriate and costly'' (Schwartz, 1989:133).

Extralegal Factors Affecting Juvenile Justice

Social, religious, and political factors have long played an important role in the handling of juvenile offenders. From the very beginning, it was the lower-class children whose behaviors were selected to be penalized, such as roaming the streets, engaging in sex, drinking, frequenting dance halls, fighting, and staying out at night. Anthony Platt argues that juvenile justice has reflected a class favoritism that resulted in the processing of poor children through the juvenile justice system while middle- and upper-class children were more likely to be excused (Platt, 1969).

This class bias has continued to affect the operations of juvenile justice in this nation. The police worker is less likely to refer the middle-class youth to the juvenile court, the intake worker is less likely to detain the middle-class youth, the juvenile judge is more likely to place the middle-class youth in a psychiatric or community-based setting rather than in a training school, and the middle-class youth who is committed to a training school is more likely to be sent to a privately administered one.

The police officer, as well as other participants in the juvenile justice system, would defend this less restrictive decision making by saying that the middle-class youth typically has more resources available than does the lower-class youth. The parents can afford psychiatric intervention or drug rehabilitation programs. There is also the matter that the middle-class youth is generally perceived as less dangerous than is the lower-class youth.

A gender bias has further blighted the performance of the juvenile justice system. Adolescent female arrest rates are five to six times lower than those of adolescent males, but females are treated more harshly than males for lesser offenses. For example, Yona Cohn found that females constituted only one-sixth of her sample but one-half of the juveniles sentenced to secure institutions (Cohn, 1963). What is of interest here is that these females violated sexual taboos but did not engage in serious or violent delinquency. Yet they were given harsher punishment than males who engaged in more serious offenses.

Hunter Hurst, director of the National Center of Juvenile Justice, articulates why the public fears the sexual misbehavior of adolescent females: ''Status offenses are offenses against our values.'' Adolescent females are ''seemingly over represented as status offenders because we have had a strong heritage of being protective toward females in this country.'' He contends that it offends ''our sensibility and values to have a fourteen-year-old girl engage in sexually promiscuous activity; it's not the way we like to think about females in this country'' (Quoted in Chesney-Lind and Shelden, 1992:116).

Finally, social injustice is found in the mounting evidence of unfair treatment of African-American and Hispanic males in the juvenile justice system. They are both overrepresented in arrest, conviction, and incarceration with respect to their population base. Carl E. Pope and William H. Feyerherm's highly regarded assessment of the issue of discrimination against minorities reveals that two-thirds of the studies revealed "both direct and indirect race effects or a mixed pattern (being present at some stages and not at others) (Pope and Feyerherm, 1990:333–334). They argue that selection bias can take place at any stage and that small racial differences tend to accumulate and become more pronounced as minority youth are processed through the juvenile justice system.

There is some concern that the crack cocaine epidemic of the late 1980s and the rise of youth gangs across the nation in the 1990s may be causing a significant increase in social injustice with minorities. The fear of violent crime has skyrocketed in the United States, and youthful minorities are being blamed for their overrepresentation in violence and drug-trafficking street gangs. The consequences of this is a dramatic increase in the institutionalization of these youths in the late 1980s and early 1990s (Bureau of Justice Statistics, 1989).

SUMMARY

The history of juvenile justice in the United States has been one of the declining authority of the family. The approach to the social control of juvenile crime appears to go through cycles of reform and retrenchment (Bernard, 1992). The most recent period of retrenchment, or repression—which began in the 1970s—proposes a "get-tough" strategy, especially with hard-core juveniles, as the most effective way of dealing with youth crime. The means to accomplish this goal have not proved satisfactory in the past and are likely to be no more successful in the future.

The juvenile justice system is probably under greater criticism today than ever before in this nation's history. The quandary about juvenile justice has resulted in various proposed strategies. There are even those who argue that perhaps the best approach would be for the juvenile system to become part of the adult system. The reality is that the juvenile system is presently turning to the adult system far more than it has since the juvenile court was founded at the end of the last century. Juvenile offenders are increasingly being granted the due process rights that adult offenders have, receiving mandatory and determinate sentences in juvenile court, being transferred to adult court and tried as adults, and being sentenced to prison with adults. Juveniles have even been sentenced to the death penalty and executed.

In the midst of the "get-tough" talk, which has been spurred by the rise of drug-trafficking gangs and drive-by shootings, informal procedures continue to exist, and both status offenders and hard-core offenders have been affected by these procedures. Adolescent female status offenders have been the most adversely affected, especially when they are involved in sexual behaviors. But African-American and Hispanic offenders have also been affected, because the public's fear of violence and drug trafficking has resulted in more punitive treatment of these juveniles. The increased rates of institutionalization have been one of the consequences of this more punitive treatment.

Reform in the juvenile justice system obviously requires that social changes in the wider society take place first. Too many homes do not provide adequately for the needs of children. Individual communities must become more involved in the prevention and control of juvenile lawbreaking. Improvements must also take place in the public schools, especially with high-risk children. Conservatives are probably correct that juveniles must experience greater cost for their illegal behaviors, but liberals are also right in asserting that only a humane and fair justice system will have a positive effect on youthful offenders.

REFERENCES

American Correctional Association. *1988 Directory.* College Park, MD: American Correctional Association, 1988.

Bartollas, Clemens. *Juvenile Delinquency,* 3d ed. New York: Macmillan, 1993.

Bartollas, Clemens, and Stuart J. Miller. *Juvenile Justice in America.* Englewood Cliffs, NJ: Prentice-Hall, 1994.

Bartollas, Clemens, Stuart J. Miller, and Simon Dinitz. *Juvenile Victimization: The Institutional Paradox.* New York: Halsted, 1976.

Bernard, Thomas J. *The Cycle of Juvenile Justice.* New York: Oxford University Press, 1992.

Bordua, David. "Recent Trends: Deviant Behavior and Social Control." *Annals* 359 (1967): 149–163.

Breed v. Jones, 421 U.S. 519, 95 S. Ct. 1779, 1975.

Bureau of Justice Statistics. *Children in Custody, 1975–1985.* Washington, DC: U.S. Department of Justice, 1989.

Chesney-Lind, Meda, and Randall G. Shelden. *Girls: Delinquency and Juvenile Justice.* Pacific Grove, CA: Brooks/Cole, 1992.

Cohn, Yona. "Criteria for Probation Officer's Recommendations to Juvenile Court." *Crime and Delinquency* (1963): 272–275.

Feld, Barry. *Neutralizing Inmate Violence: The Juvenile Offender in Institutions.* Cambridge, MA: Ballinger, 1977.

———. "The Transformation of the Juvenile Court." *Minnesota Law Review* 75 (1991): 691–725.

Fogel, David. *". . . We Are the Living Proof": The Justice Model of Corrections.* Cincinnati, OH: Anderson, 1975.

In re Gault, 387 U.S. 1, 18 L. Ed. 527, 87 S. Ct. 1428, 1967.

In re Winship, 397 U.S. 358, 90 S. Ct. 1968, 25 L. Ed. 2d 368, 1970.

James, Howard. *Children in Trouble: A National Scandal.* New York: Pocket Books, 1971.

Kent v. United States, 383 U.S. 541, 86 S. Ct. 1045, 16 L Ed. 2d 84, 1966.

Krisberg, Barry, Ira M. Schwartz, Paul Liskey, and James Austin. "The Watershed of Juvenile Justice Reform." *Crime and Delinquency* 32 (1986): 5–38.

Lerner, Steve. *Bodily Harm: The Pattern of Fear and Violence at the California Youth Authority.* Bolionas, CA: Common Knowledge Press, 1986.

McKeiver v. Pennsylvania, 403 U.S. 528, 535, 1971.

Miller, Jerome G. *Last One over the Wall: The Massachusetts Experiment in Closing Reform Schools.* Columbus: Ohio State Press, 1991.

Miner, Joshua L., and Joe Boldt. *Outward Bound USA: Learning through Experience in Adventure-Based Education.* New York: Morrow, 1981.

Murphy, Patrick. *Our Kindly Parent—The State.* New York: Viking, 1974.

National Advisory Committee for Juvenile Justice and Delinquency Prevention. *Serious Juvenile Crime: A Redirected Federal Effort.* Washington, DC: Office of Juvenile Justice and Delinquency Prevention, 1984.

Platt, Anthony M. *The Child Savers.* Chicago: University of Chicago Press, 1969.

Polsky, Howard. *Cottage Six: The Social System of Delinquent Boys in Residential Treatment.* New York: Russell Sage Foundation, 1963.

Pope, Carl E. and William H. Feyerham. "Minority Status and Juvenile Justice Processing: An Assessment of the Research Literature." *Criminal Justice Abstracts* 22 (1990): 333–334.

President's Commission on Law Enforcement and Administration of Justice. *The Challenge of Crime in a Free Society.* Washington, DC: U.S. Government Printing Office, 1967.

Ratliff, Bascom W. "The Army Model: Boot Camp for Youthful Offenders." *Corrections Today* 50 (1988): 90–102.

Richette, Lisa Aversa. *The Throwaway Children.* New York: J. B. Lippincott, 1969.

Rothman, David J. *The Discovery of the Asylum.* Boston: Little, Brown, 1971.

Rubin, Ted. *Juvenile Justice: Policy, Practice, and Law.* Santa Monica, CA: Goodyear, 1979.

Schall v. Martin, United States Law Review 52 (47): 46, 81–96, 1984.

Schramm, Gustav L. "The Judge Meets the Boy and His Family." *National Probation Association Yearbook,* edited by Majorie Bell. New York: National Probation Association, 1945.

Schwartz, Ira M. *(In) justice for Juveniles: Rethinking the Best Interests of the Child.* Lexington, MA: Lexington Books, 1989.

Schwartz, Ira M., Marilyn Jackson-Beeck, and Roger Anderson. "The 'Hidden' System of Juvenile Justice." *Crime and Delinquency* 30 (1984): 372–384.

Shichor, David, and Clemens Bartollas. "Private and Public Juvenile Placements: Is There a Difference?" *Crime and Delinquency* 36 (1990): 286–299.

Vaughn, Joseph B. "A Survey of Juvenile Electronic Monitoring and Home Confinement Programs." *Juvenile and Family Court Journal* 40 (1989): 4–22.

APPENDIX

Key Personnel

Aftercare officers

Child care staff for residential and institutional programs

Juvenile court judges

Juvenile court referees

Probation officers

Professional staff for residential and institutional programs

Key Agencies

Bureau of Justice Statistics
U.S. Department of Justice
Box 6000
Rockville, MD 20850

Juvenile Court Statistics
National Center for Juvenile Justice
701 Forbes Avenue
Pittsburgh, PA 15219

Office of Juvenile Justice and Delinquency Prevention (OJJDP)
742 Indian Building
633 Indian Avenue
Washington, DC 20530

Uniform Crime Reports
Federal Bureau of Investigation
Washington, DC 20535

INDEX

ABOUT THE EDITOR
AND CONTRIBUTORS

ANA JOSEFINA ALVAREZ is Professor of Criminal Justice at Universidad de Nacional Autonoma de Mexico. She has published several books on crime and drugs, including *Traffic and Use of Drugs: An Alternative Vision* (1991), *Anthology in Criminology* (editor) (1992), and *Drug Policies in the American Continent,* in press. She has also published articles on delinquency in the Dominican Republic and child abuse in Mexico. Research interests include drug policies, child abuse, and adolescent juridical socialization in France.

W. TIMOTHY AUSTIN is Professor of Criminology at Indiana University of Pennsylvania. Recent publications include a co-edited book, *Criminological Thought*, and numerous articles and book chapters on terrorism and conflict in the Philippines. Research interests involve studies of conflict resolution and terrorism, particularly in the Philippines.

CLEMENS BARTOLLAS is Professor of Sociology at Northern Iowa University. Recent publications include the fourth edition of *Juvenile Delinquency* (in press) and a co-authored book, *Juvenile Justice in America* (1994). His current research interests focus on post-Newtonian paradigms, and a biography of Larry Hoover, gang chief of Gangsters Disciples (Growth and Development).

SIGISMUND O. A. AKIN BULUMO is Professor of Sociology at Ondo State University in Nigeria. He has published articles on such topics as wife battering, public concern for crime and crime prevention in Nigeria, and indigenous behavior in Nigeria. Research interests include insurance fraud and feminist perspectives of criminality in Nigeria.

HERMAN CONRADIE is Professor of Criminology at the University of South Africa. Recent publications include articles on child abuse, and other forms of violence. Two forthcoming books concern child abuse in South Africa and attacking and murdering police in Gauteng, South Africa. Research interests include child abuse, vehicle highjackings, and attacks on police in South Africa.

RAYMOND R. CORRADO is Professor, School of Criminology, at Simon Fraser University. Recent publications include a co-authored book, *Juvenile Justice in Canada* (1992), and an article on the Young Offenders Act in Canada, co-authored with Alan Markwart. His areas of research interest include youth violence, mental disorders among youth, and youth justice.

JAMES O. FINCKENAUER is Professor of Criminal Justice at Rutgers University. Recent publications include a co-authored book, *Organized Crime in America,* and *Russian Youth—Law, Deviance, and the Pursuit of Freedom* (1995). Current research interests include a project funded by the National Institute of Justice on Soviet emigre organized criminal networks in the United States.

MARK S. GAYLORD is Associate Professor of Applied Social Studies at the City University of Hong Kong. He is the co-editor of *Introduction to the Hong Kong Criminal Justice System* (1994). Other publications include articles on policing and the death penalty in Hong Kong. He is now studying police accountability in East Asia and lawmaking in the People's Republic of China.

HIROKO GOTO is Assistant Professor of Economics at Fuji College in Japan. She has published on the topics of women's crime, crime and delinquency, and juvenile justice reform. Research interests include due process in juvenile justice and juvenile law reform in Japan.

NAGWA A. HAFEZ is a Professor in the National Center for Social and Criminological Research in Cairo, Egypt. Recent publications include *Changing Trends in Juvenile Delinquency in Egypt* (1994). Research interests concern juvenile delinquency and the social aspects of road accident victims.

CLAYTON A. HARTJEN is Associate Professor and Chair, Department of Sociology, Anthropology, and Criminal Justice, Rutgers University. Recent publications include *Comparative Delinquency: India, the United States, and Other Countries* (1996), co-authored with Sesha Kethineni, and other comparative analyses of delinquency. Research interests focus on Indian delinquency and juvenile justice, international aspects of youth crime and justice, and criminological theory.

J. DAVID HIRSCHEL is Professor of Criminal Justice at the University of North Carolina at Charlotte. Recent publications include *Criminal Justice in*

England and the United States (1995), co-authored with William Wakefield, and book chapters and articles on police arrest practices in England and the United States. Current research interests are on comparative criminal justice systems, drug use and the criminal justice system, and criminal victimization.

CÉSAR BARROS LEAL is Professor of Juvenile Law at the Federal University of Cearas, Brazil. Recent publications include *The Statute of the Child and Adolescent Law 8069/90* (1992), *The Human Rights Protection in the National and International Levels: Brazilian Perspectives* (1992), and *Basic Studies on Human Rights* (1995) (all co-authored) and articles on female criminality, crime and punishment in the U.S., and prisoners's rights and treatment in prisons in Brazil. His current research interest concerns community service as a socio-educational measure for juvenile offenders.

SESHA KETHINENI is Assistant Professor of Criminal Justice at Illinois State University. Recent publications include *Comparative Delinquency: India, the United States and Other Countries* (1996), co-authored with Clayton Hartjen, and other publications of comparative analyses of Indian delinquency. Research interests include comparative studies of delinquency, jury selection procedures, and the condition of jails in the United States.

ALAN MARKWART is a youth justice policy analyst with the Ministry of Attorney General, British Columbia, Canada. Recent publications include book chapters and articles on Canadian juvenile justice, which is also the topic of his current research interest.

REYNALD OTTENHOF is Professor of Criminology and Criminal Law at the University of Nantes in France. Recent publications include writings on criminology, the new French Penal and Juvenile Law Codes and specialization and functions of juvenile courts. Research interests concern delinquency, criminology, and penal and civil law.

VASSILIKI PETOUSSI is a doctoral candidate at Virginia Polytechnic Institute and State University. The title of her dissertation is "The Feminist Revolution in Legal Scholarship: Is it Missing?" She is also working on the topic of patriarchy and women's criminality.

XIN REN is Assistant Professor of Criminal Justice at California State University, Sacramento. Recent publications include works on prostitution and the second economy in China, and a forthcoming book on law, in press with Greenwood. She is studying career criminal legislation and robbery in northern California.

JEAN-FRANCOIS RENUCCI is Master of Conferences, Faculty of Law at the University of Nice, France. Recent publications are *Penal Rights of Minors*

(1994) and *Delinquent Youth, Youth in Danger* (1992). Current research interests include civil, criminal, and juvenile law and issues concerning human rights.

ELIZABETH SAMMANN is an Associate at Donovan Newton Leisure & Irvine in Paris, France. She published an article on the topic of family preservation in the *DePaul Law Review*.

JOHN SEYMOUR is a Reader in Law at the Australian National University. Recent publications include *Fetal Welfare and the Law* (1995), a co-edited book titled *Children Rights and the Law* (1992), and an article on *parens patriae* and wardship. Research interests involve juvenile justice and medico-legal problems in obstetrics.

DONALD J. SHOEMAKER is Associate Professor of Sociology, Virginia Polytechnic Institute and State University. Recent publication include *Theories of Delinquency, Third Edition* (1996), and articles concerning juvenile delinquency and juvenile justice in the Philippines. Current research interests examine youth deviance in the Philippines and the Netherlands.

KALLIOPI STAVROU is an attorney-at-law in Greece. Professional interests include the adjudication of penal cases and theory of penal law.

ICHIRO TANIOKA is Professor of Sociology at Osaka University of Commerce. Recent publications include an article on school uniforms, social control, and delinquency in Japan. His research interest concerns gambling as deviant behavior.

IVONNE VINAY is an English translator/interpreter and professor at National University, Acatlan Campus, Mexico. Her translations have been published by the University, PEMEX, and various publishing companies in Mexico. Her current research interest is the design and development of a Reading Comprehension Program based on intellective mental processes.

WILLIAM WAKEFIELD is Professor of Criminal Justice at the University of Nebraska at Omaha. Recent publications include *Criminal Justice in England and the United States* (1995), co-authored with J. David Hirschel, and articles on comparative criminal justice issues. Research interests include the criminal and juvenile justice systems in England.

DOBROCHNA WÓJCIK is Professor and Head, Department of Criminology at the Institute of Law Studies, the Polish Academy of Sciences. Recent publications include a co-edited book, *Selection of Offenders at Family Courts* (1990), and articles and book chapters on violent crime and aggressive criminals, rights of youth and victim perspectives. Research interests focus on juvenile justice, victims of crime and offender-victim mediation.

NANCY TRAVIS WOLFE is Professor of Criminal Justice at the University of South Carolina. Recent publications include the second edition of a co-authored book, *History of Criminal Justice* (1995) and *Policing a Socialist Society: The German Democratic Republic* (1992), plus book chapters and articles on comparative juvenile and criminal justice. A current research interest is the transition of the former East German legal system.

ISBN 0-313-28895-X

90000>

EAN

9 780313 288951

HARDCOVER BAR CODE

TEXAS A&M UNIVERSITY - TEXARKANA